MW00451412

Jean Seberg — Breathless

GARRY McGEE

Best always —
Garry McGee 08/15/15

Jean Seberg — Breathless
© 2008 Garry McGee. All Rights Reserved.
No part of this book may be reproduced in any form or by any means, electronic, mechanical, digital, photocopying or recording, except for the inclusion in a review, without permission in writing from the publisher.

Published in the USA by:
BearManor Media
P O Box 71426
Albany, Georgia 31708
WWW.BEARMANORMEDIA.COM

ISBN 1-59393-127-1

Printed in the United States of America.
Book design by Brian Pearce.

Front Cover Photo courtesy of Independent Visions.
Title Page Photo filming *Paint Your Wagon*, courtesy of Seberg Family Collection

Table Of Contents

Prologue 7

Chapter One: *1938-1956* 13

Chapter Two: *1957-1959* 41

Chapter Three: *1959-1962* 77

Chapter Four: *1963-1966* 109

Chapter Five: *1967-1968* 143

Chapter Six: *1968-1970* 173

Chapter Seven: *1970-1971* 197

Chapter Eight: *1972-1976* 227

Chapter Nine: *1977-1979* 259

Chapter Ten: *1979-1981* 285

Epilogue 307

Acknowledgments 313

Selected Bibliography 315

Index 324

Prologue

"[She was] one of the most appealing and enigmatic movie stars of the 1960s."
— film critic Vincent Canby, 1979

"She, the farm girl, dines with de Gaulle, visits the White House, gets handwritten letters from André Malraux... is as American as boysenberry."
— film critic Rex Reed, 1968

"Jean Seberg ... should be neutralized."
— FBI director J. Edgar Hoover, 1970

In front of Notre Dame, 1967. COURTESY OF SNORRAMYNDIR

Jean Seberg had it all: beauty, talent, wealth. At least, so it appeared.

To the public her life seemed, as she herself described it, a "roller coaster" of personal and professional highs and lows. Yet the Jean Seberg saga is colored, for most people, by one of a number of sharply divergent and simplistic views. She was, for example, either an opportunist or a benefactor. For some, this was an attractive yet calculating woman who used men to further her career and social standing, for others, an intelligent actress whose talents and grace threatened the men in her life. On the one hand, she was a realist ahead of her time, on the other, it will be said, a naive idealist who allowed herself to be exploited. There are those, however, who see the Jean Seberg story as something more, perhaps even as "the genuine American tragedy."

As an international film star and Continental sophisticate, it was especially her beauty and charm that captivated men. For an entire generation of women, she was the epitome of freshness as the free-spirited American in Paris, and she made every young girl's dream of fame seem possible.

With the news of her death at the age of forty on September 8, 1979, the press allegations of a suicide shattered such illusions. Yet, beyond the public image, there was a Jean Seberg that neither her fans nor the media ever understood.

Six days after the discovery of Jean Seberg's remains in the backseat of her Renault car, a graveside ceremony took place at Montparnasse Cemetery in Paris, the city in which she spent most of her adult life. Simultaneously, an ocean away, a memorial service was held in Marshalltown, Iowa, where Jean had grown up.

Next to the lectern, a basket of chrysanthemums was placed alongside an enlarged, framed photograph of Jean in the role that brought her first stardom, Joan of Arc. The picture had been taken twenty-three years earlier by Marshalltown photographer Patton Apgar, shortly after it was learned the local girl was selected to play the role in director Otto Preminger's film, *Saint Joan.* Apgar captioned the work in 1956, "Saint Joan in Despair."

Family members and close friends of Jean and the Sebergs attended the memorial service. As the immediate family sat in the balcony and friends below in the nave of Trinity Lutheran Church, they listened as Pastor Warren Johnson eulogized Jean.

"She took unpopular stands. It was not easy to be in the forefront," Johnson said. "The noisy gongs and clanging cymbals did not understand. She bore the burden until she staggered beneath its weight." He continued, reminding the mourners that "most of us cannot understand the pressure a celebrity endures. We are not here to make a goddess of Jean, or a saint. We are here to tell the other side of the story. She, like Joan of Arc, whom she emulated, was a warrior against injustice … She seemed to sense a call from which she could not be dissuaded."

Although words were comforting, no amount of sympathy could heal the loss. The fact that the news media reported Jean committed suicide was an added burden to those close to her. The *Marshalltown Times-Republican* noted: "Family and close friends ... find it difficult to think of her having tendencies for self-destruction." The death of Jean Seberg, however, was not a closed case, for new information was made public in the following hours, days, and years.

As unconventional as Jean's death was, so too was her life. Her film career was not in the usual Hollywood pattern, but was international, spanning almost forty films, almost half of which were not produced in English. There was the groundbreaking perennial French classic *Breathless*, the critically rediscovered *Bonjour Tristesse*, and *Lilith*, which brought her a Golden Globe nomination for best actress in a drama. There were the Hollywood hits, *Paint Your Wagon* and *Airport*. Two of Jean's personal favorites were the French-produced success *The Five-Day Lover* and the Italian-made *Dead of Summer*.

Her personal life was as diverse as her career. There were three failed marriages, to a French-born lawyer, a French diplomat/writer of Lithuanian origin, and a budding American-born film director. Nothing about Jean completely surprised her family or close friends, except her death and the events that followed.

After the memorial service in Iowa, Jean's parents, Ed and Dorothy Seberg, returned to their middle-class, one-story home on Kalsem Boulevard, together with several friends and family members, including her siblings Mary Ann and Kurt. In dire times, such as a death or a serious illness, it is a given that friends and relatives offer baked goods and casseroles so that meals need not be a concern. This was the case with the Sebergs, but much of the food remained untouched.

Although news reporters had gathered outside the church during the service, one aggressive reporter continually telephoned the family afterwards. Ed did not wish to talk, but he finally relented. He had been through this countless times since Jean became an actress. The media usually wanted a quote, and he normally gave them a generality to indicate how proud he and his wife were either of Jean or of her latest film work. He was tolerant and kind, but not long-winded when it came to reporters. With this particular call, however, the reporter did most of the talking.

As Ed Seberg listened, the expression on his face changed from grief to shock. What he was hearing was almost beyond belief, something out of a movie. The caller informed Ed that the FBI had had an "active, discreet investigation" of Jean beginning in 1969. He was also told that the FBI admitted to planting a well-publicized rumor in 1970 to discredit Jean. The reporter said that this revelation had just hit the news wires and that it was, strangely, the FBI who just released the information while the memorial service was being held. Ed thanked the reporter, but gave no comment since the shock of this news proved unbearable.

Ed relayed the reporter's story to those who gathered around him. "My brother kept saying, 'No … It's not true … It's not true!' as he paced the floor," Ed's sister, Velma Odegaard, recalled. "He was in total agony."

Yet the information fitted like pieces of a puzzle, making a clearer picture of his daughter's life, and beginning to explain certain events from the past several years. Jean had confided in a few people, suggesting that the FBI was the force behind certain stories and events surrounding her. Some shrugged off Jean's accusations, while others were dubious; wondering why the FBI would bother with her, of all people. Now it all made sense to Ed Seberg …

Shock and disbelief, however, turned to anger and bitterness later that day as Ed received confirmation of the story. He then telephoned several government officials for an explanation, but was not given a satisfactory reply. "He never was the same after all this," Odegaard said.

Ed walked outside his front door to the spot where he proudly flew the US flag, a symbol of freedom and democracy. Every day he would display the flag, in the evening returning it indoors. After hearing what had happened to his youngest daughter, Ed could not bear the sense of betrayal he felt. On this day of his daughter's burial, he carefully removed the flag and took it inside, setting it down in the back corner of the living room behind a chair. There it stayed for the remaining days of Ed Seberg's life.

The FBI's admission provoked controversy over government intrusion in a citizen's private life, as well as to what degree a public figure's life should be made accessible. Newspapers criticized each other for spreading idle gossip, and many fingers pointed to one person responsible for Jean Seberg's downfall: former FBI head director J. Edgar Hoover, who had agreed that Seberg should be "neutralized" and publicly humiliated.

The revelation of the FBI's intrusion resulted in expressions of outrage by a majority of the American public. It also caused a flurry of editorials and news reports for several months following Jean's death. Journalist Pete Hamill, who met Jean at a party in Los Angeles in the late 1960s, wrote in the *New York Daily News*, "A lot of people were tougher than that old fraud J. Edgar Hoover, but Jean Seberg wasn't one of them. And so she's dead and we the living can choose to react with indifference or rage. One baby and one beautiful, troubled adult are dead, possibly as the result of government actions. Those actions were moral, if not illegal crimes. And if civilization is to mean anything, the agents of justice must rise in outrage and make someone pay."

The darling of Paris, who helped shape contemporary cinema, who had moved between the worlds of show business and politics, from middle-class, small-town beginnings to international stardom, wealth and influence in her own unique, uncompromising manner, was gone. Jean Seberg was, whether by her own hand or not, finally neutralized. But the question remained: why did the head of the FBI and principal government officials wish to destroy an American-born actress who lived primarily abroad?

CHAPTER ONE
1938-1956

"I'm going to grow up and be a movie star."
— Jean Seberg in her childhood

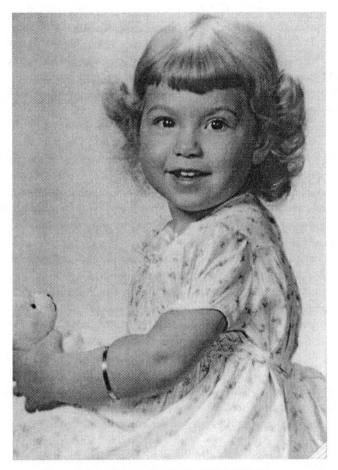

COURTESY OF SEBERG FAMILY COLLECTION

1

"From the time she was born she was ahead of her time. She was interested in things that young girls her age were not interested in — probably ever. She knew people, and about their problems and concerns. She was an amazing person."
— Mary Ann Seberg

"I'm still the girl from Marshalltown, Iowa," Jean Seberg said many times. While she never completely rejected her Middle-American roots, many of her visits to Iowa were quiet affairs, unannounced, to protect her and her family from the curiosity of the media and townspeople. "When she came home to visit, it was a secret," said Reverend Warren Johnson. "Otherwise, people wouldn't let her alone. When she was home, people would drive by, stop, take pictures. She didn't like that."

Marshalltown did not always know what to make of its famous daughter. "Some people turned up their nose and said, 'Oh boy, she's living it up,' but they'd be the first to stand on Main Street for a parade for her," Marshalltown resident Armon Adams remarked. Other residents loved Jean as one of their own. "Picture, if you will, a beautiful flower in your hand," one Marshalltown resident said of Jean. "Now take that flower and close your hand. That is what Hollywood professionally, and the FBI psychologically, did to Jean Seberg."

When Jean Dorothy Seberg was born on Friday, November 13, 1938, at 5:15 in the morning, 18,000 residents lived in Marshalltown. The primarily conservative town was the county seat of Marshall County which included the attractive stone courthouse situated at the highest point in the county. Its statues with the scales of justice facing north served as a symbol that inside the courthouse justice prevailed, as it did throughout all of the courts in the United States. At least, that is what Marshalltownians were raised to believe.

Elm and maple trees lined the neighborhoods and a large number of two-story houses with porches and large backyards provided for lazy days of summer. The main street had several businesses, including several clothing stores, Lillie Mae's candy store, two movie theaters, and the *Times-Republican* newspaper office. The largest employer at that time was Lennox Furnace Company, and Marshalltown was regarded as a pleasant place to live and raise a family. Des Moines, fifty miles southwest, provided for additional entertainment and necessities; Ames, forty miles west, for a university education.

Seberg was an American name. Jean's paternal grandparents arrived in the United States from Sweden in 1882 after having petitioned the King of Sweden for permission to emigrate. Edward Carlson changed his name to Edward Seberg because, as Jean later explained, "there were already too many Carlsons in the New World." The name Seberg was a combination of sea and mountains, which reminded Edward of his native land. Edward Seberg, Sr., was employed in a clothing factory in Marshalltown, then in the railroad yards, and later as the janitor at Trinity Lutheran Church.

Jean's maternal grandparents, Ernest and Frances Benson, farmed near La Moille, a community ten miles west of Marshalltown. Frances' ances-

Jean, Kurt and Mary Ann Seberg. COURTESY OF SEBERG FAMILY COLLECTION

try traced back to John Hart, thirteenth signatory of the Declaration of Independence. It was said that as a child Frances wanted to run away from home and join the circus. Frances was an affectionate, but independent lady who kept journals that numbered over six thousand pages when she died. An optimist who lived her life with abandon, she wrote in her journals:

"I read a book and wish to quote its author, Alexander King: '... keep your eyes and your heart wide open, and all the wonders of the world will constantly come home to you.' I don't think one can possibly conceive of all the miraculous and surprising things that have fallen into my life merely because I've always been so avidly alive to the rich potentials of my daily existence.

"I think it is true that each and every individual has, at sometime or another during their lifetime, had the same dream as I. A dream of faraway places; of a better understanding of our fellow man; of a desire to travel and explore."

Ernest and Frances' daughter, Dorothy Arline, left the family farm and attended Iowa State Teachers College. She then taught elementary school for several years. Ed Seberg, Jr.'s ambition was to become a doctor; however, the cost was too extreme. Instead, he decided to become a pharmacist. After working part time as a bottle washer to pay for schooling, Ed graduated from the State University of Iowa (later renamed University of Iowa) School of Pharmacy in Iowa City in 1931. He then secured a pharmaceutical job in Marshalltown.

Ed Seberg and Dorothy Benson married on September 4, 1933. Guests recalled how Ed left his wedding reception early because he was scheduled to work until nightfall at the drugstore. Dorothy, a lovely, good-natured and gently-humored woman, and her husband, who, she once remarked, "resembled James Stewart because he was tall, quiet, and kind," settled into their South Fifth Street home. The couple had four children in the next sixteen years. Mary Ann, born in 1936, was followed by Jean in 1938, Kurt in 1941, and David, born in 1949. The Sebergs moved to 305 North Sixth, then across the street to number 306, when David was born, where they remained for the next several years.

It is the general consensus among residents that the Seberg children had an average, normal childhood growing up in Marshalltown. Jean later recalled that her father "pampered his wife and 'spoiled' us kids."

"Mary Ann was a brilliant girl, but she was more reserved and quiet," recalled Velma Odegaard, Ed Seberg's sister. "Then there's Jean. She just had that determined look — one look at those twinkly blue eyes and smile — you knew exactly what she was going to do! Kurt was like Mary Ann and loved the outdoors and helping at the pharmacy. David was an ambitious boy, like Jean in that way. But ... he didn't have much of a chance ..."

When Jean was a toddler, she was fascinated by her aunt's baby grand piano. "She'd try to scramble up on the bench, but she couldn't do it because she was a little chubby. So I'd help her up," Odegaard said. "And then, when she was tired of pounding on the piano, she'd scramble down and over would go the piano bench. She did that for several years and the leg kept getting looser and looser."

"I [was] a bit of the family ham," Jean later admitted.

Odegaard never reminded Jean in her adult years of the piano bench because, "Knowing her and her kindness, there's no telling what she'd do! I was afraid she'd buy me a new piano bench and piano since she was always so generous."

While Grandpa Seberg could not pronounce the English "J," he called Jean "Yen" or "Yeena." In adult life, whenever Jean wrote or telegraphed her family, she usually signed her name "Jeana." "I remember Jean combing her grandparents' hair," Odegaard said, "and asking them if there was anything she could do for them. So caring and taking the time for them. None of the other grandchildren took the time like Jean did."

Everyone agreed that Jean Seberg took after her grandmother Frances

Benson, who was a great and perhaps the earliest influence in Jean's life. While Frances tried to be fair in spending time with her other grandchildren, she saw similarities to herself in Jean. As Jean grew, the two developed a close, lifelong bond.

A streak of independence developed early in Jean's life. Her first complete sentence was "I can do it by my 'lone." Acting in little "Jeana" also

Jean and Mary Ann Seberg. COURTESY OF SEBERG FAMILY COLLECTION

emerged at an early age. At the age of four she used her talent to fool a pair of neighbors.

"My parents used to always tell this story," Mary Ann Seberg recalls. "One day Jean decided she was hungry and she went to a neighbor's door and asked if she could have a banana because [she said] she hadn't had a thing to eat all day. And so the neighbor gave her a banana and she sat on their front porch and ate it. Then she went to another neighbor and gave the same story and got another banana. Finally, the neighbors got together and told my parents the story."

Jean's scheming continued throughout her childhood, although it was not done to be cruel. One time while at church, she walked up to a woman wearing a tri-corn hat and asked her if she was Paul Revere.

Since Velma Odegaard lived across from Rogers Elementary School,

Jean also made a habit of visiting her aunt with a group of friends on baking day: "Jean would say 'Hi, Aunt Velma' really sweet. I knew what she was doing — she wanted some cookies for her and her friends. It never failed. She would be there every time I baked cookies — the scent must have carried over to the school yard or something. But I didn't mind."

Family was important to Ed and Dorothy Seberg. On Sundays they attended Trinity Lutheran Church together, they ate their meals together, and at times they worked together in Seberg Pharmacy, which Ed opened in 1940. On Thirteenth Street, the pharmacy's slogan was "the Suburban Drugstore with the Downtown Service."

Ed ran a tight ship and stressed the importance of responsibility to his children. "We have several generations of families who count on us," he once said. "We've always believed in waiting on the children when they come in, because someone's at home waiting for them to return."

"I always worried about Ed when he received middle of the night calls," Dorothy Seberg remembered. "But he never seemed to have any problems. He got along with everybody, regardless of race or creed." Once, Ed personally dropped off a prescription to an elderly, ill man who had planned to walk to the pharmacy in the rain. Ed scolded the man for not staying in bed, and regularly checked on the man to make sure he was resting. In all practicality, Ed Seberg was a physician of experience, but one without the benefit of an actual degree.

"I wonder how many people in Marshalltown he helped in his own humble, quiet way just because he liked people and wanted to relieve their suffering, never expecting anything but a 'thank you,'" recalled Marshalltown resident Florence Barker years later. "I remember him coming to the drug store at a late hour at night to give us medicine for a very sick baby. When we tried to thank him, he just said, 'Take care of that boy.' That's the kind of person Ed Seberg was."

The Seberg children, at one time or another in their childhood, worked for their father at the family business. When Mary Ann was six, she and Jean took an old popcorn machine outside the pharmacy and sold popcorn streetside. At the soda fountain in the front of the store, the children made "green rivers" (which was lime syrup with soda water), cherry Cokes, and chocolate sodas concocted with a secret recipe.

"When there was ice-cream, the farmers would stop in; the last thing they'd do on a Saturday night," Mary Ann says. She also remembers veterans from the Iowa Veterans' Home across the street from the pharmacy walked down every morning for a bromoseltzer. Mary also recalls hearing that during the Prohibition years, when alcohol was not available, the soldiers bought green aftershave and drank it for effect.

Jean later reminisced about different memories and incidents from her childhood: seeing the Iowa River overflowing onto its banks, or the family dog, Rusty, a constant companion who stayed by her side while she walked in the rain, feeling the rain bathing her cheeks and running into her shoes.

One time when Jean returned home from a walk, she entered the house and heard on the radio of a tornado warning for the Marshalltown area. Ed telephoned Dorothy from the pharmacy, telling her to take the children into the basement. Although the Seberg home was not damaged, Jean later

Jean and Lynda Haupert. COURTESY OF SEBERG FAMILY COLLECTION

wrote that after the danger passed, "we climbed up from the basement and watched the black vortex moving into the distance, the shark of the skies looking for prey to snap up and destroy."

During her childhood, summers usually entailed a short family vacation and Bible study camps for the children. For two weeks Jean and Mary Ann stayed on their Uncle Bill's farm near Indianola. In her writings, Jean recalled Grandfather Benson accompanying her on the bus. She recalled in her writings: "I sat next to him and the smoke of his cigar made me feel nauseous. But that didn't matter to me, I was so fond of Grandpa. What happiness. Grandpa said, 'Jean, you are a strange girl, you really are.' Dear Grandpa, so bald and so cheerful."

Mary Ann remembers another time traveling on a bus to their uncle's farm when Jean befriended a man. After talking with him, she gave him the only money she had — a ten-dollar bill from her father to pay for expenses on the vacation — because she felt sorry for him.

In the wintertime, Jean walked a short distance to Wolfe Hill to sled or ice skate, which was a passion. With her siblings and the neighborhood children, including her best friend Lynda Haupert, hours were spent playing behind the Veterans Home on the banks of the Iowa River. There, they took walks in the woods, played in the trees, and climbed the great sand bank in order to slide down to the bottom. When Haupert and the others asked her to "hunt for game," Jean begged off and spent time composing poetry.

One of Jean's poems written during her pre-teen years shows her serious nature:

> You laugh
> And say I'm too naive.
> Not really.
> I just prefer to believe.

Not all was fun in Jean's childhood. For instance, when she wished to be part of a girl's group, her name was submitted and each member voted by placing a small ball into a box. If all the members placed a white ball into the box, the girl was admitted. However, if there was one or more black-colored balls found inside, the girl was dismissed. In the first round of voting, Jean was blackballed. Several weeks later, however, the girls voted again and Jean was admitted.

Ed and Dorothy encouraged, but did not force, their children to broaden their own individual interests. Jean was signed up for dance classes. "Tap, toe, ballet, acrobatic," says Haupert, who was also in dance class. Mary Ann and Jean sang duets at church ("I can't believe we ever did that," Mary Ann says), and Jean joined the Red Feather Kids, a United Way campaign, where she won an award. "She always had a cause, even as a child," says Haupert. "If it wasn't an animal, it was other things. She always had something she was working toward not only to better herself, but society."

Jean's interests expanded into several areas and subjects that were not taught or even contemplated at the Marshalltown schools. Dorothy Seberg claimed Jean held the record for the largest number of books borrowed from the Marshalltown Public Library. "You never saw Jean without a load of books under her arms," Odegaard confirmed. "She was always reading. I remember asking Ed about them and he'd say, 'they're beyond me.'"

"Jean was interested in many things: brain surgery ... politics ... medicine," says Mary Ann. "She had many interests beyond those of most girls her age." Jean's interest in medicine prompted her to nurse sick animals back to health. Each time Jean brought an injured animal home,

Dorothy would sigh, "Oh no, Jean. Not another one!" After the animals were brought back to health, however, Jean found homes for them around Marshalltown.

In the fourth grade and at the age of ten, Jean wrote a play for Be Kind to Animals week. She presented the play before the entire student body at Rogers Elementary School and it won top prize at a Marshalltown Animal Rescue League contest. The award was a puppy. Jean refused, fearing a new dog would hurt Rusty's feelings. Soon after declining the award, Jean talked about Rusty on *Uncle Ray's Doghouse*, a radio program on Marshalltown's KFJB radio station.

Although Marshalltown is far north of the Bible Belt, with its strict religion and rigid uniformity of values, the Sebergs were considered a religious family. Blessings preceded each meal, the children said prayers before going to sleep every night, and the family attended church regularly. After her confirmation into the Lutheran church in June 1952, Jean became a Sunday school and Bible school teacher. When Jean attended a Boston youth convention in the summer of 1953, she wrote the following, which combined her religious beliefs and penchant for poetry:

"Sir, why do I live?" he asks the sun,
And "Why was I sent?" he questions a star.
He said, "You are here to love and be loved,
To give of yourself to all mankind in whole,
To make others happy,
To brighten a soul,
To follow the path your Saviour trod,
My son, you are here to serve your God."

The poem was a far cry from one which she wrote when she was ten years old and her grandfather Seberg had died. "It was a poem of great irritation," Jean recalled in her adult years. "I [felt], 'How dare you all call yourselves Christians and believe in a hereafter and then be sobbing because this man left you, when, if you believed in his goodness, as you say you do, you know he's much happier?'"

Ed Seberg, Sr.'s death nevertheless affected the young Jean deeply, and whenever she needed to cry in her future films, she thought back to his passing. "I have to touch something cold. It could be an ice cube, a stone, or a damp wall," Jean later recalled. "The coldness brings back the memory of his funeral, and the tears come automatically."

While Ed and Dorothy Seberg did their best to divide their time and interest equally among the four children, they noticed their second daughter was not average. Jean was unlike other children in that she took each project she became involved in with an overabundance of enthusiasm and earnestness. This caused her parents great concern. They felt "Jeana" should be more carefree and less serious in her childhood.

"Jean was always what the town felt as 'different,'" Dorothy Seberg said in 1957. "...she lived a rather lonely life of her own choice in a world of her vivid imagination. I guess little Jean was getting ready all along for something special to happen to her."

Mary Ann, an honor student who later graduated from the State University of Iowa, also felt something extraordinary was going to occur in Jean's life. There was no sibling rivalry, but an ideal respect without indifference for each other's hopes and plans in their individual futures. Jean wanted to be an actress; Mary Ann to be a teacher and have children. "Jean loved her family very much, especially Mary Ann," says high-school friend Dawn Quinn. "She would tell me about Mary Ann being in the Scottish Highlanders [an acclaimed university band which included bagpipes and drums, as well as its members dressing in native costumes] and touring Europe with them. She was very proud of her."

As Jean grew into her teenaged years, her primary focus of interest appeared to shift onto two areas: acting and politics.

Not unlike Frances Benson, Jean loved watching movies at the Odeon Theatre and the Strand on Main Street. An early favorite was Betty Grable and *The Shocking Miss Pilgrim*, but this was displaced by the likes of James Dean, Piper Laurie, and Tony Curtis. Ingrid Bergman soon became Jean's favorite actress. Hours were spent leafing through the movie magazines at Seberg Pharmacy, where Jean daydreamed about becoming a movie star.

"I thumbed through a mail order catalog searching for the dresses I would wear when I and Rock Hudson drove across America together in his big, black, highly polished automobile," Jean recalled. "The dress for crossing the desert, the dress for posing in front of this or that monument. And then, the arrival in Marshalltown, my folks. 'Mom, this is Rock Hudson. No, we can't stop here. We need to push on to California.'"

"Whenever I think of Jean and I as children," says Mary Ann, "I think about us lying in our twin beds and Mother telling us it's time to get busy, and Jean's standard response was, 'I don't have to learn how to do that. I'm never going to have to do that. I'm going to grow up and be a movie star and I'm going to have a maid who will do all of my work.' From the time she was tiny, she was acting, she was performing. She was always going to be a movie star. That's all we ever heard."

A hint of Jean the actress was seen one morning when Dorothy Seberg was busy preparing food for her female friends, who were to visit the Seberg home shortly. Everything was in order, except for her second daughter's appearance. "Jean, please go to your room and put on something presentable," Dorothy told the jean-clad teenager. Jean turned and left the kitchen. After the guests arrived, Jean floated in, wearing a purple formal gown. Dorothy gasped as the nonchalant Jean served refreshments to the bemused women.

One afternoon when she was twelve, Jean saw the Marlon Brando film *The Men*. In it, Brando debuted as a paraplegic serviceman adjusting to life after the war. "Maybe the combination of medicine and acting had something to do with it," she later recalled, "but I was really very deeply impressed, and I left the movie feeling strangely shaken. For some reason the film made me aware of the power in acting, although Marlon Brando was certainly not my conception at the time of a typical movie star." She subsequently added she viewed the film as a way "to do something constructive, and help people."

After watching the film, Jean was determined to become an actress. "The next day I went to the public library in Marshalltown and told them I wanted to be an actress," Jean said in 1974. "There were a couple of books they could recommend, both by Stanislavsky, *An Actor Prepares* and *My Life in Art*. Well, I took them home, and couldn't make heads nor tails of them."

Brando's performance, nonetheless, inspired Jean to write a fan letter to the actor. "Dear Mr. Brando," she wrote. "I know that you must get tired of all those reporters and photographers annoying you, so if you would like to, you are very welcome to come and stay with me and my family as long as you want." Jean did not receive a response. Years later, when she met Brando and told him of her letter and offer, he replied, "Why don't you ask me now?"

Jean learned at an early age that not all people were created equal. Some lived in big, fancy houses, while others lived in cramped, one-story homes. She discovered there were different classes in society, and although the Sebergs were considered middle class, these disparities bothered her. Some families had a new car annually, while others drove the same old Ford year after year. (Mary Ann recalls her parents having a 1937 beetle-shaped Ford "for way too many years. I can remember being embarrassed and complaining to my folks about it. I think their next car was a Hudson.")

Jean later told of reading a book when she was eight, the story of a little black girl who was riding a bus with her mother. The girl noticed people were looking at her as if she were odd. The girl's mother said: "They're looking at you because you're very beautiful and have coffee-colored skin which they don't have, and that's why they're envious." "In short, that childhood reading revealed a whole new world to me," Jean recalled. "I understood that racial prejudices existed ... I saw how far [blacks] were excluded, isolated from the others. I understood the problems of human relations which they had to confront every day and the objects of contempt they had become."

One summer, while working as a counselor in Riverview Park, Jean befriended several black children. Observing the difference that existed between whites and blacks in her hometown, Jean decided to do something. "Marshalltown had no real problems with the blacks," Jean offered years later in Paris. "They lived apart — the poorest, the most underprivileged down by the railroad tracks. They had their own churches, their own social life. The whites ignored them. Only when racial tensions began to mount did I become involved."

While Jean was elected co-president of the student body in her ninth grade year, she mailed an application for membership in the Des Moines chapter of the NAACP. She was fourteen at the time. This act — in the years of McCarthy and his hunt for un-American subversives — sent the locals gossiping, shocked her friends, and surprised her parents. "Jean," her concerned father told her, "[people] will say you're a Communist." Jean replied, "I just don't care what they will say."

In the late 1960s, Jean tried to explain her reasons for joining the NAACP: "I really don't know why I did it," she told *Cosmopolitan* writer Joan Barthel. "There was a black athlete at our high school who fascinated me. There would always be after game parties at which he'd dance with the white girls. He could hold them as aggressively close as he wanted to, which he sometimes did with a vengeance. But when the dance was over, the iron curtain fell and that was it. One night he asked to walk a white girl home and he [was] beaten up.

"I can think of a thousand reasons for my joining the NAACP that make me sound terrific, but the only valid reason I can think of is a kind of alienation. I was raised in a rather 'strict' atmosphere, and I thought that other people who were alienated in other ways must feel much more deeply."

By the time Jean Seberg entered Marshalltown High School in 1953, she had developed from a cute little girl into an attractive young woman. With her five-foot-four frame and green-gray eyes, accentuated by shoulder-length sandy-blonde hair, she caught the attention of others. It has been said that even when the teenaged Jean walked down the street, it was not uncommon for the local men — regardless of age or marital status — to take a second glance at her. In more ways than one, Jean Seberg was becoming a distinct individual in the public's eye.

2

"I don't believe I've changed, although people's attitudes toward me have. I've found you can go anywhere and get along with anyone if you're honest and not afraid to be yourself."
— Jean Seberg

Carol Houghton Dodd Hollingsworth was a Marshalltown High School speech teacher who had years of experience on the stage and in the classroom. She began her theater career in vaudeville and taught courses ranging from French to physical education. Hollingsworth was also one of the most influential people in Jean Seberg's early life. She had married and been widowed, had traveled extensively; and had acted in the legitimate theater. Hollingsworth would tell her students stories of her life experiences, but they were never flamboyant, only straightforward accounts of her past. To them, Hollingsworth was someone who had broken through the invisible confines of small-town Iowa and had gone out into the world.

Although Hollingsworth had known Ed and Dorothy Seberg for several years, her earliest memory of Jean was as a junior high student. Hollingsworth and some of her friends were giving a group of students a ride to a basketball game. Mary Ann and Jean were among them.

"Jean got in the backseat and she was just thrilled to death," Hollingsworth recalled. "She announced she was going to be an actress." Hollingsworth had heard countless other girls make the same statement. Usually she would smile and not respond to such a comment, but one day she went to see Jean act. "She was outstanding," Hollingsworth remembered. "I thought, well, she does have a little something."

While in high school, Jean enrolled in Hollingsworth's speech classes. When Hollingsworth's doorbell rang at 10:30 one evening she was tired and almost did not answer it. "Well, there was Jean, and she wanted to know if I thought she could become an actress," Hollingsworth reminisced decades later. "So I delivered my usual speech on DDT — drive, determination and talent. You have to have all three to succeed. And I told her 'it isn't all beer and skittles,' meaning it's not glamorous. My feelings are if you can't keep kids from going into the theater, fine. But I would never urge anybody into it."

To her students, Hollingsworth was known as Coach in the classroom and as Ma outside of school, even long after her students had graduated and moved away. When Jean's friend Hannah Druker-Heyle had her eighteenth birthday, Jean, Hannah, and Lynda Haupert invited Hollingsworth to a party. "We had ginger ale in champagne glasses," Hollingsworth remembered. "They were a lot of fun."

Jean and her friends enjoyed Carol Hollingsworth's speech class so much that she and a few other students, without Hollingsworth's knowledge, begged Marshalltown High School principal B.R. Miller for a second-year speech class. Their plea was successful.

Jean entered oratorical competitions and one-act play contests. She was an immediate success, a natural actress. Her performance in Thornton Wilder's *The Happy Journey to Trenton and Camden* won her first citation at the Drake University Play Festival in Des Moines. One of the judges went so far as to say Jean "was the best Beulah I've ever seen."

On one occasion Jean replaced a student who had suddenly taken ill for a speech contest. With only a day's notice, she pulled a convincing performance. "She was the kind that you don't find very often, who can pick up a part and know how to read it," Hollingsworth explained. "She could play straight or character, and she was very smart and took direction well. If I ever asked her to make a change in her delivery, and very often there wasn't any, but if there was a change, you just tell her once and that'd be it." On another occasion, Jean was given three days to learn a role in *Fireman Save My Child*. Again, her performance was convincing.

Jean's first stage assignment was as an understudy in *Ladies of the Jury* in her junior year. "When she wasn't busy learning lines as the understudy, she'd be busy doing other things associated with the play. Several times I saw her sweeping the stage floor," Hollingsworth recalled. "She was so wrapped up with theater."

Whenever Hollingsworth directed a school play, she invited the cast and crew to her home on the last night. "We would play charades," Hollingsworth said. "We would use play titles and the room would be filled with kids. '*Tis a Pity She's a Whore* was one title, but *Blithe Spirit* was the hardest to do."

In a self-evaluation written for Carol Hollingsworth, Jean wished to "… lower my voice pitch and develop a wider range … I want to, and should, know more about acting and not over-act or drop lines. My participation in the oratorical contests has practically abolished my fear of audiences (though I'm still a little nervous before plays). Probably what I consider most valuable was the reading of plays. It opened a whole new field of interest to me. I loathe work — I hate dusting, cooking, clerking and waitressing. This year I've found a kind of work that requires thought and preparation and use of every part of a person, and I've really enjoyed it. I'd like to continue, as it's my favorite class. P.S. Thank you for being so patient with me."

After her junior year in high school, Jean enrolled in acting workshops in the summer of 1955 at the State University of Iowa. While there she played Moy Fah Loy in *The Yellow Jackets*. Gail Rhodes, who also attended the workshops, remembers Jean as "really serious about acting: very proud of her family, yet very much a lady." Rhodes also recalls Jean giving her tips on how to act around boys: "Jean said, 'If you can't cry beautifully in front of a boy, then you shouldn't cry at all. Because then you've had it.' She really made an impression on me. I then wondered to myself, 'How do I cry?'"

Although Jean's primary goal was the theater, she honored her parents' advice to be involved in a variety of activities. She played the glockenspiel in the band, sang with the mixed chorus and studied Latin and Spanish for one year. She also participated in the extramural girls' basketball league and joined G-Y (Girls Y), the Marshalltown YWCA social club for teenagers. In her bobby socks and calf-length skirts Jean went to Bible camp, and once, when the band formed the outline of a sombrero during the half-time show of a football game, Jean dazzled the crowd with a Spanish-influenced dance.

Despite her activities, Jean found time for socializing, which included dances and watching movies. She was struck by James Dean's performance in *Rebel Without a Cause* so much that she watched it several times, once dragging Carol Hollingsworth to the theater. Saddened by Dean's unexpected death, Jean sent a letter of condolence to his aunt with $5 for flowers to be put on his grave for his birthday. She received a note of thanks from the aunt and showed it to only two of her friends — Dawn Quinn and Lynda Haupert. She feared the others would make fun of her.

Jean later recalled going to parties with her friends where the girls whispered about the affairs of a contemporary. "You never knew what to expect from Jean," says Lynda Haupert. "She was very caring, always considerate. But she also loved to shock people. I remember she took me aside one day and told me she was going to tell her boyfriend she was pregnant. My jaw must have dropped. Then she said, 'Just to see what his reaction would be.'"

Jean's taste in boyfriends varied throughout her high school years. After Jean's death, gossip concerning her alleged promiscuity as a teenager ran rampant throughout Marshalltown. One schoolmate claimed to have dated Jean for two years while both were in high school — obviously a false claim to fame by a man who was probably rejected by Jean in their youth.

"I have never heard of these stories," says Lynda Haupert. "She may have 'necked' in her early teen years, but she was not sexually active at an early age. As for those who say they dated Jean for years on end, I find it hard to believe, since she had dated several boys in high school." It would not have gone unnoticed by her best friend if Jean had dated one person exclusively for two years.

One man who did catch Jean's interest was Paul Richer, an instructor at Marshalltown High School who earlier had been fired for his controversial teaching methods in Riceville, Iowa. *Time* magazine reported then that Richer taught a two-and-a-half-week course on Communism and read his students passages from *Of Mice and Men*. Richer's teaching style caused a lot of gossip in Marshalltown, but to the young and impressionable Jean Seberg he was a man not afraid to express his beliefs, no matter how extreme. "She was quite taken with him and was going to quit school," Carol Hollingsworth said, but she dismissed the suggestion that Jean's relationship with Richer was serious. "She was funny. She had crushes." When Richer left Marshalltown for military service, the relationship dissolved.

Not dismayed, Jean invested her time in other interests, including politics. In the summer after her junior year in 1955 Jean was chosen to represent Marshalltown High School at Girls' State, a youth forum sponsored by local auxiliaries of the American Legion. The three hundred attendees voted her "most representative Girls' State," and in a mock election she was appointed lieutenant governor, which sent her to Washington, D.C. There, she was nominated the vice-presidential candidate of the Nationalist party, and although Jean did not win, she was voted "All-Round Girls' Stater."

In December 1955, Jean was named the first teenage chairperson of the

Iowa March of Dimes campaign, an honor she was thrilled to receive. A rare promotional film of an interview between Jean and then-Iowa Governor Leo Hoegh was made, in which she gave her reasons for joining the fight against polio:

"Teenagers see the need to help in the polio campaign. We're in the age group where we see our friends on crutches, mothers and fathers in wheelchairs. We see whole families handicapped because crippled fathers can't work. And to me, the saddest sight of all, we see people in iron lungs. Possibly there for the rest of their lives …

"… and, Governor, we're growing up. Soon it will be our responsibility that you and other people in Iowa and America have. And we want to show you and other Iowa grown-ups that we can do that job. We appreciate our way of life, our health and our need to know how to assume and carry out responsibility."

The film reflects Jean's compassionate interest in politics and society, but at the same time it reveals the love affair the camera had with her, even as a teenager. The piece shows the beauty, poise, and diction that singled her out later in life, beginning to take form.

3

"If I had made it clear at the start that I was only interested in screening girls with talent, I would have saved many, many girls some unhappiness. Many of them [thought] that I would make them into a movie star by some magic."
— Otto Preminger

In January 1956 Carol Hollingsworth selected the play *Sabrina Fair* for the school production. It was the story of a girl who goes to Paris, becomes a sophisticate, then returns to her chauffeur-father's workplace in Long Island, where she is pursued by two brothers. Hollingsworth chose Jean to play Sabrina, and on the first day of rehearsals, Jean knew all her lines.

When the play was performed to the sold-out 1,000-seat auditorium, patrons left amazed. "I remember thinking she was awfully good," says Marshalltown resident Pauline Smith. "There were rumors then that if she wanted to be an actress, she could." Warren Robeson agreed: "My wife said to me as we were walking down the steps after the play: 'That girl's going to be a movie star.' And a year later she was."

The *Times-Republican* raved over Jean's acting, her "outstanding talent, perfect enunciation" and her French. Since the school did not offer French as a course, the accomplishment was applauded even more. (Carol Hollingsworth, who was fluent in French, coached Jean with the language.) A repeat performance was held a month later to benefit the Community Hospital, with Jean going door-to-door selling tickets. Jean's Sabrina was so memorable that to this day residents who attended the play vividly recall her performance.

"She played the lead in *Sabrina Fair*, and my policy was if a student played a lead in a play, they wouldn't play lead again," Hollingsworth said. "Of course I'd like to have had her play lead in several things — but she didn't."

As the lead in Sabrina Fair. *Lynda Haupert stands in the doorway.*
AUTHOR'S COLLECTION

To fill the void, Jean concentrated on readings and dramatic pieces for competition. Throughout the spring of 1956 in her senior year, Jean won several honors, including an American Legion oratorical contest. She repeated the previous year's outstanding player award honor at the State University of Iowa Play Festival, when she played Emily in Act III of *Our Town*. She then earned a Division I top rating in the Iowa High School Speech Association competition for her twelve-minute excerpt from, prophetically, Maxwell Anderson's *Joan of Lorraine*.

While it appeared that Jean Seberg was headed for bigger and brighter things, however, schoolmates began to criticize her for her ambitions. "She'd tell people that she would meet Marlon Brando someday," says Dawn Quinn, "and that she was going to be a big movie star. But people would laugh at her — they did not believe in her talent. Once she received some anonymous phone calls and letters running her down, asking her who she thought she was. She told me about them."

Quinn also reveals a deep-seated insecurity in Jean which rarely surfaced in those early years, one that questioned loyalty and trust. "[Jean] broke down and said, 'Dawn, I'd trade all of my honors and talent for some true friends and a boy who really loves me.' Jean was more sensitive and caring than most people thought. She'd go out of her way to befriend 'unpopular' kids that you weren't supposed to be interested in. When my parents and

Sightseeing in Massachusetts while performing summer stock, 1956.
COURTESY OF SEBERG FAMILY COLLECTION

I moved to Marshalltown in my senior year, I didn't know anybody. Our backyard touched the Sebergs' and one day she came over and introduced herself. We became friends immediately. Her parents would sometimes call her Jeana, and she was 'Jeana' to me all her life."

"I'll never forget how she was for the underdog," Carol Hollingsworth stated. "This one boy in her class had had some trouble, and he was just going to leave school and go into the Navy. Well, this was another ten-thirty call at night, and in came Jean with her little friends telling me I have to do something about this kid. 'He couldn't go into the Navy — he was in the play. He couldn't leave the play' and so all of us finally persuaded him to stay in school and get his diploma. Quite a few years later he wrote to both Jean and me and thanked us for convincing him to finish school."

In June 1956 Jean graduated from high school, eleventh out of 197 students. Her yearbook, *The Post Script*, shows a caricature of her running after a motorcyclist, calling out "Marlon, Marlon." The caption reads: "Same Old Chase." The class poll named her "Best Dancer," "Most Sophisticated," and "Most Likely to Succeed."

Gazing into a crystal ball, the high school newspaper, *Pebbles*, predicted twenty years from then, "Jean Seberg has become a second Helen Hayes and in her spare time she's a soda jerk at Seberg's."

Carol Hollingsworth arranged a scholarship for Jean to apprentice at a theater in Cape Cod, which took her to the east coast. Jean then auditioned before the staff at Priscilla Beach Theater, located outside of Plymouth, Massachusetts in June. She was the youngest of the forty-odd young actors and actresses, and performed a selection from *Joan of Lorraine* which had won her citations earlier that spring. The directors immediately cast her in the lead female role of Madge in *Picnic*, William Inge's drama of a wayward man's impact on the lives of a group of small-town people in Kansas.

She was cast opposite John Maddox, a slim, curly-haired young actor from Fort Worth, Texas who played Hal, the vagrant. Before long, Jean fell in love with the handsome Maddox. Years later, after Jean became famous, Maddox told friends he and Jean would drive out to the country in an old pickup he had, and make love under the star-filled skies. Once summer stock was completed, Maddox said he and Jean planned to move to New York together and try to secure work in the theater. Friends believe this was Jean's first serious romance.

Jean reveled in the tight-knit company of the PBT (dubbed "Peanut Butter Theater" by the actors), the late-night talk sessions, and camaraderie of the actors. The actors called Jean "Grace Kelly" because of her poise and distant beauty. Mornings at the theater were spent with classes. Rehearsals began after lunch and often continued through the late evening. The more she experienced of summer stock theater, the less promising the prospect of studying at a university in the Midwest looked to Jean.

After completing *Picnic*, Jean worked the rest of the summer at the Cape May Playhouse in New Jersey. "I was paid fifteen dollars a week," Jean recalled, "and ten dollars of it went to the landlady. She was the kind you see in the movies. You know, on payday she was at the door with her hand out and steel in her eye." At the Victorian rooming house, Jean bunked with two other girls and "we made stew in a big kettle in the yard out in back of the theater," she recalled. At the playhouse Jean played several leading roles, including Sally Carroll in *The Two Mrs. Carrolls*, the title role in *Claudia*, Susie in *The Late Christopher Bean*, and concluding with the role of Sorel in Noel Coward's *Hay Fever*.

On one August night, Jean and some of her friends went to the Cape May movie theater, where they saw a trailer announcing that director Otto Preminger was searching for a young woman to be his Joan of Arc in the upcoming film production, *Saint Joan*. Interested females between the ages of sixteen and twenty-two were asked to fill out application forms in the theater lobby. Jean dismissed the contest as a gimmick. She felt a studio contract player or an already established actress would play the role.

The contest was genuine, despite her scepticism. United Artists backed Preminger's campaign with $100,000 to find his Joan of Arc. Three million printed appeals were distributed around the world, and eleven thousand trailers pushing the contest appeared in movie theaters across North America and Europe. In a few weeks, the news media touted Preminger's contest as the biggest talent search since David O. Selznick's quest for his Scarlett O'Hara in *Gone With the Wind*.

In Marshalltown, news of the contest caught the attention of J. William (Bill) Fisher. In addition to being the millionaire head of Fisher Controls, Fisher was a staunch supporter of the arts. He subsidized operas at the New York Metropolitan Opera, and he owned a multi-million-dollar collection of Impressionist paintings and ceramic pieces which were later donated to and permanently displayed in Marshalltown.

Fisher telephoned Carol Hollingsworth. "I'm going to submit that girl who presented me with the gold cuff links in the ceremony at the YMCA last year," Fisher announced.

"You mean Jean Seberg?"

"Yes. Have you recommended her for that movie contest?"

"No, I haven't," Hollingsworth replied.

"Bill Fisher told me that he and the theater manager recommended Jean for the contest, and he told me to go down to the theater and also recommend her," Hollingsworth maintained. "Well, I talked it over with my husband and thought, 'If anything does come of this, and she or her folks don't want her to do it, all they have to say is 'no.' Neither one of us thought anything would ever come of it.

"But I was the fourth person to recommend Jean. Her summer stock group in the East also submitted her name, and she knew it. But I get either the 'credit' or the 'blame,' when actually I was the low man on the totem pole."

Regardless of the support, Jean did not think she would be given the role. She kept telling people "I'll never get it." What she hoped for, however, was to meet Preminger and impress him enough to get an encouraging word to show her parents. Jean felt perhaps that would convince her parents to let her take acting lessons in New York.

Jean knew little about Otto Preminger. She was aware that he was a powerful Hollywood director, but that was about all. She remembered seeing his film *The Man With the Golden Arm*, a breakthrough film that dealt with illegal drug use, starring Frank Sinatra. "I saw it in Marshalltown," Jean recalled years later, "with a boy I didn't like, and I had a stomach ache. So all I remember is that it was a great pain to me."

At the end of the summer Jean returned to Marshalltown and discovered she was among the 3,000 finalists for personal auditions with Preminger.

She was not the only one from Marshalltown. Jayanna Welsh, then a student at Stephens College in Columbia, Missouri, was also a finalist. "A rather pretty girl," Carol Hollingsworth said. "She had a great desire to become an actress." Welsh's interview in St. Louis was held in mid-September. It ended there.

Jean's audition was set to take place at 10:00 a.m. at the Sherman Hotel in Chicago on September 15. Ed and Dorothy agreed to take her to Chicago, but told their daughter she must first enroll at the State University of Iowa. At the Iowa City campus, Jean declared herself a drama major and pledged her sister's sorority, Kappa Alpha Theta. "I took my suitcases into the University and met my room-mate, and then left immediately for Chicago," Jean recalled.

"Our parents were always supportive," says Mary Ann Seberg, "and they always encouraged us. I never remember them being upset other than going to Chicago to let Jean tryout for *Saint Joan*. At the time it was a big trip, and it was expensive. They thought it was a fluke — they didn't think there was anything that would come of it. And I think they might have been afraid of what might happen if something did come of it."

Although excited about the prospect of personally meeting Otto Preminger, Jean downplayed any chance of winning the role of St. Joan. "What bothers me most," she wrote a friend, "is that I'm going to miss the big Woody Herman concert," which was to take place back home while she was in Chicago.

In the Sherman Hotel's Bal Tabarin room on the fifteenth, Jean found herself among one-hundred-fifty other potential actresses auditioning. Seated next to Jean, in alphabetical order, was Julie Sommars, who was fifteen years old at the time and also from Iowa. Sommars remembered Jean, as they had been competitors in the Iowa State oratorical contest earlier in the year. When Jean was called to read for Preminger, "She dumped her street shoes in my lap and told me to watch them when she went in to see him," Sommars recalled.

Preminger and his assistants held court on a raised platform in an adjoining room, in which two bright spotlights enveloped the stage. The director was unseen in the room, invisible to those reading in the darkness. Each of the girls was asked to read a three-minute passage from the play:

"Perpetual imprisonment! Am I not then to be set free? ... Go, light your fire! ..."

Jean Seberg walked onto the stage, smiling, fresh, optimistic. She recited the first of two speeches from the play to the unseen Preminger, when he stopped her.

"How old are you?" he demanded.

"Seventeen," she answered.

"I don't believe it," he replied.

Preminger then noticed she had not worn a cross from her neck like the other girls. He asked her why.

"My family is too poor to afford one."

Knowing a line such as that would not work with a seasoned professional as Preminger, Jean then laughed and said, "Because I knew all of the other girls would be wearing them." She then recited a second speech that Preminger had asked the girls to memorize. "She was in there for what seemed like forever," Julie Sommars remembered. "When she came out, she grabbed the shoes and said, 'He listened to both my speeches,' and marched away."

Sommars was then presented to Preminger, but was dismissed because he felt she was too young. Sommars, however, went on to an acting career that included roles on *The Loretta Young Show*, *Matlock*, and *The Governor and J.J.* on television.

Later that day Preminger asked Jean to read a second time. After she finished, Preminger smiled. "You're a very talented girl." After Jean's reading, the *Chicago Tribune* reported "… Jean Seberg may cop the Saint Joan role in Otto Preminger's movie. She auditioned at the Sherman Hotel un Herr Otto did der flip!" Preminger then met with the Sebergs and told them he wanted Jean in New York for the final rounds of auditions. "You have a very talented daughter," Preminger told the speechless couple.

Ed Seberg recalled that first meeting with Preminger in Chicago. "He was walking around his room chewing a great big, red apple. He said 'You vant an apple?' and I said, 'No.' 'You vant a drink?' I said, 'No.' He said, 'Vell, we vant to take your girl to New York.' And I said, 'I don't want her to go.' 'Ve do not gobble up little girls in New York.' So what are you going to do? Jean was determined to go. The thrill of a lifetime."

Despite personal reservations, Ed and Dorothy allowed Jean to attend the next set of auditions. She flew to New York two weeks after the Chicago tryout to prepare for a screen test. While in New York, Jean went to several plays and visited friends from summer stock. Before checking out of the Ambassador Hotel, where the Preminger group had secured her room, Jean paid for her meals and telephone calls, much to the director's chagrin. She did not wish to take advantage of Preminger hospitality, preferring to show him she was a mature and independent-minded young woman.

Jean returned to Marshalltown, waiting for word on the contest. Her romance with John Maddox had come to an end, with Maddox certain Jean was destined for fame. While friends later claimed that Maddox was obsessed with established actors who had extraordinary careers, Maddox himself was unable to achieve a successful acting career. Friends claim he became seriously manic-depressive. Years later, he chartered a sailboat for an excursion along the Virginia coast and was never seen again. Maddox mysteriously disappeared, allegedly in the Bermuda Triangle.

By October 17, Jean was back in New York. The 18,000 entrants were now reduced to a group of four: Kelli Blaine, a New Yorker who studied at the Actor's Studio; Doreen Denning, a Swedish actress; Olga Bielinska of Milwaukee, Wisconsin; and Jean Seberg, the pharmacist's daughter from Iowa.

Each finalist was asked to act out scenes from the play for a second screen test. After Jean delivered her initial scene, Preminger asked her if she would be willing to cut her hair for the rest of the test. Jean agreed, and the resulting short crop gave prominence to her cheekbones, while her eyes gained a distinctive spark.

"I wanted to win; I had to win," Jean recalled years later. "Wasn't I Joan's age; didn't I come from a small farming town? And I didn't want to marry the boy next door, either!"

Preminger drove Jean through rehearsals that day, forcing her to repeat scenes over and over. He tore into her with an onslaught of criticism, including, "You're nothing but a ham and a phony. You can't act and you will never be able to." The harder she tried, the more tired she became, which resulted in Preminger saying after one scene, "Well, you did that almost as well as Rita Hayworth." The Preminger personality was only beginning to show.

Nonetheless, Preminger had found his St. Joan in Jean Seberg.

After the final test he went into her dressing room and noticed some violets on the table.

"Who bought you these violets?" he asked.

"I bought them myself. They are my favorite flower."

"Well then, I will see you have fresh violets in your dressing room every day when we are in England," the director replied as he hugged her. It was then that Jean learned she had been given the part.

Preminger announced his choice at a press conference at noon on Sunday, October 21. Arrangements were made so that Ed and Dorothy Seberg could be in New York when the announcement was made, although they were told beforehand that Jean had won the role. Reluctantly, Ed Seberg found a neighbor to mind the store, and he and Dorothy flew east and registered at the St. Moritz Hotel in New York, courtesy of Preminger.

"I think I was disappointed that she wasn't going to be my sorority sister. I really was," says Mary Ann Seberg. "I was looking forward to having her at [University of] Iowa, and I know my parents were really concerned about her life. My Dad was disappointed that she wasn't going to get her college education. I thought that this film was going to be it for her — that she would do this one film, and then come back to Iowa and go to school."

At the press conference Preminger introduced Jean and then Richard Widmark, who was signed for the role of the weakling Dauphin. Later that afternoon Jean placed a call to Carol Hollingsworth to tell her the good news, but she was not at home at the time. A former student who lived in New York called Hollingsworth with the news.

That same evening Preminger presented Jean to the world on *The Ed Sullivan Show*, which featured singer Marion Marlowe, the boxing Scimpini chimps and comic Jack Paar. After introducing the victor of the *Saint Joan* contest, Sullivan described Jean as "the girl who caught lightning in a bottle." Sullivan then introduced Ed and Dorothy Seberg, who were in the audience. While a spotlight searched for the couple, the pair momentarily rose from

Preparing for the Marshalltown festivities after it was announced Jean was chosen to play Joan of Arc. AUTHOR'S COLLECTION

their seats, only after being told to stand. Jean then reenacted her audition scene before sixty million viewers.

"Do I need to tell you," she gushed, "that I am the happiest girl in the world?" Preminger explained that his reason for choosing Jean was not so much her acting ability, but "her personality. It's very difficult to describe it in words. She has an enchanting personality and she captivated me. That's the best answer: she captivated me."

The next day, Jean was interviewed by Dave Garroway on the NBC *Today* morning show. Later that week, in a further stage of her transformation into his idea of an actress, Preminger had moles removed from her face. Just one beauty spot remained high on her left cheek.

Upon her return home to Iowa, Jean was met at the Des Moines airport by her family, Iowa Governor Leo Hoegh, a group of local and national news reporters and photographers, and a large crowd of well-wishers. "I was so shocked when she came off the plane with that haircut — almost boyish," Carol Hollingsworth recalled. "I thought to myself, 'Is this Jean?'"

Riding in the back of an open Cadillac convertible, Jean was driven to Des Moines City Hall where she received an orchid corsage, a key to the city, and a small gold-plated ear of corn, lest she forget her roots.

"I think the whole community was excited about that," says Pauline Smith of the win. "After all, there's this young girl that was selected from our town to play this important part. It seemed that it was going to be a very important movie, it was a well-known director, and there was so much publicity about it. The whole town was extremely proud of her at the time, and excited about the prospects of her being in a movie."

At Seberg Pharmacy with her father Ed. COURTESY OF INDEPENDENT VISIONS

A police escort led Jean and her family on the fifty-mile drive northeast to Marshalltown, with a two-and-a-half-mile procession of vehicles following them. Along the way, Ed told his daughter, "Remember old Mr. Mendenhall? He came into the store after *The Ed Sullivan Show*, and every time he tried to tell me something, he'd burst out crying. 'Oh, Ed,' he'd say, 'she can do so much good!' And then, 'Boo hoo!'" Jean laughed, but when she wisecracked, "I guess I'll marry Elvis Presley and reform him," her father did not find her response amusing.

Hundreds of people lined the streets of Marshalltown to show their excitement and to catch a glimpse of the future star. Placards proclaiming "We're Proud of You, Jean" covered store windows. The Marshalltown High School band marched down Main Street in front of an open convertible where Jean sat, waving to the crowd.

At the Community YMCA, an eight-foot portrait of Jean hung outside the spot where she was presented with a key to the city of Marshalltown. After speeches from town officials, Jean spoke to the crowd. "First of all, I'd like to know if this key will open any banks," she giggled nervously. "It'll be a big help to know that you are all encouraging me. I hope that I can make this role come to life. I'll do my best."

With classmates and high school drama teacher and lifelong friend Carol Hollingsworth.
COURTESY OF INDEPENDENT VISIONS

That evening at the Orpheum Theater, a thirteen-minute clip from Jean's screen-test was shown. The *Times-Republican* commented that "her portrayal of St. Joan brought a lump to the throat and a tear to the eye. Viewers came away certain that stardom was assured." Local girl had made good.

Dawn Quinn recalls the celebration differently: "Marshalltown never really accepted Jean, even before her career. Her beliefs and support of causes were too liberal. That town had been mean to her in the past. All of a sudden, everyone was fawning all over her. She was still the same girl, though. It was terribly hypocritical, and by the end of the day Jean was exhausted and close to hysterics because of those people."

"There was a sense of pride, of course, in Jean. I'm sure there was some envy because, after all — especially girls my age — that was something to be chosen and become a movie star," says Pauline Smith. "That was everybody's dream, even in the back of your mind."

Jean was not the only girl from Marshalltown with stars in her eyes. Within two years of the *Saint Joan* contest, no fewer than five young girls from Marshalltown publicly emigrated either to New York or to Hollywood to find their fame and fortune. After all, they thought, if Jean Seberg could become a movie star, why couldn't they? Unfortunately, none went on to the reach the status in the film world which Jean achieved.

During Jean's week at home, Marshalltown High School held a special assembly in her honor at which the school's drama club, Masque and Dagger, initiated the annual "Jean Seberg Award," to be given to the most promising drama student. The recipient's name would be engraved beneath Jean's on a plaque to be displayed at the school. In addition, the recipient would receive a small scholarship provided by Jean. Years later, the original plaque mysteriously disappeared.

Discussions of her newly signed seven-year contract with Preminger led Ed Seberg to suggest Jean should live on a $25 weekly allowance, with the remaining amount deposited into her savings account. The contract gave her a flat rate of $250 a week the first year, while Preminger paid for her living expenses himself. The second year her salary was to increase to $400 a week for forty weeks. By the seventh year she would be earning $2,500 a week if still under contract to Preminger.

On November 13, her eighteenth birthday, Jean boarded a plane for New York on her way to London, where *Saint Joan* would be filmed. Alongside other news media, Preminger's publicity personnel recorded the departure. Clutching a white leatherbound Bible from Dawn Quinn, the golden ear of corn, and a satin mouse for luck from Frances Benson, Jean waved goodbye to her family and well-wishers as she boarded the plane, bound for an uncertain future.

After her landing in London and meeting with the English press, Preminger and his entourage of photographers and publicists took Jean on a four-day trip to France to visit sites associated with the saint. While Preminger stayed in Paris, Jean, American journalist Tom Ryan, and still photographer Bob Willoughby went on a pilgrimage to Domrémy, the village where Joan of Arc was born and first heard the voices. The group then went on to Orléans, where the Maid defeated her enemies, to Compiègne, where she was captured, and to the Cathedral of Rheims, where she crowned a French king. In the archives, Jean read the records of the original trial. "It was terribly exciting, so eerie," she enthused, "just as though you were there in the court, inside Joan."

The highlight of the tour for Jean was Paris. Since childhood, she had dreamed of visiting the city of lights. "What a place and amazing people!" she exclaimed. "In Paris I walked up and down the Champs-Élysées, bought dresses at Dior's," she said, "and saw Ingrid Bergman in the play *Tea and Sympathy*. Oh, she was kind — she told me my haircut was the shortest yet. I have it cut every three days." Bergman had played Joan of Arc in the 1948 film of that name.

At her first press conference in Paris, Jean told reporters that the only person in her family remotely connected with show business had been her grandmother Frances Benson. She elaborated that Frances "wanted to be a bareback rider in a circus but never made it." The next day one newspaper reported, "Miss Seberg's grandmother wanted to ride a bear." Another wrote, "Miss Seberg's grandmother wanted to ride bare."

While Jean "really loved" Paris, her strongest impression was of the countryside, with its gently rolling hills, which reminded her of eastern Iowa. She found it beautiful and breathtaking.

Jean returned to London for *Saint Joan*. Jean admitted she was not nervous — not until the first rehearsal, when she was introduced to her co-stars. Sir John Gielgud was the first one she met. "I was petrified," she admitted. "I didn't know what to call him — Sir John, Mr. Gielgud, or what? I blurted out, 'I'm so glad to meet you, Mr. Sir John Gielgud.'"

Jean sat at a table with other cast members and read the script out loud. "I sat there and looked around me at all those great people of the stage, and I was afraid when I opened my mouth the words would not come. I thought, 'You poor little innocent. What on earth are you doing here?'"

But as time passed, Gielgud, Widmark, and the other cast members talked with Jean, invited her for tea, and gave her small gifts, making her feel more comfortable and less tense.

However, Preminger did not want his new star to become too close to the other actors. His carefully calculated daily scheduling was so precise that there was scarcely time for Jean to socialize off set.

"She was terribly lonely during *Saint Joan* that Christmas Eve," Carol Hollingsworth said. "She had to stay in Europe rather than return home for the holidays. Preminger had no thought at all for that child. He really was a beast."

CHAPTER TWO
1957–1959

"To take an actor's belief in himself away is like cutting off the wings of a bird and saying to it: 'and now try to fly, if you can.' "
— Jean Seberg

Celebrating her birthday with François Moreuil on the set of The Mouse That Roared.
COURTESY OF SNORRAMYNDIR

4

"Forget who you are and what you were. You must be Joan of Arc."
— Otto Preminger to Jean Seberg

While in Britain, Jean was named among a group of Iowans who had brought "exceptional glory and honor to themselves, their respective communities and our state," according to a resolution passed by the Iowa senate. Others honored included 1956 Miss Universe Carol Morris of Ottumwa, poet Paul Engle, and the Rose Bowl-winning State University of Iowa football team. "People tell me that I'll do for Iowa what [the musical] *Oklahoma!* did for Oklahoma," Jean quipped. "The only thing, they don't say what *Oklahoma!* did for Oklahoma."

Filming *Saint Joan* commenced on January 9, 1957. Despite the huge publicity campaign Preminger built for finding a new Joan, he could do nothing to control gossip leaked to the press. One account had the director demanding the replacement of his suite door at the Dorchester because he did not like the design. Another said Preminger had rows at a British airport because planes did not wait for him. As a result a new publicity man was hired, but it was to no avail, and the negative press continued. Sir John Gielgud had already replaced Richard Burton as Warwick, and now French cameraman Georges Périnal took over from the Briton Desmond Dickinson. In addition, Paul Schofield asked to be released from the role of Ladvenu, a part now taken by Kenneth Haigh.

"How that man works," said Archie Duncan, who had a part in the film. "Even on a day off when he doesn't intend to shoot a foot of film, it's rehearse and re-rehearse. I never worked so hard in my life."

Nor had she. Jean was awakened at 5:00 a.m., breakfasted at 5:30, at 6:15 left the hotel and was driven to Shepperton Studios twenty miles away. Then followed make-up at 7:00, rehearsal at 8:00 and filming 8:30 through noon. After a half-hour lunch, filming resumed until 6:00 p.m., followed by viewing the previous day's rushes from 6:00 until 7:00, an hour's drive back to the hotel, dinner at 8:00 p.m. in her hotel room and bed by 9. Seldom did this schedule change, but once Preminger allowed Jean to accept the dinner invitation of Vivien Leigh and Laurence Olivier in London. Preminger also introduced her to Harry Belafonte, whom Preminger had directed in *Carmen Jones*. "Harry was just what I needed then," Jean said. "I was confused by everything, and he gave me good advice about acting."

Despite wearing a suit of armor that weighed thirty pounds, Jean was the consummate professional until taunting by Preminger caused her to speak back.

"What's the matter? Can't you do this scene?" Preminger prodded her.

She stood, looked him straight in the eye, and flared defiantly: "I'll do this scene 'til you drop dead!"

Another time he asked her, "You're a short thing. What makes you think you can act?"

"Well, Helen Hayes isn't very big," Jean shot back.

"At first she was intimidated by Preminger," says Mary Ann Seberg. "But she stood up to him when he frightened her. My feeling was that it was a hate/love relationship. She appreciated the opportunity to work with him, but really didn't like the way he treated her at times." Jean had allies in many cast and crew members, including Gielgud, who felt that Preminger's haranguing was taking its toll on the inexperienced actress. Jean and Gielgud engaged in long conversations and played chess, and she sought his advice. "Don't worry about fame as an actress. Fame does not change a person," Gielgud told her. "People who know you least will say you've changed — but those who love you the best will see that you are still the same." Not long after, he presented Jean with a gift: a cup and saucer that had once belonged to his great-aunt, the celebrated actress Ellen Terry.

Jean did not tell her parents of every tirade she suffered from Preminger, but one letter betrayed a hint of the stresses: "I am very happy in this work. It is intensely difficult and exhausting and sometimes infuriating, but it is what I wanted."

Roger Furse, the designer of costumes and sets, wrote Ed and Dorothy Seberg an encouraging letter during the filming:

"I have seldom, if ever, known someone who has been less affected by all that is happening to her. She is so genuine, and so modest, and at the same time so full of zest for her work and the interest she finds in meeting new people, that everyone is charmed by her goodness and her simplicity as well as her quickness to learn from a multitude of new experiences.

"I have met in the course of my professional life many young people who have been on the edge of success — many of whom have got it, and hold onto it — and I can honestly say that I have never yet met one who came to it with more buoyant, but modest spirit than your little Jean. She will deserve, and I think will have, great success. And it is good to think that she will know how to value it and how to use it."

In one highly charged scene the Inquisitor (played by Felix Aylmer) sentences Joan to life imprisonment and then surrenders her to the English. Aylmer turned to Jean apologetically after the scene was shot: "My dear, I hate to say such dreadful things to you."

Before filming the climax in which Joan is burned at the stake, Preminger opened the set to the press. It was a carefully orchestrated scene. Jean was chained to the stake with brushwood piled under her feet while extras yelled, "Burn her, burn her!" Beneath the wood were cylinders of gas which were supposed to ignite when the extras playing soldiers applied their flaming torches. There was to be a quick fire which would rapidly die down. At this moment the cameras were to stop rolling and Jean would be replaced by a mock-up dummy before completion of the scene.

As the cameras filmed, something went terribly wrong. The gas flared up too fiercely, and in an instant Jean was enveloped in fire. She uttered a scream and instinctively tried to cover her face. The extras now cried out for

Preparing to film Saint Joan's *climatic burning at the stake scene.*
COURTESY OF SNORRAMYNDIR

help while fire extinguishers smothered the flames. Stage hands removed Jean from the chains and she was carried off the pyre. Her hands were burned, as was her stomach and knee, and her hair was singed. Scars on her stomach stayed with Jean the rest of her life.

Preminger was accused of using the scene as a publicity stunt. "What do they think?" he asked. "Would I risk burning the star of my picture?" The incident, nonetheless, made front page headlines and pictures in newspapers and magazines across the world, and many like *Life* devoted an entire page or more to a sequence of dramatic photographs. Preminger saw fit to include seconds of the accident in the finished film.

"It was a very traumatic thing for her in that she didn't think that the people [on the set] really understood that she was being burnt," says Mary Ann Seberg. "She was really scared. I remember her saying she put her hands up to her face. It was terrifying for her." Always the professional, Jean publicly joked to the press: "I smell like a singed chicken," and added, "I felt so sorry for Otto Preminger. He must have been terrified."

As to what went wrong with the fire, Roy Whybrown, the special effects expert in charge of the scene, explained: "There were seven gas jets under the faggots. The soldiers who were supposed to light them failed to light two. So there was a certain amount of unburnt gas which accumulated and suddenly flared up."

Less than twenty-four hours after the incident, Jean again made the news. Riding to the set for additional filming, she was involved in a car accident with Preminger and photographer Bob Willoughby. Apparently, the car lost control on a patch of ice and slammed into a post. The director received some bruises and a sprained wrist, and some of Willoughby's camera equipment was damaged. Apart from a nosebleed Jean was not hurt, but she was shaken.

For publicity purposes, Preminger arranged for photographs to be released showing his protégée safe, sound, and happy despite the recent mishaps. News photos flashed across the globe with a smiling Preminger holding Jean's bandaged hand. Jean telephoned her parents to reassure them she was all right. "What I really want," she confessed, "is to be home for two weeks without a reporter within a hundred miles."

Soon after the recent chain of events, Jean sent Preminger a postcard showing a green monster cracking a whip. The caption read: "My, but we do have fun, don't we?"

While riding back to the Dorchester shortly before the completion of *Saint Joan*, Preminger told Jean he recently acquired the film rights to Françoise Sagan's best-selling novel *Bonjour Tristesse*. Confident of her work in *Saint Joan*, he gave the lead role of Sagan's French heroine Cecile to Jean.

Despite the calm exteriors Ed and Dorothy Seberg presented publicly, Dorothy was privately excited about the prospects of Jean's film career. Ed, on the other hand, was concerned about the disruption the press and Preminger's publicity people had caused in their otherwise tranquil lives. "Some of the things that happened to Jean were awfully hard on her parents," says Warren Robeson. "They were always supportive, but Ed would have been happy if Jean had never gotten into film. But he and Dorothy were very supportive and they never acted different because their child was a star."

"Mother's quite bewildered by it all," Jean told *Cue* magazine at the time, "but grandma loves it and keeps a huge scrapbook. Dad says that in about ten years from now he'll know better if he likes the whole idea."

Ed and Dorothy took part in the CBS television series *Stand Up and Be Counted* in February 1957. In the program, the studio audience was asked to give their views on certain subjects. When the Sebergs were asked, "Will you continue to live in Marshalltown or move to where your daughter goes?" a majority of the studio audience believed they should stay in Marshalltown. In reality, the Sebergs never even contemplated moving away from their home.

Returning to Marshalltown that spring, Jean found herself on the defensive when an article in the women's magazine *McCall's* appeared. The article contained quotes from the previous November's homecoming celebration. Doubting the sincerity of the community during the festivities, Jean had told *McCall's* reporter Helen Eustis, "I never felt as if I belonged here. I'd look at all the people in this town who just get up in the morning and go to work and go home to bed and I'd think 'If that's all there is to life, I don't want it.' I was always pretending I wasn't afraid, and I'd blustered and bluffed my way to all kinds of prizes and things. But I've never really been a happy person.

"I used to have a dream where I was being chased through the backyards by somebody who was going to stab me in the back. I always thought I'd die young."

When the quotes appeared, Jean told her friends, "Don't believe what you read about me in the papers." To smooth any ruffled feathers, Jean informed the *Des Moines Register* in a public apology that "I always wanted to act, and I wanted to go where I could act. There is more opportunity elsewhere. But that doesn't mean I don't love Marshalltown. I hope that people won't be mad at me. It's a wonderful place to grow up."

"She knew, like we all did," says Mary Ann, "that she was headed for something bigger than she could find in Marshalltown."

While at home, Jean took swimming lessons at the YMCA and studied basic French to prepare for her upcoming role in *Bonjour Tristesse*. Filming was set to begin in July 1957 on the French Riviera. David Niven was cast as the playboy father and Deborah Kerr as his love interest, with Jean excited by the prospect of playing Niven's disillusioned daughter. "She was thrilled to be in *Bonjour Tristesse*, I think more than *Saint Joan*," Carol Hollingsworth divulged. "In high school, she and the other kids told me that I must read *Bonjour Tristesse* — they just loved the book."

Although Jean was looking forward to her second movie role, the public and critical reception of *Saint Joan* had not yet been determined. Jean privately felt she could have performed better in different circumstances - if, for example, she had been closer to her family during the filming, rather than in England, if Preminger had been more understanding and less domineering, or perhaps if she could have taken private classes in film acting techniques.

The *Saint Joan* premiere was held on Joan of Arc day, May 12, 1957. There was generous coverage in the Paris newspapers, and tickets to the event priced from $100 to $1,000 benefited the French Polio Foundation. Since the annual Cannes Film Festival was in full swing, many personalities traveled to Paris specifically for the occasion. Among those who clamored for seats were Olivia de Havilland, Yul Brynner, Anita Ekberg, Bob Hope, Salvador Dali, Maurice Chevalier, and François Mitterand.

Jean, whose hair had grown out, wore an aqua Givenchy dress courtesy of Preminger. "I was going up the stairs," she recalled, "very ritzy in all my finery, trying hard to be sophisticated. But people kept crowding around, stepping on the train of the gown and I had to keep jerking it out from

With Saint Joan *director Otto Preminger at the film's premiere in Paris, May 1957.*
COURTESY OF SNORRAMYNDIR

under feet. It isn't exactly easy to smile and be dignified while you're pleading, 'Please get off my train.' Sophistication-wise, I had the distinct feeling I was falling on my face." Figuratively, she was.

Concerned with the reception of the film, Jean's parents sent a cablegram to her just before the premiere: "WE DON'T CARE WHETHER IT FAILS OR NOT. YOU'RE STILL OUR STAR." Unfortunately, the words of the Sebergs proved prophetic. The film was coolly received by those present at the screening, and few of the notables went on to attend the post-premiere party at Maxim's. "Everybody came up to me and said, 'You were wonderful,'" Jean later told Mike Wallace. "I was so gullible. I thought the film was a huge success."

Although Jean knew there were problems with the film and with her performance, only after seeing the audience's reaction at the premiere did Preminger realize *Saint Joan* was a flop. Years later, Preminger reflected that many blamed Jean and her inexperience for the film's failure. "That is unfair," he reported. "I alone am to blame because I misunderstood ... Shaw's play." Rather than a direct dramatization of St. Joan's life and legend, Preminger later revised his view of the play as "a deep but intellectual examination of the role religion plays in the history of man." Yet he never regretted making the film.

But it was Jean who bore the most criticism and blame when the film failed to live up to expectations. One critic wrote that her method of registering emotions as "the slightly pained expression of a well-bred young girl at a party who is trying to conduct a conversation with a beau and, at the same time, to conceal the fact that her dress is coming apart at the seams." *Time* magazine offered: "Actress Seberg, with the advantage of youth and the disadvantage of inexperience, is drastically miscast ... by physique and disposition, is the sort of honey bun that drugstore desperadoes like to nibble with their milkshakes." One New York critic suggested Preminger should send his protégée "back to the Iowa high school where he found her."

"That was nasty," Jean said shortly after reading the latter. "It wouldn't have been so bad if [the critic] had said 'Mr. Preminger should send Miss Seberg to dramatic school.'" Jean continued, "One thing that gives me strength is to know that I'm not the first this has happened to. I'm not comparing myself to her, but I know that Katharine Hepburn was knocked unmercifully by the critics when she was getting started. The most famous crack, of course, was Dorothy Parker's: 'Miss Hepburn ran the gamut of emotions from A to B.'"

"There are things in my performance I'm not happy with," Jean acknowledged in 1957. "But I don't believe it's all bad. I believe some of it is good. When [the critics] say I'm immature, that I'm inexperienced, that I lack emotional depth, they aren't saying anything I don't know already.

"In Paris, they said I wasn't as embarrassing as Ingrid Bergman."

Today, Mary Ann Seberg recalls that she felt Jean was "fine" in the role: "it was better than I had expected, after hearing some of the reviews. *Saint Joan* was my introduction to filmmaking and film critics," she says. "We knew the film wasn't being well-received, but I was afraid of what the critics would write, and that their reviews would hurt Jean's feelings."

Jean's performance, however, impressed Italian director Vittorio de Sica. He felt she was "very exciting" in *Saint Joan*, and wanted her to appear in his next film, *The Last Judgement*. But Jean could not do the film as she was still under Preminger's rule.

Despite several mixed reviews and an "excellent" rating from *Photoplay* magazine, the damage was done, and Jean Seberg's career appeared finished before it truly began. "I think part of the failure of Joan is that people are tired of her," Jean said. "There's no suspense. And in my case, an unknown, people and critics say, 'Show me.' And 36,000 mothers saying,

'My Hazel would have been better.'"

In his autobiography, Preminger recalled one of those mothers. In the late-1960s, he met a woman whose daughter was one of the 18,000 *Saint Joan* applicants. "My name is Streisand," the woman said. "I am Barbra Streisand's mother. I just want to tell you that my daughter auditioned for *Saint Joan* and you did not give her the part." Her voice was rising. "You, a famous director! And you didn't recognize talent when you saw it."

"My dear, Mrs. Streisand," Preminger soothed. "Please, compare your daughter's career with Jean Seberg's. You should be grateful I didn't cast her in *Saint Joan*. It might have ruined her future."*

With several million dollars at stake and smarting from the damaging reviews, Preminger again geared up his publicity machine and sent Jean on a promotional tour. In twenty-seven days and twelve cities in North America, Jean conducted over 100 radio interviews, sixteen press conferences, more than thirty newspaper interviews, and made such appearances as opening a new supermarket.

During the promotional tour, Jean met Paul Desmond, a thirty-two-year-old saxophonist who was part of the Dave Brubeck Quartet. The two met again in San Francisco while Jean was still on the *Saint Joan* tour. "He is much too old for me," she told Lynda Haupert. "He isn't attractive at all. He's just beautiful." Once again, Jean Seberg had fallen in love.

While on a flight to attend the London premiere of *Saint Joan*, Jean nonchalantly wrote part of a poem on the margin of a newspaper:

I run too fast
I fly so high
I hit so hard
Too wide my eye
Too full my heart
Too deep my pain
So short the kiss...

Unable to finish the last verse, Jean tossed the writing aside. When the flight landed in London Jean posed for photographers, clutching a copy

* Note: Interestingly, Preminger was making *Skidoo!* while Jean was involved with *Paint Your Wagon*. Both films were Paramount productions; however, then-studio head Bob Evans and owner Charlie Bluhdorn felt *Skidoo!* was "a mess." The latter said the film belonged in the sewer, not on the screen, and he vowed Preminger would not make another film at the studio. Bluhdorn disliked Preminger's dictator-like approach to people, as well as his later films under the studio banner. Bluhdorn ordered Evans to give the director "a very slow death" in the remaining years of his contract with the studio. "Hitler himself," Evans described Preminger. In his autobiography, he wrote: "It took three years. His arrogance finally broken, Preminger exited the Paramount gates for good, one shattered kraut."

of *Catcher in the Rye* and the newspaper. The London *Daily Mail* spotted and enlarged the poem in one of the photographs, featuring the unfinished piece in their newspaper. Readers were offered five pounds for the best line to finish the poem. Jean was irritated when she learned of the contest. "That poem was just for me and about me," she protested.

Saint Joan had its Western Hemisphere premiere in Marshalltown on June 25, 1957. On the day of the premiere, several local businesses paid for a full-page congratulatory advertisement in the *Times-Republican*, with an open letter to Jean:

"...While we are immensely proud of your original selection from the thousands of young women to the title role of Saint Joan, we have been prouder of your modest acceptance of the honors and public adulation that have come your way in the meteoric rise from a 'home town girl' to a star of international recognition.

"Too, we are grateful for the worldwide publicity you have given Marshalltown ... basking in the limelight of your activities ...

"Our every good wish goes with you as you continue your acting career."

The Orpheum Theater was filled to its 914-seat capacity, with Jean's family in attendance. Although Jean could not attend the premiere, she prepared a tape-recorded message which was played to the audience before the screening. "I hope you enjoyed the movie as much as I enjoyed making it," her message declared without conscious irony. While her brother David fell asleep during the showing — his snoring quite audible at times — the eyes of the rest of the family were proudly fixed on the screen and on their Jean.

The *Times-Republican* critiqued Jean and *Saint Joan* the following morning after the Marshalltown showing: "Those of us who have known Jean from childhood may have difficulty separating the Jean Seberg we know from the Maid of Orleans she plays ... Her performance was more than her home-town fans had a right to expect."

Saint Joan grossed less than $500,000 in its initial run. Jean's bosses sent her flowers to ease the disappointment. "Thank you very much," she wrote them. "But I should be sending you some flowers!" Regardless of the largely negative reviews, Jean was awarded the "best feminine lead" honor — in Belgium, no less — for her work in *Saint Joan*.

Many expected *Saint Joan's* critical and financial misfortune would cost Jean the role of Cecile in *Bonjour Tristesse*. "I could have understood if Preminger had decided not to put me in *Bonjour*," Jean said. "But he showed a faith in me no one expected him to show."

"It is true," Preminger said of his $2-million film, "that if I had cast Audrey Hepburn instead of Jean Seberg it would have been less of a risk. But I preferred to take the risk." To show his faith in Jean, Preminger arranged a photo opportunity for seventy-five reporters in which author Françoise Sagan was introduced to Jean.

"I feel as sorry for Françoise Sagan as anyone I know," Jean told a reporter shortly after the meeting, "because people just won't let her alone. She was very quiet. She said she was interested in a play that she was writing about middle-aged people. 'Ze are ze only kind zat interest me,' she said. She is like a little cat, walking around quietly, seeing everything, chewing it over. Her court follows her everywhere; she seems to need people who need her."

Sagan's book became a literary phenomenon, especially among young adults. Translated as "Hello Sadness," its story recounts one summer on the Riviera, when the bond between Cecile and her father (David Niven) is threatened by the visit of Anne (Deborah Kerr) to the carefree household. While plotting to defeat Anne's wish to establish a conventional household, Cecile's actions result in Anne's death, and she is left to live with this burden on her conscience.

In addition to the casting of Niven and Kerr there was a young French starlet named Mylène Demongeot who made her English-speaking debut in the film. "When I saw Preminger," Demongeot recalls, "I was shooting a movie in Nice and he told me Jean had to learn some French for her role. So he asked me if she could come and stay with me and my husband in my home for one month. So she came and stayed with us."

Jean quickly became friends with Demongeot, and continually called her *mon cher* (my dear). Demongeot remembers Jean being very tired from *Saint Joan*, but was looking forward to *Bonjour Tristesse*. However, she was somewhat disillusioned with show business. "She was saying, '*Mon cher*, I want to be a writer. If I can't be a great actress, I will be a great writer.' She brought with her a large case, and in that case she had a typewriter and the books in digest [form] — Faulkner digest, Hemingway digest, and I don't remember what else. We thought it was very funny to have great literature in digest, so we made fun of her. She was very sweet and charming and fresh and naive."

The two also became confidants. Jean told her about Paul Desmond and showed her a bracelet which had been a gift from Desmond. The bracelet had music notes engraved on it. "Jean knew I was a pianist, so she told me, '*Mon cher*, Paul wrote this music for me. Can you play it for me on the piano?'" As Demongeot played it, the two discovered the music was a simple music scale. "She was very disappointed."

While in Nice, Jean wrote to Lynda Haupert in June that she was "alternating between such mad heights of happiness and depression I think I will die." The "depression" stemmed from the *Saint Joan* disaster; the "happiness" was Jean's relationship with Paul Desmond, although an ocean kept the couple apart. Jean was in love with the saxophonist, but friends felt she was only a passing fancy to Desmond. "I am, in my usual, awful impetuous way, sending flowers and gifts and calling from Nice," she informed Haupert. "My father will flip because I'm not that rich. But I can't help it."

The filming of *Bonjour Tristesse* replayed the filming of *Saint Joan*. Tempers flared between the director and his stars. On a private beach at Le Lavendou, Jean stood by the water's edge in a Givenchy swimsuit. The scene was to show Jean coming out of the sea with a happy smile to greet David Niven. "Do it again!" Preminger screamed to Jean. Rather than getting in and coming out of the water, she was doused with water. An assistant dutifully approached Jean with a bucket of water and emptied it forcefully on her. A shiver shook her body.

"No! You must smile!" Preminger screamed. Another bucket of water was thrown on her. On the seventh take Preminger was finally satisfied. Seeing her shake from the cold, the crew sympathized with her. By now, they referred to the director as "the Fuehrer."

Witnesses felt Preminger no longer believed in Jean, and that she was made to suffer for his mistake and her own inadequacy. Although the crew was somewhat secluded on the Riviera, somehow stories of Preminger's treatment of Jean permeated film centers all over the world. Perhaps the leaks came from crew members who were sympathetic to Jean. "[She's] got plenty of guts, plenty of talent and plenty of stubbornness," said one. "Don't underestimate her. In the first place, I think the picture will click. And in the second, I think Jean will go on to stardom even if she has to take a longer path than she thought she would."

One night while at Le Lavendou Jean had a dream. In it, she was in a tiny, dark room. No sunlight came through the windows, but the room was filled with shadows and an invisible, yet menacing presence. Frightened, she left the room and ran outdoors. There she saw George Thomas standing by Preminger's Chrysler convertible. He had tears streaming down his face. Jean told him he must get out the entertainment industry. "I can't stand what it's doing to you," she said.

Later, Jean told Thomas about the dream. He was puzzled and replied that he actually liked his work. "You just have to learn how to handle it, and the people in it," he replied. "Stay in the business, Jean."

At one point, Preminger barked unmercifully at her in front of the cast and crew. Niven and Kerr went to the director and said, "Listen, lay off this girl, because she's had it, and if you continue, we don't want to carry on working." Niven told Otto that he wasn't going to get a performance out of Jean by ranting.

Jean was not the only one singled out by the director. Preminger was difficult with most of his talent. When David Niven, Kim Novak, and Eleanor Parker were asked if they felt he was a hard taskmaster, each of them replied: "No comment." Marlon Brando told Jean he "wouldn't work for that bastard, not even for ten million dollars." Dyan Cannon said while making Preminger's *Such Good Friends*, "discord and mayhem on his set sent me reeling." Cannon refused to speak to the director again. Faye Dunaway described

Preminger as "autocratic and dictatorial." Actresses Maggie McNamara (who debuted in Preminger's *The Moon is Blue*) and Dorothy Dandridge (*Carmen Jones*) were both victim of Preminger's explosive temper and verbal abuse. Both women also ultimately committed suicide.

"He was a nasty man," says Mylène Demongeot. The memory of making the film is still fresh in her mind decades after the fact. "I didn't speak a

Relaxing with Mylène Demongeot, Otto Preminger, Deborah Kerr and David Niven during the filming of Bonjour Tristesse, *1957.* COURTESY OF SNORRAMYNDIR

word of English — only what I learned in school. The big scene when [my character] is in bed with David Niven was a one-shot scene — six minutes of speaking English. It was terrible. Preminger wasn't very happy when he saw the rushes, so we did it another time. I worked as well as I could, but to do six minutes of English, which is not my language … And he did it, I'm sure, on purpose because he was like that. He was terrible."

Demongeot, however, stood her ground with Preminger. "I was very young and a very sarcastic person. So once when he shouted, I told him, 'Don't shout like that because you'll become violent. If you become violent, you'll have a heart attack.' He didn't know what to do," Demongeot laughs. "He thought, 'Those French people are crazy.'

"But Jean was the victim because he had that contract — a long contract with her, so he could do what he wanted. And he was very hard on her."

From the Hotel Prince De Galles, on July 26, Jean wrote to her parents:

Finally I am taking the time to write you a letter. I feel ashamed for being so slack before, but there has been so much going on, and I have so much today. Today was our first really warm, sunny day in Paris, and now it is early evening and I am already in my nightgown and ready to study — something I haven't done enough.

Life is a little ironical. I am right back where I started. After experimenting hours with different coiffures for the role, they whacked it off today, to the stage (only a bit better shaped) that it was when I arrived home last time and Mama made her historical, hysterical quote.

Anyway, I really do like it and feel more myself in it.

How is everyone? Have you seen about the air-conditioning? Is it still so awfully hot? I am thinking of moving to another more quiet hotel, along with George and Libby [Jean's cats]. This is nice, but they are now working on the roof, which is pretty noisy.

Kurt, today I drove the Mercedes through the whirling traffic of Paris. It is just wonderful. Otto said if I wanted to buy it after the film, I could probably get a huge discount, but it would still be very expensive. The drivers here are insane and it's pretty frightening. Monday we may do my driving shot through the streets.

Yesterday Brando called. Maybe you read he's in the hospital here. He spilled hot tea on his lap and was badly burned. Anyway, he invited me to come visit him last night at the hospital which I did (for heaven's sakes, don't let the papers get this) and we sat and talked for three hours. I see why he is a great actor. He has an unlimited curiosity about everything.

He is also very honest and nice, and I'd love to be his friend. His elderly aunt is here in the hotel and this morning we went shopping. She is so much like Granny, and we have lots of fun.

Did the clothes I sent ever come? I bought two new dresses
the other day — that's one reason I wired for money, Daddy.
It arrived today. They are both very simple, one straight
and tomato, the other full and aqua. Just street dresses.
I'm getting so sleepy. Better start studying before I drift off.
Will write later. Please write. Maybe Dawn can read this.
I'm so far behind on mail. I love you all. Jeana.

Although Jean tried to paint a picture of contentment to her family, she
was terribly lonely. She was a foreigner in a strange country which spoke an
unfamiliar language, and although she was taking French lessons, her command of the language was far from adequate. "My French is so bad, I can't
understand unless I concentrate," she confided to Lynda Haupert. "When
'I vant to be alone,' I just let my mind wander and bango, they [the French
people] are shut out as deftly as if I'd turned off a hearing aid."

While biding her time shopping on a day off, Jean parked her rented car
in a No Parking zone. A French traffic policeman began to quote several
traffic rules to her in French. Two tears rolled down her cheek. The policeman asked for her identification and she gave it to him. Her name and face
looked familiar to the policeman before he realized whom he was lecturing.

"You have played Jeanne d'Arc?" he sputtered.

"Yes," Jean replied quietly.

The policeman looked at her closely, threw the identification onto her
lap, then declared, "Jeanne d'Arc never cried!" before peddling away on his
bicycle.

Jean dried her eyes and murmured, "And Jean Seberg won't do any more
crying either."

"For a while, she had everything in her hands to have a successful career.
So everything was fine," says Mylène Demongeot. "Then she went to St.
Tropez for filming, and when I arrived, she had fallen in love with François
Moreuil. She said, '*Mon cher*, I'm in love! I just met a marvelous man. He is
a noble. He is the Count Moreuil.'"

It was during a break in filming that Jean, Preminger, Niven, and Kerr were
invited to lunch at La Reine Jeanne, the villa of millionaire Commandant
Paul Louis Weiller. After meeting Charlie Chaplin and other guests at the
lunch, Jean changed into a bathing suit and walked to the edge of the estate.
There she saw a young man water skiing, and Jean asked if she might try. The
man was François Moreuil, a twenty-three-year-old lawyer who was staying
at the villa, a guest of Weiller. Friends described François as a young man
of immense charm and ambition. His first impression of Jean Seberg was,
however, that of "a little girl, all white, no tan, rather small, and no hair."

The two began talking. "There was a mutual attraction immediately,"
Moreuil remembers. "Otto was there, watching us, and he did not like it

very much because Jean was his property. I felt that immediately.

"I met Otto at that house, and he thought I was rich because I was in this house. Of course, that was not the case. I had a family who had some money, but I was, by no means, a very rich person. And Otto always had respect toward very rich people."

A friendship quickly developed between Jean and François Moreuil, and the pair began dating.

Commandant Weiller disliked his guests leaving his estate in the evening. "The younger guests would push their cars, not to make any noise, and would bribe the guard at the gate, which was two miles away from the house," François says. The younger guests who dared to defy their host usually spent their evenings nightclubbing in St. Tropez. François was one of them. "Every night I pushed my car and went to see her. We saw each other every day."

Cast and crew members noticed a change in Jean. She was more relaxed and did not let Preminger's demands bother her. One friend jokingly quipped at the time, "For *Saint Joan*, she went to church every Sunday. Now that she's playing in *Bonjour Tristesse*, she's having three romances simultaneously!"

Perhaps this was an exaggeration, but François Moreuil was the one man with whom Jean was spending more and more time. Although a lawyer, he had a keen interest in filmmaking. Hollywood director William Wyler was the second cousin of his mother, and many budding French directors were among his friends. Jean found in François a man who understood and supported her, and listened to her when she needed someone to confide in. She told him of her problems with Preminger. "That relationship, although not sexual, but a psychological one, was a strain for her," he recalls, "which means that when I met her she was a very unstable person, and somewhat neurotic."

Jean had long decided Paul Desmond was no longer interested in her, and François was not only available, but filled the void she felt with no man in her life. "You asked me about Paul," Jean wrote Dawn Quinn. "Well, it took me a long time to realize it, but everything ended as soon as I left San Francisco. He didn't write, didn't call, didn't do anything. And I became a very bitter girl. But now I've met someone who has taken his place wonderfully — a tall, thin, very black-haired Parisian lawyer named François Moreuil." Soon, the couple fell in love.

One friend could not believe Jean was in love with this Frenchman. "She wanted to marry a nobleman, and he told her he was a count. So, she wanted to marry him and become the Countess François Moreuil. We told her, 'He's not a Count! Why do you believe he's a Count? He's nobody!'"

François vehemently denies he ever told anyone he was a count. "This is totally preposterous," he says, "and must have come of the delusion of somebody else." The truth is he was never a count.

"He is a count," Jean wrote Dawn Quinn, "but his family doesn't use the title, and he is a wonderful writer. He wants one day to be a film director. And he loves me. When I was sick here, he was my nurse. When I cry, he cries. He has such a lovely soul, and thank goodness, he speaks perfect English."

To another friend Jean wrote: "First, since my heart is bursting like a ripe plum, I'll tell you I am really in love. And I can see Lynda laughing now and saying 'Oh, no, not again!' and I can hear her again laughing as she says 'Now she'll say — "but this is different.""

Publicly, Jean wanted to keep her involvement with François quiet. "I don't want to talk about it," she replied when an interviewer inquired. "It's cheap to use your private life to further your career, and it seems to me it would damage any kind of deep emotional relationship."

François recalls the first dinner he had with Jean in Paris, where he witnessed the mixed blessing of his girlfriend's celebrity in practice. "She said to a journalist, 'There are so many forks, I don't know which one to pick,'" he recalls. "It was a joke. But it was amplified that she came out of a little town to go into a world of big films and lead that jet-set life, which she didn't like at all.

"Jean had not had a tremendous education, but she was a very bright girl, very clever," François insists. One time when the couple visited an art museum, François asked Jean which painting she liked. "She immediately chose the best," he says.

François joined Jean in London when the *Bonjour Tristesse* cast and crew moved to finish the film at Shepperton Studios. After completing the film, Jean and François slipped away to Paris where he introduced her to his family. Jean immediately connected with his mother, a politically conscious woman who later became involved with Amnesty International.

While Preminger still held her under contract and did not tell Jean if he had any future use for her, she decided to move to New York to take acting lessons. Preminger also returned to New York where he had an office. François soon followed and moved in with Jean.

"When I went to New York, I left my law practice, sold my car, and went without my papers. I started [there] by working in a darkroom for ten hours a day developing photos for a photographer," François recalls. "There we had a life that was quite funny. Jean was making $200 a week and I was making $75 a week with the photographer. We couldn't afford to eat at restaurants, so I started to cook. And I remember a delicatessen where I'd return used bottles to get the refund. We were really short on money."

Their fixed income did not prevent the couple from having an active social life. Several times they were invited out for dinner or on a weekend getaway upstate. "One week would be enormous and great luxury," François muses. "The next would be fried eggs."

*"I refused to believe that I was so wrong and the critics so right, that this girl was
so completely void of talent."*
— Otto Preminger of Jean Seberg

Returning to Marshalltown and her parents' new home on Kalsem
Boulevard in October 1957 (which, because of her frequent trips home,
caused her brother David to quip, "Guess we got to drive all that way to
get the actress again!"), Jean told her family she was dating François, but
she withheld the fact the two were already living together. A week later,
François flew to Minneapolis and was met by Jean at the airport.

In Marshalltown, Jean introduced her new boyfriend to her parents,
brothers, and friends. "She brought him to dinner one evening," Carol
Hollingsworth remembered, "and I looked out the window and I saw them
coming up the walk. I thought, 'Oh Jean, you've done it again!' I didn't care
for him. I thought he was ill-mannered."

Jean and François attended the Junior College Players production of
My Sister Eileen and then visited Mary Ann and her boyfriend Ed in Iowa
City. "François was an interesting man," recalls Mary Ann. "I wish I could
meet him today, because he was leading a completely different lifestyle than
what we were leading at the time. He exposed us to a lot of things that
were unfamiliar with our family. I think he was as fascinated with small-
town Iowa as we were with him. None of us knew how to relate to him. He
seemed to make Jean happy at the time, and that's all we were concerned
about."

In early November, Dorothy Seberg held an open house to introduce
François to over one hundred neighbors and relatives. The Frenchman, while
hinting at an upcoming engagement, openly told anyone who wanted to listen "I have a good job and Jean doesn't need to work. Any time she wants to
quit is fine with me. This Hollywood — it is one big blah."

Jean invited Dawn Quinn over for a long visit, which included mention
of Otto Preminger's presence in New York. "He just isn't human," Jean told
her friend. "He buys me beautiful clothes, but he never makes me happy on
the inside. It's terrible, but sometimes I wish he would just die!"

When the couple returned to New York, Preminger caught up with them
at her apartment and told Jean he was renewing her contract for a second
year. Believing that *Bonjour Tristesse* had the potential for success, Preminger
had no intention of letting Jean escape from his control.

The *Bonjour Tristesse* premiere was held in New York on January 15, 1958.
Ed and Kurt Seberg flew east to attend the event with Jean. "Didn't seem
like you," Ed Seberg said to his daughter. "Looks pretty bad," Dorothy later
admitted.

The reviews were decidedly mixed, better than those for *Saint Joan*, but far from what had been expected or hoped for. One critic wrote "almost everything about this picture manifests bad taste, poor judgment, and plain deficiency of skill." *Time* wrote, "Jean Seberg ... blooms with just the right suggestion of unhealthy freshness, a cemetery flower." *Newsweek*, however, said "Miss Seberg is still an amateur actress ... as to where the career which began so suddenly and joyfully less than two years ago will proceed now, only time, and possibly Mr. Preminger, can tell."

"I don't think *Bonjour Tristesse* was quite as bad as it was made out to be," Jean reflected years later. "Actually, of all the pictures based on Françoise Sagan's stories, I think it came off best. I was still nervous and unsure of myself. My tension is apparent through much of the picture but I was not quite as bad as in *Joan*. As Preminger has said since, he treated me all the wrong ways ..."

At the time, however, with two films to her credit, Jean was feeling like a failure. "I've never known Jean to be depressed about her films," says Warren Robeson. "Her attitude was always like 'Well, it's time to move on.'" Jean later recalled: "My self-confidence had been ravaged, but I decided I wasn't going to quit. I was determined to give acting the good old college try."

It helped that, while Susan Hayward won the Best Actress Oscar in 1959, the French cinema and arts weekly magazine *Arts* voted Jean Seberg the winner of the annual "Best Feminine Interpretation" award for *Bonjour Tristesse*. When the film opened in France, *Cahiers du cinéma* put Jean on its February cover, calling her "the new divine of the cinema." Jean was slowly becoming the darling of Paris. François Truffaut wrote: "When Jean Seberg is on the screen, which is all the time, you can't look at anything else. Her every movement is graceful, each glance is precise. The shape of her head, her silhouette, her walk, everything is perfect: this kind of sex appeal hasn't been seen on the screen. It is designed, controlled, directed to the nth degree by her director, who is, they say, her fiancé. I wouldn't be surprised, given the kind of love one needs to obtain such perfection ... Jean Seberg, short blond hair on a pharaoh's skull, wide-open blue eyes with a glint of boyish malice, carries the entire weight of this film on her tiny shoulders. It is Otto Preminger's love poem to her."

As with *Saint Joan*, Preminger had several million dollars at stake in a film which had garnered less than glowing reviews. He again sent Jean on a promotional tour, and, at one stop in February, Jean and François made an appearance at the Italian premiere of *Bell, Book and Candle* to help promote *Bonjour Tristesse*. The couple took along their cat Bip, which François had bought in New York. At the premiere, Bip was presented with "the first 'Oscar' ever presented a cat," Jean wrote Dawn Quinn, "which she's supposed to forward to Pywacket, the cat who starred in the picture. Isn't that silly? But the Italians loved it."

In Miami, a Lincoln convertible with a banner reading JEAN SEBERG IN 'BONJOUR TRISTESSE' taped to its sides was at Jean's disposal. She rarely used the car because she did not want the attention. But being in Florida, and François being a huge fan of the film *Key Largo*, they decided one day to tape over the signs and drive to Key West.

"We never got there, because I was doing what I did in St. Tropez," François remembers. "It was sunny, I had no shirt on, just a pair of shorts and barefoot, like we do in St. Tropez. And I was going 80 or 90 miles an hour. Suddenly there was one police car in front of us, and one in back, then a screech of tires and I stopped. They got me out of the car, hands up, and said to me, 'Man, you're gonna be killed.' I pretended immediately not to know a word of English. They were very rude.

"I was joking with Jean in French: 'These are morons. I'll handle it.' But in three or four minutes, it turned really bad. Then Jean did something I never would have done. She talked to them rudely, and took a $100 bill and threw it out at them on the road and said, 'Leave us alone.' And that was the end of the story. We didn't go to Key West, and I didn't drive as quickly after that."

Preminger then flew Jean to Hollywood to meet with Louella Parsons, who was arguably Hollywood's most powerful gossip columnist to the studios. Parsons escorted Jean to her backyard, where she showed Jean a bright blue statue of the Virgin Mary with spotlights shining on it. Rather than talking about *Bonjour Tristesse*, Parsons asked Jean point blank: "Are you going to marry Otto Preminger?" Parsons had heard rumors that Jean was to be the next Mrs. Preminger. "Certainly not!" Jean replied, shocked at the suggestion. Then, knowing enough of the person she was dealing with, she added adroitly: "He's much older than I am, and he has been like a father to me."

"If you marry Otto after his divorce from Mary is final, you will have lost my confidence," Parsons warned. She later noted Jean "got under my skin, which doesn't happen very often to me." After the two dined at Chasen's, Parsons wrote in her column how Jean had "won me over with her youth and her apparent wish to have me like her."

The rumors that Jean and Preminger had planned to marry were simply idle gossip. Nothing could have been further from the truth, especially in view of the animosity now existing between the director and his protégée. The closest to any real intimacy the couple came was a New Year's Eve kiss he gave her shortly before filming *Saint Joan* or other such occasional photo opportunities.

"It was a bad time for me," Jean recalled. "*Confidential* magazine came out with a piece about me and Preminger entitled 'Svengali and the Druggist's Daughter.' It was horrible." When that particular issue of *Confidential* arrived in Marshalltown, Ed Seberg's pharmacy was one of the first businesses to receive it. He read the article and promptly removed the piece from his pharmacy shelves. He then went around the town to each store that carried the magazine, all the newsstands and the bus stops, and purchased every issue they had on sale. "Then he burned them all," Jean recalled, "to show his contempt."

Returning to New York and François, Jean concentrated on learning more about the craft of acting. She studied speech with acting coach Alice Hermes for several months, and took mime lessons from Étienne Decroux, mentor of Marcel Marceau and an acquaintance of François.

Now that she was residing in New York, Jean hoped to study at the Actor's Studio, then the most prestigious establishment for learning the craft. In Jean's case, it was rather a question of relearning everything Preminger had taught her. "I think the low of that particular period was when I moved to New York and applied at the Actor's Studio. I went to see Lee Strasberg," Jean told *Cosmopolitan* in 1968.

"I was going through a psychologically painful period — very painful — and I really had difficulty walking into a room with three people in it. I said to Strasberg, 'I can't possibly stand up and audition, but I've heard you let people audit. May I? I know I'll be so swept away by the excitement of what I'm seeing, and the experimentation, that I'll want to take part.'

"I found him an extremely aloof man. He said, 'That's true. We do have such instances.' And he told me to go home and write to the Actor's Studio for formal permission to be an auditor. I did write — three times — and I never even got a reply. That was kind of the final blow, because I had taken a step; I had at least decided. Well damn! They say I'm not an actress — so I'll learn. I thought that would be the best way to do it. I find it kind of amusing now, and I'm not bitter, but it was a big put-down at the time."

Despite the deadends Jean's film career had taken, François encouraged Jean to develop other creative interests. One thing he did was buy Jean a painting kit, hoping she would take an interest in that art form. She didn't. She admitted that she made an effort to appreciate classical music, but she went "all out for progressive jazz," and favored the likes of Frank Sinatra and Ella Fitzgerald over Bach and Dvorak.

François secured a job working for an international law firm on Madison Avenue during the day, and at night the couple began to socialize more. When they attended the "April in Paris" Ball at the Waldorf, they sat at the same table with then-Senator John F. Kennedy and his wife Jacqueline. "It was very nice," recalls François. "Jacqueline was of French origin and spoke French. [But John] was just some guy. I had a cousin who was a member of Congress, so I wasn't entirely impressed."

Both he and Jean were impressed, however, with Roscoe Lee Browne. Through the black actor, they were invited among a small group to spend a weekend at Steepletop, poet Edna St. Millay's 800-acre estate in Upstate

New York. After her death in 1950, Steepletop became the residence of her sister and brother-in-law, Norma and Charles Ellis.

"Browne was acting in the South — Tennessee or somewhere," François recalls, "and he spoke with a wonderful English accent. And the people there couldn't believe he could speak so well. Someone asked him, 'How did you learn to speak so well?' and he said, 'I had a white mammy.' It was fantastic."

In this setting, among a small group of people, Jean was most comfortable. François believes it was one of the few times he saw Jean truly happy. He encouraged her to mingle more with people her own age. At their apartment they received several friends from Paris, including artist César, actor Christian Marquand, as well as Françoise Sagan, and dined with Suzy Parker and Jane Fonda, among others.

But while Preminger was in New York the director continued to keep Jean under his control. "Otto used to call at eleven o'clock at night: 'Jean, I left you a book last week and I want it back right away.' And he was serious," remembers François. "I'd take the phone from Jean and say [in a British accent], 'Dear Otto. Good evening. This is François. I'm afraid it's a bit late to call. Miss Seberg has no intention of returning any book at eleven o'clock at night. Good-bye, Otto.' And I'd hang up."

François concluded that the only way to enable Jean to move on with her life and career would be to wrest her from Preminger's control. "Otto had let her down," François feels. "He had made two films with her which were flops and he was not doing anything with her anymore. So from that point of view, her world was coming to an end. I thought something should be done about that."

In the spring of 1958, François and his employer, lawyer Claude Lewy, approached Preminger to sell the remaining years of Jean's contract to Columbia Pictures. After four months of negotiating, an agreement was reached in August. Preminger telephoned Jean. His last words to her were "Jean, I have sold you." Although he stipulated the right to use her in one film a year, Preminger never again offered Jean a part in his productions, which included *Exodus* and the 1959 classic *Anatomy of a Murder*.

Preminger could, had he wished, have used Jean Seberg in the latter film. When Lana Turner walked off the set of *Anatomy of a Murder* in a rumored dispute over costumes, Preminger vowed to replace Turner with "an unknown and make her a star." He then cast Lee Remick as a woman who alleges she was raped by the man her husband is accused of killing. The film was a critical and financial success, and made Remick a star and respected actress.

"Preminger," Jean said, "dropped me like a used Kleenex."

"Every time I read about poor little Jean Seberg I have to laugh," said screenwriter Thomas Ryan, who had worked with Preminger, in 1963. "This was a tough little dame, very resilient, who knew exactly what she wanted.

And Otto, despite the stories, did try to make it up to her. That's why he put her in a second movie, *Bonjour Tristesse* — to give her another chance. Of course, he also wanted to prove he was right when he picked her out of [her father's] drugstore."

"I feel very much responsible for her because I discovered her and put her in two leads," Preminger told Mike Wallace. "It's a strange thing. In the Eastern Hemisphere she became a star but in America she has not been accepted by the critics. I think they resented her fast success and the publicity, for which Seberg was certainly not responsible. But I do believe she will go on working hard because I know her character and I believe she will eventually succeed."

Although grateful to Preminger for "discovering" her, Jean had mixed feelings toward the director. She acknowledged that he had instilled in her a professional discipline which would stay with her for the rest of her life. For example, Jean was punctilious regarding appointments and calls to the set, and controlled her temper while in the studio. However, she believed that all of Preminger's publicity efforts had disastrously harmed her film career. He had thrown her into the public eye whether the public wanted her or not.

"I hit rock bottom," Jean later recalled. "I went personally and professionally bankrupt. Then all the people who had surrounded me with fond attention disappeared — many forever — and there were no more flowers …

"The shock was greatest because I had divorced myself from life in Iowa. My girlfriends had married and led lives that I no longer had any touch with, and I hadn't developed a circle of friends in the new life I was projected into at seventeen, and that was suddenly finished at twenty. I was a stranger everywhere."

In August 1958, Jean returned to Marshalltown for Mary Ann's wedding. Three weeks later, Jean and François were to be married. She opted for a quiet ceremony in the church she attended as a child. "Mary Ann is so happy, I don't want to take away from her wedding while planning mine. Ours will be extremely simple and I hope fairly small," she wrote to a friend. "We still want to make it dignified and pretty. Suzy Parker and Lynda Haupert will be bridesmaids (it's an informal church wedding, so it's customary to just have two)."

Suzy Parker was unable to serve as a bridesmaid, and Mary Ann could not attend the ceremony because she and her new husband had moved to Utah for work and additional schooling. Despite this change of plans, Jean and François vowed to keep the wedding small and special, yet memorable.

"They wanted a very lovely wedding and have a reception at a restaurant and have champagne. At that time it was not in our way of life," says Mary Ann. François agreed, and the ceremony and reception which was to follow were planned as modest but elegant.

Marshalltown and the press had other ideas.

"If my personal life seemed on the surface replete with men desiring only to make me theirs forever, that was just a plant by the press agents."
— Jean Seberg

"I didn't want a mob there, reporters crowding around, flashbulbs going off in my face," Jean said of her upcoming wedding. "François and I planned to elope. But then I thought how I'd hate to leave my folks out … and my best friends … and some of my favorite relatives … So we sat down with my parents to plan a nice simple ceremony and make out a small guest list. At least that's how we started."

Although François' parents grew to like Jean very much, they tried to have his passport taken away at the airport when he left Paris for the wedding in Iowa. "An actress was not an ideal woman for me as a wife," François admits. "They did not attend the wedding."

The locals chatted and gossiped about the upcoming wedding for weeks. François' over-the-collar hair was frowned upon so much that a group of local boys talked about wrestling the Frenchman to the ground and giving him a haircut. When Jean went for a fitting of her wedding dress, an oyster white silk gown with an empire waist and a balloon skirt specially designed for her by Guy La Roche, her fiancé crouched down and peered to make sure the hemline met his specifications.

One day François went shopping for underwear at a local department store. After changing into the selected items he walked out of the dressing room to ask Jean if she liked them. At that time, no men in Marshalltown, or in the rest of the United States for that matter, asked women their opinion of undergarments. Both stories made the newspapers.

"I think there were people looking for things," Mary Ann recalls. "People were looking for something sensational to write about, and every little eccentric thing François did was for the newspapers."

"In France," François adds, "there isn't that kind of prudishness."

"I must say Marshalltown was a surprise for me," he continues. "Although her mother and father were very nice to me — terribly nice — it was still a surprise to me. It was not the world I was accustomed to."

The feeling was mutual.

François regularly cut Jean's hair. He was trimming her hair in his future in-laws' bathroom, when a friend walked in.

"Gee, that's lovely," the girlfriend said. "I'd like to take a picture of that."

"No," he barked. "But if you wish, I'll show you my ass."

"I didn't want this photographed — it belonged to us, our life," he says today.

At Lloyd's, the restaurant where the wedding reception was to be held,

François mentioned there was to be a silver bowl in which caviar would be served. "And the lady there said, 'What is it? How do you spell it?' It was crazy," he remembers. "It was a different world." He asked owner Lloyd Barlow for the roasted turkey to be deboned and then reassembled for the dinner centerpiece.

"But that's impossible," Mr. Barlow announced.

"Why?" he asked. "I've seen it done so many times."

"Well," Barlow countered, "maybe it's done in France, but I wouldn't think of doing such a thing to an American turkey."

François' anger built, but Jean took him aside and spoke to him in French. To settle the disagreement, Jean suggested there should be two turkeys, one for show and one cut beforehand to serve the guests. The three agreed on this compromise.

Taking charge of all wedding arrangements, François gave Jean's aunt, Eula Mae Seberg, a detailed blueprint for the flower arrangements, consisting of yellow roses and ferns to decorate the altar. Using local millionaire Bill Fisher's private plane, he flew to Chicago to pick up two cases of champagne specially sent from France.

Although Jean's studio promised *Look* magazine an exclusive on the wedding, the French news media were infuriated by Columbia's attempts to keep them away. "Try and keep us out," one warned. In the days prior to the ceremony, reporters and photographers from *Paris Match* and *France-Soir* arrived in Marshalltown to cover the wedding. Following suit, *Vogue* and *Life* were among the two dozen news organizations which dispatched staff to the town to cover what Lynda Haupert described as "Cinderella's wedding."

"She's made two movies, both very bad," a representative from Columbia Pictures commented. "She hasn't done anything for two years, but she's still popular. It's just that any girl can look at Jean and feel she might do it, too. Jean gives hope to American teenagers — that someone may discover them."

Seeing that her wedding plans were increasingly escaping from her control, Jean became irritable. It was supposed to be one of the happiest days of her life. Now it was looking like another one of Preminger's publicity junkets.

At the wedding rehearsal the evening before the ceremony, Jean and François had a heated debate over the ushers' ties. Dorothy Seberg took her daughter aside and tried to reason with her. Dorothy felt Jean was under a great strain, and later had a heart-to-heart talk with her about married life.

"My mother said then she didn't think I should get married," Jean later confessed. Jean had debated whether she was indeed making a mistake in marrying François. She told one friend that she had to go through with it "because Otto's making me do it."

Rain fell on Marshalltown the morning of September 5, 1958. By the time of the wedding, it was uncomfortably hot and humid. Shortly before four o'clock, Jean arrived at the church in a black Cadillac. Thirteen hundred spectators gathered outside the church to catch a glimpse of the bride in her wedding dress, but Jean hurriedly walked into the sanctuary of the church.

Allowing the press a photo opportunity inside the church before the wedding, Jean cut the session short by saying, "I think we should call it quits on the pictures now." Later, the press failed to honor Jean's requests that no pictures should be taken during the ceremony.

Mr. and Mrs. François Moreuil, September 5, 1958. COURTESY OF LYNDA HAUPERT

When François arrived to the church, he cooperated with the photographers and the television cameramen by climbing the church steps twice. Even his careful planning of the day did not prevent him from locking his keys in the borrowed car. A garage mechanic had to break the car window to retrieve them.

In putting their personal touches on the wedding, the Sebergs had eight-year-old David carry the rings on a satin pillow embroidered by Frances Benson. Jean put a sixpence from Mary Ann in her shoe for luck, while Dawn Quinn and Marshalltown High School music teacher Stephen Melvin sang "O Lord Most Holy." As she began her descent down the church aisle, Jean turned to Lynda Haupert and whispered, "I think I'm making a mistake."

The guests wiped perspiration from their faces in the stiflingly hot church, and as Jean and François stood before the altar the Rev. Christenson advised that "There are adjustments to be made that will need patience and understanding," and that marriage is "one of the great adventures man is privileged to enjoy."

After the twenty-minute ceremony, François kissed his new bride on both cheeks before sobbing out loud.

As a thunderstorm raged outside the reception for 250 guests at Lloyd's, the newlyweds sipped champagne from a sixteenth-century goblet. The roasted turkey was displayed and then switched in the kitchen with the carved one, and no one noticed there were two turkeys. Despite Jean's invitation to him, Otto Preminger did not attend the wedding.

Since Columbia Pictures had put Jean on hold for a possible role in an upcoming film called *The Beach Boy*, co-starring Kim Novak, to be directed by King Vidor, the newlyweds planned on spending their wedding night in New York. With a police escort and a caravan of cars filled with wedding guests, the couple continued with their champagne in their limousine on the drive to the Des Moines airport. After the pair boarded the airplane, the Marshalltown friends raced back home to watch reports of the wedding on the evening news.

In New York, the doorman at their apartment building read of the wedding ceremony in the newspaper. He was quite angry. There was a big fuss," as François recalls. "He said that we had 'lived in sin' for one year. In '57-'58, New York was a very prudish town and people lived by WASP-ish standards."

When the offer to act in *The Beach Boy* fell through, Jean and François flew to St. Tropez for a three-week honeymoon at Paul Louis Weiller's estate where they had met. The newlyweds then returned to France and moved into an apartment with a garden in the Paris suburb of Neuilly.

As Mrs. François Moreuil, Jean acted the dutiful 1950s housewife, seeing her husband off to work in the morning and being there to greet him in the evening. "I thought at the time we had a very normal life," observes François. "The only thing we didn't agree upon was politics. I am a Gaullist, and a very determined one, and my mother was to the left and still is. Jean and my mother shared the same political beliefs — radical."

Jean's mother-in-law once told her, "If you don't busy yourself with politics, politics will busy itself with you."

"She got along with my mother very well," François remembers. "They saw each other often, and were both having a little conspiracy against me, saying what a 'bad boy' I was."

Jean also spent her time reading and writing, which François supported wholeheartedly. "She wanted to write more than act," he says. He recalls one article she wrote which was published in the *Herald Tribune*. "It was not an important piece, but she had that urge to write."

The marriage, however, was beginning to show strains. Jean was not the kind of woman who relished the role of housewife, and she also disliked crowds, while François enjoyed socializing in groups. "François was sort of an overgrown French version of a fraternity boy," Jean later told writer

In The Mouse That Roared *with Peter Sellers, 1959.* AUTHOR'S COLLECTION

Hollis Alpert. "He had a compulsion to go out every night to either a night club or some ratty Whiskey a Go-Go jukebox kind of place."

François, on the other hand, discovered his wife had deep, unresolved insecurities. "She was either unhappy because she was making a movie or unhappy because she wasn't making one," he says. "It really was always a drama with Jean."

Fifteen months had passed since the completion of *Bonjour Tristesse* when in October 1958 Columbia quite unexpectedly put Jean in the low-budget comedy *The Mouse That Roared*, co-starring Peter Sellers. The story told of Grand Fenwick, the smallest country in the world, which, in order to rescue its economy, declares war on the United States in the hope of swift defeat and generous reconstruction aid.

Filming took place in Great Britain, with three weeks on-location on the Channel coast and in Surrey. On November 10, the production moved to the Shepperton soundstages, where production for Jean's previous films had taken place. From the beginning the film belonged to Sellers who, in a *tour de force* performance, played three roles: chain-mailed high constable Tully Bascomb, Prime Minister the Count of Mountjoy, and the Grand Duchess Gloriana. Jean's supporting role had little for her to do other than act as Tully's love interest, give the proper reactions as dictated by the script, and deliver a few lines of dialogue.

Jean admitted she was feeling a bit rusty in the acting department, and director Jack Arnold encountered some problems with her on the first day of shooting. In the first shot of the day, Jean took a step forward, said her line, and then stepped back again. On the second take she did the same. Arnold took Jean aside and politely told her to just deliver the lines, don't take a step. "Was I doing that? I wasn't conscious of that," she said. Arnold kindly told her to be conscious of it. But by then she became so conscious of it she didn't know what she was saying. By take twenty-five Peter Sellers didn't know what he was saying either. Arnold stopped and resolved to shoot the scene another day.

"She'd come fresh from her indoctrination by Preminger into film acting," Arnold remembered. "Preminger was a screamer and a yeller. He waited until he got her into hysterics, then he'd turn the camera on her. I don't yell or scream, so this was a new experience for her. She went on to become quite a good actress."

For the first time in her career, the film gave a glimpse of her talent for comedy. One humorous scene takes place as Jean, her on-screen father and several important government officials are being kidnapped into Fenwick through a French border. In the scene, Jean rushes up to the guard and, speaking in French, pleads for his help. "Good appetite, mademoiselle!" the guard says to her as she is being dragged away. He then turns to Sellers and asks, "Tell me, sir ... What language was she speaking?"

Although not primarily hers, *The Mouse That Roared* was a huge success. It played for two years at the New York Guild Theater, and one year at both a Beverly Hills and a Paris theater. Budgeted at $400,000, it grossed over $50 million in all markets by the mid-1980s.

While vacationing in Rome with François in early March 1959, Jean became violently ill. François rushed her to the American hospital in Paris, where she underwent an emergency appendectomy. This hospital visit, coupled with a misunderstanding of a quote Jean gave the following month, resulted in columnists reporting she was pregnant. During a stop in New York that spring, Jean told a columnist, "We're expecting a family, you know." The columnists led his column with an item saying Jean and François were "imaging," not realizing she was referring to her cat Bip. Jean quickly remedied the rumor and assured her parents they "would be the first to know" if she were pregnant.

Columbia arranged for her to attend acting classes with other contract players in an attempt to develop more film projects for her. The classes, taught by Paton Price, were held on the old Columbia lot, in California. Leaving François behind in Paris, Jean rented an apartment in Los Angeles, and began her first class with Price in April 1959.

A former teacher at the American Academy in New York, Price believed in Jean's talent and left an indelible mark on her life. He was unwilling to force her to the point of hysterics, and Price believed in the principle that if an actor did not know and accept himself as a human being, then he or she could not play a character.

"Paton's whole concept of life is to stand open, to learn not to withdraw from it," Jean later said. "He showered me with warmth at a time when I really needed it. I think it's because of him that I am not bitter about the *Saint Joan* period and I don't feel I have to play her again to prove anything." She credited Price for "giving back [my] lost confidence."

From this point on in her films, one can see a change in Jean's acting. The self-consciousness of her acting in the two Preminger films, including the stiff movements, dialogue delivery, and facial expressions, have mostly disappeared.

During a visit to Marshalltown in May with François, Jean was called by Columbia to replace an ailing Doris Day for the film premiere of *It Happened to Jane* in Boston. Jean received a telephone call from Bob Ferguson of Columbia Pictures the day before the event. She agreed to replace Day and help her studio.

"I never dreamt I'd be up at 5:30 this morning at home and running to catch a Chicago-bound plane in Des Moines so that I could make connections for Boston," Jean told a reporter. "I don't feel tired at all!" Although the crowd would yell out Doris Day's name, Jean waved and signed autograph books obligingly. Jean's cooperation did not go unnoticed by the press. One columnist wrote: "…with all the charges being thrown around loosely these days about how the younger generation of motion picture stars doesn't know its important place in the industry and especially in its public relations … [Jean Seberg] has demonstrated she is not open to such charges."

Jean resumed Price's acting lessons in Hollywood, and then in June returned to Paris and François. Although he was still employed by a law firm, he began thinking seriously about film directing. The "New Wave" was just sweeping across France, with young filmmakers taking to the streets with a camera and no script, to capture an improvisational way of life. François, like Jean, knew a number of these nouvelle vague directors and wanted to be part of the scene.

One summer evening in 1959, François told Jean that an aspiring director by the name of Jean-Luc Godard was interested in talking with her about a new film. "Who's he?" she asked. He explained that Godard was a critic for the journal *Cahiers du cinéma*, and, along with Chabrol, Truffaut, Rohmer, and Rivette, belonged to a circle of promising filmmakers who had liked her work in the Preminger films. François added that Godard had made a short film which he wanted Jean to view.

Since Columbia had no roles for her to play that summer (she had been a leading candidate for the role of Milly Wormold in *Our Man in Havana* but was not offered the part), Jean met with Godard one morning and viewed his short. The film, *Charlotte et son Jules*, starred a young former boxer named Jean-Paul Belmondo. "I found his film very fresh and different," Jean recalled. When Godard asked her if she'd like to work with him, she responded, "I think I would."

Shortly after, Godard and François Truffaut met with Jean. Godard pitched his idea to the bewildered Seberg: he outlined a story in which a car thief kills a policeman, then, while hiding out with his girlfriend, discovers she has turned him in to the police. Truffaut had written a two-page synopsis based on a real-life account, but there was no script. While Godard felt Jean-Paul Belmondo would be perfect for the role of the gangster Michel Poiccard, he told Jean he wanted her to play the girlfriend Patricia Franchini. The film's title was to be *À bout de souffle* (*Breathless*).

Godard said that the character would be a continuation of her role in *Bonjour Tristesse*. "I could have taken the last shot of Preminger's film and started after dissolving to a title, 'Three Years Later,'" Godard said. Originally, the character was said to have been based on the heroine in John O'Hara's *Butterfield 8*.

Jean hesitated. She had no script to study since none existed; the budget was almost non-existent; there was not even a full production crew. Nevertheless, François urged Jean to accept the role, as did Truffaut. She also realized she was Godard's last chance to get *Breathless* on film. He had little money, the producer was going bankrupt, and as Jean said, "I was [Godard's] last trump card."

A few days later, Jean-Paul Belmondo visited Jean at her apartment in an attempt to persuade her to star with him in the film. But she had already made her decision. With no other acting offers that summer or that fall, Jean cautiously agreed to star in *Breathless*.

7

"Jean really enjoyed making Breathless, *and much of it was ad-libbed. It showed what Jean could do when left to her own devices."*
— Carol Hollingsworth

Since Jean had a contract with Columbia, she could not work as a freelance actress. Moreover, since the studio had never heard of him, Godard needed simultaneously to impress and convince them he was a serious filmmaker. He sent a twelve-page telegram to Columbia offering the studio either $12,000 for Jean's services or half the worldwide profits from the film. *Breathless* producer Georges de Beauregard also tried to get permission from Columbia, and since François Moreuil was a lawyer and knew America, he sent him to see Columbia head Harry Cohn.

François had heard a story concerning a movie deal in which Nicky Hilton had threatened 20th Century-Fox head Darryl Zanuck he would take

With Jean-Paul Belmondo in Breathless, *1959.* AUTHOR'S COLLECTION

his then-wife, Elizabeth Taylor, away from movies forever if his demands were not met. Since Hilton was wealthy, Zanuck caved in to his demands. François decided he would try the same ploy. "I thought, what the heck," he says. "They won't have time to verify the story. I'll be very arrogant."

François met with Harry Cohn and said he would take his wife away from the film world forever if permission were not granted. "I said, in an English accent, 'You either draw up the contract and give her permission to do that movie… and if you don't, I'm very rich, I don't need you. She doesn't need you.' And it worked. And it was a total bluff." Columbia accepted the $12,000 offer (roughly one-sixth of the film's budget) rather than the percentage, a choice that eventually deprived the studio of several million dollars.

On the first day of shooting, August 17, 1959, Jean still had her doubts. By the end of the day, she nearly walked off the production. "Godard had just emerged from a miserable love affair and was feeling bitter about women," Jean remembered. "He wanted to make me more terrible looking than I already was. [Jean was wearing her hair in a modified *Saint Joan* style.] We agreed to disagree, shook hands, and I left. He followed me, and we made up."

When Godard suggested that for the last scene of the film, after Patricia turns in her lover, she should steal his wallet, Jean protested. She felt that her character would already be sufficiently disreputable without going to this extremity. After discussions, it was decided Patricia would not steal the wallet.

Years later, Jean recalled she did understand if her action was the result of nervousness or "simply a deeply Puritan mentality, but I refused to be a thief. Jean-Luc was grieved. I think there was always between us this misunderstanding of this refusal, a misunderstanding that was, I confess, entirely my fault."

On the third day of the shoot, Godard and Jean had another clash. What the disagreement entailed has been forgotten over the years; however, François recalls the scene was "so childish. Godard, thinking he was very shrewd in that he was dealing with an American actress, said, 'If you aren't behaving well, I won't do any close-ups of you.' A silly thing to say — absolutely preposterous. And Jean said, 'OK. I won't do the film.'"

There never was a final script for *Breathless* while it was being filmed. Jean received her instructions at the start of each day, usually from a crumpled or torn piece of paper. "Jean-Luc would arrive every morning with a pocketful of striped yellow notebook pages like students have, filled with what he'd written the night before," Jean said. "He was afraid what he was making wouldn't last long enough to be a full-length film." At times, Godard read the text out loud and Jean and Belmondo simply repeated the director's words.

Godard wanted to retain the identity of Patricia as an American visiting abroad, so Jean spoke French with a Midwestern accent. On many occasions, he recited lines in French to Jean, and then asked her, "Now, how would you say it?" Jean then offered the director her version of how an American who does not know the French language might speak the lines, confusing the masculine and feminine genders at times. "It became much more colloquial and much more foreign in a way," Jean said later.

François did not visit the set often because "I did not want to be known as 'Mr. Seberg.'" He did, however, have a cameo as a photographer in the finished film and also admits to writing some of the scenes, mainly parts of Jean's dialogue. "She was very disabled because there wasn't a script and Godard would bring, every morning, pieces of paper — not even pages," he remembers. "And when she would ask him, 'How do you want me to act that?' he'd say, 'How you want to.' It was not the way she was used to acting."

"We did a lot of improvising," Jean later recalled. "And I believe Belmondo and I often thought we were creating more than we really were. [But] Godard was very much in control of it all."

When *Breathless* cameraman Raoul Coutard first met Jean in person, his first thought was "How on earth am I going to film her?" Coutard said Jean did not have good skin, but with the help of makeup, he found she had a

In costume with Breathless *director Jean-Luc Godard.*
COURTESY OF INDEPENDENT VISIONS

rare gift: she was photogenic. Even when the lighting was poor, Jean could be filmed wonderfully. Coutard admits the relationship between the director and leading lady was "tense. She didn't let herself be pushed around, but she did cooperate. After all, she was an American professional."

Still, there was a lack of organization, there never was a script, and a café restroom served for her dressing. Jean could not help but think how far she had plummeted from the Hollywood productions of Preminger only two years earlier. But, on the other hand, she was actually having fun making a film this way. It was easier for her to concentrate on her character and her acting rather than having producers and a crew of a hundred impatiently waiting for her to deliver her lines to the satisfaction of the director.

Most of the *Breathless* filming took place in room twelve of the Hotel de Suède on the Left Bank. "…there was hardly anybody else in the room," Jean recalled, "except for one electrician who'd come in and out to fix up the lights, and a girl who tried to keep some kind of a script."

In the film, Jean and Belmondo romp around the cramped room, ad-libbing their lines, and hide under the stark white sheets, implying intervals of lovemaking. Jean demanded she remained fully clothed while the scene was filmed, and later admitted, "I did start to get qualms" about the way their improvised intimacy was being filmed.

The film's $90,000 budget was so tight that Jean's wardrobe for the film came from Prisunic, a French discount store. Godard himself pushed a mail-delivery box from which Coutard, unseen by pedestrians, filmed the now-famous Champs-Élysées sequence. The final scene was filmed by Godard himself as he sat in a wheelchair and was pushed along, in a traveling shot.

The atmosphere on the film was casual. On some days when Jean did not feel like working, she would say so. Then Godard would say the same and both decided to take the day off, which meant everyone took the day off. "Godard is like a Paul Klee painting, always hiding behind those funny dark glasses," Jean later reflected, noting that this man rarely looked her in the eye when he spoke to her. "Belmondo insists Godard had a mad crush on me, but I was unaware of it at the time."

After less than two weeks of shooting, the film wrapped in mid-September. Jean was still bewildered about the film itself, wondering whether it would, or could, be shown publicly. "We knew when we saw the rushes that we were doing something very unusual. Very new in its style," Jean later said. "And we didn't know if the film would ever be seen — if the public would ever like it."

In retrospect, Jean realized she was "too young, too introspective, and … too unhappy to profit fully from an adventure which ought to have been much more rich for me."

In the meantime, Columbia found a bit part for her in *Let No Man Write My Epitaph*. Jean flew alone to California in the fall of 1959 for the film. In Los Angeles, she rented an apartment on Olympic Boulevard and contemplated her future. She decided she had married her husband for all the wrong reasons. He had been her support during the years with Preminger, and she appreciated his help when dealing with her former director. But Jean and François did not and could not get along. They were no longer compatible, and it did not help matters that she was not in love with him anymore.

While Jean was in Los Angeles, director Joshua Logan invited her to the Beverly Hills Hotel to read for the lead role in his upcoming Broadway play, *There Was a Little Girl*. Carol Hollingsworth said, "She tried out for the play, as did Mia Farrow, Brooke Hayward, and Jane Fonda," as well as Piper Laurie. "Jean wrote me and said, 'Of course, Jane Fonda will get it because she's his Goddaughter' — and Jane did get the role. I was hoping that maybe Logan would be interested enough in Jean to put her in a Broadway show at a later time. That's what I would have liked to have seen her do.

"I remember Josh Logan was interviewed on the radio show called Omnibus when he was starting the play with Fonda. He actually spent more time talking about Jean than he did anyone else. He really praised her ability."

Logan sent Jean a personal note to express his appreciation:

> … At this moment we felt that to tell our story and with the misgivings we have about certain aspects of the play we should cast a certain way. It has nothing to do with talent or beauty or ability in your case. Here it was so close that we almost had to draw straws — I'm not sure we made the right decision and should we find out in time we might come begging. At any rate you are a wonderful girl, a gifted actress and I hope I have the privilege of working with you soon. Best always, Josh Logan.

Logan did not forget Jean Seberg, or her reading.

Jane Fonda's performance in the play drew mixed notices and closed after a limited run on Broadway.

CHAPTER THREE
1959-1962

"Seldom has an artificially created young celebrity been extinguished so utterly and rekindled so luminously. Never has an American actress been so nearly destroyed by Hollywood and so fondly embraced by Europe."
— Robert Emmett Ginna on Jean Seberg, *Horizon* 1962

Shortly after moving into the rue du Bac apartment, 1961.
COURTESY OF SNORRAMYNDIR

"I'm an American, and I would hate to have anyone think I was an exile or an ex-patriate or anything else because I feel totally that I'm an American. I live in France because ... for the time being my work keeps me here."
— Jean Seberg

When Jean arrived to Los Angeles in the fall of 1959 for *Let No Man Write My Epitaph,* she discovered she was not even assured of the supporting role offered her. Rather, Jean was expected to make a screen test as the Chicago society girl.

"I went to the studio to check in," she recalled. "When I went to the casting office and asked for my script, they said, 'Here's your test scene.' I said, 'What do you mean test scene?' They said, 'Yes, you have to test for this tomorrow with two other girls.' And after having tested for *Saint Joan* and all that followed, this was dreadful.

"But I tested, and very foolishly I went back and said, 'All right, I won the test, now give me my part.' I should have just said, 'All right, I won the test, now I don't want the part.' I should have just gone away. I regret that I didn't."

While Shelley Winters, Burl Ives, and Ella Fitzgerald had plum roles, Jean's part only provided the girl for James Darren's character to marry. Illnesses among the cast, coupled with production delays, caused the filming to go over schedule, much to Jean's dismay. She claimed that she never saw the finished film ("I wouldn't go see it. I refuse to see it"), and when the film played in Marshalltown, she said, "I hope no one here goes to see it." Nevertheless, she had at least made herself visible at Columbia, and felt this might result in better offers in the future.

In late November while Jean was in Hollywood, François reported a theft in their Paris apartment. Jean's engagement ring, reportedly valued at $6,000 had been stolen. In addition, a collection of 150 solid gold and silver humidors belonging to the Countess de Sainte-Croix were missing. Several pieces of art had been taken, including a small painting by Drouais also valued at $6,000. Another victim of the thefts was former boxer Georges Carpentier, who also lived in the same building. His wife's jewels, $600 in cash and other objects were stolen.

A Marshalltown jeweler recalled having seen the ring when Jean brought it in to be cleaned. "They [Jean and François] told me it was a family heirloom from his side of the family — hundreds of years old. It was a nice ring with a diamond and rubies, but its value was only sentimental. It didn't have much value to it." The ring and the other stolen objects were never recovered.

In late 1959, François flew to Los Angeles to be with Jean and luxuriate in the social night life Hollywood offered. While there, he visited the French consulate. "Being brought up a certain way," François explains, "one of the first things I did when I arrived anywhere was to go to the general consul and leave my card."

Charles Lucet, the French Ambassador to the US at the time, related what happened next: a vice-consul asked the Consul-General if he would like to see a young Frenchman and his wife, a "ravishing young woman." He said he had more important things to do. The vice-consul replied: "You're wrong, Mr. Consul. She's worth seeing."

A few days later François and Jean received an invitation to a dinner party at the consulate. Jean did not want to go because she was tired from working on *Let No Man Write My Epitaph*. In addition, she did not know anyone who was going to the party. But her husband insisted. Grudgingly, Jean changed into an evening dress suitable for the occasion and to meet the stares of strangers. She did not imagine that the invitation was more than a courtesy. The Consul-General who sent the invitation was Romain Gary.

Gary was born in Vilnius, Lithuania, on May 8, 1914, the son of merchant Arieh-Leïb Kacew and Mina Owczynska (often known as Nina). Much concerning his early life remains obscure, not least because in his admired 1960 autobiographical account (translated as *Promise at Dawn* the following year) and other reminiscences, he often applied a novelist's imagination to what he knew and remembered of his past. He saw little of his father, and his parents separated in 1925, leaving his mother to struggle single-handedly with the boy's upbringing in turbulent times. As his memoir vividly testifies, she was a remarkable and resourceful woman, ready to make every sacrifice for a son who, she felt, was destined for fame. In Mina's imagination France represented the pinnacle of civilization, and one day Roman would doubtless represent this nation as ambassador.

The blueprint for Gary's future moved one step closer to realization when he accompanied her from Poland to Nice in 1928. With little money, they survived by selling antiques or other items until Mina assumed management of a boarding house close to the Russian Orthodox cathedral. By strange coincidence, its name, "Pension Mermonts," combined the elements of sea and mountains in the same way that the name "Seberg" had done for Jean's forebears, the Carlsons. Roman, now Gallicized as Romain, received a solid French education in Nice, enrolled at the Faculty of Law at Aix-en-Provence in 1933 and continued legal studies in Paris the following year.

Both mother and son were fascinated by the cinema, and somehow the idea arose that Gary's real father might have been the great Russian silent era star Ivan Mosjoukine, a myth that he continued to toy with as a plausible resemblance became more striking with passing years. His conviction grew, however, that it would be through writing that he could fulfill his mother's ambition for him, and this was encouraged by the acceptance of two stories by the weekly review *Gringoire*.

In 1935 Gary was granted French nationality. Three years later he entered service with the French Air Force in which he served as navigator and instructor, but which, perhaps owing to his Jewish immigrant background, denied him a commission. After the fall of France and the creation of Pétain's Vichy régime he made his way via Morocco to England, joining with those who rallied under the leadership of de Gaulle to fight on for liberation. In August 1940, now "Romain Gary de Kacew," he was enrolled in the Free French air service and served as a gunner on bombing missions over Germany, but was soon posted to Africa. It was here that he heard belatedly from a friend of his mother's death from cancer, news which affected him profoundly, and which perhaps only intensified his lifelong drive to repay her belief in him through achievement.

Returning to England with the Groupe Lorraine, he flew many missions over occupied France. One of these, in January 1944, resulted in serious injury, permanent partial paralysis of the face and transfer to administrative duties under de Gaulle. It was in London that he met and married Lesley Blanch, a cultivated writer for *Vogue* magazine with a passion for all things Russian and ten years his senior. His war service had earned him the Croix de Guerre, the Croix de la Libération and membership of the Légion d'Honneur and had made a career in the exclusive French diplomatic corps now a possibility. He had simplified his name, and it was as Romain Gary that he founded his literary career in France with the novel *Éducation européenne* (*A European Education*, 1960) which received the Prix des Critiques in 1945.

Successive diplomatic postings took the couple to Sofia, Bulgaria, to Berne and to New York, where Gary served as spokesman for the French delegation to the U.N. In 1956 he became Consul General in Los Angeles. Lesley Blanch had overtaken her husband's literary celebrity in 1954 with her best-selling account of intrepid female travelers, *The Wilder Shores of Love*. Her husband's piqued pride, which he himself mocked in an article for *Elle*, was quite soon to be salved. In 1956 his novel, *Les Racines du ciel* (*The Roots of Heaven*, 1958), which drew on his wartime experiences in Africa and was well in advance of its time in dealing with ecological concerns, was awarded France's most prestigious literary award, the Prix Goncourt. The 1958 film, *The Roots of Heaven*, directed by John Huston and starring Errol Flynn, Juliette Greco, Trevor Howard and Orson Welles, was only the first of a series of lavish screen adaptations of his novels.

Some viewed the Gary-Blanch marriage as a mother-son relationship, while others saw the union as one of an outspokenly independent Englishwoman and a moody Slav. Despite the difference in ages, this appeared to be a partnership which worked, cemented as it was by shared cultural interests. Many women were intrigued by Gary's background and exotic appearance. Blanch was well aware of her husband's passing amours, which hitherto had not seriously threatened the continuity of their lives.

François Moreuil well recalls the meeting which took place in December 1959: "The first thing [Gary] said to me after 'Hello' was 'You've got nice shoes. Do you mind if I try them on?' I found that terribly incongruous. But I let him try them on." Gary slipped the shoes on, and removed them. His attention then focused on Madame Moreuil.

What Romain Gary saw in the twenty-one-year-old Jean Seberg was a strikingly beautiful young blonde woman with warmth, poise and an air of innocence. After several more dinners with Romain in the company of François, Lesley Blanch, and several others, Jean came to realize that she had indeed married the wrong man. She was attracted to Romain's maturity, his fund of stories, his humor and his charm. He was eight years younger than her father.

Jean's parents had no idea there were marital problems between Jean and François when the two visited Marshalltown during the Christmas, 1959 holidays. Mary Ann and her husband Ed were also there to celebrate the holidays, and the *Times-Republican* recorded the event with a family picture and story. A family photo of Jean and François in Marshalltown, however, shows Jean in a pensive mood with François sitting behind, looking as if he has accepted the fact that their marriage is over.

While the couple was in Marshalltown, the December 28 issue of *Life* magazine hit the newsstands. In the magazine's photo essay on love, Jean and François were featured. They portrayed their love in a mannequin-like head-shot by Phillippe Halsman. While the theme of the issue was "The Good Life," the couple's inclusion was far from idealizing anything good.

"You could tell the marriage was on its way out," says Lynda Haupert of this time. Reports of a separation appeared, but Jean denied them, believing that her private life did not belong to the public.

In an effort to dismiss the rumors, Jean arrived with François in Salt Lake City, Utah to narrate a March of Dimes fashion show. As the chairwoman of the event pinned three white orchids to Jean's shoulder, someone remarked, "I thought a columnist said your husband had left you and gone to Paris."

"Obviously not. Here I am," he quietly intervened. "When I go, Jean goes. Maybe in a few weeks. We have an apartment there."

"Unlike love and marriage, or even ham and eggs, miracles and fashion shows seldom go together," Jean offered, changing the subject. "A show like the polio one provides both glamour and miracles …miracles from the funds it spills into such worthwhile coffers."

The couple returned to Los Angeles where Jean continued acting classes, but François needed to attend to his work in Paris. Before he left for France he asked Romain Gary a favor. As he later recounted, "I said to Romain Gary, 'Please take care of my wife. She'll be alone.' And he said, 'Sure, I'll do that.' And he did. He sure did."

Romain and Jean dined together several times, but always in the company of others. The couple shared an intellectual, and at the time, platonic relationship.

At her parent's home with François Moreuil, Christmas, 1959.
COURTESY OF SEBERG FAMILY COLLECTION

Prior to her own return to France, Jean visited Romain. "I told him that I was going to miss him," she admitted years later. "Somehow, I felt that if I didn't tell him, I was going to by-pass something significant in my life." That spring, Romain took a temporary leave from his diplomatic post and flew to Paris.

In Paris, Jean and Romain began seeing each other secretly. "Terrible things happened because she wanted to see him," François remembers, "and I didn't want her to see him." But Jean defied her husband. One day François, his father, and Jean-Paul Belmondo confronted Romain. "We went to his hotel room. My father said to Romain, 'a man of your age, who's fought in the same war as me, how can you behave that way?' and we almost broke his nose. We punched him first." The incident did not alter

Romain's attitude toward this new romance.

In March, Jean dazzled Parisians at the Paris Artists' Ball, where she paraded around center ring as a clown and led two trained seals in a beach ball toss. Also that month, *Breathless* was released, creating a considerable stir in the film world. *The New Yorker* proclaimed the film "a masterpiece" and wrote, "It is far and away the most brilliant, most intelligent and most exciting movie I have encountered this season ...it may even threaten the Kennedys as the warmest topic of local conversation for weeks to come."

Godard was hailed a hero and Belmondo became a French heart-throb and much sought-after leading man, while Jean relished the unaccustomed accolades she was receiving on all fronts. Sophia Loren said she was "Fabulous!" and one columnist wrote Jean was prettier and a better actress than the France's own Brigitte Bardot. "The greatest difference: Jean seems to have a brain and growth potential."

American critic Pauline Kael singled out Jean's performance: "As Jean Seberg plays her — and that's exquisitely — Patricia is the most terrifyingly simple muse-goddess-bitch of modern movies." Kael continued: "Patricia, a naive, assured, bland and boyish creature, is like a new Daisy Miller — but not quite as envisioned by Henry James. She has the independence, but not the moral qualms or the Puritan conscience or the high aspirations that James saw as the special qualities of the American girl ... she is so free that she has no sense of responsibility or guilt. She seems to be playing at existence, at a career, at 'love'; she's 'trying them on.' But that's all she's capable of in the way of experience. She doesn't want to be bothered; when her lover becomes an inconvenience, she turns him in to the police."

In retrospect, some felt Jean's role in the importance and success of *Breathless* had been exaggerated. Cinematographer Raoul Coutard said in 1995, "*Breathless* did well because it was *Breathless*. Not because of Belmondo and Seberg." In truth, however, the film's success came from the combination of all its elements, from the cast and crew to the director and editor.

One cannot deny Jean's involvement in the film was a leading factor in its success. As she pointed out, she had been Godard's last chance to get the film made because of her name recognition. If Jean had not been part of *Breathless*, and the film had been made with an unknown actress, it is doubtful whether many American critics would have bothered to view, let alone review the film, even supposing that it had found bookings in American theaters at all. *Breathless* was Jean's first true leading role after Preminger, and the critics were willing to give her another chance to redeem herself as an actress. She did this, and simultaneously critics discovered an important film. In time, critics and historians would rank *Breathless* as one of the turning points in the evolution of the cinema, alongside *The Birth of a Nation* and *Citizen Kane*.

With *Breathless*, Jean's career galvanized and her bankability status as an actress was suddenly transformed. François Truffaut publicly called her "the best actress in Europe," and no other actress in France, apart from Brigitte Bardot, commanded as high a salary for a film. She agreed to star in François' directorial debut film in the summer, and chose two further films from the others now offered.

In addition to her husband's *La récréation* (*Playtime*), which like *Bonjour Tristesse* was based on a story by Françoise Sagan, she signed to star in Jean Valère's *Les grandes personnes* (*Time Out for Love*), followed by a light comedy, *L'amant de cinq jours* (*The Five-Day Lover*), directed by Philippe de Broca.

"I did a very bad thing for an actress who supposedly cares about her work," Jean said, referring to the films. "I felt at the time, for financial reasons, that I should accept — or at least consider — the offers I was being given on the basis of my work in *Breathless* ... Columbia was talking about dropping my option, so I had absolutely no financial guarantees." Noting her popularity abroad and the success of *Breathless*, Columbia not only increased her weekly salary, but increased her loan-out fee to $20,000 per picture. The payment to Columbia for the use of Jean's services usually represented the single highest cost in the French filmmakers' budgets.

"*Breathless*, opened all the doors for her," says Vony Becker, who later became a close friend. "She had character. Her face, her hair, her look — it was new. A little American star here in Paris."

Jean became the prime example of liberated womanhood. Her trademark close-cropped hairstyle was copied worldwide. Although many felt Jean looked better with shoulder-length hair, she preferred the short-look throughout her life. Jean would not always be remembered exclusively for "the Seberg cut." Mia Farrow later copied the style while starring in television's *Peyton Place* and was credited with the cut in a 1992 *People* magazine issue of idols and fads. But it was Jean who had popularized the style for that generation.

Privately, Jean was pleased, but surprised. What was more perplexing was the French interest in her. "I still don't know why I should have meant anything to the French. This strange, awkward creature with rather bad teenage skin and extremely short hair — what could she possibly have symbolized? But it was a triumph ...It was fantastic for all of us," Jean reflected later.

The French idolization of Jean was so great that one girl from Paris (complete with la coupe Seberg) left her home to study in Iowa. Françoise Guilne went to Iowa because she wanted "exposure to the sort of society that produced the qualities in Jean Seberg," according to a newspaper account. Guilne had seen Jean in Paris nightclubs, and met her when she played a bit part in *Breathless*.

"We thought she was darling," Guilne said while visiting Ed and Dorothy

Seberg. "She was so graceful — as she was in *Saint Joan*." Only through visiting with Jean and talking about America did Guilne decide to study abroad. "She talked about Iowa in a romantic way [and said] I would meet more genuine people in Iowa," Guilne offered. "Jean loves this state. She talks about its beauty. And I have the same feeling."

The public interest in Jean Seberg after *Breathless* grew to a level comparable with Preminger's publicity campaign during *Saint Joan*. This time, however, she was not being forced upon the public. Now the public craved for her. They wanted to know what Jean Seberg was thinking, wearing, reading …and whom she was seeing.

The surge in media attention, albeit positive, reminded Jean uncomfortably of Preminger's publicity campaigns. This, added to her involvement with Romain Gary and the unsteady state of her marriage, pushed Jean to the point of exhaustion and confusion over how to cope. François believed she was having a mental breakdown. In April, he drove her to the American hospital in Paris in the convertible he had purchased for her. Along the way, he remembers, "the conversation was probably not a very nice one between us. With her high heels, she broke all of the instruments on the dashboard." Shortly after, Jean was admitted to a clinic under psychiatric care.

"She was there for a week and it was agreed between the doctors that no one was to see her," François recalls. "Romain and I agreed to that because there was too much pressure on her." Shortly after, he learned that Romain, disguised as a doctor, had been to see Jean during her recuperation in the hospital. "That made me absolutely furious because I thought it was unfair," he says today. In addition, he remembers how Romain had put Jean under the care of one of his friends who was a psychiatrist. He did this, François believes, in order "to take hold of her."

François relayed his feelings to Jean. She didn't believe a word of it. "When I'd say something, she'd say, 'You're lying,'" he recalls. "I've had many faults, but I was never a liar."

François spoke with Ed and Dorothy Seberg about the situation. The trio agreed Jean should recuperate in Marshalltown, away from Paris and the spotlight. Jean flew to Marshalltown on April 20. The press reported she had returned home to recover "from a kidney ailment brought on by overwork." Although his involvement in Jean's life was unknown to her family, Romain had also agreed to leave Jean alone for the time; however, François learned that his rival secretly visited her in Iowa during her convalescence.

At home Jean told her parents she and François could not reconcile their differences, and that she was going to file for divorce. Ed and Dorothy supported their daughter, especially when she told them François frightened her. "They took it very well, considering there had never been a divorce in our family," Jean said. She went into more detail with a close friend, saying François had physically abused her on several occasions. Jean did not care about how her hometown would gossip about the upcoming divorce. It was her life, and she was going to live it.

Although Jean exaggerated the spousal abuse angle, it was nonetheless acceptable grounds for divorce. She went to her lawyer in Marshalltown and discussed the matter.

Jean's stay, which again went well recorded by the *Times-Republican*, consisted of making May baskets with David, flying kites, and taking long walks alone. *Breathless* had not yet played in Marshalltown, but she apologized ahead of time to her hometown. "Yes, it has some naughty four-letter words," the former Sunday school teacher said, "but I don't say any of them, and I expect the English version will be censored." Later she added, "I'm not sure I'd want my friends here to see it, but if they do, they'll just have to remember I'm not the type of person portrayed in the movie."

François scheduled the first day of shooting on his film for June 6, which meant Jean was needed beforehand for meetings. Uneasy at the prospect of dealing with her estranged husband alone, Jean asked her mother to accompany her to Paris. Dorothy, however, was preparing for Kurt's high school graduation and felt it unfair not to be with her son during the commencement exercises.

One day while Dorothy was trimming Jean's hair in the basement, Frances went inside to see how her daughter and granddaughter were progressing. "Out of the clear sky," Frances later wrote, "Jean asked, 'Granny, would you like to go back to Paris with me?' And all under one breath she said, 'You know you'd have to fly.'" Never one to decline an adventure, Frances immediately accepted and practically started packing her bags that moment. She then began a journal of the trip which she entitled "Eight Weeks of Ecstasy."

Jean flew to New York a few days earlier for business meetings, so Frances took a train there and met her granddaughter at Grand Central Station on May 22. For eight days the pair stayed at the Plaza Hotel, and Jean took her grandmother on a tour of the city and introduced her to her friends. They also went to the theater and saw *West Side Story* and *The Sound of Music*, which Frances thoroughly enjoyed.

Jean and Frances left for Paris on June 2. Aboard the TWA flight in New York, Frances was comforted to know that the recent years of Jean's life had not changed her granddaughter, but that she had become a confident young lady. "Jean was somewhat amazed with me, and a little disappointed," Frances wrote. "She was so sure that I was going to be frightened as I had never flown in a big plane, let alone a jet. Jean is a veteran of twenty-three flights across the Atlantic, but she is not too confident. She always has the feeling 'this could be it.'"

During their flight in the first-class cabin, Frances remembered "a young mother with her baby sat opposite us. They were homeward bound to Rome. The child became uneasy, and the poor mother was frustrated. She had only two hands with which to work and she could not speak a word of English. Jean, seeing her plight, spoke to her in Italian and volunteered to hold the baby while the mother made the necessary repair — a dry diaper."

Reporters noted François was not at the airport to greet his wife. The next day, a reporter asked Jean if she did indeed plan to divorce her husband. "Nothing is decided," she answered, stretching the truth. "We have our personal problems to sort out."

One week later, however, Harry Druker, Jean's Marshalltown lawyer, filed divorce papers for her in the Marshall County District Court. "CAT IS OUT," SAYS JEAN IN ADMITTING MARITAL RIFF headlined the *Marshalltown Times-Republican*. In fact, Jean confided in Warren Robeson at the newspaper that she was having marital problems. She composed a statement that "our backgrounds, our upbringing, our ways of life, and many of our interests are incompatible; and we have mutually agreed that it is best that we part. There is no bitterness involved, only sincere regret," Jean dictated. In her own handwriting she added: "This statement should be released to Warren Robeson of the *Times-Republican* on the day the notice of divorce is placed with the paper."

9

"I love to act, but at some point I would like to settle down and have some children. It seems to me a very sad life to go on and on, just acting and to end up at age fifty without any children or husband."
— Jean Seberg

This was Frances Benson's first visit abroad. In fact, the only country she had visited outside the United States was Canada. The different culture, and ignorance of the language in Jean's adopted home country, did not discourage Frances. She relished the mysterious surroundings of which she previously had only read and seen photographs.

Jean and Frances stayed in a suite at the Berkeley Hotel in Paris. Frances related how she liked to sit by a window and look out "upon the busy street and the park across the way. On the street below us was a flower stand, also a news stand. The park was full of sidewalk benches and they were usually all occupied. Many children came each day, and there was a merry-go-round for their entertainment. The French children seem so fleet of foot, it almost seems they run instead of walk.

"At the far side of the street in a thicket was some sort of 'john,' or retreat for men. There was a constant stream of men going in and coming out, always in the act of buttoning or zipping up their pants."

On their first evening together, the pair went to dinner at the Eiffel Tower. Jean was recognized there by autograph seekers, and when she and her grandmother exited the tower, "one of the money-making photographer schemers snapped some pictures of us," Frances later recorded.

Frances witnessed first hand the busy life Jean was leading: modeling for Dior, dress fittings at Givenchy's, interviews, and public appearances, one after the other. "Jean hardly gets a chance to breathe without some kind of interruption," Frances wrote.

She also saw how little privacy her granddaughter had in public places. In a restaurant, Jean, Frances, and a small group of friends were dining. "Suddenly, a black sports car drove by with a 'Hi Jean!' circled around us and came back. He was a director whom Jean had met, and with him, his wife. Then curious people began asking for autographs and cameras were clicking all over the place, and another enjoyable evening had ended."

In *Playtime*, Jean was cast as the daughter of an American NATO officer, enrolled in an upper-crust boarding school in Versailles. Attracted to a sculptor who lives next door, her playtime is spent with him. The sculptor's mistress encourages him to seduce the American girl, knowing that his infatuation will pass. It does, and the daughter returns to America, hurt but wiser from her experience.

The atmosphere on the *Playtime* set was strained, mainly owing to the relationship between the director and the star. The press reported Jean and François argued openly during filming. "There have been fiery moments during the shooting of [*Playtime*]," one news article dramatized. "M. Moreuil keeps making script changes between scenes, and Jean insists she can't memorize dialogue on the spot. He's said some unkind things about her acting and those visiting the set say the off-camera flare ups are more entertaining than the Sagan plot."

However, Françoise Prévost, who appeared in *Playtime* as the sophisticated mistress, does not recall any arguing between husband and wife during the filming. "Jean was extremely nice, always trying to help," she remembers. "I never saw her making, as we say, caprice."

Privately, Jean wanted out of both the film and her husband's life. "It was pure hell," she later said. "He would scream at me and then I would cry and Grandmother would try to patch things up."

"When we were doing the film," François remembers, "she was seeing Romain Gary. She'd come home and change, leave dirty clothes in the house, then leave and go out with him. I was very hurt.

"When I knew our marriage was finished, I threw all her things away. I said, 'You want to leave me?' And I threw them out the window. Everything. And I said, 'Leave.'" The film still needed to be completed, so the pair's relationship was far from over. Also, François claims Jean had charged several haute couture dresses for her wardrobe. "It took me months to pay Givenchy for dresses she had not paid for," he says.

During the filming, Jean and her grandmother moved into an apartment at 52 rue de Bourgogne, subleasing from John Gallihera, whom Frances Benson described as "a fashionable bachelor or 'playboy.'" Weekends and evenings were spent touring the city's more famous landmarks and museums, socializing with Jean's friends, and visiting nightclubs. One evening the pair went to the Blue Moon to hear singer Bobby Short. Short saw Jean in the audience and later spoke with her and Frances, thanking both for attending his performance.

Frances Benson relished this new setting, enjoying almost every moment in Paris and at the apartment, meeting new and different people. While Jean and her friends spoke in French, Jean translated the conversations into English for Frances. Despite the language barrier, Jean's friends asked Frances if they could call her Granny, as Jean did. Frances gave them permission to do so.

Just prior to Frances Benson's return to the United States in early July 1960, Jean had a pleasant surprise. She quite unexpectedly spotted her former high school instructor, Paul Richer, walking across the street while she was stopped at a traffic signal. Richer introduced his wife Linda and their baby son to Jean and Frances, and told Jean they tried to contact her, but since her telephone number was unlisted, they had given up trying to locate her. Jean invited them to her apartment and later to dinner, where Richer told her he was teaching in Nigeria. Jean found Linda Richer charming, and when Linda confessed she did not realize how cool the evenings in Paris became, Jean loaned her a coat to wear in their remaining days in Paris.

On July 14, Bastille Day, Jean and Frances attended the huge celebration and military parade, and also ran into Jean's *Let No Man Write My Epitaph* co-star Burl Ives in the crowd. Jean and Ives spoke for a few minutes, and Jean introduced him to her grandmother. "Imagine," Frances later enthused, "shaking hands with a celebrity!"

Frances left France the same day, crossing the Atlantic on the *S.S. United States*. When she returned to Marshalltown in August, Frances, revitalized by her experiences in Paris and with a newfound taste for independence, found herself an apartment. She moved out of the Seberg household one month short of her seventy-ninth birthday.

Jean completed her scenes for *Playtime* in July. When released, the film did not achieve much success. *The Village Voice's* Andrew Sarris reviewed the film in 1963: "*Playtime* was directed by Francois Moreuil while he was still married to Miss Seberg, and no von Sternberg is he! At the risk of sounding naive about such matters, I would say that such indifferent direction as this constitutes ample grounds for divorce."

In time, Jean felt badly about the way she treated François, and in a 1970s interview, she praised his direction of *Playtime*: "François had the misfortune of coming in on the last crest of the new wave, when the producers began to back away from all these young men. It was bad luck for him. I thought while we were making the film that he was a good director. Gentle. Terribly passionate, though, about what he was doing. The film had quite a few good reviews but unfortunately didn't make any money — and it's a merciless industry."

Today, François says *Playtime* "wasn't a very good film." In fact, he does not have a copy of the film in his collection.

In late summer 1960, Jean began work on her second French film of the year, *Les grandes personnes* (*Time Out for Love*). In it she played a nineteen-year-old from Nebraska who is in Paris for a three-month vacation. She falls in love with a playboy race car driver, and after an affair leaves for America, wiser to the ways of Europe and its men. Looking back ruefully, Jean confessed she had done the film for "very base commercial reasons," and she dismissed the production later in her career. "*Time Out for Love* is absurd," *Newsweek* agreed, " — but Seberg is not. She has an individual, unimpaired quality and it is enough to rescue even this ball of fluff."

Françoise Prévost also appeared in *Time Out for Love*. "Jean Valère was a good director, but a little too wise for my taste," Prévost says. "He was not very original. At the moment it was filmed with the nouvelle vague style of Godard and Truffaut. It was a new style, and Valère was still the old style. Jean Seberg accepted the part because it was a very good story.

"When I saw it again recently, I said this film is really quite Jean's own story: This little girl coming from the United States to study in Paris, and she meets these people who are a little cool, cynical, but actually she is a smashing success with them. She falls in love with this guy who is actually nothing at all, so selfish and who uses other people for his own interests. Jean's character is destroyed by these people. And I think that is a little like her own story."

During filming *Time Out for Love*, Jean read Romain Gary's autobiography, *Promise at Dawn*. "Gary's book is beautiful, lovely to read," Jean told a *Newsweek* reporter who was visiting the set. "As a birthday present, I sent him my own translation of two chapters, and he told me I had done a good job."

In late August Jean dashed off a letter to Dawn Quinn:

"... As a result of the divorce proceedings and my extravagant life with François before, I'm on a strict budget.

"I understand there have been rumors in the States that we reconciled and I just want to assure you that's nonsense. It was a sad and painful mistake, but not one I intend to begin again. I'm living here quietly with my cats and work for company."

On September 20, the Marshall County Court granted Jean a divorce on grounds of her husband's cruel and inhuman treatment. Dorothy Seberg appeared on Jean's behalf at the proceedings, with Jean's deposition having been filed earlier.

François says he did not know that the divorce had been filed and first heard of it while editing *Playtime*. "The story was lurid, was so awful," he remembers, "that I immediately cried. And when the tears were over, I called my boss in New York and said, 'What are we going to do?'" What he actually did was counter-sue Jean for divorce on the grounds that she had not notified him of her planned divorce. "By that time she had been taken mentally, totally, by Romain Gary," he believes.

At the time François angrily told the press, "She owes almost everything to France. She became a star in France. She became a Frenchwoman when she married me. But she took refuge in the States rather than apply to a French court when she felt it more convenient."

Jean filed for divorce in Marshalltown for several reasons: It was after she spoke with her parents personally at home that she decided to divorce. Jean had not given up her American citizenship and was still legally a citizen of the United States. Petitioning for divorce in Iowa was not simply convenient, but made perfect sense to her.

Still, François was angry. "I was not even summoned, warned or questioned by this court," he fumed. "I learned I got a divorce through the radio and newspapers ...Now she has left home again, but she will have to appear before a French court, and this time I am filing for the divorce — for a fair, legal one."

Immediately, Jean's attorneys, Boardman, Cartwright and Druker, fired back this statement: "...contrary to [his] statement, he was properly notified of the divorce action and was aware of its pendency of the proceedings. On two separate occasions he was personally notified to appear before the court but chose to ignore the summons. Whether or not Mr. Moreuil chooses to recognize the divorce of the Iowa court is of no importance. Its validity is not dependent upon his whim. He was given due notice and an opportunity to be heard. The divorce is fully effective, and Mr. Moreuil cannot set it aside by attacking it in the press."

Today, François says he was never notified of the divorce action or the proceedings by Jean or her lawyers. It was this technicality that allowed him to file for divorce against Jean in France and under French law. By charging Jean with adultery and naming Romain Gary as the other man, he obtained the court's ruling in his favor. Jean did not attend the hearing.

"The French court would never have granted me the divorce," he says, "if Jean could have produced the slightest evidence of my knowledge of [receiving the notification] from the Iowa courts." In addition, the French court relieved him of the payment of alimony to Jean. "When we divorced," Jean recalled in 1961, "he thought I'd ask for alimony. I wouldn't dream of it."

"It was quite courageous of me," François admits today, "because I was still very much in love with her. It left me in a very hard period for two to three years after. It was not fair, but life is not fair."

In regard to the cruelty charge, François said at the time, "My only cruelty consisted of giving up my profession to help further my wife's career." Today, however, his feelings have changed. "Everyone around me laughed about that. Mental cruelty is when a girl comes into your house, leaves her dirty clothes on the bed and goes out with another man. I think that's mental cruelty."

As for the physical abuse Jean reported to confidants in Marshalltown, François finds the accusation shocking and denies it strenuously: "I never hit Jean. Never. I never touched a woman. I never touched my [present] wife."

Jean later viewed her first marriage as a "youthful folly": "I got married for all the wrong reasons. I married because I was afraid and beaten, because I wanted to be protected. It never could have worked. I mean, you don't marry to run away from yourself, and if you do, it's always going to be disastrous. But I owe François a great deal; he gave me friendship when I needed it."

"In my bitter moments," Jean confessed years later to film critic Hollis Alpert, "I often think it was François' itchy desire to be part of the film world, a director, if possible, that was his primary motive for marrying me. Certainly, I wouldn't have existed in his eyes if I had been Miss Nobody from Iowa." This, too, he denies, explaining that he was attracted to that "pale girl with short hair" who wanted to water ski before he learned she was Jean Seberg the actress. "She might as well have been a clerk in a department store - I would have loved her as much."

Looking back on their life together, he remembers how the press referred to him as Mr. Seberg. "That was one thing I was avoiding very much," he says. "I did not want to be 'Mr. Seberg,' and I don't think I ever was." As for his former wife, he admits "Jean was ahead of her time. She was a very strong personality," and adds: "There was something in her that kept her moving from man to man, moving from one country to another country, moving from one part of herself to other parts of herself. And it all led to a very tragic end."

In retrospect, it was not a marriage without warrant: François had helped to get Jean's contract out of Preminger's hands and to a leading Hollywood studio; he had taken her to France and persuaded her to act in *Breathless*; and he introduced her to her future second husband.

Jean moved in with friend Aki (Hersay) Lehman, who had worked on *Saint Joan*, and who remained a close friend of Jean's even though she was also friendly with Otto Preminger. "It was not Jean," Lehman once said, "but Otto who played Joan of Arc."

Lehman did not care for François or his circle of friends: "[He] always struck me as the kind of snob who would look down on her small-town Iowa background. She was dropped very quickly by most of the people who knew her through François — no loss, I must say, for they were part of a little snobbish group here given to amorality and shock-the-bourgeoisie jokes in dreadful taste. What was refreshing about Jean was that she had never become spoiled, and she had meanwhile developed a fantastic thirst for knowledge."

The person who satisfied that thirst was Romain Gary, whom Jean discreetly continued to see in the following months. Through him she analyzed her life and career. In an article she wrote for the *Oxford Opinion* in the fall of 1960, which confidants felt Romain helped her compose, Jean discussed her qualms about acting on screen: "It is a very difficult craft, film acting. Understanding it intellectually means very little. Some of the most believable actors are 'intelligent' actors. A camera traps you, the true you — not a distorted reflection in the mirror, but a pure critical reproduction in a magnifying lens. It is difficult to lie to a camera."

She also realized that acting is "a profession which few can leave even when they know their time has come ... Perhaps the day arrives when what he [the actor] has to offer is a la mode — the little-boy lost quality of James Dean, Van Johnson's freckles, the soft-hearted gangster face of Bogart. What happens? The audience identifies him with this special personal quality, and the movie moguls capitalize and produce it on a mass market. He has, suddenly, no self to sell anymore; he has the carefully mimicked imitation of himself as he once was. And finally the public will feel this too."

Jean Seberg privately concluded that she should no longer continue playing the American girl in France. She felt a need to change her onscreen image as a "free spirit." If not, there was the danger of being typecast in a way which would severely limit her renewed career.

The change came in October when Jean began her third French film of 1960. *L'amant de cinq jours* (*The Five-Day Lover*) was her first French comedy, and she pulled it off well. Complete with a shoulder-length brunette wig, Jean was cast as Claire, a married Englishwoman with two young children. Reserving weekends for her family, Claire has a daytime affair from Monday through Friday with a playboy after her husband has gone to work and the children to school.

Filming was enjoyable, but, in addition, Jean revealed a new subtlety in her acting and displayed little of the self-consciousness that had been evident in some of her previous performances.

"Humor is always the hardest thing to understand in a foreign language. But Jean did. She was very gifted for comedy," director Philippe de Broca reflected. "She played the character of the free-spirited Englishwoman delightfully." De Broca felt her leading man, Jean-Pierre Cassel, had fallen in love with her. "I always felt there was a little wickedness to her delight.

Jean was very flirtatious, and could certainly tease men, although it was never done with cruelty."

When released, *The Five-Day Lover* was not an overwhelming success in France. "They thought it was really outrageous," Jean recalled. "You would see me one second in the arms of my lover and the next shot would be of me holding my children. It became a bit shocking." The film was a hit in

In The Five-Day Lover *with Jean-Pierre Cassel.* AUTHOR'S COLLECTION

art houses, especially in New York. Brendan Gill of *The New Yorker* wrote: "It's ungallant for me to say so, but I was astonished by the tact and delicacy with which Miss Seberg played her tricky role. She, it turns out, is an actress, and, oh, how beautiful!" *Time*, the *New York Post* and the *World-Telegram* all placed *The Five-Day Lover* on its annual "Ten Best Pictures of the Year" listing.

"It's one of my favorite films," Jean said. "For me it was first of all a change of pace and I learned a great deal from de Broca about comedy technique, about pace and timing." *The Five-Day Lover* remained one of Jean's favorites later in her life.

After *The Five-Day Lover* Jean took a break from films. She pursued other interests, which conspicuously involved Romain Gary, whose marriage to Lesley Blanch was clearly coming to an end. At the end of the year

Jean and Romain quietly moved from the small apartment they had rented on the île Saint-Louis to an opulent apartment at 108 rue du Bac.

On the Left Bank, the gated rue du Bac building is situated in an elegant neighborhood with art galleries and antique shops. The couple's twelve-room apartment was on the third floor, overlooking the street. In the courtyard behind the building was a large, private garden of flowers and vines.

The revelation of Jean's involvement with Romain brought a reaction of mixed confusion and surprise from her family. "When we first learned about Romain, my first reaction, and that of my parents, was that he was very old. He was about my father's age, and we didn't quite understand that relationship," Mary Ann Seberg says.

During this time Romain concentrated on his writings and was completing his novel *The Talent Scout*. Its story revolves around José Almayo, a ruthless dictator of a Spanish-speaking country, and the young American woman who becomes his mistress.

The unnamed woman was loosely based on Jean, as became evident in details from her unblemished, creamy skin and turned-up nose, to her short blonde hair. Like Jean, the woman was from the Midwest and had joined the NAACP when she was fourteen. The similarities continued when the young woman writes long letters to her grandmother, in which she unburdens herself of her problems and sins.

The girl also educates the man of the finer things in life; however, in 1968 Romain commented, albeit affectionately, that it was the other way around with himself and Jean. "Romain really thinks I'm still a dumb farm girl," Jean retorted.

Upon the book's completion, Jean immediately saw what Romain had done and at first felt flattered, despite being the obvious butt of some of the satire. In time, however, she would grow to resent his continual use of her persona as a basis for his characters.

10

"Her films and her way of life were considered risqué in the 1960s, but today they would not be blinked at."
— Dawn Quinn

In January 1961, Jean departed on a six-week trip to the Far East, an invitation from the Japanese film industry. She toured Bangkok and Hong Kong with Romain, which not only proved an enjoyable trip, but additionally brought a welcome escape from the news media. Back in Paris, *Playtime*, *Time Out for Love*, and *The Five-Day Lover* were playing simultaneously around the city, with one critic commenting that the barrage was a Jean Seberg film festival.

In Marshalltown, the *Times-Republican* ran a full page of publicity stills from Jean's three recently released French films. While *Playtime* and *The Five-Day Lover* eventually played in her hometown, *Breathless* was the first one that opened, in 1961. Ed and Dorothy Seberg first viewed the film in Des Moines. Both liked the movie and Jean's acting, and Dorothy added, "She isn't anything like that!" "I'm not a good critic of my daughter's movies," confessed Ed. "I watch her and not the picture."

When the film opened at the Strand Theater in Marshalltown shortly after, manager Bryan Rowley warned that no one under sixteen would be admitted to view the film. Ed Seberg felt the move was a bit extreme, and said he doubted *Breathless* would harm the average teenager. "It's up to other parents to decide if they want their teenagers to see such movies."

When asked, considering the nature of her French films, if she believed in censorship or making alterations in films, Jean answered: "Oh no. The old Hollywood thing of the studio taking von Stroheim films or Welles's and cutting them - I think it's shocking. The censorship I believe in is self-censorship. Obviously, no censors — or very few — are going to have the taste or discrimination, or the cultural background or sensitivity and delicacy that a great artist in any field will have dealing with his own work. Censorship can be a very dangerous thing." The uproar provoked by Seberg's French films at that time is surprising, considering that if released today the films would probably receive no more than a PG rating. But in 1961 they were considered racy.

"I think at the time the French films started coming out, the town ... I think they were still proud of her," says Pauline Smith. "But, of course, Marshalltown, being a small town in the Midwest, had certain values, and the movies were frowned upon in some areas. But you just expect that in a small town.

"The films were different. They weren't like the usual Hollywood movie. No one understood this 'New Wave' that they talked about. The method of filmmaking was entirely different than the Hollywood system — the splashy Technicolor musicals and all."

Some Marshalltownians felt Jean had changed, and believed that the acting they saw onscreen was the life she was leading in France. "I am an actress," Jean answered. "To label a girl 'good' or 'bad' is silly, stupid and cruel." When asked if she had been "Europeanized," Jean replied: "In many superficial ways I've been extremely influenced by Europe ...I've always felt a wonderful closeness with the French and they've been very good to me, and France is home for me now. Most of my happier moments, some of my unhappy ones, and most of my work and most of the respect I have from people have been in France."

Concluding their trip to the Orient, Jean and Romain flew to New York and stayed at the Plaza Hotel. After living in France and having visited the

Orient, Jean re-evaluated the United States. She told Hollis Alpert while in New York, "I find myself believing more and more in American culture. And I'm getting more and more fed up with those who pooh-pooh America. It's far and away the most humane country and the one with the least compromise."

During a taxi ride there, Jean listened to the cab driver sound off racist lines to her, but she kept quiet. At the end of the ride she lied to the driver by remarking, "I happen to be very happily married to a Negro and have two lovely children with him. What do you think of that?" The driver sniffed, "I pity you." The cab driver's remarks angered her for days.

While in New York, Jean appeared on *The Tonight Show*, then hosted by Jack Parr. She spoke to Parr about her improbable American film comeback and the roller coaster career she had endured in three short years. When he asked about Otto Preminger, Jean put her hands to her face in disgust, not wishing to talk about him. Surely these questions about Preminger and her films with him would have subsided by now, she felt.

Later in the year, Jean did comment on Preminger: "I realize that his bullying methods work with some people, but he destroyed my confidence in *Saint Joan* ... I'm glad he discovered me, and I'm glad he starred me in *Saint Joan*. But after that picture, there was only one way to go — to the bottom."

When asked what was behind her improvement as an actress (was it lessons?), she replied sharply: "Living."

Jean flew home alone to Marshalltown in the spring for a quiet Easter week. Helping color Easter eggs with David, and visiting friends and relatives, Jean remembered to congratulate the Bobcats basketball team which had won the state championship. Columbia offered her a part in *Sail a Crooked Ship* with Robert Wagner and Ernie Kovaks, but she declined.

Gossip columnists continually fed the public with fictitious goings-on of the offscreen Jean Seberg. One item claimed she was dating Australian cattle baron Charles Pearlfuss. Another linked Jean with Sidney Poitier after she attended the premiere of *A Raisin in the Sun* with him at the 1961 Cannes Film Festival, where she publicly entertained several members of the American film industry. Her main concern at this time was not her career, but still her relationship with Romain Gary.

After completing an eighteen-month course on Roman and Gothic art, known as Cours du Louvre, Jean's certificate was personally signed by novelist André Malraux, the Minister of Culture and a significant figure in France. He also did not speak to "just anyone," as one person remarked, indicating how far the actress had come in terms of acceptance in Europe. Jean described Malraux as "a Renaissance man lost in our century," and the two retained a lifelong mutual regard.

"I could see you as Anna Karenina," Malraux once said to Jean. She felt highly flattered by the compliment implicit in the suggestion. "Have you ever wanted to play Anna Karenina?" Malraux continued. "You know, if I could begin life all over again, I would be a film director and that is the film I would do. But I have never directed women. I think it must be a very special thing."

The two attended Alain Resnais' prize-winning film, *L'année Dernière à Marienbad*, which Malraux dismissed as "nonsense." When Otto Preminger's

Presenting Sidney Poitier and members of the A Raisin in the Sun *delegation at the 1961 Cannes Film Festival.* COURTESY OF SNORRAMYNDIR

film *The Cardinal* opened in Paris, Malraux invited Jean as his personal guest and allowed her to sit with him in a private theater box, and she and Romain attended the premiere party for the film held at Maxim's. Jean and Malraux remained friends and kept in touch until his death in 1976.

While Jean preferred small groups at dinner parties and for conversation, she was at times frustrated with the French social life. "The French system seems to be based on saving the maximum of yourself to those nearest you. Perhaps that is better than the other extreme in Hollywood, where people give so much of themselves in public life that they have nothing left over for their families," she analyzed. "Still, it's hard for an American to get used to. Often I will get excited over a luncheon table, only to have the hostess say discreetly that coffee will be served in the other room. I miss that casualness and friendliness of Americans, the kind that makes people smile."

One of Jean's French friends commented, "She can detect French phonies faster than any American girl around."

In late summer, Jean contemplated but turned down a part in the play

Sunday in the Park on Broadway. "Columbia suggested it might not be a good idea to tie myself up that long," Jean cited as the reason. Columbia considered casting her in *The Ugly American* with Marlon Brando, but when she wasn't offered this part she accepted a role in the Franco-Italian production *Congo Vivo*.

This film was partly filmed on-location in the former Belgian Congo, and Jean arrived in Leopoldville in early September. "The Africans are so child-like and sweet," she wrote Dawn Quinn, "but, as you read in the papers, they have child-like brutality, too! And the babies: the women carry them on their backs — like little black beans." Jean commented to the press there were few European women in Leopoldville, that out of the 350,000 residents of the city, only 20,000 were white. "Every time I went to the hotel lobby or restaurant, I was treated gallantly."

Jean's role in the film as a frigid, suicidal wife of a Belgian colonist has her drifting into an affair with an Italian journalist. The affair is unconsummated because of the trauma she has suffered as a victim of rape.

While filming *Congo Vivo*, Jean recited her lines in French and then was answered in Italian by actor Gabriele Ferzetti, the famed actor of *L'avventura*. A reporter asked Jean if it was difficult to act under these conditions: "Not at all. It's the eyes that matter. I watch his eyes. They express everything there is to say. They tell everything," she explained. "If an actor's eyes say nothing, then he is a bad actor."

At one point during the production, Jean served as an interpreter for American newsmen when they interviewed a high Congolese official. Tensions on the set, however, mounted when political unrest closed in near the filming location. The fighting was over the Katanga province, which had seceded from the Congo, and the land's mineral-rich deposits.

"The Belgians bungled things badly in the Congo," Jean later told reporter Sheilah Graham. "They wouldn't educate their natives. It was only last year that a colored doctor was able to practice. The Belgians built two universities that presumably were open to all. But to get in, you had to know Greek, which automatically kept out to Congolese. The fact is the natives are very kind, and it is surprising after the treatment they received from the Belgians they are not more brutal."

In addition, the heat and humidity were high, the food suspect, and water dirty. Jean contracted a case of amoebic dysentery, and months later she would become irritable and ill. When the crew arrived on location to film a ferry scene, "we found soldiers with big guns trained on us," Jean recalled. Only when United Nations Secretary General Dag Hammarskjöld died in a suspicious plane crash in the jungle, on his way to a meeting with President Moise Tshombe, did the uneasy crew flee to Rome to complete filming.

Congo Vivo — part documentary, part love story in the Hollywood style of the 1930s — had little impact on the film world. Jean knew the film had its flaws; primarily that the two stories did not mix well. "There are fascinating things in the film — interviews with [prominent Africans General Mobutu and President Kasavubu] — but then there are other shots of me in my bathroom, combing my hair and taking sleeping pills. It doesn't fit together at all." In additon, "There's a sequence [over which the producers] might have some trouble with the censors," Jean offered. I dance with an African."

When Romain flew to Rome to meet with Jean in October it did not go unnoticed by the press. The couple allowed themselves to be photographed and consented to a handful of interviews. In a conversation with the French magazine *Elle*, Jean was open about her feelings toward Romain:

> *Elle:* It seems that in America the notion of divorce is not the same as it is in Europe. What do you think of that?
> *Jean:* I'm for divorce. I think, in general, Americans are less sophisticated than Parisians.
> *Elle:* What do you mean by sophisticated?
> *Jean:* Here in Paris, even if people get along very well, they prefer to cheat on one another as much as possible. Each one has his little life on the side, and I don't like that. Americans divorce. It's more honest.
> *Elle:* If you had to get married in the near future, would you marry Romain Gary?
> *Jean:* I have no idea. All that I can tell you is that he's a marvelous man, a great friend for whom I have admiration and esteem, on the human as well as the professional level.
> *Elle:* Do you know the wife of Romain Gary, the novelist Lesley Blanch?
> *Jean:* Yes, I met her in California. She's a very nice woman, I must admit. But she's been separated from Romain Gary for a very long time.
> *Elle:* Do you expect a man to be responsible for you?
> *Jean:* Yes I do. It's a man's job.

Lesley Blanch had apparently been willing to let the affair run its course, as she had with Romain's previous liaisons, but she could not remain blind to the fact Romain and Jean were serious. They were, after all, now living together. Although Blanch would not agree to a divorce, Jean and Romain continued their affair, regardless of any legal impediment that kept them from marrying. Romain was aghast at the ruinous terms of separation proposed by his wife. For her part, Blanch apparently believed she was acting in his interests in remaining unyielding, and that marriage to Jean Seberg would be a disaster for him. On Jean's side, the situation was a highly uncomfortable one. René Agid, a friend from Romain's early days in Nice, and his wife Sylvia were witnesses to this tug of war and employed as confidants by all the parties when they expressed their frustration.

The gossip concerning the Seberg/Gary/Blanch triangle eventually found its way to French diplomatic circles, where many found the affair unaccept-

In Venice with Romain Gary, November 1961. COURTESY OF SNORRAMYNDIR

able. An interview which Blanch gave to *Paris-Presse* in November 1961, in which she openly responded to questions about her marriage, prompted Romain to angrily accuse her of destroying his career. Prominent Gaullist and Minster of Foreign Affairs, Maurice Couve de Murville, prevented Romain from receiving any further promotions. Romain decided to relinquish his post until the scandal ended.

In his 1974 book, *The Night Will Be Calm*, Romain largely attributed his decision to his friendship with and loyalty to Charles de Gaulle. "I couldn't work next to Charles de Gaulle because I wanted to keep my sexual liberty … It was a question of rectitude. De Gaulle had an ethic of respectability for his public servants that I didn't want to take on myself. I had to choose between a double life of lies or refusals …I wasn't going to sacrifice my nature and my love of life to ambition and the desire to make it."

Ultimately, the news of Jean's involvement with Romain Gary worked its way to the United States and to Iowa. In January 1962, the *Des Moines Register* published a Paris news story under the headline: "Jean Seberg, Idolized, Is Saddest American." Describing Jean as a home wrecker, the article acknowledged that the seventeen-year Gary marriage had "been on the rocks for a long time."

"I may be very *vieille vogue* [old fashioned] but I'd rather not wash any dirty linen in public," Lesley Blanch commented. "Romain and I met during the bombardments of the war, we lived through hard times together and we had our successes together. You can't tear all that down in one day or even in many years. We've had crises before, but we've always surmounted them," she insisted, referring to Romain's previous affairs. Romain simply stated, "This is our business and ours alone."

She continued to find herself on the defensive, especially when she returned for a visit to Marshalltown the same month. In addition, *Breathless* had already played in Iowa during her visit home. One Sunday after a service at Trinity Lutheran Church, the minister took her aside and asked, "Jean, why don't you come back to us for a while?"

Jean could not understand why her hometown or the state had such an interest in her, especially in her private life, or why they judged her choices in films, clothes, and men. But she did have an ally in Warren Robeson and the *Times-Republican*. "We always tried to be fair in what we reported and what we didn't report concerning Jean," Robeson says.

During her visit, the *Times-Republican* reported that Jean was "scheduled to discuss with NBC television officials the possibility of doing dramatic tele-plays next fall even though she vowed 'never to do a television series.'" Although nothing resulted from the meetings, such niceties did not keep quiet the public gossip of Jean and Romain in the press or in the backyards of homes.

Jean's parents remained tight-lipped about her life, the uproar over *Breathless*, and the articles about her Parisian lifestyle. Witnessing the adverse press accounts and the small-town talk during this visit home, Jean kept one secret to herself. She was pregnant with Romain's child. Jean intended to carry full term but could not bring herself to tell her parents or her friends. "With her upbringing, it was a difficult position to be in — pregnant and unmarried — at that time," Lynda Haupert remembered. "She should have been born twenty years later, when sex and morality were freer."

"If a girl falls from grace occasionally, that doesn't make her bad," Jean said at the time. "What we call sin isn't easily pinpointed. There are women who are the most horrible, hurtful bitches you could imagine, but they're 'good' because they haven't succumbed sexually. Does that make sense?

"If a man marries a virgin it's hardly a guarantee that he's got himself an angel — or vice versa."

Returning to Paris, Jean told Romain of the pregnancy. He was delighted, but cautious, wanting to keep the impending arrival quiet until he could finally convince Lesley Blanch for a divorce. He also felt the public knowledge of the pregnancy would prove disastrous to his relations with Charles de Gaulle and also to Jean's film career, as in the case of Ingrid Bergman a few years earlier when Bergman, while still married to her first husband,

The Seberg family in 1962: Mary Ann, David, Kurt, Dorothy, Ed and Jean.
COURTESY OF SEBERG FAMILY COLLECTION

became pregnant by director Roberto Rossellini. Although circumstances differed in the two cases, an unmarried pregnant actress was nonetheless unacceptable to the public in 1962. Jean agreed to Romain's wishes and kept silent.

Shortly after, Jean and Romain dined with *Look* editor Joseph Roddy. In the article "The Restyling of Jean Seberg," Romain discussed Jean and his novel *The Talent Scout*.

Romain revealed that "I used the [main] character to represent the idealistic and unrealistic attitude of Americans, the American naiveté. Jean loses her naiveté rapidly under my influence in real life. In the book, and maybe in real life, too, she takes people for what they are on the surface. And she does this with frequently disastrous results. She can be in the middle of the most criminal sort of setup, and she can't see it. That's the American side of her character."

"I never knew until I came here that somebody can be really nice to you for years and really hate your guts. Happens all the time here," Jean replied. "She has brains and, what's more, intellectual curiosity," Romain continued. "And when you think of where she came from — "

"You mean to sit there and say Marshalltown High School is not an intellectual atmosphere?" she countered. Romain did not respond.

Although Romain believed Jean possessed a degree of naiveté, Jean was realistic in regard to acting. "I know that the greatest of actresses has about twenty good years of acting in her and that she will go on living for thirty or fifty years as a human being. So the conclusion I have come to is that I can't make acting my whole life …I'm lost to Debbie Reynolds roles, and I'm not going to give Liz Taylor a run for her money.

"I went through a very rough period at first in Paris, when the French thought the highest compliment they could pay me was that I didn't act like an American at all. And you know what Frenchmen think about American girls, don't you? They think you have to break an American girl in like you break in a horse. You have to comb it, run it, beat it. Same as a horse. That's what Frenchmen think about American women.

"But American movie stars! You should hear Frenchmen on that. When absolutely great French actors, I mean the very best ones, hear that I was in Hollywood and had lunch with John Wayne, they can hardly stand it. 'Just think,' they say, 'John Wayne. You had lunch in Hollywood with John Wayne?'

"Now, you know absolutely everything about me, including the fact that I was conceived, born and married in Marshalltown and that I will probably be buried there in the fourth most beautiful cemetery in the world."

11

"[Jean Seberg] has arrived."
— A critical review of *In the French Style*

By 1962 Jean Seberg had become the third highest ranking female star in France — as a French actress. Her success was reflected in the salary she earned from Columbia Pictures at the time: $1,750 a week. Five years earlier, Jean was making $250 a week under her contract with Otto Preminger.

In the spring of 1962 Columbia wanted Jean to star in the film *In the French Style*, which was to be financed and distributed by the studio. Based on two short stories by Irwin Shaw, "In the French Style" and "A Year to Learn the Language," with direction by Robert Parrish, both men agreed to co-produce the project.

Seeing her success in Europe, the brass at Columbia felt Jean was the ideal choice to play the role of the American girl who travels to Paris to study art and learns the ways of Europe. For Jean, the role marked a possible breakthrough in a Hollywood film.

Irwin Shaw, however, had Barbara Harris in mind for the lead. "My brother David kept telling me that Jean Seberg was my girl," Shaw recalled. "David pointed out that not only had she lived in Paris for five years and that in *The Five-Day Lover* she had shown herself to be an actress of charm and ability. Bob Parrish and I went to see the movie and we decided David was right about her."

Mike Frankovich, Columbia's European head of production, read the screenplay and gave his tentative approval for Jean to appear in the Shaw/Parrish film, although she had the right to veto the project.

Meanwhile, in addition to her pregnancy, Jean was also suffering from the recurring amoebic dysentery she contracted while making *Congo Vivo*. Recovering from treatments for the illness, she retreated to Romain's vacation home in Barcelona, Spain for a three-month stay beginning in May.

Accompanied by her maid Eugenia Munoz, Jean wrote Dawn Quinn while there: "I am recuperating from my cure, which about finished me off for good. But if it did that to me, it must have been worse for my amoebas, which are smaller. At least that's what we hope. All seems well, but I have to take it easy for a few weeks and decided to get away from the hurlyburly of Paris and take a little sun… The Spanish are such absolutely lovely people — so clean, honest, proud and generally nice. It has been a revelation."

In the letter, Jean did not let slip any hint that she was pregnant.

After serving as a judge at the 1962 Cannes Film Festival, Romain joined Jean in Barcelona. There they lived quietly and in seclusion until Robert Parrish asked to visit Jean to discuss *In the French Style*. Jean pretended to have a broken foot, so she sat up in bed with her leg elevated. Romain concocted a wire cage to keep the weight of the blankets off her foot — and to hide the fact she was nine months pregnant. She received Parrish in her bedroom and discussed the project, but the "broken foot" concerned the director.

"How long do you think you will be laid up?" he asked. "We're supposed to start filming in three weeks."

"That won't be a problem," Jean replied. "The cast comes off next week."

The charade worked; however, Parrish thought Jean had gained weight. She promised the director the added pounds would be gone before filming. Parrish left, convinced Jean was perfect for the role.

Jean told the director she would read the script that evening, and then would give him her answer the next day. She arranged for Parrish to stay with Romain at a nearby cottage he had rented by the sea. The two men had known each other socially, and spent the evening talking about the film industry and politics. At one point Parrish brought up the subject of *In the French Style*, and asked Romain whether or not he thought Jean would accept the lead role. Romain replied he did not get involved in Jean's work.

"She makes her own decisions," he said.

After reading the script, Jean telephoned the next day and told Parrish, "If I don't get this part, I'll never speak to you or Irwin again. I love it!"

Shortly after, Jean gave birth to a healthy son by cesarean section.

Years later, Jean acknowledged that Alexandre Diego Gary was born on July 17, 1962. Through his contacts, Romain arranged the proper legal

Filming In the French Style, *1962.* AUTHOR'S COLLECTION

papers to state officially that Diego was born in the small French village of Charquemont on October 26, 1963. But in the summer of 1963 Jean was filming *Lilith*, and one month prior to her son's alleged birth date, she was attending the premiere of *In the French Style*. A pregnant Jean Seberg would not have gone unnoticed.

It was not until July 1965 that Jean told Dawn Quinn about Diego: "I have a big surprise for you. Now hold onto your seatbelt. Romain and I have a two-year-old son. Really! He is a beautiful boy and his name is Alexandre, but we call him Diego. He was born shortly after our marriage, and because of all that we have kept it very quiet. I imagine around this fall it will come "out," but we will have avoided by then the kind of press we feared and it will be alright. I had him by Cesarean section. It's a rather fantastic story, but I'll have to tell you when I see you."

Jean's other friends were told of Diego in the months and years that followed. Carol Hollingsworth learned the news in 1966. "She kept Diego's birth a secret from everyone," Hollingsworth recalled. "Jean wrote me a letter and said, 'Why is it so hard to tell the people you love what is going on in your life?'"

While Jean reported for rehearsals for *In the French Style* in early August, Diego was cared for by Eugenia, who eventually became a surrogate mother to the boy. Filming began on August 27, and during the course of the production, Diego was safely hidden away with Eugenia in Spain. Frequently, Jean either telephoned Eugenia to ask about Diego, or snuck away during her days off to visit her infant son.

As Christina James in *In the French Style*, Jean was given the chance to show her acting range more convincingly than in any previous film. The story, spread over a four-year period, begins with a pony-tailed innocent in Paris and ends with Christina as a sophisticated, yet disenchanted member of the jet-set who returns to the States to marry a doctor.

"She's the most professional, technically proficient actor I think I've ever directed," Parrish said of his star. Parrish had directed several actors, including Gregory Peck, Jack Lemmon, and Rita Hayworth, and added, "[Jean's] knowledge of what the camera wants is kind of staggering."

Jean, however, remained modest but retained her sense of humor when she told a reporter, "The whole movie is very fine. I wrote my parents back in Marshalltown that they'll be able to see this one." One highlight of the script is a scene in which Christina and her father discuss her life sympathetically but candidly during his visit to Paris. Shaw questioned whether this was valid and real in the 1960s, but Jean told him it was "because I'm always playing the scene with my parents."

Ed and Dorothy Seberg flew to Europe and paid their daughter a visit during filming. Parrish invited Jean and her parents to dine with him one evening, and shocked Jean when they went to eat at a topless restaurant. Feeling embarrassed for her parents, she scolded the director for subjecting them to half-nude women. Parrish thought the adventure would be humorous. The usually proper Ed Seberg just laughed and assured Jean and Parrish that it was "all right"; however, Dorothy did not look beyond their table throughout the meal. Jean made no mention of Diego to her parents.

With filming taking place in Paris, the Riviera, and the Studios de Billancourt, Jean did not have to leave France to make a Hollywood picture. Despite a few minor problems on the set, including one in which Shaw had an argument with a hairdresser over how Jean's hair was to be combed, as well as almost daily script rewrites, filming went smoothly. Both Parrish and Shaw called the shoot a "happy" experience, and in an unheard move for a Hollywood film, brought the film in on schedule in eight weeks and $26,000 under its $557,000 budget.

After shooting the last scene late at night, Shaw and Parrish invited the crew and cast to a quiet dinner to celebrate the end of filming. Although the restaurant was closed for the evening, the maitre d' allowed the group inside after recognizing Shaw and Jean. After eating, one of the workers began playing an accordion, while another person produced a harmonica. Parrish called the impromptu celebration the best wrap party he had ever attended.

While Parrish danced with Jean later that evening, she confessed the truth behind the "broken foot" story. He was dumbfounded. "And you kept it a secret through the whole picture?"

"It's still a secret," she corrected. "Only you and I and Romain know."

"Why did you do it?"

"Because I loved Irwin's script."

Upon *In the French Style's* release, the *Daily Mirror* wrote: "Jean Seberg makes an engrossing and surprisingly efficient heroine as the innocent abroad … her performance indicates the judgment of Preminger, who launched her (disastrously) in *Saint Joan*. He predicted, however, that she would become an important actress. She has arrived." *The New York Daily News* gave the film its highest rating, and a majority of the reviews were positive.

Jean viewed herself fully rehabilitated after "Hollywood's cold shoulder." With the film's critical and financial success, Jean said, "I don't want to sound pompous, but I find it very gratifying." As a result of *In the French Style*, Shaw and Parrish were offered backing for other films, and Columbia renewed Jean's contract for six more pictures.

Indeed, Jean Seberg was living out her life and her dreams. Although some things had not worked out the way she had planned — the failure of Preminger's films, the success of *Breathless*, the romance with Romain — she kept searching and continued fighting for her goals. Her principal goal at this time was to marry Romain.

In late 1962 rumors covered Paris like a cloudy fall day: Jean would give up her career to fight for Romain. Lesley Blanch would not hand Romain over to Jean. Romain and Jean were to be married very soon. One newspaper account said, "Jean Seberg will have to wait awhile to marry author-diplomat Romain Gary. Mrs. Gary is still in New York and is not returning to France until the end of November. As far as she's concerned, she says there are no problems." Another rumor went so far as saying Jean and Romain were already married.

"It's absolutely untrue," Jean said to *France-Soir* in December. "We're in exactly the same situation we've been in for the last three years. Romain Gary is still married, which cripples our plans. If we were married, we wouldn't hide it. On the contrary."

CHAPTER FOUR
1963–1966

"I've become Europeanized, but staying in Europe has made me realize, I think more than ever, how American I am."
— Jean Seberg

With Moment to Moment *director Mervyn LeRoy and co-star Sean Garrison, 1965.*
AUTHOR'S COLLECTION

12

*"I think for an American girl living in Paris who is doing films, my private life
is probably more my private life… whereas if I were living in Hollywood, I
imagine my life would be much more of the public's knowledge."*
— Jean Seberg

In January 1963, Jean went to work for her *Breathless* director Jean-Luc
Godard in the film vignette, *Le grand escroc* (*The Big Swindler*), one of five
shorts of international thievery which would comprise the film *The Greatest
Swindles in the World*. In it, Jean replayed her *Breathless* character, Patricia,
who four years later is a reporter for a San Francisco television station.
While investigating a story in Morocco, Patricia interviews a counterfeiter
who gives fake money to the poor.

Le grand escroc was cut, however, from the film and did not have its own
separate release until the 1967 London Film Festival. While the twenty-
minute sketch did not capture the verve and innovation of *Breathless*, the
seldom-seen piece was not without its merits. Godard's style remains fresh,
with its editing and improvisation; Jean's Patricia is polished and mature.
It is not understood why the short was excluded from the film other than
the producers deemed it as "weak"; however, the other four shorts themselves (by Roman Polanski, Claude Chabrol, Ugo Gregoretti and Hiromichi
Horikawa) were not widely applauded when *The Greatest Swindles in the
World* was released in 1964.

After completing the filming in Marrakesh, Morocco, Jean's return to
France later that month caused a flurry of media interest. At Tangiers she
boarded a ferry en route to the Spanish coast with 121 other passengers,
including several American diplomats. Once at sea, a powerful storm tossed
the boat onto rocks, leaving its occupants stranded for thirty-eight hours
while the storm raged. Throughout the ordeal Jean kept her composure, caring for frightened Moroccan children and elderly people onboard. "The second night out," she recalled, "one man took several of us aside and suggested
we bribe a crew member to lower a boat and get away — just the four of us."
Jean rejected the idea, and she and the others were rescued by two fishing
boats the next day.

"I don't know what we would have done without Miss Seberg," said one
British passenger. "She was absolutely wonderful, and kept us all going. So
calm!"

In the context of her life at this point the experience was nothing, and
Jean joked that it was better than being burned at the stake. "We ran out
of food and water yesterday," she told a reporter upon being rescued. "There
was only wine to drink. But the captain gave us all a large tote of brandy
before we were taken off this morning."

The next month, Jean appeared on the cover of *Life* magazine. Unlike most other screen personalities who had graced the cover, Jean was not featured for her acting career. Instead, she modeled the latest Paris fashions, wearing a demure black lace Yves St. Laurent gown. Inside, in the company of Sophia Loren and Romy Schneider and other screen celebrities, Jean modeled a French nun's headdress also by St. Laurent. "I wish I could wear it every day," she was quoted as saying.

In the early months of 1963, Jean learned that director Robert Rossen was adapting J.R. Salamanca's novel *Lilith* for Columbia. *Lilith* had been greeted with widespread acclaim when published in 1961, and it went through five hardback printings before selling more than half a million copies in paperback.

Jean had read the novel when it was first published, during recovery from the amoebic dysentery she contracted while making *Congo Vivo*. Bob Gottlieb, an editor at Simon and Schuster, had personally sent her a copy. She thought the book was very good, but at the time she did not see herself as Lilith if a film were ever made. In fact, Jean originally saw this as a role for Audrey Hepburn.

Her feelings changed when she learned the book was to be interpreted on film. She immediately signaled her interest, but so did Samantha Eggar, Yvette Mimieux, Sarah Miles (all of whom were ultimately considered for the role), and Diane Cilento. Not only did Jean feel the role could rid her of the American in Paris stereotype, but she also felt it would provide ample opportunity to display her acting range. Although not discontented with her career so far, she believed she still had more to offer. "It was the first time I really fought to get a part," she later said.

Rossen's script showed how Lilith, a young woman in a fashionable mental institution, lures an orderly named Vincent into her self-conceived world. Warren Beatty had already signed to play the orderly, and it was Beatty who suggested Seberg for the role. In March 1963, Beatty telephoned Jean from London to ask if he and Rossen could meet with her. The pair then flew to Paris to see if their Lilith existed in Jean Seberg.

"It was a tough talk," Jean said, recalling the meeting. "They kept asking whether I was as bad as people said, and I was not really being myself but giving them what I thought they wanted to hear." Accompanying the two men was Rossen's secretary, who sniffed, "Lilith ought at least have long hair." Jean recognized the woman. She had once worked for Otto Preminger. "I find myself very attractive with long hair," Jean answered rather sharply. Turning to Rossen, she found he was amused by her retort. Shortly after this she was given the role.

Signed for a salary of more than $60,000, Jean left Diego in the care of Eugenia. In April 1963 she flew to New York for pre-production work on the $2 million film, to be filmed on the East Coast. On one weekend, Jean slipped off to Marshalltown for a quiet visit. As in many of her visits, she made no public appearances, and confined herself to telephone calls to friends and relatives while staying with her immediate family. "Jean always tried to be as unobtrusive as she could when she came home," says Lynda Haupert.

Robert Rossen was very definite about how he wanted Lilith character-ized in the film: feminine, while being virile at the same time. He wanted Jean to avoid falling into a mad Ophelia-type portrayal. Jean agreed with the director's idea. But when a photographer took pictures of Jean in a Greek style, pleated white dress, running through a meadow, Rossen barked, "That's exactly what I do not want!"

In preparing his actors for their roles, Rossen arranged for the cast to visit Chestnut Lodge in Rockville, Maryland, an expensive sanitarium on which Salamanca based Poplar Lodge, the country club-type hospital. In a piece written for *Cahiers du cinéma*, entitled "Lilith and I," Jean recalled meeting with a female patient at an asylum who called herself Rita/Sylvia: "If one said 'Good Morning, Rita,' she replied, 'I am Sylvia,' and the oppo-site. Besides this doubling, she took herself for God as well, and she com-plained endlessly of the work that that caused her. But she knew how to do nothing but knit, and as she was God, she knitted hearts, lungs, ovaries, human organs.

"I developed a great respect for mentally ill people. They remind me of very fine crystal that cracks because it's almost too fragile to be touched."

"Aren't you the star of *Breathless*?" a young male patient asked Jean.

"Yes, I am," she gently replied. "Why do you ask?"

"Because you are so beautiful that you made me crazy."

In addition to Jean and Beatty, the cast also included Peter Fonda, Anne Meacham, Gene Hackman (who regards *Lilith* in his résumé as his film debut, although he actually appeared in a low-budget horror movie prior), and Kim Hunter. An Academy Award Best Supporting Actress winner for *A Streetcar Named Desire*, Hunter had endured difficulty in finding film work after she was accused of being a Communist in the 1950s. Regardless, Rossen realized her talent and cast her as a doctor in *Lilith*.*

Production on *Lilith* began May 6 in Great Falls, Maryland, and pro-ceeded over the next three months. The role was a genuine departure for Jean, allowing her to use her wholesomeness as a cover for Lilith's malevo-lence. In one beautiful, yet haunting scene, Jean lifts her skirt to her knees, wades into a misty lake, and bends over to kiss her own image, an act that

---

* Note: Interestingly, around this time, producer Arthur P. Jacobs had secured the film rights to Pierre Boulle's book *La planète des singes* and was compiling a list of actresses who he thought could play the lead female role. Jean Seberg was included, alongside Eva Marie Saint, Shirley MacLaine, Claire Bloom and Joanne Woodward. Three years later when the film was made, the role went to Kim Hunter. It was of Zira, the kind-hearted chimpanzee in *Planet of the Apes*.

shows not only the character's destructive narcissism but also Jean's delicate grace:

"Look at her," Lilith says in the film. "She wants to be like me — she's lovely. My kisses kill her. She's like all of them. Destroys them to be loved."

Jean liked Rossen as a director because he had a "European method" to working. One day she was sitting on a box, deep in thought. Rossen told

A break in filming Lilith. *Warren Beatty and director Robert Rossen are on Jean's right and left respectively, while hairstylist Frederic Jones stands behind her.*
COURTESY OF FREDERIC JONES

the cameraman to film Jean without her knowledge. After a few minutes she realized she was being filmed. "Well, Jean," the director said, "you're on *Candid Camera*."

"Rossen was a man who knew and felt my insecurities," Jean later recalled, "and helped me with them. I think that's why a kind of liberty came across that I haven't had in many other films."

Jean admired her director, and sympathized with his past. In the 1950s, Rossen became embroiled in the House Un-American Activities Committee's witch hunt of Communist party members and sympathizers in the United States. He had been a member of the Communist Party between 1937 and 1947, and named other supporters to the Committee in 1953. According to his closest friends, Rossen never fully recovered from being blacklisted in Hollywood or his decision to testify to the HUAC group.

As with her other films, the actress was well liked by and close to the crew on *Lilith*. One new friend was Frederic Jones, the hairstylist on the film. "Jean was always nice and considerate," says Jones. "Jean was cheerful while doing her hair and would always say 'thank you' and comment that her hair 'looked lovely.' She was never difficult in any way. It was a pleasure to work with her. She was delightful." Jones points out that Jean always either arrived on schedule for her daily makeup call or was there before she was due. This made his life easier, as he needed to work on other actors' hair each day.

"I just fell in love with her," he says. "She was absolutely wonderful. She never came in, flipping around, acting 'the star.' She was always studying her lines, going over everything. Of all the people I've worked with on movies, Jean and Lynn Redgrave were two of the nicest."

On the evening of June 20, Jean and Romain were the invited guests of President and Mrs. Kennedy at the White House. Frederic Jones styled her hair for the occasion. "I think she was nervous because she was going with Romain, who was still married," Jones recalls. "They were trying to keep [their affair] as secret as possible. She was quite honored to be invited."

Despite arriving half an hour late at the White House, due to traffic and delays, the pair found only one other couple in attendance, speechwriter Richard Goodwin and his wife. Jean and Romain believed they were invited to a state dinner or something similar, and had not realized it was a private dinner. Their initial embarrassment was quickly overcome by the First Couple's hospitality and conversation. Jean recalled how the President "kept questioning Romain about the General [de Gaulle]. How had he gotten on with his soldiers in the war, that sort of thing. Kennedy was obviously fascinated by de Gaulle."

"Do you know him well?" Kennedy asked Romain.

"Nobody really knows him well," he replied. "And anyone who says he does is a liar."

Romain recounted "My Dinner with Kennedy" for the French weekly *Candide*. Among the many subjects that were discussed that evening — from the United States' reputation in Europe to Jean-Paul Belmondo — Romain felt President Kennedy failed to understand him on the subject of US dominance. "I remember his saying, 'You don't believe America wants to dominate anyone, do you?' I said, 'No, but it is a fact of life. You do, whether you like it or not.' He didn't understand that, not at all."

"[Kennedy] was like an IBM machine, digesting everything," Jean recalled. "I swiped a menu and wrote Malraux a long letter about it." Romain reported he had never had met a brain that functioned as relentlessly as the President's.

Later that evening, the First Lady, who was not only of French descent but an ardent Francophile, took Jean aside and asked if she and Romain were planning to marry. When Jean told her that they might, Mrs. Kennedy warned, "Don't. They lose all interest in you once they do."

"They had a very enjoyable evening. They were very comfortable and made to feel at home," says Mary Ann Seberg. "But Jean was upset. She said the men were all invited to go to one room and given cigars, and the women had to go to another room to talk about 'lady things.' She would have much rather preferred being in on the political discussion with the men.

Before departing for the White House, June 1963. COURTESY OF FREDERIC JONES

"Looking back on her life, I think if Jean hadn't been an actress, she probably would have been a politician — and a very good one. She understood people, their needs, and of the problems in society."

Jean was later informed that Mrs. Kennedy requested a print of *In the French Style* for a White House showing. "My husband will like anything," Jacqueline told author Irwin Shaw, "as long as it's in English."

Upon completion of filming in Maryland in June, the *Lilith* production team moved to a Long Island estate in Locust Valley that became Poplar Lodge. The estate, named Killingworth, was the former summer home of Myron C. Taylor, chief executive of US Steel. Only two weeks of studio filming were needed, and they took place at the Long Island Studios in New York.

Both filming and the role were demanding. "I'm dead — my hours are from 5:30 A.M. to 7:30 P.M. And it's such a tough role," she wrote Dawn Quinn. "Plus the fact that Warren Beatty's behavior is just unbelievable. He's out to destroy everyone, including himself."

To another friend, she wrote that Beatty gave new meaning to the word "complicated." Beatty's unprofessionalism was "long and fatiguing ... we lose a staggering amount of time every day." In pre-production, Rossen and Beatty had developed an almost fraternal accord. This stopped abruptly on the first day of filming when Beatty tried to take control and alter scenes. The working relationship between director and star deteriorated more and more as the production progressed. Once, when journalists visited the set, Beatty turned his back on them and walked over to Rossen to ask a question. Although the director was busy preparing a scene, Beatty interrupted him. "Do you think my hair is too long behind the ears?" he asked.

"I was winning Oscars when that son of a bitch was a baby pissing in a pot," Rossen later growled about Beatty.

At one point Beatty suggested his line, "I've read *Crime and Punishment* and *The Brothers Karamazov*" would be more effective if changed to, "I've read *Crime and Punishment* and half of *The Brothers Karamazov*." Rossen suggested he recite the line as written.

"You know, Warren," Jean offered, "I don't think you'll ever be really happy until you've produced or directed your own film."

Robert Rossen was dying from a rare skin disease and ingested large quantities of pills for his illness. Fatigued, at times he fell asleep in the middle of filming a scene. *Lilith* was to be Rossen's last film, and his experience with Beatty allegedly led to his telling friends that when he died, it would be because of working with Beatty. "At the end of filming, [Rossen] was in a complete state of exhaustion," Jean recounted. "And the permanent confrontation that opposed him to Warren did not help matters; [Beatty] wanted to bring a lawsuit against him, and other childish things ..."

Further problems added to delays. While filming near Oyster Bay, Jean accidentally stepped into a patch of poison ivy. Her legs and face broke out into a rash, and scenes were rescheduled while she spent a few days recovering.

One physically challenging scene involved Beatty walking into an abandoned barn where he finds Jean and Anne Meacham (who played another patient) in a compromising position. He throws Jean down on the floor before tossing Meacham outside. "It was rough," says Frederic Jones, "but I don't think Warren was doing anything to hurt her. My main concern was that the hairpiece would stay on. There was a lot of pushing, pulling and knocking down. But Jean didn't complain."

When another scene required Lilith to slap Vincent on the face, the conflict between Jean and Beatty came to a head. Peter Fonda claimed Beatty kept resisting Jean's slap with his arm after each take. This caused bruising on Jean's arm. "It was really hurting her," Fonda alleged. He told Beatty if he continued, he'd "beat the shit out of him." Shortly after the confrontation, Columbia sent a representative to the set and informed

Fonda that if he even touched Beatty, "they'd sue my ass." To get his point across to Beatty, Fonda showed up shortly thereafter with several friends — black belts in karate, who positioned themselves menacingly on the sidelines.

During a break in filming, Fonda met with his father, Henry, and his sister, Jane, in New York. During their meeting, Peter and Jane discussed Jean

Preparing for a scene in Lilith *with Warren Beatty. Frederic Jones combs the wig Jean wore in the film.* COURTESY OF FREDERIC JONES

Seberg and her film career abroad. Jane became fascinated with the success of the French film industry and decided that perhaps her career's future lay in France. Shortly after this she moved to France, where she appeared in a handful of films.

Fonda's biographer, Fred Lawrence Guiles, later noted "Jane was bright and scintillating onscreen, but impressed few off-screen as being an original thinker. Seberg held her own in the company of filmmakers, writers and philosophers, and was probably too intellectual to be a fine actress."

Rumors of Jean having an affair with Beatty on *Lilith* circulated, as they had with almost all of Beatty's previous — and would with future — leading ladies. But unlike many of the others, Jean was not added to the list of Beatty's conquests. "Romain Gary was right there with them when we were in Georgetown and when we were in New York, they stayed at the Plaza," Jones offers. "The girls were after Warren like crazy every place we'd go. They'd be crawling out the windows. But Jean never had an affair with him."

Although there was no affair between Beatty and Jean, she was constantly pursued by others while she was in New York. Flowers by the armful were sent to her suite by the numerous suitors hoping, in vain, to win her affections.

"She was happy because Romain was with her," Jones recalls, "and she wanted to marry him. But she was also unhappy because Romain's wife wouldn't give him a divorce. And evidently, Romain was in love with Jean. He certainly seemed that way because he was always concerned about how she was doing, how she was feeling, and if she was doing well. In fact, Romain Gary asked me once what I thought about her acting, and I said I thought she was very good. And I did. In fact, she was a very unusual person, as far as I'm concerned. She was sweet, kind and considerate, and I think she tried her very best."

Jean and Frederic Jones found they had one experience in common: both had worked with Otto Preminger. The pair spoke a great deal not only about the director, but *Saint Joan*. "Otto was a very difficult man to work for, and if you don't understand him, it's extremely difficult," Jones says. In fact, Jones once almost quit Preminger's *Hurry Sundown* because he could not tolerate the director's verbal abuse any longer. He was lured back by Preminger's wife who said, "Please don't leave. He does it to everybody. He does it to me."

Jones feels that if Jean had not done *Saint Joan*, she might have become a more famous actress. "Jean really did talk more about her future than she did about her past. She planned to get married to Romain, and try to live a simple life. I don't really think Jean liked the nightlife and all the publicity. She wasn't at all that type."

At the end of July, an overzealous press agent divulged to newspapers that Jean would film a partially nude love scene with Beatty, and that Rossen was ordering a closed set. Jean immediately denied this and spoke to the chiefs at Columbia. "I've received an apology," she reported, "and I imagine heads will roll."

"I have never done a nude scene or a nude to the waist scene, and the way I feel about it, I never will," she told columnist Earl Wilson. "It's a decision that every actress needs to make. I'm not objecting on moral grounds. It's just that I didn't do it." The denial did not receive nearly as much coverage as the original announcement. That angered Jean, who confided to friends: "It wasn't true, but what can my parents say when everybody reads it?"

By the time the denial was printed, Jean's parents had read the initial story and wrote her a letter about it. "They reported," Jean said, "that a couple of their friends had already mentioned the stories about their little daughter going naked in front of a lot of people. They were more concerned about their friends who hadn't mentioned it."

Filming on *Lilith* concluded in August, and a wrap party was held to celebrate the film's completion. Warren Beatty did not attend. It was reported that the animosities between Beatty and Peter Fonda continued brewing, with Fonda going so far to arrange a group of local men to beat up Beatty at the party. Frederic Jones was asked by the film's operations manager to drive Beatty from the Long Island location, complete with a police escort, to the main highway. Fonda and friends had to be content with tearing apart Beatty's dressing room trailer.

Jones returned to the production site and escorted Jean to the party, as she and Romain still wished to keep their involvement as private as possible. "We had so much fun," he says. "It was a great evening." The party was held on the estate's gardens, and large candles with glass shades were lit throughout the grounds.

Shortly after, Jean, Beatty, Jones and a make-up artist converged in New York for a photo shoot. Jones relates one of his fondest memories of Jean: "We had done several photos, then [the photographer] wanted to change the lights and set, so we had to wait. Warren stretched out on a small bed as he was tired.

"We were talking and kidding around. Jean whispered to me, 'Let's play a trick on Warren. Take my scarf and put it around your head, and I'll apply lipstick on your lips, then go over and lie down beside Warren and see what happens.' I said, 'OK,' so I went over and started to lie down next to him. He turned over and pulled me down on the bed and kissed me — we didn't know he had heard us. Of course Jean and everybody were laughing. Warren said, 'You wanted a kiss, so you got one!'"

The filming left Jean exhausted, but also exhilarated. She felt she had done her best film work ever. "I don't want to make any more mistakes," Jean said, referring to some of her previous films. "I used to be in a terrible rush — when I was little, I assumed one might as well commit suicide if one had tottered on to thirty — but now that I've reached twenty-five, I see there's more useful time left than I supposed. I can even imagine quite a pleasant life after thirty."

Jean returned to France to dub the French version of *In the French Style*, then flew on to London on September 21 to promote the English version of the film. At the gala midnight showing, guests were given breakfast boxes containing croissants, Robertson's jam, Nescafé, and Piccadilly cigarettes, all in the French style.

In addition, Lesley Blanch had finally decided to end her marriage to Romain and agreed to a divorce. Meeting with reporters in her suite at the Dorchester Hotel in London, Jean admitted (upon hearing of Blanch's consent), "I've found happiness and love in Paris, and very soon I hope I shall be married."

On October 10, 1963, Jean and Romain took out a marriage license in

Paris. On the sixteenth they went to the Mediterranean island of Corsica. There, in the small village of Sarrola-Carcopino, they were privately married by Mayor Noël Sarrola in a civil ceremony. That same afternoon, the newly-weds flew to Nice to celebrate the nuptials quietly. They spent the following week traveling by car to Switzerland for a two-week honeymoon, and then to the Riviera, "mainly," Jean wrote, "to avoid the press, etc." Jean was one month shy of her twenty-fifth birthday, Romain was forty-nine. Ten days later, Diego was "officially" born.

Jean wrote to her *Lilith* friend Frederic Jones shortly after the marriage announcement. The note displayed not only her happiness, but her sense of humor: "Thanks for your wire. Needless to say, we're both terribly happy after all these years of living in sin to be a respectable old married couple. In fact, we were amazed it leaked out to the press. We rather hoped to keep it quiet awhile …Sorry to type this, but I'm practicing up for a secretarial job in South Africa, which I'll take after the premiere of *Lilith*…"

On November 18, Jean and Romain made one of their first public appearances together as man and wife. The program, "Do the church and the theatre need each other?" was held at the American Church in Paris. The couple were invited guest speakers who spoke on behalf of the theatre side. Jean's and Romain's opinions mattered little, however, since their mere attendance at the event was the main draw with reporters and photographers. They were the most celebrated couple in Paris.

13

"[Jean Seberg] is the most celebrated American girl in Paris."
— *Life* magazine

"People are always asking me what I'd like to do next," Jean said in the last months of 1963. "So much has happened to me in such a short time that I feel like a compressed car. I know what I don't want to do," she continued, "[which is] to end up like so many other actresses do. Everything in this business conspires to make you brutal and tough, finally, like a man, and you end up all alone at 60 …What I'd like to do right now, for a little while, is to be bored."

"I was very happy she married Romain Gary," says Mylène Demongeot, "because she said it was the dream of her life to marry a famous writer. So I was happy for her to achieve that dream. Her other dream was that she had also wanted to be a writer, she told me many times."

As the wife of a famed novelist, Jean hired a maid and a secretary and entered her haute couture period, wearing the latest fashions from Yves St. Laurent, Givenchy, and Dior. Her tastes in fashion designers also extended to Chanel and Courrèges. She also purchased outfits for friends and her family. "Jean was always so considerate," her friend, Vony Becker, recalls. "Once, when I didn't have a lot of money, she took me into a boutique and bought me a beautiful, simple black dress that I liked. I didn't ask for it, but she wanted me to have it."

"A lot of polish has come — if there is polish — since my second marriage," Jean said. "Romain kind of took me in hand and said, 'Listen, you have to stop wearing those coats that make you look like a graham-cracker carton with two feet sticking out.' And he told me always to wear my hair short, the way I wore it in the beginning, because he felt that my features got lost when I had a lot of hair around my face. And, of course, because of him I met many people I would certainly never have had any occasion to meet otherwise."

The "polish" also extended to the decor of the apartment at 108 rue du Bac. White walls featured expensive abstract paintings, sofas complemented by low tables for glasses and ashtrays, shaggy fur throw rugs from Greece, sculptures that rested on slate floors, and Diego Giacometti bookcases filled with books and objets d'art.

"We are putting ardoise tiles in the living room — my cigar-smoking husband — and we are both great coffee drinkers, you know. We'll have pink salmon cork on the walls as background for the paintings with carmel, beige and salmon tones," Jean informed a writer. But the apartment also had a lived-in feel, with items propped against the wall waiting to be put away. "[Romain] says that an apartment that is too well organized has a definitive feel which makes him want to leave," Jean said, "which deprives him of the thing he cares most of all for: availability." She also added that she and Romain were "stay-at-home types. We like dinner parties of six or so. Our idea of Chinese torture is The Big Dinner."

"It was one of those typical grande bourgeoisie apartments," director Nicolas Gessner remembers. "Since in Paris it's very seldom to get 'the view,' they had these dark and closed curtains. With these narrow streets, you are next to your neighbor. In a way it was stuffy, but it was still grand and big, and a nice place with corridors."

The free spirit evolved into the American sophisticate. She ate breakfast in bed and had a part-time secretary who helped with correspondence. Jean slept eight to ten hours a night in designer nightgowns on a pair of twin beds pushed together, with the mattresses placed crossways. She often wore a Chinese robe around the home, and preferred to bathe in a tub rather than shower. In social and literary circles, Jean was not addressed as "the actress Jean Seberg," but as "Madame Gary." She began developing other interests as well in her role as the wife of a prominent man. "I love flowers and try to grow them …I'm also studying Japanese floral arrangements. I design earrings which I have made in Spain. They have good jewelers there," Jean offered.

"Did I tell you Romain will probably go back to the diplomatic service?" Jean wrote Carol Hollingsworth in February 1964. "I know he misses it and they'd like him back, probably as counsel general somewhere for a year or so, and then ambassador. This means that a certain party I know from Iowa who can't even make her bed properly is going to have to learn how to run gigantic houses and plan meals. Ugh! But it's an exciting life and a wonderful way to see the world. And the people at the Foreign Office say it's perfectly alright for me to carry on an acting career."

Although Jean had previously dined with presidents, ambassadors and other political figures, she finally met Charles de Gaulle and his wife on February 18, 1964, when she and Romain were invited to lunch with the French leader. Meeting de Gaulle privately furthered Jean's acceptance in France, and enhanced her status on the social ladder. She was more than pleased. She felt honored.

"De Gaulle is a very nice person," Jean confided, "and he knows all of the films that I have made."

As Romain Gary's wife, Jean could have functioned as an ever-smiling goodwill ambassador between the United States and France; instead of this, however, she opted for a private life with Romain and Diego while continuing her career. Still, she found herself on the defensive when people criticized her living in France rather than America. "It annoys me when a Frenchman comes up and says, 'oh, you're so unexpectedly Parisian.' He means to compliment me, but I can't help snapping: 'I'm an American — Iowa American.' I can't imagine pretending to myself that I am anything but an American."

Romain Gary added, "Because she comes from Iowa and now lives in Paris, many American reporters say she's an expatriate. Not true. Every few months she flies back to Marshalltown — her roots. People there — maybe they're shocked at the kind of films she's made in France, but she is one of their own and they are extremely kind to her. She comes back always a glowing gem of a girl, shining and bright and splendid."

When asked whether the Gary/Seberg relationship wasn't Pygmalion and Galatea replayed, Romain said: "You think I am wise and she is naive. I am knowledgeable and she is not. You are mistaken... She reads omnivorously, everything — Tolstoy, Pushkin, Flaubert. And she retains what she reads... Failure diverts most young people... [but it] has strengthened her, fortified her, made her more determined than ever."

Romain returned to this "Pygmalion" theme so beloved of the press in his autobiographical work published in 1974, insisting that Jean had influenced him much more than the converse. He pointed out how Jean had drawn him from diplomacy into the world of cinema. It was his career, not hers, which had changed. There was also an ongoing private joke between them which suggested that Jean was in some ways the elder.

The on-screen reunion of Jean Seberg and Jean-Paul Belmondo was announced in the spring of 1964. The project was a French chase film, *Échappement libre* (*Backfire*), under the direction of Jean Becker. The film has Belmondo attempting to steal the three-hundred kilos of gold concealed by a gang in the Triumph automobile he is being paid to deliver. Jean plays the photographer accomplice with whom he falls in love. Smoking slender cig-

In 1964. COURTESY OF SNORRAMYNDIR

arettes and wearing stylish suits, Jean was presenting a new image as a chic, confident professional woman.

For nine weeks, the crew criss-crossed throughout Europe and the Near East, filming at different locations. During the production, Jean developed a lifetime friendship with the director's wife, Vony Becker. "Jean was a little provincial girl," Becker says today. "When Jean had a lot of money, she was very generous and spent it freely, giving it around. Jean loved to behave like a star — long cigarettes, generous gifts. We got along because we were both too sensitive and too vulnerable."

Becker had a cameo in *Backfire* in which she snubs Jean-Paul Belmondo in a bar. Becker relates that, while the on-screen chemistry of Jean and Belmondo sizzled (as it had with *Breathless*), off-screen Belmondo had no interest in Jean — and vice-versa. Although many of the French movie-going public had wanted the pair to have a real-life relationship, that was never realized. Jean was devoted to Romain Gary — and to their son, who was still being kept in seclusion.

One day during the production of *Backfire*, Jean and Vony Becker dined with Jean and Romain. The four had met at a restaurant and were talking. Quite unexpectedly, Jean "suddenly burst into tears," Becker recalls, "and said she had a son and was hiding him in Spain." Romain comforted his wife, and the two quietly told their bewildered guests about Diego. After a few minutes, Jean composed herself and the conversation returned to *Backfire*.

The resulting film was another hit for all involved, with the *New York Times* commenting, "Like *Goldfinger*... high-level tension and lively, suspenseful entertainment. Intrigue, danger, willing sirens, road-racing and mayhem...the danger filled chase is in high gear fun."

After the success of *Backfire*, Jean was looking forward to working with other New Wave directors, since it was to this group that she owed her triumphant return to the screen with *Breathless*. "I owe a great deal to François Truffaut because he was sort of the spearhead of all of it, and made the most wonderful pronouncements about admiring me and thinking I was a good actress ... at the time it was terribly important for my morale," she reflected.

Jean hoped to work with Truffaut on a film in the near future: "It's Ray Bradbury's *Fahrenheit 451*, with Lewis Allen producing." But when the time came to film in 1965 the role went to Julie Christie, whose acting in the critical and commercial successes *Darling* and *Doctor Zhivago* (both in 1965) catapulted her to worldwide fame. Jean was doubly disappointed. She had not only lost the dual role in a film which might have showcased her talents as much, if not more, than *Lilith*, but she had also missed the chance to work with Truffaut.

Outside the world of films, Jean and Romain were busy with other things, especially in Majorca, where Romain was having a vacation house built in the village of Puerto de Andraitx. Named "Cimarron" upon its completion the following year, this "superhouse" was entered by large wrought iron gates. It had two parallel wings, which comprised a dining room, a large kitchen, a gallery the length of the structure, suites containing three bedrooms and baths, a salon, "interminable corridors" as one guest recalled, terraces, and a swimming pool with a view of the bay beyond it.

With her career moving forward and her marriage finally realized, Jean still had not told her parents about her son. She felt it was time to tell them the truth. In the summer of 1964, Jean invited her parents to visit her in

Europe. In Majorca, Romain collected his in-laws at the airport, and when they arrived at his and Jean's villa, she came out with the child at her side.

"This is how I envisioned [the meeting]," says Mary Ann Seberg. "They were standing outside and Jean said, 'There's someone I want you to meet,' and it was Diego, and he was almost two. I don't think my parents were overwhelmed by it. I feel they were delighted to have a grandson. But I don't know why Jean and Romain never told us earlier. I know [my husband and I] were really surprised because Diego came between our two daughters. I think Jean just didn't want to hurt our parents' feelings."

When the Sebergs returned home to Marshalltown, Romain wrote them with specific instructions concerning Diego's birth, in the event a reporter asked them. Romain penciled the date of birth as October 26, 1963. Jean's parents did not question Romain's request as both were ecstatic to have another grandchild. This joy far outweighed concern that Jean should have had a child out of wedlock. To them, the circumstances did not matter.

Although they were legally married, Jean and Romain continued to keep Diego's existence hidden from the public. While keeping him in Spain with Eugenia, Jean and Romain based themselves in Paris, regularly shuttling to Spain and back for visits. Romain continually told his wife that this arrangement was in the best interests of all involved, despite her many objections.

In August 1964 the long-awaited completed version of *Lilith* was submitted as the official American entry at the Venice Film Festival. "Jean is going to surprise the hell out of a lot of people. This girl is an actress," Robert Rossen stressed. "Not just a star, an actress."

Realizing that the theme was not as commercial as current film releases, Columbia hoped that the film would be well received for its artistic merits. However, Luigi Chiarini, the chairman of the festival selection committee, was not an admirer of *Lilith*, and suggested the Americans might wish to submit another film instead of this one. Angered, and accusing the committee of judging his work unfairly and prematurely, Rossen called Chiarini's action "tyrannical" and "typical of the new cult of snobs." The film was pulled from the festival.

Jean and Romain flew via Air France to the US, where *Lilith* had an advance screening on September 19, 1964. The venue chosen was at the New York Film Festival, although it is unknown whether the couple actually attended the event. The main objective of reporters at the festival was to note the audience's response to the film: in this case it varied between polite applause and scattered booing. Critics broadly agreed with the audience and panned the film. *Time* complained the film was an attempt "to deliver the same old Hollywood sexology in a fancy wrapper."

Lilith certainly deserved a more appreciative reaction than the one it received in 1964. Almost every aspect of the film has its distinctive merits, from its haunting musical score, through its editing, direction, and screenplay. "The reason it failed was that the film was too sophisticated for that time," says one film historian. "Perhaps it is too sophisticated for today."

In Europe, *Lilith* met greater acceptance, and in France it was named one of best films of 1964 by *Cahiers du cinéma*, which proclaimed it an "incontestable masterpiece." *Cahiers* film critic Jean-André Fieschi wrote that *Lilith*, along with Alfred Hitchcock's *Vertigo*, was "the most complete realization in cinematographic form of the indefinable, the inaccessible, which the coupled plays of beauty and of illusion shape into a sumptuous and fatal mirage."

It was not that critics in 1964 found the entire work without merit. On the contrary, if *Lilith* received nearly unanimously negative notices, Jean earned just as many glowing special mentions. Bosley Crowther in the *New York Times* lauded her "fresh, flighty, fearsome performance." *Life* called her "a revelation … every nuance of her delicate interpretation is convincing. [She is] more than just another dumb blonde. Perhaps there is still hope for Kim Novak and Tippi Hedren." Critic Larry Rummel wrote "[the] performance from Miss Seberg must rank with the best of the year. If not with the best on film."

The majority of the American critics agreed that Jean Seberg, the actress, had finally arrived. Howard V. Cohen wrote the following under the headline "The Crow Eaters": "The indigestion critics so frequently complain of probably comes more often than not from eating crow. Jean Seberg has been feeding it to them in ever increasing quantities of late. She may well be the finest young actress operating in the movies these days. On second thought, eliminate the qualification and make it a fact. Miss Seberg IS the finest young actress operating in movies these days."

"[*Lilith*] was a very meaningful experience for her. It was very dramatic and believable," says Mary Ann Seberg. "I think it was the first film Jean did in which I really didn't think about her being my sister."

Jean's performance, however, could not bring the ticket buyers into the theaters, and *Lilith* was a financial failure. When the film played in Marshalltown, the *Times-Republican* applauded the acting but felt "the average viewer may come away wishing to see Marshalltown's pride in something light, bright and frothy with a touch of corn that we Midwesterners like in our entertainment."

When Jean wrote Frances Benson on November 14, 1964, she did not mention the film:

> Dearest Granny Grunt,
> Well, here I am 26 years old and I haven't learned a thing yet! It's amazing to think I've lived over a quarter of a century. I had a very nice birthday — flowers from Diego in Spain, flowers from Romain's cousins and niece, books

and a little jewel from Romain, etc. etc. The folks sent me a much needed nightie and very pretty sweater.

We have decided to bring Diego here to the house at the end of the month. I couldn't stand the separation anymore, and I was really getting very depressed. Besides, Romain was sad. So they'll [Diego and Eugenia] come here soon. I suppose the neighbors will gossip, but we don't care, and there's not much they can say anyway.

We are busy re-furnishing the apartment. It is so big and formal, I'm trying to make it homier. With my great gift for housekeeping!

I'm also busy with dress fittings for the movie that begins in January.

We still don't know who my partner will be. And next week we have a dinner with De Gaulle's cabinet head and with Malraux so I sort of wonder if they aren't going to offer Romain a diplomatic post.

Take care, Granny. I'll see you soon. We love you.
Jeana

Early in 1965, Jean began work on Universal's *Moment to Moment*, a romantic suspense drama which might have been directed by Alfred Hitchcock, since Jean had earlier commented that they were to make a film together. As things turned out, it became the seventy-fifth film for veteran producer/director Mervyn LeRoy. Filming began in France, and Jean found an immediate rapport with LeRoy.

Looking back on the failure of *Lilith*, Jean figured she might never have made another Hollywood-produced film had it not been for LeRoy. "He told Universal that he wanted either Audrey Hepburn, who was unavailable, or Jean Seberg," she disclosed.

"The entire plot evolves about the character of the wife," LeRoy offered. "It is difficult to find 'lady actresses.' Aside from Audrey Hepburn, Grace Kelly and Ingrid Bergman, there are very few. But I happened to see Jean in *The Five-Day Lover*, and after that I studied all of her films and decided, though we had never met, that she was the girl for the role. She has the elegance, sweetness and charm required."

In the film, Jean played Kay Stanton, a young wife who accidentally shoots a Navy officer with whom she has had an impulsive affair. Believing he is dead, she panics and dumps his body into a ravine. The man survives, but is the victim of amnesia, and Kay's husband, a psychiatrist from Columbia University, is called in by the police to help the sailor recover his memory. The truth is revealed, but Kay is ultimately forgiven.

While part of the film was shot on the Riviera (much to her delight), Jean was shocked at the amount of money spent on the film. Estimates had LeRoy spending $25,000 a day. Cameras were brought in from Paris, wind machines from Rome, and English-speaking extras from Paris and London. LeRoy also shipped in a dozen plastic palm trees from Hollywood to the Riviera, since Mother Nature had neglected to provide real ones in some of the sites chosen for shooting.

For a scene which involved Jean with co-stars Sean Garrison and Arthur Hill in front of two ancient statues of Hercules and Atlas, LeRoy asked if the sculptures could either be moved or (in shades of future US attorney general John Ashcroft) modestly draped with fabric. LeRoy feared that American censors would disallow the showing of statues with exposed male genitalia in the film, regardless of their cultural credentials. French officials, however, did not sympathize with American sensitivities and denied the request. Provision was made in the camera placement to satisfy all parties.

"It is a good 'woman's' picture — in color and pretty clothes," Jean wrote a friend. "The camerawork is done by same man who did *My Fair Lady*, so I'm being spoiled! It is a nice group of people, although my partner (a new boy — Sean Garrison) is rather stiff. Romain is here with me, so we live pretty much curled up in our suite with the TV! It's quiet and nice."

During the shoot in France, the media attention surrounding Jean and her star role in another American film soared. A French interviewer inquired if film was her life.

"No," she replied, "but I was very lucky. I got to perform in Europe. I gained experiences instead of lying underneath California's palm trees waiting for some or other little main part. I was very lucky in life. I had the luck of meeting my husband. So film isn't everything to me. That's the tragedy of film; that's why it ends badly. This exclusiveness takes you up completely."

"You won't let yourself be devoured?"

"No," Jean smiled.

When the weather on the Riviera turned unusually chilly, LeRoy decided to return his cast and crew to the Universal lot in Los Angeles, where the Riviera was reconstructed at a cost of $350,000 — nearly four times the cost of *Breathless*, as Jean pointed out.

Jean telephoned her mother shortly after she arrived. "I have a wonderful role, fabulous sets, beautiful gowns by Yves St. Laurent. We've rented a home with a pool…" She continued on and on. Dorothy Seberg was happy for her daughter, but then finally asked, "That's wonderful dear. Are you doing any television?"

In fact, Jean was on television, if only for a moment. She was nominated for a Golden Globe for Best Actress in a Drama for her work on *Lilith*. This was presented by the Hollywood Foreign Press Association, and Jean and Romain attended the awards ceremony held at the Ambassador Hotel on February 8, 1965. The major awards were televised during NBC's *The Andy Williams Show*.

With Romain, arriving as a nominee for the Golden Globe Awards, 1965.
COURTESY OF SEBERG FAMILY COLLECTION

Although the Golden Globe for Best Actress in a Drama award went to Anne Bancroft for *The Pumpkin Eater*, several critics and magazines predicted Jean would receive an Academy Award nomination for Best Actress. Perhaps if the film had been a commercial success, or if the critics had applauded *Lilith* as much as they had its star, she might indeed have been the recipient of the Oscar. Whatever the reasons may have been, the predictions proved mistaken. The 1964 nominees, announced while Jean was still in California filming *Moment to Moment*, included

Anne Bancroft, Sophia Loren for the comedy *Marriage Italian-Style*, Kim Stanley in the drama *Seance on a Wet Afternoon*, Debbie Reynolds in the musical *The Unsinkable Molly Brown*, and the victor, Julie Andrews in the musical *Mary Poppins*.

Mary Ann Seberg feels Jean was not upset that she did not receive a nomination, and that these things were not important to her. "I'm honest with myself," Jean said two years earlier. "I know I will never be a star in the Hollywood sense, and the truth is acting could never be my whole life again. There are too many [other] things to do." Dawn Quinn, however, believes "Jean wanted, more than anything in her career, to be accepted as an actress in America. But she never got that recognition. It really did hurt her feelings."

The American press was hailing *Moment to Moment* as Jean's first Hollywood film, oddly overlooking *Let No Man Write My Epitaph*. She was besieged by reporters wanting details of her life abroad. When asked if she had been able to improve Franco-American relations herself, Jean replied that she felt Parisians had become more polite to Americans due to the decline in the tourist trade. "Actually, Americans are too nice," she offered. "They submit to poor service and high prices without complaining. Not me. When Frenchmen hear my American accent and try to be rude, I bring out my dirtiest French words. That gets action."

A reporter asked Jean if she would ever make another picture with Otto Preminger. "I don't talk about Otto anymore. It has to be forgotten," she said. "Let's just say that I matured in [*Saint Joan*]. I was burned at the stake."

While in Los Angeles, Romain drove Jean to work every morning during the filming, and sometimes he stayed on the set to watch the filming. "Either he loves me very much," she joked, "or he wanted the car." On the Universal lot, Jean was allowed use of Doris Day's dressing room, which, as she wrote Warren Robeson in Marshalltown, "had a refrigerator, complete bathroom and even telephones and attractive paintings."

LeRoy tried to make the set as comfortable as possible as well. He knew what Jean had been through with Preminger, and although it did not show in his films, he was also aware of the new European methods of filmmaking and of Jean's contributions to the nouvelle vague.

Jean was grateful to LeRoy for the role and respected his work. When actor Elliot Gould told *Time* that he hoped he'd never have to make a picture with LeRoy, Jean came to the director's defense. "When his attack was printed, I kept my peace," LeRoy recalled. "But I did have a champion. Jean Seberg went to bat for me and sent a letter to the editor of *Time* [in which] she listed some of the pictures I made and concluded, '…he is one of the gentlest, most civilized human beings around.' That made me proud because nice words from someone I had worked with, who knew me, meant more than unkind words from someone I had never met could hurt." LeRoy also believed in Jean's acting ability and predicted she would be one of the Top Ten box office stars in a few years.

While LeRoy himself was a powerful director in Hollywood for several decades, he had been investigated by the Federal Bureau of Investigation before he could direct the film version of *The F.B.I. Story* in 1959. LeRoy was approved as director of the film only after FBI head director J. Edgar Hoover was satisfied that, according to one FBI agent, "we had enough dirt to control him."

In the eyes of the world, Jean had become a sophisticate. Writer Peter Bart reported in 1966: "Jean Seberg eagerly tries to convince her interviewer that she is no longer the scared starlet from Iowa but is, instead, the suave Parisian dame, the worldly wife of a Parisian intellectual. To fortify this image, Miss Seberg positions her bored-looking husband within shouting distance and they periodically exchange torrents of French during interviews."

But in several ways Jean remained the star-struck girl from Marshalltown. One day at the Universal commissary, Cary Grant walked up to Jean while she was being interviewed by Don Alpert for the *Los Angeles Times.* "So nice to see you again," Grant said. "You see, Jean, I put on a clean shirt just for you." Alpert duly noted Jean remained speechless during the short visit. Returning to the interview, Jean talked about her French career: "*The Five-Day Lover* also gave me a taste for comedy which I haven't been able to Cary Grant — excuse me — carry through."

While in Hollywood, Jean also attended a Screen Producers Guild banquet attended by, among others, James Stewart, Jack Warner, Elke Sommer, and Eva Marie Saint. Stewart presented Alfred Hitchcock with the Guild's highest honor, the Milestone Award.

When Princess Margaret visited Universal Studios during her 1965 goodwill tour of the United States, Jean was selected by her as one of the people in Hollywood she wanted to meet. Among others included were Natalie Wood, Rock Hudson, Shirley MacLaine, and George Cukor. On the day of the occasion, Jean was to sit at the head table while Romain was assigned to a less prominent one. Jean was not informed of the seating arrangement, so she sat next to Romain and failed to take her place next to Princess Margaret's husband, Lord Snowdon. A studio official blamed her for the mix-up: "We were told Miss Seberg wouldn't sit there unless her husband were allowed to." When Jean heard this, she was understandably angered. "How dare anyone accuse me of such bad manners?" she fumed.

In addition to attending other industry fetes while in Hollywood, Jean constantly granted interviews. In many of these she showed herself as determined to defend her background as her own private life. "I get so mad when people make cracks at Iowa. A lot of very talented and creative people come from my hometown.

"I'll never give up my American citizenship. I think your roots are important. I can't imagine pretending to myself that I am anything but an American." Jean added, "When I make a picture in French they still have to alibi my accent and put in a line explaining that I'm a 'foreigner' of some sort."

To paint a picture of domesticity to the press, Jean said, somewhat humorously, "Life is less complicated for the housewife who knows how

With Alfred Hitchcock at the Screen Producers Guild, 1965.
COURTESY OF INDEPENDENT VISIONS

to cook. And it's more rewarding and satisfying to be the one who can take bows for a beautifully prepared and served dinner.

"I can prepare simple things like broiled steaks and roasts, and I make good salads and dressings, but I don't claim to be a cook because of that," she pointed out, adding that when she and Romain entertained, they preferred only a small number of guests. "Never more than four," she claimed. "We like one conversation going at a time, where all guests can contribute. Occasionally we do give large cocktail parties."

After completing *Moment to Moment* in March, Jean and Diego went to Marshalltown for an unpublicized visit, while Romain and Eugenia returned to France. Jean and Diego also visited Mary Ann and her family, who were then living in Cedar Rapids, Iowa. There, Jean introduced Diego to his cousins.

"We had a very nice time," recalls Mary Ann. "Jean brought Easter dresses and bonnets for my daughters to wear, and when Diego saw them, he wanted to try one on. So he did," she laughs. Diego quickly established a camaraderie with his cousins and neighborhood children. "We introduced him to all the little neighborhood children and said his name was 'Diego.' One day a little neighbor boy came by and knocked on the door, and he asked, 'Can 'the eagle' come out and play?' He didn't understand 'Diego.' That was a fun time."

Unsure of the outcome of *Moment to Moment*, and leery of the Hollywood welcome wagon treatment, Jean was happy to return to Paris. "I'd like to achieve a precarious teeter-totter of doing good films in Hollywood, then going back to Europe to do small, low-budget films. I'll go on working as long as they ask me." Still, Jean did not accept a role she did not like simply for the sake of working. "One producer gave me a script in which I was to play Marilyn Monroe. Now wouldn't that have been just the thing to send me back to Marshalltown?"

In Paris, Jean and Romain hired a second Spanish maid, Celia Alvarez, as Eugenia had taken over the duty of being Diego's nanny. Jean wrote her parents about Sandy, a dog she had brought from California, who "seems to have forgotten that apartments don't have fire hydrants, and we don't know what to do, as he is lovely that I keep hoping that he'll shape up and Romain mumbles threats about sending him out in the country."

Romain was also suffering from a hernia of the esophagus, which was checked earlier by doctors at the Mayo Clinic in Rochester, Minnesota. "We are almost always at home now because it's impossible to follow the Mayo diet if we eat in restaurants. So far Romain has lost eight pounds, and I have lost five, which was really necessary," Jean wrote her family. She added: "P.S. Diego looked at the big globe in Romain's office yesterday and wondered where 'Paca and Granny live.'"

Almost immediately upon her return to Paris, Jean began *Un milliard dans un billard* (*Diamonds are Brittle*) in April. In this film she plays the glamorous voluptuary Bettina whose mother is leader of an international jewel theft ring. The leading man, Claude Rich, portrays a middle-of-the-road, cautious bank clerk who dreams of making a big heist. With four weeks of work on the Swiss-German-French film, it was a happy return for Jean, and the lighthearted theme that crime does sometimes pay seemed to be the perfect antithesis to some of the conventionally moralistic films Hollywood was churning out at the time.

"I really got my start as a director thanks to her," says *Diamonds* director Nicolas Gessner. "I had this project, it was a good script, and the producer said, 'We need names! We need names!' So we went to Jean Seberg and she loved the script. I thanked her for trusting me as a first-time director, and she said something that's very true: 'That's when people are at their best: when they do their first movie.' She was a specialist of people who do their first movies.

"She was a recognizable name. She had star quality. Everybody was interested in Jean Seberg. You knew that meant something good."

"Jean Seberg had a sunny side and a darker side, and that showed in everything she said and did," Gessner says. "She had this clean look, but

With Diamonds are Brittle *co-star Claude Rich and director Nicolas Gessner, 1965.*
COURTESY OF SNORRAMYNDIR

people thought there was more to it. And this is what I used in the movie." A scene in the film which exemplifies Gessner's notion involves Jean and Claude Rich taking a steamboat ride on Lake Geneva.

Rich says, "I'd like to do a caper."

"You're not the type," she retorts. Then she changes her mind. "OK, let's go ahead. Let's steal the whole ship."

"He's very frightened by the immediacy of Jean," Gessner explains. "And this is very much in character with Jean. Afraid of nothing."

Gessner remembers Jean's best quality as a person was "her sense of humor, combined with her utter, utter beauty. A sense of humor — which in a way is the tip of the iceberg that emerges — and nine-tenths of a sense of humor is intelligence. And for intelligent people, life is a comedy. But she was not the giggling type of person. She was very serious about her sense of humor."

Another of Jean's qualities, according to Gessner, was her ability to adapt to the European method of filmmaking while keeping intact her "American technique of perfectionism."

Romain Gary was impressed with the finished film. "You are the first one to discover Jean's talent for comedy. Let's write a comedy for her," he suggested to Gessner, curiously overlooking Jean's work in *The Five-Day Lover*. The two men began writing a screenplay specifically for Jean, but it was never completed. "It went off in all directions," Gessner remembers. "Every day he was pounding out thirty or forty pages. It was too crazy."

With son Diego, summer 1965. COURTESY OF SEBERG FAMILY COLLECTION

That summer Jean and Romain rented a vacation house on the Riviera sight unseen — "which is my fault," Jean wrote a friend. "It turned out to be completely unpractical — situated between a railroad track and a national highway (just the kind of silence a writer needs!), and too far from the beaches to go without a car. We finally decided that life in Paris is more pleasant and are back here and having a big row with the owner about next month's rent, as she didn't tell us the truth." In Paris Romain worked on a follow-up to his successful novel *The Ski Bum*, while Jean spent time with Diego, relaxed, and read.

"I'm going through a phase where I'm a little tired of acting," she wrote Dawn Quinn. "It will pass, but I think it's mainly a disappointment over the quality of roles and scripts one sees. Sometimes I wish I had another, second 'craft' to have satisfaction from and not be dependent on just acting."

In August, Jean accepted a supporting role and star billing in *A Fine Madness*. Offered a fee of $125,000 (co-star Joanne Woodward received

$100,000 for a lead role), she and the household returned to California for filming in late September 1965.

This time she would star with Sean Connery as a rebellious poet and a cast including Colleen Dewhurst and Patrick O'Neal, and Jean thought this could be the break-through critical and financial Hollywood success that had so far eluded her. She appreciated the easy-going working atmosphere among her fellow actors. Patrick O'Neal remembered how, during the making of *A Fine Madness*, the actors and their spouses met every Friday night in the screening room of the Beverly Hills Hotel to watch a film that one of them chose.

"Paul Newman brought beer and popcorn — made it himself," O'Neal recalled. "It was just a social evening after work — we all felt very close. Each of us got to choose our favorite film." O'Neal selected *Singin' in the Rain*, while Woodward chose Alfred Hitchcock's only American comedy film, *Mr. and Mrs. Smith*, starring Carole Lombard. Jean opted for less traditional fare. Her choice was *The Lady with a Dog*, a beautiful, haunting Russian film based on a Chekhov short story. "I thought her choice was wonderfully appropriate [since] Jean was a little girl from Iowa."

At Thanksgiving, Jean and Romain dined quietly with Woodward and Newman, and then Ed and Dorothy Seberg managed to steal a few days away from the pharmacy and flew to Los Angeles for a short visit.

By December, when *A Fine Madness* was in its final weeks of filming, Jean's role seemed to have been reduced to little more than continual complaining. When the time came to shoot the scene in which Connery pulls Jean into the sanitarium ripple bath, she hesitated. She had not performed in any state of nudity in her previous films, and she declared that she would not in this one. The problem was resolved when Jean consented to wear "pasties" which concealed her breasts. Despite her modesty, *Playboy* ran a double-page spread of the scene.

Once filming was completed, Jack Warner could not comprehend the comedy and ordered the film re-cut to his specifications. The result was a critical and financial bomb. The disappointments of her two 1965 Hollywood films disenchanted Jean with the film capital still further. She disliked Los Angeles, with its smog, and the all-too-often insincere camaraderie between many people in the industry.

"There are none of the friendly, family feelings that I get when I work in France," she commented privately. "In France, you know if you're making a movie, you're going to sit around waiting in a café, which is not disagreeable. Here, they give you some superb trailer with a Frigidaire and a stove. I keep expecting to find a warmth to the work in Hollywood which doesn't exist. The unions have imposed so many people for each job that there is no longer a sense of responsibility. I'm a lot less nervous when I get up in the morning to go to work now. But some of the joy has gone out of acting for me."

Returning to Paris just before Christmas, Jean sent her yearly holiday personal check to her family and a special gift and note to Frances Benson relating to a family ancestor:

"The enclosed document concerns John Hart and I had it purchased for you in New York. It was written in 1865 (April 5) and signed by the Civil War Governor of New Jersey, authorizing construction of a proper monument to the memory of a man who 'made so many sacrifices to his country at the formation of our National and State governments' and who at the time was buried in a farm graveyard.

"It sums up nicely the things John Hart did and I thought it would have a special meaning for you and the family."

After three films, and traveling halfway around the world for two of them, Jean was happy to be at home in Paris, and quietly spent the holidays with her husband and son. It was also time to reflect on the direction her career, and most importantly, her life, was currently taking.

14

"America is waking up."
— Jean Seberg

While Jean and Romain had a marriage based on love and a deep admiration for each other, some privately felt that by 1966 it was developing into a father-daughter relationship. Publicly, Jean asserted that the romance between Romain and herself was alive and well.

Several people wondered how many men of Romain's age could find a beautiful actress like Jean Seberg. "That's not fair," remarks Frederic Jones. "Romain was a brilliant man and he understood Jean. That's why she loved him so much."

Jean respected Romain's intelligence and literary talent, but continually denied to the press that he guided her in choosing movie roles. It is doubtful whether Romain had much of a hand in steering his wife's career, nor indeed was she likely to have yielded control over anything which mattered so much to her. As an experienced writer he would quickly have spotted weaknesses in screenplays such as *A Fine Madness* or *Moment to Moment*, and, as she told the press, he was always free with his advice. Yet he stressed that she made her own decisions, and he went with Jean on location simply because he wanted to be with her. While he did not enjoy moving from Paris to Los Angeles twice in one year, he was prepared to do this for her sake.

Some (including Romain's first wife) believed Jean had trapped Romain into marriage, and used his standing in society to raise her own. Others thought it was Jean who had been used by Romain. She was, after all, a famous actress. "Romain wouldn't have brought anything to her career," one friend says. "But [the union] would certainly help him."

When Romain retired to his den to work on his writing for weeks on end, Jean became anxious. Sometimes she tried to make a joke of it: "His concentration is incredible. I can play Trini Lopez records full volume and he just goes on writing. He wears a shin guard on his legs because I kick him under the table when we have guests and I see him thinking about his books." This conflict had made their life together especially difficult in the early days. Jean's work would come in fits and starts, but for Romain the creative demons could be remorseless.

In February Jean learned her *Lilith* director had died of a coronary occlusion. She sat down and wrote a touching epitaph to Robert Rossen, for whom she held a deep appreciation and admiration: "I remember the Jewish Passover spent among Rossen's family, the Jewish dinner, the thousand candles that burned in the room, while Rossen chanted the ritual songs with his sons, and I had the impression that there was in Rossen, and in his film, something very precious and very secret that I would never find again."

There was talk that Jean would star in a film based on Romain's story, *The Ski Bum*, whose film rights had been secured by producer Joseph Levine. The character of Jess, the independent daughter of an American diplomat, was clearly modeled in part on Jean, and Romain had already completed a screenplay. Unfortunately, the deal fell through, and it was not until 1971 that Bruce Clark's film, starring Charlotte Rampling, appeared. Instead of this project, in the early part of 1966, Jean began work on *La ligne de démarcation* (*The Line of Demarcation*), a film that dramatized French resistance to the Germans in a village situated on the border between the occupied and Vichy zones. Jean's character, the British-born wife of an aristocrat, helps two Allied agents escape to freedom, and is eventually imprisoned by the Germans for her actions.

In the British monthly *Films and Filming*, Jean discussed the film and its director, Claude Chabrol: "Chabrol is such a strange man. I think with *La ligne de démarcation* he believed that he was going to make almost a parody of the Resistance, and of that whole period of French life...I also suspect — knowing Claude, and liking him for this — that he probably had heard that we might be able to shoot this story in a place where there was a very comfortable hotel with an absolutely superb restaurant.

"When you make a film with him you can't help putting on weight. You spend the morning in the make-up department, ... deciding what you're going to ask them in the kitchen to prepare for everybody to eat that night. Otherwise I don't really know why he made that film."

While *The Line of Demarcation* did little business in Paris, it was seen as a tribute to the French underground in the provinces.

In March, the Garys went on a tour of Poland and Hungary, where Romain gave a series of lectures and the couple attended several official banquets. Jean wrote her parents while en route to Budapest: "Our trip was fascinating and sometimes terribly depressing. The people we met, particularly in Poland, were very warm and very charming, but life in those countries is so difficult and so harsh that everyone who is pro-Communist should be given a free ticket by the U.S. government so they can change their minds. Don't repeat that where it might be printed, because we were on a good-will tour and don't want to seem ungrateful. I was sick with the flu and a terrible cold most of the time, and you cannot imagine the trouble I had just to find a fresh orange to eat! Daddy will be amused to know that the doctor in a little town in Poland gave me American vitamins bought in the black market because he said they were better than their own."

While Jean was recognized less on the tour than in southern Europe, several times she was approached by young people.

A few weeks later, in April 1966, Jean wrote her parents that "*Moment to Moment* has done pretty well — better than *Judith* with Sophia Loren, and better than Natalie Wood's picture (*This Property is Condemned*) — but I don't want to do another movie where I am without support from a well-known male actor. It's too much responsibility alone."

Although *Moment to Moment* was not the blockbuster Universal had hoped for, it was not a complete disappointment in financial terms. Critics, however, dismissed the work. "If only it had Alfred Hitchcock instead of Mervyn LeRoy as director," the *New York Times* lamented. "The bait is all there, but don't expect to be hooked."

Despite the poor reviews, for once Jean was in a film role that became a real hit in her hometown. Today, *Moment to Moment* is arguably the favorite Seberg film among Marshalltownians. Of the few photographs Carol Hollingsworth kept of Jean, one was a publicity still from the film. When Jean gave her former teacher the photograph, she joked, "I'm at the airport with my husband telling my lover good-bye."

In May 1966, Jean returned to the US on business, then quietly visited her family in Iowa. Upon her return to France, she told a reporter: "In the United States we have a tendency to replace culture with Freudianism; the way you appear intelligent is to talk about your neuroses. I was very struck by that during my last stay there, during meetings or luncheons. The feeling of guilt continues to dominate American psychology. I know very few creative people — creative in the true sense of the word — who don't go, sooner or later, to a psychiatrist."

Jean could not completely understand the ways of the US, Marshalltown, or her parents. She had at times, an underlying sense she had failed her parents, especially her father. Unlike her sister, Jean had not completed her college education, something which was important in Ed Seberg's eyes. In addition, Mary Ann was leading a life her parents could relate to — she lived in middle-class comfort, with her husband, their two children, and a dog. But Ed and Dorothy were very proud of Jean; however, with their upbringing, they did not incessantly exude that pride publicly.

While Marshalltown appeared the same, during the visit Jean noticed the changes taking place in American society. "[Things] are beginning to happen there. Bob Dylan — a real poet — is somewhat the symbol of the rising generation looking for new values," Jean said. "As for the Vietnamese war, one finds it's acceptable for young men who want to avoid [the draft], some of them from the highly patriotic families of the Midwest. The beatniks have almost become respectable. Ginsberg is giving lectures at American universities. It's undeniable: America is waking up."

Jean took with her back to Paris the latest recordings by artists in America, and played her favorite songs to her friends. "We would sit down and listen to her American music," recalls Vony Becker, one friend who was an audience for Jean's musical preferences, "and Jean would translate the words for us. She introduced us to the music of Bob Dylan and Joan Baez. Jean had a passion for them."

On June 15, Romain and Jean slipped away to the Greek island of Mykonos. They traveled four days by car and spent the following ten days vacationing, while Eugenia took Diego to Spain where she visited her relatives.

With no other offers that summer (Jean had turned down a film in London with Yul Brynner because "the script was so bad"), she accepted a role that took her on a two-month shoot in South America in late August. In *Estouffade à la Caraïbe* (*Revolt in the Caribbean*), Jean plays the idealistic daughter of a mobster who joins a rebellion against the country's dictator. Her hair was dyed blonder than she normally wore, and her skin tanned more than usual.

Foreseeing uncomfortable living conditions, Jean sent Diego and Eugenia back to Spain while she and Romain left for Cartagena, Colombia, where the film was shot. Although they stayed in a luxurious hotel, Jean couldn't help noticing the degradation of society in Colombia and the crime and poverty all around her. "If I had lived in South America," she said two years later, "I would have fought with Che."

Jean found the heat of Colombia almost unbearable, and the make-up literally dissolved on the actors' faces. Jean was also required to swim in shark-infested waters for the film, although two men swam nearby, just out of camera range, to keep the animals away.

It was while in Colombia Jean discovered lumps in her breasts. Fearing cancer, she had several benign tumors removed and underwent hormonal treatment when the film crew returned to Paris to complete production.

Although Jean never used Diego for publicity purposes and went out of her way to shield him from the spotlight, the public was hungry to see what the boy looked like. It was only a matter of time before the paparazzi caught up with and photographed him. While in Paris in late October 1966, Jean was unexpectedly captured on camera with Diego for the first time. "[Diego] was coming home straight from the Costa Brava," *France-Soir* reported. "He

Taking a break during the filming of Revolt *in the Caribbean, 1966.*
COURTESY OF SNORRAMYNDIR

rushed to the Saint-Maurice Studios to find his pretty mom who is finishing her latest film *Estouffade aux Caraïbes* [sic]." The photograph gracing the front page of the newspaper showed Jean crouching down with her son, holding his hand while both smiled. "To surprise her," the copy read, "he spoke Spanish to her."

The last weeks of 1966 were spent quietly in Paris. A few days after Christmas, Jean wrote her parents: "I am having a post-Christmas lazy spell. Romain and I have had a dreadful time getting back on Paris time after our travels — have been going for walks at 5 A.M. because we can't sleep. He's just about done in as he tries to work all day but can't sleep at night."

She then told of their traditional Christmas gift opening and the excitement in Diego's eyes: "He received so many lovely toys that I'm taking all the old ones to a school for blind children here. I gave Romain a beautiful Italian leather armchair for his office and he gave me a pretty gold bracelet and two small statues, one Chinese, one Egyptian dating 600 and 200 years B.C. I hope you'll all use your checks for what you want most. Wish they were bigger, but it seems the more I make, the less I see!"

CHAPTER FIVE
1967–1968

"I'm tired of living a gypsy life."
— Jean Seberg

With Romain and Sandy the dog in their rue du Bac apartment.
COURTESY OF SNORRAMYNDIR

15

*"Although she has retained her American citizenship ('and will never give it up')
she is devoted to her adopted country...France has deeply loved and respected Jean."*
— columnist Dorothy Manners

By 1967, Romain felt an urge to return to public service. He visited with
his and Jean's friend, André Malraux, who headed the Ministry of Culture,
to discuss various possibilities. In the spring, he accepted a post as an adviser
to the Ministry of Information, where his responsibilities were to include
developing new cultural programs for French television. Romain was eager
to take up the position, but he accepted the job only after two of his conditions were met. Having declined a salary, he could insist on freedom to
travel and flexible work hours, so that he might accompany Jean in the event
that she needed to leave France to work on a film.

Shortly after, Jean and Romain traveled to Athens to begin work on
Claude Chabrol's *La route de Corinthe* (*The Road to Corinth*), once again
entrusting Diego to Eugenia's care. In this deliberately silly color comedy/
spy film, Chabrol has Jean searching for her husband's murderers before they
can complete their mission to destroy NATO radar installations in Greece.
Romain plays a non-speaking cameo role in the film as an Orthodox priest,
wearing a black hat and robe, while Chabrol himself plays an informer who
appears in various disguises until he is knifed in a cemetery by assassins
dressed as priests.

"This film has been hard, hard work," Jean wrote Carol Hollingsworth.
"Up every day around 5 A.M. and the old eyes are getting weaker and weaker
under those awful arc lights. I'll be miserable when it's over. It's the most fun
I've ever had (which, alas, doesn't mean it will be the best film) and I've done
comedy with a freedom and relaxation I've never known before. Chabrol
loves actors so much that you feel a positive force coming to you from him
while you work."

The fun continued when Jean agreed to be dangled 300 feet over the
Corinth Canal after her stunt double balked. "So I just thought what the
hell and did it myself," Jean recalled. "They attached me by this leather belt
to a crane, and swung me around until I was hovering over the canal which
was far below. It was a comedy sequence and I had to scream 'Let me down,
let me down.' The cameraman thought I was going to pieces so he stopped
shooting. So I had to go through the process all over again. Of course, once
I'd done it I was very proud.

"When I saw it in the completed film, I was furious. Claude had used two
cameras, and for once in his life he placed them very clumsily. And I don't
think you get the sense of danger of it. I was so disappointed because if I was
going to do something show-offy and breakneck, I wanted it to look super."

During one scene, which was shot at the Athens Hotel, Jean ran into Harry Druker, her Marshalltown lawyer, and his wife Rose, who were on their way back to the US from a trip to Israel. That evening they dined together. "Jean and Romain were living in a beautiful apartment," Mrs. Druker recalled, adding that although Jean wore a simple, flowing robe and no make-up, "she was absolutely breathtaking in that setting." Mrs. Druker reminded Jean of when she was younger and used to daydream of becoming a famous actress. "'Your dreams really did come true, didn't they, Jean?' She smiled and put her arms around me. She was so beautiful and unassuming, I almost wept."

In June, the Garys returned to Paris and were reunited with Diego. Jean felt that, with her recent schedule, she had neglected her child much too long. She spent the next weeks with Diego, mounting a display of his paintings throughout the rue du Bac apartment, where she invited friends to view them.

"Jean was trying to be a mother," Vony Becker says. "She invited us to the rue du Bac many times. She and her friends would have small parties for the children, and they were wonderful and detailed. Once, at Halloween, there was a magician for entertainment. Jean was really happy at the parties, and they would take place in the big living room. And at Christmastime she'd have a tree and presents for all her friends — but she'd prepare a whole month before. But I never saw Romain interact with Diego."

One day Jean and Diego met Vony and her son, who was approximately the same age as Diego, at a restaurant in the country. "Jean wanted to go there with Diego," Vony recalls. "But he was raised by those Spanish ladies and he was unbearable — destroying everything. My son and I met them there, and at first the two [boys] had a lot of trouble getting along. Then they began to act up. At one point Jean and I stomped our feet and yelled, 'That is enough!'" Vony laughs. "They stopped in their tracks and looked at us like, 'What is going to happen to us, Mother?'"

In July, Jean, Romain and Diego took a family trip to Cimarron in Majorca. Romain loved the home and spoke to Jean of moving there permanently. "To some, that would sound like heaven on earth," Jean later said, "but to me it sounded like retirement. And I thought, 'Listen, I'm only 28 years old. I'm not ready to retire.' Romain has his writing to keep him busy, but I couldn't see myself working with potted plants. I'm a spoiled brat, you see."

Back in Paris at the end of July, Jean acquired a new green Austin 1100 car. The following day, she had been at Studios de Billancourt and was driving into the heart of Paris with her friend and frequent co-star Maurice Ronet around 7:00 P.M. when her car crashed into another vehicle which had pulled out in front of them. A seventy-six-year-old pedestrian was struck and badly injured. Although she emerged unhurt, Ronet had been thrown from the car and was hospitalized with broken ribs, a suspected concussion, and cuts to the face which required stitches. The press reported Ronet's concern that he might be left disfigured, and although she had not been at fault Jean was "devastated" by what had happened.

Ronet, however, quickly recovered and was cast in Jean's next film, which was set to begin in October. It was not to be a Hollywood movie this time as Jean had been offered a role in the Bob Hope comedy, *The Private Navy of Sgt. O'Farrell*, but the role did not impress her and she turned it down. In fact, when an American reporter saw Jean that summer, he asked her what he and others could do to get her back to Hollywood. She laughed, "Just offer me a good role, a good story and a good director — and I'll be there."

Romain, meanwhile, was anxious to do just that. He had learned much about the film industry from his time in Los Angeles, where he had got to know many leading figures such as John Ford and Gary Cooper. David O. Selznick had asked him to adapt Fitzgerald's *Tender is the Night* for the screen in 1958, and although this came to nothing there had been other screenwriting assignments. Together with James Jones, he became involved in writing the screenplay for Ken Annakin's 1962 *The Longest Day*, another enterprise of the producer of *The Roots of Heaven*, Darryl F. Zanuck. While accompanying Jean on location he had seen more of the processes of film-making. Furthermore, the screen adaptations of his novels (notably Huston's stodgy interpretation of *The Roots of Heaven* and Ustinov's overblown *Lady L.*) had not impressed him, and he was convinced he could do better. Now, he felt, was as good a time as any for him and his wife to work together. The result was *Les Oiseaux vont mourir au Pérou* (*Birds in Peru*), a turning point in the careers and lives of both of them.

Romain completed a script from his 1962 short story with this title (from the collection *Gloire à nos illustres pionniers*), which was translated in *Playboy*, winning a *Playboy* writing award, and was also included in his 1964 volume of translated stories, *Hissing Tales*. He envisioned Jean as Adriana, a married nymphomaniac who searches for fulfillment on a remote beach littered with the remains of dead birds. When he dedicated the story to her, Jean had said, "I don't think Romain and I will ever work together. I don't think it's a good idea for people who are very close to collaborate professionally." However, she now felt obligated to help her husband realize his dream of making a film, even if it meant going against her previous instinct. Having Jean's name associated with the project, Romain was able to secure backing from Universal Studios.

"I, myself, have never known a nymphomaniac," Romain stated, "but I do know they are pitiful creatures because the compulsion which drives them into one affair after another is that they never find satisfaction — and for a woman, nothing can be more tragic. Adriana is such a pitiable figure, so when she pleads to die, you know this is a blessed release for her and for everyone around her."

The French board of censors was uneasy about the nature of the story, but gave Romain approval of the script, feeling that he would handle the delicate matter tastefully. He planned to have a closed set during certain scenes, as the emotional strain on Jean in them would be heavy. Romain warned that his film would have no "wild" sex scenes, and Jean reiterated the nudity clause that was included in all her movie contracts. "I'll never play a scene in the nude," she said. "Even my husband can't demand it of me."

In the autumn, before filming commenced, Jean took an eight-month lease on a three-acre farm two hours outside of Paris. Located near the fishing village of Honfleur, five Holstein cows grazed on the "vibrant green" grass which reminded Jean of Ireland, and she planned to use the place to escape the confines of Paris. "I'll try to get there with Diego — maybe I can find him a pony to ride," she hoped. "Anyway, I really needed something like that and the air in Paris isn't good for Diego all year round."

Now enrolled in school and "extremely intellectual," Jean boasted, Diego was also developing a penchant for playing cards with his schoolmates, much to his parents' dismay. "Romain and I detest gambling. Diego must get that from Romain's White Russian ancestors," Jean fretted, "who all ruined themselves."

On September 30, Jean wrote her grandmother:

Dearest Granny Grunt,
I am in bed with the flu so decided to take advantage of a rare moment of peace and isolation to drop you a line. When I think how I used to rebel against the routine and monotony of small town life: now sometimes I'd give anything to be able to get "bored" once in awhile and not have fifty phone calls a day to cope with. I'm not complaining really, but sometimes it's just all a strain.

We begin filming Monday on Romain's picture. Heaven knows how it'll be, but he's all excited about it. Maybe it'll pull him out of his bear's den a little more often.

Iowa must be in her autumn dress by now. It always smells so good with the bonfires and all.

Love to all,
Jeana

P.S. How's your money stand?

Filming *Birds in Peru* began in early October 1967 with a star-studded cast, including Maurice Ronet, Pierre Brasseur, Danielle Darrieux, and Jean-Pierre Kalfon. While filming interior scenes at the Paris Joinville Studios, Jean and Romain were visited by columnist Radie Harris. Romain told Harris the part of Adriana "is an extremely demanding role, but I'm sure Jean will be marvelous in it."

On the set of Birds in Peru *with co-star Danielle Darrieux and Romain, 1967.*
COURTESY OF SNORRAMYNDIR

"It's wonderful working with Romain," Jean offered. "He has caught on so quickly that you'd think he's been directing all his life! Maybe that's part of his soldier and diplomatic training," she laughed.

Harris noted before leaving the set, "I thought how wonderful that Jean has found such fulfillment in every area of her life over here, and yet still remains as American as blueberry pie."

Roderick Mann was another who visited the Garys on the set, and he asked them about working together, considering their private relationship.

Romain admitted he was worried about this while planning the film, confessing friends advised him "not to play Svengali. Don't do that to your wife. Many a marriage has broken up that way. But to tell you the truth," Romain said, "the moment she walks on the set I forget she is my wife. I call her Seberg. 'Where is Seberg?' I say."

Appearances were deceiving. The film production was running into trouble, and Jean was concerned about how she would be presented in the finished film.

Later that month the company moved to the south coast of Spain, to a deserted stretch of beach used as a setting in the film. "We're living in a rather plain little summer house," Jean wrote Carol Hollingsworth, "and we can't get the hot water to function. Last night Celia and I heated two canisters of water so Romain could take a sorely needed bath. The first days it rained here and was awfully depressing — our cars and the camera equipment kept sinking into the sand."

Conditions were not ideal, and the film, being Romain's first directorial effort, was not well-planned. Faulty equipment, trouble with set construction, and the inevitable problems with the other members of the cast hampered the production. Whole days were lost waiting in cold weather for better filming conditions. In addition, trouble brewed between husband and wife. "She had complained about making the film because Romain made her do some things that she felt were kind of degrading," says Mary Ann Seberg. "She was a little afraid and not very happy with their working relationship."

The seclusion and waiting continued. Reporter Thérèse Hamel arrived to view the filming, but instead learned more of the Seberg/Gary relationship. Sitting literally in a shack, Jean honestly spoke of the filming ("Everyone's going nuts here. Days of waiting, it's awful"), then turned the subject to her husband. "I'm certainly the elder of the two. Romain is a boy of fourteen inside the shell of a fifty-year-old. He has enthusiasms, love of childish laughter and games which I no longer have. Life is strange. I married him for security. It turned out the opposite way ... I don't think you can offer much to a man like Romain. But a woman could harm him."

The production team returned to Paris in December and completed filming before Christmas. Interest in the film abounded throughout France, and reports claimed the Seberg/Gary film had all the earmarking of a success, especially when Romain said, "[Jean] gives the best performance of her life. I didn't have much to do to get it out of her because she felt the part admirably."

Jean had no idea how the finished product would turn out, but believed that in her husband's hands the film would be a success. She could not resist reviving her old joke from the Preminger days, "I guess you might say I've gone from saint to sinner."

December 1967 was busy for the Garys. In addition to filming *Birds in Peru,* Jean attended a UNICEF gala, and the pair went to the Élysée for the Réception des Arts et Lettres on December 8. Christmas was spent in Paris, and the holiday made Jean homesick for the ones she had spent in her childhood.

"There's never a Christmas I'm not dissolved in tears halfway through Christmas Eve. We always went ice-skating on the Iowa River and everyone sang carols and asked us in for hot chocolate and then we'd end up at midnight church." On this Christmas, Diego woke up three times during the night and asked his mother, "Is Père Noël here yet?"

"Diego loves it," Jean said, and jokingly added, "Romain hates Christmas. He's a Scrooge. He never gives presents to anybody."

In early 1968 Jean was asked to participate in a curious, little-known project that was planned to be a series about European cinema. Publicist Malcolm Thompson brought the idea to producer Tom Parkinson and his Silverscreen production company. John Crome was assigned to direct. Crome had been working at the BBC making programs aimed at the youth market. "This was 'Swinging London,'" Crome explains, "and I had made film interviews with most of the rock/pop stars at the time, and the fashion people, so I was an obvious choice for this."

The Girls was the pilot episode for the series. "What the premise is in Europe was that [with] women and sex, there was a different attitude in the cinema toward those matters than in the United States," Crome says. "It was in effect comparing Europe and America, and it wasn't just about actors. It also included interviews with film directors and producers who were women, but with some eminent producers who were male as well."

The Girls chiefly consisted of a series of interviews. Producer Joseph Janni (*Darling*) spoke about Julie Christie because she was unavailable, Godard actress and independent producer Macha Méril described her experience, and there were contributions from actresses Anita Pallenberg, Joanna Shimkus, and Susannah York. Also featured were Jane Fonda and then-husband director Roger Vadim, and Jean Seberg.

Jean's participation in *The Girls* was completed in one day. She suggested filming in the Paris salon of designer Ungaro (who claimed to have designed the miniskirt) where she was being fitted for a dress. "My impression of Jean as a person was that she was charming and polite, pleasant and helpful to us, and she saw us as a group of young Brits in our twenties with long hair and what have you, who needed helping out, and she would do anything to help us out. She came across as very self-assured, confident, loving her life. She was living a life of a rich bourgeois Parisian woman who got her clothes made by a top designer, ate at the best restaurants, knew all the right people."

Crome says the filmed interview was not terribly deep. "It was basically about her feeling of freedom in Europe ... that the films were more intelligent. She was happy to promote the thesis that in European film, there was a greater freedom for women to express themselves."

The Girls was completed, but the series didn't continue because the production company went into liquidation. The film was shelved, never shown publicly, and generally overlooked in the participants' filmographies. "It was a typical story of films at that time," Crome explains, "of things getting made and never getting shown."

16

"[Seberg] is anything but bland, yet she has been constantly accused of blandness.
She is anything but humorless, yet she has frequently been described as unquotable.
She is anything but frivolous, yet she has often been dismissed as superficial."
— Joyce Haber

After the astronomical success of the film musical *The Sound of Music*, Hollywood studios rushed to develop similar projects in musical genre, hoping for equally rich pickings. By 1968, it was estimated that twenty-eight musical properties were bought by the studios for production. Jean's alma mater Columbia had *Funny Girl* and *Oliver!*; United Artists was set with *Fiddler on the Roof* and *Chitty Chitty Bang Bang*; Warner Brothers, *Camelot*; Universal, *Thoroughly Modern Millie*; MGM, *Goodbye, Mr. Chips*. At the Paramount offices, *Darling Lili* had Julie Andrews starring in the lead; Barbra Streisand was signed for *On a Clear Day You Can See Forever*; and the pairing of Clint Eastwood and Lee Marvin was set for the musical screen adaptation of the play *Paint Your Wagon*.

Learning of the $15 million investment in *Paint Your Wagon*, a sum unheard-of at the time, Hollywood observers touted this to be one of the biggest potential box-office winners, even before the film began production. Alan Jay Lerner collaborated on the story with Frederick Loewe, a partnership which had produced several hits including *Brigadoon, My Fair Lady, Camelot*, and *Gigi*. Lerner and director Joshua Logan wanted Jean for the lead female role. Paramount did not. In fact, Faye Dunaway claimed she had been offered the role but had turned it down in favor of another film. "It was all an accident, really, but I've had one of those peculiar careers anyway, so nothing really surprises me anymore," Jean said.

She was considered and ruled out, then reconsidered before she was asked to go to Los Angeles in March 1968 for a screen test. At first, Jean refused to do the test, but after reading the screenplay she found it the "most commercial script I ever read." The role of Elizabeth struck her as one of "a nineteenth-century flower child." Now she agreed to the screen test, one in which she had to lip-synch to Eydie Gorme's voice in a musical number. Jean had no misgivings either about the role or the castings. Privately she felt Shirley MacLaine would be the eventual victor.

Borrowing one of Romain's revolvers for the test*, Jean calmly walked into the Paramount offices and played a scene with Lee Marvin, who had already negotiated a $1,000,000 salary, in person. "Jean came into Josh Logan's office wearing a real pistol to get in the mood," Marvin recalled. "I was there and I thought, 'what kind of cuckoo bird is this?' Yeah, she wanted the part all right! I said, 'What the hell. I'm here, I'll do the scene with her.' And I was impressed."

"There's this womanly quality about her," Lerner said about the character of Elizabeth. The actress selected for the role "had to be a woman, but she had to be a young woman. She had to be attractive. She had to be capable of some kind of a decent love. For all those reasons, [Jean's] absolutely ideal for the film."

"Jean had that little girl quality we wanted, but also enough maturity to carry a love story with two grown men," said Logan. "She's no longer the ingénue; she's grown mentally and spiritually, she has strength and technique."

Coupled with her screen test, Logan and Lerner convinced Paramount that Jean Seberg was more than capable of playing the pivotal role. Shortly afterwards Jean signed for a salary of $120,000, plus expenses, and secured a large rental home in Beverly Hills.

Ray Walston, who played "Mad Jack" Duncan in the film, recalled the selection of Jean for the film: "I knew nothing about her. I had not seen her in whatever films she'd done," Walston confessed. "As a matter of fact, when she was cast in the role, I raised an eyebrow — not because of her talent or anything, but because of the fact that I had been a very close friend of Josh Logan, and he asked me specifically about the casting of the girl in that role. I suggested three actresses — I think one was Jane Fonda, another one was Joanne Woodward, and also Lee Remick.

"I was very surprised he chose Jean Seberg. The only thing I knew about Jean Seberg was that she was in *Saint Joan*."

Meanwhile, in Paris, an edited version of *Birds in Peru* was submitted to the French censors for final approval. By a vote of 10 to 9 the board refused certification and banned the work from French theaters. Stung, Romain appealed the decision directly to the Minister of Information, Georges Gorse, to whom he was still an advisor. One of the objectives which had encouraged him to take this post had been the liberalization of censorship. The Minister overruled the ban, instead applying minor cuts, but Romain's anger with the censors resulted in his resignation in May 1968.

* Note: It was reported Jean borrowed "one of Romain's .45 automatics for the test"; however, it may very well have been a .38 Smith & Wesson, which he was given a permit to own in 1960. It was this gun that Romain used in 1980 with catastrophic results.

"If people think it is pornographic," Romain said, "I have failed. To me the difference is this: When a film ceases to be artistic, at that point eroticism stops and pornography begins."

When Jean saw the final cut of the film, she could not conceal her dismay — she was simply appalled. The film opened with a head shot of her, as her head pushed against the sand in a sexual rhythm, and things went downhill from there. She could not believe Romain had presented her in such an embarrassing fashion. She felt used, hurt, and angry, but kept her true feelings from the public, saying simply to the *Los Angeles Times'* Joyce Haber: "*Peru* is provocative and may be shocking to some."

Many critics were scathing. "If we remember that Jean Seberg is Romain Gary's wife," reproved a film critic from *La Croix*, "we shall fully measure the depths of the abyss into which he has fallen."

Under the newly formed production code of the Motion Picture Association of America, *Birds in Peru* became the first film to receive an X rating. This did not signify that it was regarded as pornographic (*Midnight Cowboy* also received an X rating shortly after — and the Best Picture Academy Award), but the film was considered for mature audiences only.

Although *Breathless* was a surprise to Marshalltown residents when it played there, *Birds in Peru* was so startling to those who saw it that the film was seldom even discussed. Unlike her previous works, the *Times-Republican* did not bother to review it.

Lynda Haupert puts *Birds in Peru* in perspective: "At the time it was pretty risqué, but it wouldn't be today. Marshalltown was shocked. Her parents were probably embarrassed by it. But again, there was a part of Jean that liked to shock people — do or say something shocking, doing the unexpected. It goes back to when she greeted her mother's guests in that formal gown."

"Most people didn't understand that film," Jean said in retrospect. "It was a literary film, not a visual one. There's a place for that. People who went to see it expecting to see a dirty film were disappointed. People who went expecting to see a visual film were disappointed. Romain learned a lot on that film.

"For me, and I hope I'm not betraying Romain's intentions, it was a kind of ritualistic dance of death."

Romain and Jean separated for a period of time as the result of *Birds in Peru*, with Jean working on *Paint Your Wagon* and Romain staying in Paris. "Gary was a good writer, but not a good filmmaker," Romain's close friend Roger Grenier remarks. A neighbor of the Garys on rue du Bac, Grenier often saw Jean, Romain, and Diego on the street walking the dogs. Grenier was also employed at Gallimard, the French company which published Gary's works.

"*Birds in Peru* was not a very good movie," Grenier says. "It was the beginning of when things went wrong with Jean in her personal life." Nonetheless, their separation did not last; even if the trust Jean once had in her husband was shaken.

After the announcement that Jean was signed for *Paint Your Wagon*, producers considered her a "hot" property once again, and she received several film offers. Jean chose a small role in the police melodrama *Pendulum*, set in Washington, D.C. For one month's work on this film, produced by Columbia, she was paid $100,000. The story concerns an independent-minded police captain (George Peppard) who falls under suspicion from colleagues when his unfaithful wife, played by Jean, is murdered.

"As I recall, George was particularly keen on Jean for the role, which I thought was fine," says Schaefer. *Pendulum* marked Schaefer's debut as a film director, and he was an admirer of Jean Seberg and her films. "I resented she had been forced into *Saint Joan* because I didn't think that showed her off as she was a very lovely young lady. I really liked her in *Breathless* and the films she did after that. So, I was very pleased to have her in *Pendulum*."

On March 24, 1968, Jean had been in Los Angeles for ten days preparing for *Pendulum* when she received a telephone call from Marshalltown. Her eighteen-year-old brother David had been killed in a single vehicle car accident. After working on his car's engine that Sunday, David and a friend had gone for a drive on Highway 330 to make sure the car was running well.

"David and his friend stopped by my place earlier that afternoon, and then he went to State Center to visit my sister. On the way home it happened," Velma Odegaard recalled. Odegaard later heard David might have been dragracing with another vehicle. On a bend in the road southwest of Marshalltown, David lost control of the car when it skidded eight-hundred feet and crashed into a ditch. The two were found dead in a patch of burning grass near the car. "David's mother wanted his watch, but they could never find it," Odegaard said. "Sometimes Dorothy would go out to the scene [of the accident] and try to find the watch, I think just to have that personal memento."

It was rumored that the family of David's friend were going to sue the Sebergs for their son's death. Since Jean was wealthy, it was said, Ed and Dorothy Seberg seemed to be an easy target for such an action. In reality, the family hadn't even considered such an action, and they, along with the Sebergs, felt hurt by the lie circulating around town.

Jean immediately flew home to her grieving family. Romain had left California and was in Paris for only two days when a reporter from *France-Soir* telephoned him about David's death before Jean was able to tell him. Romain arrived in Marshalltown the following day for the funeral.

While in Marshalltown, Romain heard about what he called, "the other community 'tragedy'": a girl from a well-respected white family had married a black man. Romain quietly tried reasoning with a small group of people who were talking about the story, shaking their heads in disgust. "You don't have twenty million Negroes in France," one man said to him. "No," Romain agreed, "but we have fifty million Frenchmen in France and that ain't all fun either."

Romain realized that these sentiments were not shared by the majority of Iowans, and found most to be "pleasant, friendly, and 'un-psychological' people," he wrote, "by which I mean people who are sufficiently well-balanced, straight-forward and self-assured." He also described Jean's home state being to America "what a 1924 bottled Château-Lafitte is to French wine."

Feeling that it might help to take their minds off the tragedy of David's death, Jean invited her parents to join her in Washington, D.C. for the location filming on *Pendulum*. Romain joined them there, and the production began April 3. "We had just started shooting there, with Jean getting into a taxi and seen riding around to establish Washington as the locale," Schaefer recalls. "We were there one day. On the next day, Martin Luther King was assassinated." Riots followed in the capitol almost immediately.

The local law enforcement told Schaefer they could not protect the cast and crew, and suggested they should leave the city. "Filming there was dangerous in a way," Schaefer says. "We had a lot of extras dressed in police uniforms for a scene. We had to call off the shooting because when those extras were walking back to wardrobe, they were attacked by black youths. Fortunately, no one was seriously hurt. It was a very tense time." The unrest in Washington, D.C. was hardly a place for Ed and Dorothy to recuperate. After appearing as extras in a street scene for the film, the couple returned to Marshalltown.

The production then continued, completing the scenes featuring Jean hailing a taxi cab at Lafayette Square near the White House, then riding to Capitol Hill. "If you look at the film, you can see in the background parts of Washington literally going up in smoke," Schaefer notes. The cast and crew were then confined to their hotel rooms for two days until it was decided to complete the film in Los Angeles.

Jean wrote Vony Becker that Washington, D.C. was "horrible. The indifference of the white population is almost total. Instead of improving conditions in the ghetto, they are buying arms to defend themselves. You get the impression of being in a profoundly sick country which doesn't believe in its illness. Even Romain, who judges America less severely, senses a disturbing malaise."

Jean spoke with writer Margaret Ronan before leaving to Los Angeles. During the course of their conversation, Jean remarked she had just read a news item in which a congressman was quoted as saying the Supreme Court's "soft policy" on crime was causing more crime. "When are we going to stop trying to transfer our guilt feelings to the Supreme Court?" Jean asked Ronan. "That's irresponsible nonsense! The Court can't cause crime. It simply tries to guarantee equal justice for everyone. We help cause crime if we elect the wrong legislators, or if we don't see that the police have enough manpower to do their job properly. The Supreme Court can't appropriate money for law enforcement, or clean up the slums, or stop drug pushers. We have to do these things, and in too many cases, we're trying to pass the buck."

Ronan (who considered herself "outclassed" by Jean) asked her if she was glad to be home. "Ask me if I'm scared," Jean answered. "I'm terrified — and excited, too. Cataclysmic changes are taking place in American life. But we made them happen, and we have to learn to live with them."

Apart from the events in Washington, the filming of *Pendulum* went smoothly and was for the most part shot in sequence. Location scenes, including one with George Peppard at the National Airport which was shot instead at the Burbank Airport, were faked in California without compromise. Hopes were high for the film, and *Playboy* saw fit to bid on stills of the Seberg/Peppard love scene for an upcoming issue.

Filming the love scene was complicated. "Jean insisted on having pasties over her bosoms in case they showed," Schaefer remembers. "There was very little risk of showing; however, the little pasties caught the light, and little bits of that did show." A number of takes were made of the scene to make certain there would not be any 'squares of light' reflecting off Seberg's chest in the finished film.

"We had no intention of doing anything indecent, but wanted to make it a kind of sexy situation," Schaefer says. "But that was no problem, and there was never any temperament about it. The two seemed to work very well together. There never seemed to be any conflict between them."

Yet according to Jean's friend Lynda Haupert, there was a conflict: "Jean told me that George Peppard had wanted to rehearse their lines up in his hotel room — he had come on to Jean, and had been for some time — and Jean refused. And the next day in filming, there was a scene in which he had to slap her. Instead of faking it, he slapped her hard. She said, 'I know what they mean when they say 'I saw stars' because he slapped me so hard, I saw stars.'"

Schaefer visited Jean, Romain, and Diego at the house she rented in Beverly Hills, and only remembers the visit was relaxing and "rather pleasant." Schaefer recalls chatting with Romain a few times on the set. "He'd come on the set and sit around, just watching and talking," Schaefer also remembers Jean being "very quiet on the set. We never talked about politics or life or anything like that. But she was a delight to work with and was absolutely first-rate in her performance."

Jean completed her scenes in *Pendulum* in May. Almost immediately, she began rehearsals for *Paint Your Wagon* at Paramount. Shortly after their return to California, Jean, Romain, and Diego were visited by Grandma Benson and Mary Ann, her husband and their two daughters. Jean took her relatives to a taping of *The Art Linkletter Show*, where the host saw her in the audience. Linkletter greeted Jean and, after clasping her hand, introduced her to the audience, which gave her a warm reception.

Mary Ann does not recall Jean and Romain having any marital problems during this visit. "He was very kind and considerate to her," she says. "They seemed quite happy, and Romain was very encouraging to her." In fact, Romain helped Jean with her exercises, since any time she gained only a few

Sighted in the studio audience by TV talk show host Art Linkletter, 1968.
COURTESY OF SEBERG FAMILY COLLECTION

pounds, it showed. But the exercising was for herself, not to please Romain. "I hate girdles — that flat, ironing-board look," Jean said. "Some men are bosom men and some are bottom men. Fortunately, my husband is a bottom man."

During the visit, Mary Ann remembers Jean preparing for *Paint Your Wagon.* "She was trying so hard to learn the music because she said, 'I'm afraid they're going to dub my voice.' Romain was, as I remember, trying to encourage her without being too positive about it — trying to soften the blow a little bit. I think Romain was really good for Jean. They seemed to have had a lot of respect for one another."

Living in Los Angeles sharpened Jean's views of the racial intolerance in the United States, and the government's involvement in Vietnam. Jean began looking at the state of the world, voicing her opinion as she had for years. Only now, she was speaking out loud in the city of angels. At a party in Beverly Hills with Romain, Jean detached herself from the large group of personalities who proclaimed they were socially conscious. She was told that a young man by the pool had just returned from Vietnam, and she wanted to talk with him about his experiences. The young man, columnist Pete Hamill, recalled the meeting: "We wandered out to the pool and sat on a rock ledge in the smoggy night air, and for two hours I tried to tell her about Vietnam...She wore no makeup, and asked straight, intelligent questions. She didn't flirt. She shook her head a lot, appalled by the details, and her hands kept kneading each other. An aura of tension came off her like mist.

"'It's all connected, isn't it?' she said at one point. 'Vietnam, the oppression of blacks in America, all of it.'

"'What do you mean?'

"'I mean that it's all part of the same disgusting racism,' she said. 'If we were fighting the war against the Swedes, we wouldn't be doing these things. But because it's Orientals, we can do anything. Like Hiroshima being bombed, instead of Berlin.'

"'Maybe.'

"'There isn't much maybe about it, is there?' she said. 'It looks very clear to me.'"

Jean's views and offers to help with either a financial contribution or a signature thrust her into progressive causes. Privately, she felt the United States could overcome poverty, inequality, and especially, racism. After all, in France a black woman and a white man could walk down the street with nary a glance from other pedestrians. Jean wondered why it was still so extremely the opposite in the States.

She became involved with former athlete Jim Brown's Negro Industrial and Economic Union, which established black-owned businesses in the ghetto, and also gave money to help blacks who lived in riot-torn Watts, a section west of Los Angeles. In addition, she spoke out against the politics that had brought on the Vietnam conflict. She publicly voiced her support of Dr. Benjamin Spock, the author of baby-care books who became a war resister. In France she had earlier led the campaign to raise the standards of Arab workers residing there. In Marshalltown, she quietly set up scholarships for high school male students so that they could attend college rather than being forced to fight in the ongoing war in Vietnam. (At that time in US history, a male in college was exempt from being drafted. This policy, which catered to the wealthier classes, later changed.)

Jean did not, however, support all causes. She begged away from Resurrection City because she felt "it was humiliating for the black people. It was disorganized." At a meeting of the Southern Christian Leadership Conference, Jean alienated the fundraising guests when she was the only one who spoke out loud, demanding to know exactly where the donated money would go. "I'm tired of writing checks without knowing," she said.

In 1968 Marlon Brando held a meeting to raise money to benefit the Poor

People's March on Washington, which was started by Martin Luther King, Jr. Of the two-hundred-plus celebrities invited, which included *Mission: Impossible* stars Barbara Bain and Martin Landau, Mr. and Mrs. Lorne Greene, Mr. and Mrs. Robert Culp, Eva Marie Saint, Barbra Streisand (who delayed exiting from her car because of the photographers present), and Jim Morrison of The Doors, Jean attended this fundraiser with Romain.

Arriving at Marlon Brando's home with Romain, 1968.
COURTESY OF INDEPENDENT VISIONS

Brando's speech to the invited guests left many questioning his whole approach. While King had promoted nonviolent actions, Brando was speaking in angry, radical terms, and asked for the names of "everybody who isn't here, and I'm going to put their names in the trades."

"He kept calling the no-show liberals 'shallow,'" producer/screenwriter Abby Mann, who was a friend and active supporter of King, recalled.

Watching Brando continue to rant and lose the support of the guests, Jean deplored her host's behavior. Soon others began private conversations, ignoring the speaker. Having finally lost the group's attention, Brando erupted, shouting at a group talking by the bar. Everyone turned to see Brando glaring at novelist James Baldwin, who promptly fell silent. Jean burst out laughing, much to the chagrin of Brando.

"He just glared at Jean," Mann said. "He was so pissed off that he wasn't being taken seriously."

On May 25, 1968, Romain attended a dinner at the home of Paul Ziffren, who was one of California's most powerful Democratic leaders. After eating, Romain quietly talked to his friend Pierre Salinger, who was also at the dinner. Salinger had been John F. Kennedy's former White House press secretary, and was supporting Robert Kennedy's presidential bid on the Democratic ticket.

"You know," Romain commented during the conversation, "your guy will be killed."

Salinger remembers he had pushed the idea of assassination to the back of his mind, but now he was being directly confronted with the possibility. He asked Romain why he thought it may happen.

"He's too irresistible a temptation for the American paranoiac personality," Romain replied, "too much provocation, too rich, too young, too attractive, too happy, too lucky, too successful. He arouses in every 'persecuted' type a deep sense of injustice." Salinger told Kennedy privately about their conversation.

A few days later during an informal gathering at director John Frankenheimer's Malibu beach house, with guests including director Roman Polanski and his wife, actress Sharon Tate, and The Mamas and the Papas singer Cass Elliot, Jean and Romain met with Robert Kennedy. The subject of assassination came up again when Romain asked Kennedy what precautions he was taking to protect himself.

Kennedy shook his head and replied: "There's no way to protect a candidate who's stumping the country. No way at all. You've just got to give yourself to the people and trust them. From then on, it's just that good old bitch luck.

"In any event, you have to have luck on your side to be elected president of the United States. Either it's with you or it isn't. I'm pretty sure there'll be an attempt on my life sooner or later. Not so much for political reasons. I don't believe that. Just plain nuttiness. That's all. There's plenty of that around.

"We live in a time of extraordinary psychic contagion. Someone should make a study of the traumatizing effect caused by the mass media — which dwells on and lives by drama."

Kennedy changed the subject by asking Romain about political affairs in France. Curiously, Kennedy returned to the subject of assassination and asked how many attempts there had been on Charles de Gaulle's life. "Six or seven," Romain answered.

"I told you: luck. You can't make it without that old bitch luck."

Jean, however, was not interested in discussing her husband's theories or Kennedy's assumptions. She brought up pressing matters, including the racial problems, and about the injustices of not only minorities, but of all the underprivileged in the United States.

The topic of conversation lightened, then shifted to the election. "He said he knew he'd lose in Oregon and he didn't think he'd have a chance at the nomination," Jean remembered. When she returned to discussing social problems, Kennedy politely told her he was on vacation. "He sat on the floor, wind-burned in Bermuda shorts and a T-shirt, eating lunch with his dog Freckles," Jean recalled. "It was odd."

Shortly after, Robert Kennedy was indeed assassinated.

17

"The superb thing about Romain was that he created this Frankenstein. He pushed me to develop my own tastes. This inevitably created a conflict. The first full sentence I said as a child was, 'I can do it by my 'lone.' I'll see if I can."
— Jean Seberg

Romain returned home in May 1968 to witness the student riots taking place in Paris. His sympathy with the protesters seemed at odds with his avowed "Gaullism," inspired by personal loyalty to the wartime leader of resistance to the Nazis, and publicly re-affirmed in a newspaper article in June. No stranger to paradox, he had concluded it was time to relinquish the official role as government adviser with which he had become disillusioned.

Meanwhile, Jean and her maid Celia flew to Baker, Oregon in June to commence filming *Paint Your Wagon*. Baker reminded her of Marshalltown, and Jean enjoyed the peacefulness of the small town. Almost rediscovering her roots, Jean marveled that deer came down from the woods to feed, and that a nearby barn reminded her of a Gothic cathedral.

The film takes place in No Name City, basically a community of tents. Once gold is discovered, the commune is transformed into a sprawling town with saloons and bordellos. The greed of a few miners induces them to burrow beneath the timber buildings to recover the gold dust that has fallen between the floorboards. The underground tunnels eventually collapse, bringing down the entire town.

Paint Your Wagon centers on gold-diggers Eastwood and Marvin, who share a wife in Jean. "This is such a big picture," Jean told reporter Joan Barthel. "Even Lee was scared at first. Because in a sense, our careers are all at stake, and it's a very big load, particularly for Lee and Clint. There's less pressure on me because I'm the new-old girl they brought back, although I must say, if I really am bad a second time around, they may not be very forgiving."

With a crew of over 250, Logan was at one point spending in the neighborhood of $80,000 a day. The sets of No Name City were built on a hydraulic system which allowed the buildings to collapse, then spring back up for additional re-takes. It took two months alone for construction crews to build the sets. Traveling to the remote location fifty miles outside of Baker required, at times, three hours by automobile, so Lerner rented two helicop-

The lead actors of Paint Your Wagon: *Ray Walston, Clint Eastwood, Jean, Lee Marvin, and Harve Presnell, 1968.* AUTHOR'S COLLECTION

ters for the main cast and crew. It was reported when the road leading to the filming site was washed out and so badly eroded that the film company paid to have it repaved — forty-six miles at more than $10,000 per mile. There was also a macabre incident which some felt was a bad omen. Members of the crew discovered the wreckage of a small plane near the filming location. Inside were two human skeletons.

At the age of twenty-nine, Jean enjoyed the location and crew so much she commented, "When I was sixteen, I used to tell my parents, 'When I'm thirty I'm going to put a gun to my head.' I was one of those hopeless romantics — Madame Bovary, etc. — and I was going to end it all at thirty because life would be over. Now I'm soon going to be thirty and never before have I enjoyed life so much."

Throughout filming, Jean befriended both cast and crew, with the extras taking turns playing card games with her between scenes. Some of the extras were hippies, who flocked to the set, hoping for a chance to pocket $20 for each day they worked. "Paramount Pictures had put out ads in papers two hundred miles away, wanting the flower people, asking for guys with beards," Ray Walston recalled. "They converged on this town of Baker, with dope in their pockets and their little girlfriends. It became quite a time."

Jean offered food to the hippies as well as the use of her shower, and to wash their clothes with Celia's help. "Never let it be said," she joked, "that Jean Seberg would refuse a hippie a bath. Some of the hippies were pathetic waifs — their minds blown by drugs at 18 — but I found most of them were gentle, articulate people who didn't want to hurt anyone. They just wanted to find some real personal values."

Years later, Jean told a French reporter it was in Oregon "that I saw to what extent drugs can destroy someone. One day, I gave a news article to one of them. At 19 years of age, he had become unable to read a word. He had practically turned off his brain as one would turn off a lamp."

"Quite often I found Jean sitting in the midst of these people on the set," Ray Walston said. "She'd be sitting with all them around her. And she had a guitar and she'd be singing songs. She was really, really so nice and so pleasant to these people. I always felt a great warmth toward her."

"I've been around movie people all my life," remarked one hippie during filming, "and this Jean Seberg is one of the nicest — she seems to have complete empathy with us and the way we look on life." Jean did not think there was anything unusual about the way she acted toward them, but she did sympathize. One Sunday she helped prepare for a hippie wedding, bought a cake, and was matron of honor.

Once reports of Jean's un-starlike behavior leaked to the press, she found herself once again on the defensive. "You'd think I was a charter member of the hippies, the way people reacted to reports from Baker. Everybody talks about gaps — communication gaps, generation gaps, believability gaps. There is really only one gap, and that is a compassion gap. It exists between all of us." She also added: "I'm an incredibly privileged person in getting so many fine breaks. Look at the terribly absurd things people are unfortunately going through today, simply because of the color of their skins."

There were no communication gaps between Jean and Josh Logan, however. She deeply appreciated his choosing her for the role, especially after having missed the opportunity of collaborating with him on *There Was a Little Girl.* "Working with Josh Logan in this film is one of my great experiences," Jean said, "but I keep on thinking there must be other budding Josh Logans out there whose talent must not remain undiscovered. I'm the first to leap when a young director says, 'It's my first picture.'"

The musical aspects of the film did not worry Jean at first. She admitted "a Julie Andrews I am not," and knew Alan Jay Lerner did not want lyrical voices in the film. "That's why he cast Marvin and Eastwood. When they sing, they sound like gold miners — not Nelson Eddy imitating a gold miner."

But when it came time for Jean's one solo song, "A Million Miles Away Behind the Door," she became nervous, and her voice was shaky. Lerner recalled her voice was nice, in fact "almost good enough, but not quite." The decision was made to have her voice dubbed for the number, which was done by Anita Gordon. Lerner went to Jean with the news. "She was unhappy, of course," he said, "but understood."

Jean's singing voice was the least of the problems on the *Paint Your Wagon* shoot. Inclement weather proved a continual hindrance, and Logan's direction struck the three principals as odd. The three felt several shots were ludicrous, especially in one scene in which Jean and Eastwood were so far out in a field they could barely see the camera, on which was mounted a 1,000 mm lens. In fact, after the first few days' rushes were viewed by Alan Jay Lerner and the Paramount heads, Joshua Logan was in danger of being fired.

Ray Walston believed it was only after seeing the footage of the wife auction scene, featuring the three principals — and Walston in his first scene in the film — that the studio decided to continue with Joshua Logan.

"When Paramount saw it, they said, 'Ah, Logan's got it. This is the style — the kind of style of the period,'" Walston divulged. "The next day Josh told me 'You've saved my life. I want to thank you very much. And you also probably saved Alan Jay Lerner's life.' Now, I tell you this because when Joshua Logan cut the picture, that son of a bitch cut me to ribbons." Walston was also told he was to receive first billing below the title; however, in the official credit listing, he appeared after Harve Presnell. "That's Hollywood for you."

Jean developed a positive working relationship with Marvin and Eastwood during the filming. She described Marvin as "an interesting guy, in his own way," despite his heavy intake of alcohol, and became an instant fan of Marvin's special brand of humor. There was a scene where she bends down on the banks of a creek and puts her face into water running over a group of rocks. The cameras rolled. Suddenly, from behind her, someone roared "STOP!" Jean pulled back quickly and saw Lee Marvin.

"My God! What's wrong?" she asked.

"What's wrong?!" declared the half-drunk Marvin. "Don't you realize there are fish fucking in there?"

Everyone within earshot broke into hysterics.

But when the production wore on for more than five months Marvin grew bored and his attitude turned rebellious, spreading chaos. His drinking on the film increased, but Eastwood credits Marvin's companion Michelle Triola for at least attempting to curb his co-star's consumption of alcohol.

Clint Eastwood's career, like Jean's, had been renewed in Europe. After several years on American television with *Rawhide*, his string of Spaghetti

With Clint Eastwood and Joshua Logan on the Paint Your Wagon *shoot, 1968.*
COURTESY OF SNORRAMYNDIR

Westerns with Sergio Leone had made Eastwood an international star. A soft-spoken man with a down-to-earth personality, in Baker Eastwood stayed on a ranch and sometimes helped "slop the pigs." At times Jean assisted. Soon, as often happens between actors on film productions, the two had a discreet affair. This was not just a passing fling, however, and Jean fell deeply in love.

"Jean gave me one of those looks," says Lynda Haupert. "She didn't actually come out and say to me she was having an affair with Clint, but the rolling of the eyes told me. Jean wouldn't come out and say she was sleeping with someone. She might imply it, but she wouldn't say it." When stories of the affair began circulating, Jean said to Eastwood, "People talk if we pet the same pigs together. Perhaps we'd better stop petting pigs."

Diego had already been with Jean in Baker for a summer visit, and Romain stopped by the set in August while on a promotional tour for his novel, *The Dance of Genghis Cohn*. "Jean had a house in Baker," Ray Walston related. "She quite often gave dinner parties and I was invited many, many times. I found her a very charming hostess, in addition to being an extremely gracious young lady. I met Romain Gary at the house several times. Unfortunately for me, I did not get to know him."

Walston recalled Romain's reactions to Lee Marvin at one of Jean's dinner parties. "From the vibrations I felt between Marvin and Romain, it seems Romain was extremely cautious — somewhat wary of the bravado and outlandish talk from Marvin."

Romain returned to Paris, but was not there long before he heard of Jean's affair with Eastwood. He returned to Oregon and confronted Jean in the early morning hours in Alan Jay Lerner's kitchen. Eastwood was summoned to the Lerner house, and at 5:00 A.M., Romain challenged him to a duel. When Eastwood refused, Romain left in a bitter mood. When Romain later spoke to Jean, the couple decided to end their marriage.

On September 16, Romain called Ed and Dorothy Seberg to tell them that he and Jean were separating. He explained to his father-in-law, "I love your daughter, but I'm too old for Jean." Ed and Dorothy were deeply upset by the news, so Romain sent them a telegram:

DEAR FAMILY, YOU HAVE ABSOLUTELY NO RIGHT TO BLAME YOURSELVES FOR ANYTHING. SHALL ALWAYS STAND BY AND PROTECT HER. AFFECTIONATE REGARDS. HOPE TO SEE YOU NEXT SUMMER IN MALLORCA.

The next day, the announcement of the Garys' separation hit the newspapers, the reason given being the conflicts between two different careers on two continents. "After eight years of life and tremendous artistic achievement in France, my wife has become once again a major American star. Her work on *Paint Your Wagon* and forthcoming projects will keep her in the United States for years to come. I have crossed the Atlantic twelve times in three months. In spite of my love for Jean and America, I do not wish to become an exile," Romain stated.

Jean said: "We had eight years of happiness together and our joint concern is the security of our son, and also not to let the unpleasantness that surrounds the divorce damage memories of the past, which are important to both of us."

The grounds for divorce were "abandoning conjugal residence," according to Jean, "which is the most civilized way of getting a divorce in France." The impending divorce was "only the end of a marriage," said Romain. "It is not the end of a union." Obviously his words were more than mere rhetoric. The couple did not rush to dissolve their marriage. In fact, the legal papers were not filed until a year later.

Some felt there were "bedroom problems" between the couple, but Jean quickly dismissed that rumor. "It all depends on the man," she said. "One can be an absolutely wild roamer at seventy, another disinterested in sex at nineteen; and inside this man who is fifty-four is a sixteen-year-old who is very hard to handle."

The Garys' breakup was civil. Jean was to be given custody of Diego, but Romain insisted that the boy should be educated in Europe. To lessen the impact of a broken home on Diego, the rue du Bac apartment was to be divided in half by the installation of a new wall, so that Diego could spend ample time with both parents.

"You can't ask a child to speak three languages and to start first grade in Oregon in English and two months later to take up his French classes," Jean rationalized, citing one of her husband's favorite jokes; "because then he becomes like a chameleon: You put him on green, he turns green; you put him on white, he turns white; you put him on plaid, he explodes." She also admitted, "I'm tired of living a gypsy life. We have a little house in Greece, and property in the south of France, and a house in Majorca — and we're never anywhere. I don't think I'll live in Europe always. You can't ask a man to pack his bags and join you in Klamath Falls or Keokuk or Baker or God knows where."

It was not until 1969, through Joyce Haber and her gossip column, that the true reason for the Garys' break-up became public. Haber simply reprinted in the *Los Angeles Times* an interview Roderick Mann had conducted with Jean in Rome: "I broke up our marriage. I got a crush on someone else and because I'm a bad liar I had to tell Romain about it. I said 'Divorce me.'

"There was no sneakiness about it and that's one of the reasons we've managed to remain friends, I think ...

"He was the absolute opposite of Romain, an outdoor type, a kickback to my days in Iowa, perhaps ... it was marvelous while it lasted."

Haber added: "Who's the other man? I'll give you a clue: It isn't Lee Marvin."

Although Eastwood himself was married, he was also allegedly conducting yet another affair during the *Paint Your Wagon* shoot. An extra claims she had an affair with Eastwood before, during, and after *Paint Your Wagon.* "We had an affair for two years. Since I was involved with Clint at the time, he pulled a few strings and got me work on the film," she confides. When asked if Jean knew about Eastwood's other involvement, the woman says, "No. She had no idea."

Jean thought Eastwood was the type of man who would fit into the tight cliques of both Hollywood and Marshalltown, and was entertaining thoughts of a possible marriage. But Eastwood quite unexpectedly ended

Jean took this photo of her aunt Velma Odegaard and mother Dorothy Seberg lunching with the chauffeur, 1968. COURTESY OF SEBERG FAMILY COLLECTION

the affair. The end of the relationship hurt Jean badly. "She really loved Clint Eastwood," Vony Becker says. "The sad thing," Jean later said in reference to Eastwood, "is that my confidence in [him] was misplaced. It didn't work out."

Eastwood referred to his relationship with Seberg many years later in conversation with his biographer, Richard Schickel: "Jean and I were close buddies.' Pause. 'I really liked her a lot.' Another pause. 'I was kind of nuts about her.' [Eastwood] has had his share of location romances, but this is the one he speaks of most tenderly. It was her fragility and vulnerability that attracted him ... 'She just wanted a peaceful life.'"

Eastwood did not divulge what caused the end of his relationship with Jean Seberg.

In October 1968, the production team left Oregon and returned to Los Angeles and nearby Big Bear to finish the film. That same month Jean's mother and aunt Velma Odegaard visited her in Los Angeles. "How that girl made all those plans," Odegaard marveled. "She had a limousine for us to use, and one day we decided we'd stop traveling and have lunch at Jean's residence. We invited the chauffeur to have lunch with us, but he was hesitant and withdrew. But finally he said, 'I think you really mean it. I have driven many famous people and celebrities, but no one's treated me like you people do.' So he came in and had lunch with us. That's the way Jean always was."

Although Jean's publicist Jerry Pam believes the Eastwood/Seberg affair lasted only in Oregon — "Back in Hollywood it was strictly business and they talked only on the set," Pam said — Jean's aunt remembered Eastwood visiting Jean's home many times during her visit, and having cocktails with him. "He was a gentleman. He just seemed to be a very ordinary guy," Odegaard remembered. "And when Jean took us to the set, she introduced us to everyone, not just Joshua Logan, but to everyone who was working on that set."

Odegaard recalled one day during filming, Lee Marvin "kept flubbing his lines." After a string of profanity, Odegaard said, "He got up and said, 'I know my lines, but I can't say them. I'm done for the day. I'm not doing this anymore!' Then he got up and stormed off the set. I don't know what the problem was." Jean was embarrassed that her family should have witnessed the outburst.

"[Lee Marvin] was full of bullshit and he was a difficult man to work with," Ray Walston felt. "I felt sorry for Jean that she had to put up with that. She had the misfortune, in my opinion, of acting against a performance that was an outlandish piece of work by Lee Marvin." Walston also explained after the production company returned to Los Angeles, "Logan was very disturbed about the picture, but never said anything derogatory about Jean Seberg." The production simply dragged on, testing the patience of everyone involved with the film.

When not working on *Paint Your Wagon*, Jean took her mother and Aunt Velma to various sights around the Los Angeles area, including the Farmer's Market and Disneyland, and to tapings of *Hollywood Palace* and *The Joey Bishop Show* where Sammy Davis, Jr. was a guest. When Davis saw Jean in the audience, he asked her to stand and take a bow. Afterwards, Davis invited Jean and her relatives to dinner. "Sammy Davis, Jr. was such a nice person and so sweet to us," Odegaard remembered.

When columnists tried to link Jean with Sammy Davis, Jr., her humor disappeared. "It's sad that one cannot have men friends without it becoming a juicy bit of news for the columnists," she complained. "Despite all the gossip column stories, there is no other man in my life and I've no intention of marrying again in the foreseeable future."

In late October, French 1968 Olympic triple gold medalist Jean-Claude Killy arrived in Los Angeles to appear in a documentary film. To publicize Killy, it was arranged for him to meet Jean Seberg. Introductions were made while Jean was in costume on the set of *Paint Your Wagon* and the two posed for photographers of their first meeting. Between takes, Killy invited Jean out for dinner. The pair dined at Le Bistro with Jean's mother and aunt. Velma Odegaard admitted drawing a blank when she met the famous athlete. "Jean introduced me to him and said, 'Look at his gold medal.' And that's another thing about Jean," Odegaard added. "She loved to tease and make jokes. She said, 'Ha-ha-ha Jean-Claude. Now see? She doesn't know a thing about you — who you are or your gold medal. You're not so famous!' There was so much of the fun side of her, besides the seriousness."

Jean and Killy met several times during his visit to California: Dancing at The Factory and at The Daisy, appearing together at the world premiere of the Fred Astaire and Petula Clark film *Finian's Rainbow*, and attending the Can-Am races on October 27 in Riverside.

A few days later, the Hollywood trade papers carried an item noting that the pair "were worth watching romantically." "If so — we're the fastest blooming romance on record," Jean heartily laughed to columnist Dorothy Manners. Jean stressed the times she met with Killy was "usually with my aunt and mother present. However," Jean added mischievously, "I'm not saying I may not take up skiing when I return to France."

By November 11, Killy's work in Los Angeles was completed and he immediately flew back to France. Jean remained to finish filming *Paint Your Wagon*, which dragged on until November 17.

"There is no one else in my life, at least no one you'd call someone," Jean wrote Vony Becker in late autumn 1968. "Romain and I have left one another on the best possible terms. I'm leaving empty-handed. I want nothing. Why should I when I can earn my own living? I want only the happiness of Diego, and my one fear is that Romain will take him away from me completely. I love them both, but I was no longer able to live with all the lies. That's all. Nothing's changed."

The "lies" Jean referred to were those of her own and Romain's making, including the secret of their premarital affair and the circumstances surrounding Diego's birth date. There was also the lingering feeling that she had been used by Romain for his own ends. This was not confined to his none-too-subtly basing characters in his novels on her, but also stemmed from the *Birds in Peru* experience. Jean knew that the public would look for real-life correspondences in Romain's work, even when there was none. Romain's cousin Paul Pavlowitch, who knew Jean well, would later name seven of his books which contained characters recognizably based on her.

Despite her intelligence and being perhaps at the peak of her physical beauty, Jean was still alone. Candice Bergen once told her around this time she also had problems finding an acceptable man who felt the same way about her. "I keep going to parties and seeing Mr. Right," Bergen offered.

"But he was always leaving with Mrs. Right."

Since Jean had been spending more time in the US than France over the past year, a reporter asked her if she intended to continue living in Paris. "Not necessarily," she answered. "I love the house I've been leasing here in Beverly Hills and may buy it. It all depends on future assignments in Hollywood. You know, all people from Iowa are crazy about California!" The article concluded: "According to Paramount head Bob Evans, Jean will be back."

Jean never made another picture for Paramount. Within eighteen months, her Hollywood career was finished.

Jean Seberg — Breathless

CHAPTER SIX
1968-1970

*"If I worked in America, I would have to live in either New York or Hollywood,
and I don't especially like either of them."*
— Jean Seberg

*Talking with Marshalltown High School music instructor Stephen Melvin at the dedication
ceremony of Marshalltown's Martha Ellen Tye Playhouse, 1969.* COURTESY OF DALE SMITH

18

"Jean would be lauded today for her stands in politics and society. But back then she was brought down and considered a disgrace."
— Dawn Quinn

Hakim Jamal, born Allen Donaldson in 1931 in Boston's black ghetto, was a man with a mission. He was also an opportunist who discovered it was possible to exploit the guilt feelings of liberal white people. The harsh conditions in which he grew up soon led him into crime, alcoholism and heroin addiction, but it was the influence of childhood hero Black Muslim leader Malcolm X which changed his life and gave him a political sense of purpose. Jamal claimed to be a first cousin of Malcolm X. In reality, it was Jamal's wife Dorothy Durham who was a distant cousin to the charismatic leader assassinated in 1965. Jamal described himself as a part-time member of the Black Panther Party, and he was influential in introducing Hollywood celebrities to the Panthers. Among these were Marlon Brando and Jean Seberg. Jamal established a Malcolm X Foundation to serve as a study and cultural center. He also founded the Montessori school in the Compton area of Los Angeles for underprivileged black children. At one time, the school educated two dozen students.

In the early part of October 1968, Jean Seberg met Jamal on a plane trip to Los Angeles. During the flight she listened to Jamal tell his story, and while she sympathized and praised him for his efforts with the school, she found Jamal was not particularly friendly. He was suspicious and disdainful of whites in general. A few days later, she met him again at a film showing on the education of black children. Again, she had difficulty convincing Jamal that "all whites do not hate blacks."

On October 22, 1968, a fire partially destroyed the Foundation's headquarters in Compton. The fire department concluded that the fire began as the result of a short in the building's electrical system, but Jamal was convinced that the building had been bombed. Jean read about the fire in the newspaper, and once again made the effort to offer her help to Jamal. He now opened up to Jean. Jamal told her he had received death threats, and was afraid for the safety of his wife and children. He then asked her for money and help, which she gladly gave.

"I tried vainly to protect him, his wife and his six children," she said. Jean telephoned Sammy Davis, Jr. in Lake Tahoe where the singer was performing. She started explaining the situation with Jamal, but Davis cut her short. "I don't want to know who these people are," Davis told her, "but take my personal plane and come join me." On the weekend of November 9, Jean, the Jamal family, and her maid Celia joined Davis.

While in Lake Tahoe, Jean dashed off to her mother a promotional card with Sammy Davis, Jr.'s advertisement for his concerts at Harrah's on the front. The note, postmarked November 12, 1968, did not hint at any problems or mention the Jamals. In its entirety the note read: "Dearest Mama — The three of us are having a groovy time here, but wish that you and Aunt Velma the Swinger were with us. Love, Jean and Celia." Davis added "Me too" on the bottom.

By the third day, Jean noted Jamal's children were relaxed and did not feel afraid. But when she was speaking on the telephone one evening, Jean claimed the switchboard operator interrupted the conversation, saying, "I've had enough of those niggers and I'm cutting off the phone." After exchanging words and telling the operator she was racist, Jean decided it would be best if the group left Lake Tahoe. She rented a Cadillac, and Jean claimed that during the two-and-a-half-hour drive back to Los Angeles they were followed by five police cars.

Returning to Los Angeles, Jean invited the Jamals to stay at her home at Coldwater Canyon. One day, Jean rented a limousine and took Dorothy Jamal and her children to Disneyland. She paid for all of the expenses, and bought Mickey Mouse ear-hats for the group, including one for Hakim Jamal. "When we got home, he had fallen asleep," Jean recalled. "The kids took off the African cap he wore and put on his new hat."

She could see a positive change in Jamal, which she felt was of her doing. "Hakim is beginning to understand that there are some whites who are concerned," Jean said. Soon after, Jean began introducing Jamal to her Hollywood friends in an effort to raise money for the Montessori school.

To those who met him Jamal seemed charming, but also arrogant. Many did not even feel safe while he was in the same room with them. One night, Jean and Jamal went to a dinner at the home of Paul and Mickey Ziffren to solicit a donation for the school. Jamal was wearing a gun. Mrs. Ziffren remembers she was horrified and asked him to remove it before going in to dinner.

Jamal had reason to fear for his life. By 1968, the FBI had infiltrated the majority of black groups through COINTELPRO, the organization's counterintelligence program. With the FBI's "divide and conquer" policy, the penetrating agents provoked dissension and rivalries between several black groups, including the Black Panther Party.

The Black Panther Party had been founded in 1967 by Bobby Seale and Huey Newton. Its ten-point program promised to break "the oppressive grip of the white power structure on the black community" and "all oppressed people inside the United States." Panthers were introduced to the public in photographs wearing black berets, carrying guns at their sides, and saluting with hands clenched in a fist aimed at the sky. By 1968, the party's members were numbered in the thousands. In a matter of months, most every state in the union had Black Panther Party branch offices, including Iowa.

The Panthers were the first blatantly to reject the notion of nonviolence. Their openly Marxist organization and forthright revolutionary agenda was in marked contrast to Dr. Martin Luther King, Jr.'s peaceful demonstrations and the reform-minded Southern Christian Leadership Conference.

The official newspaper of the organization, called *The Black Panther*, regularly stated that the party advocated the use of guns and guerrilla tactics in its revolutionary program to end oppression of the black people. Residents of the black community were urged to arm themselves against the police (consistently referred to by the newspaper as "pigs"). A number of members believed the police personnel should be replaced by strictly law-abiding officers; if not, they should be killed.

In the September 7, 1968 edition of the newspaper, an article by then-Black Panther Party Minister of Education, George Murray, ended with: "Black men. Black people, colored persons of America, revolt everywhere! Arm yourselves. The only culture worth keeping is a revolutionary culture. Change. Freedom everywhere. Dynamite! Black power. Use the gun. Kill the pigs everywhere."

Future editions of the newspaper contained such threats by the party as "We will not dissent from American government. We will overthrow it," and the Black Panther's Minister of Culture Emory Douglas's: "The only way to make this racist US government administer justice to the people it is oppressing is ... by taking up arms against this government, killing the officials, until the reactionary forces ... are dead, and those that are left turn their weapons on their superiors, thereby passing revolutionary judgment against the number one enemy of all mankind, the racist US Government."

After Huey Newton was found guilty of manslaughter of an Oakland policeman in September 1968, American youth — of all races — rallied in "Free Huey" demonstrations. The conviction brought the Panthers into the national spotlight, and, through the mass media, into the homes of most every American.

A group of white liberals called Friends of the Panthers, headed by Shirley Sutherland and author Don Freed, sponsored a benefit for Huey's defense. Jamal attended, spoke with Bobby Seale, and arranged for him to visit with Jean Seberg.

The two met at her Coldwater Canyon house on November 17, 1968. Vanessa Redgrave was a house guest of Jean's when the two men visited, and she listened with Jean as Seale spoke. Jean felt the Black Panther Party's attempts to set up a free breakfast program for poverty-stricken children was not only a worthy cause, but organized and practical. She made a financial donation to the program, since the wellbeing of children was always a major concern to her. This was the first and only time Jean Seberg saw Bobby Seale.

With Thanksgiving approaching, Jean left California for a family reunion in Marshalltown. While there, a reporter from France-Soir flew to Marshalltown to interview her. Jean spoke about the social unrest in Los Angeles and her own concern for the safety of friends there. She also told the reporter she was beginning a cause called "Operation Love" to prove to minorities that not all whites are "blue-eyed devils" and that harmony could exist between all races. The reporter noticed the worry in the eyes of Ed and Dorothy Seberg, concern for a daughter who appeared to be "caught up in things they don't understand."

"Hakim thinks that he doesn't have a chance for survival. I hope with all my heart that he is wrong," she told the reporter. "But what I will say is that if he is killed, or his wife or one of his children, I will understand the anger of the blacks and will participate in the violence. I'm ashamed to admit it, for I don't think that [violence is] the answer to our problems." Several days later, France-Soir headlined: "ACTRESS JEAN SEBERG MENACED: IN THE UNITED STATES SHE HARBORED A BLACK AND HIS FAMILY, THE COUSIN OF THE ASSASSINATED EXTREMIST LEADER MALCOLM X."

Eventually, Jean grew disenchanted with Jamal and the Montessori school, believing that his tactics and her time, as well as her money, had done little to improve conditions in his programs. Although she continued to recruit other support for Jamal, the Black Panthers' breakfast program became Jean's primary concern. Because of this switch in alliances Jamal felt betrayed and vowed revenge on Jean.

"She was interested in what we were about — what was our program. Nobody ever asked us," recalled Panther member Elaine Brown, who became a close friend of Jean's. "She was not interested in giving cocktail parties for us. She was not interested in doing another number on us and being able to go there to her friends in Iowa somewhere and say, you know, 'Look at this — Black Panthers!' That was chic in those days. [But] she wanted to do something."

"Jean had her own ideals. She simply believed what she was taught in Marshalltown, embodied in the words about freedom and equality found in the Declaration of Independence," Brown later said. "To me, Jean seemed a free spirit and a true believer."

Jean began giving money to the Black Panther cause in incremental amounts, up to several thousand dollars at a time. Discreet arrangements were made whenever Jean wished to make a contribution. She would telephone, simply leaving a message using the pseudonym "Aretha" (after singer Aretha Franklin, the Queen of Soul). Then, an envelope with cash would be delivered, in several instances to the house of Elaine Brown's mother.

"Jean felt if she was known as a major contributor to the party, she would not get work in Hollywood, and would not, in turn, have the resources to continue," Brown recalls. "It was logical."

After having left for France a few weeks before, and not planning to return to the US until May, Jean-Claude Killy reappeared in Los Angeles and spent several days with Jean. It was noted in the press that the couple had been seen on December 9 at the Club Daisy, and there were whispers they were secretly engaged, a claim never substantiated. During their reunion, the pair also dined at the Italian restaurant Matteo, visited Malibu

With Romain, Diego and Sandy, 1968. COURTESY OF SNORRAMYNDIR

beach, and spent two days in Aspen, Colorado. They finally parted company when Killy returned to France on business.

In mid-December Jean jetted to Paris to spend the holidays with Diego and Romain. *France-Soir* reported her arrival at Orly airport. She was met by Romain, Diego, who gave her a bouquet of flowers, and Sandy the dog. It was noted in the periodical that Jean's luggage was lost in Los Angeles, which "irritated her considerably."

In an arrangement as unconventional-sounding today as it was then, the separated couple had decided to remain at the same rue du Bac apartment they had shared through the better part of a decade. With the new wall in the middle of the twelve-room residence, the dwelling was now divided into two self-contained units. "Since we had only one kitchen [for a time]," Jean remarked, "we met for meals quite often."

During the few short weeks in Paris they undoubtedly discussed her activism. In *White Dog*, Romain wrote about the disagreements they had had:

"All I'm saying is that you do more harm than good, because a movie star who moves in on a tragic reality always gives it an unreal touch, that Hollywood something."

"Listen, Romain, that's a too-Goddamn-sophisticated point of view. There's a school with thirty kids in it and let me tell you that their black reality is of a kind even Hollywood can't make unreal ... It's worth it. I mean, it's worth looking laughable, it's worth all the irony and the columnists' ha-ha-ha and it's worth all the bullshit, period.

"I know there's that ghastly 'film star,' movie touch about everything I try to do. I'll just stop making movies."

"If you stop being a film star, you won't need to find excuses for being Jean Seberg, the film star, and you'll probably feel no need to help them."

"Because that's my only motivation?"

"Jeannie, let's get away from it. Let's both get away. You've lived ten years in Paris. You're French by marriage."

"I'll feel, live, love, and stink American until I drop dead. I can't be anything but an American, you know that, you've just got to scratch the surface ..."

Hakim Jamal was known not to let any of his contacts lie fallow. In January 1969, he left Los Angeles en route to Europe, primarily Paris, and specifically to Jean Seberg. His trip did not go unnoticed by the FBI, as noted in Jamal's FBI file: "[It is] recommended that the Crimes Records Division attempt to place information with a reliable press contact relative to actress Jean Seberg's relationship with Abdullah Jamal." In addition, the following was typed for alleged release to the press: "It was a cold day in January when American actress Jean Seberg met her tall, dark friend at Orly airport outside Paris. The warmth of the greeting suggested something more than a business relationship. He is Hakim Jamal, a black activist from Los Angeles. A few days later, they turned up in London, where Jamal appeared on television. Now she is back in the USA, but he lingers on in London. What is going on?"

A query penciled in at the bottom of this page read: "Did Mr. Hoover approve doing this?" J. Edgar Hoover wrote in response, "I did not. Such matters should always be approved by [Clyde] Tolson or me."

By January 17, 1969, Jean was back in California. The FBI reported that on that date she appeared at the International Typographical Union in Los Angeles. The union was considering expelling Hakim Jamal from membership for failure to pay union dues. Jean paid his outstanding union fees by personal check, reportedly in excess of $200.

Jean was also in the film capital preparing to film *Airport*. Adapted from Arthur Hailey's best-selling novel, *Airport* tells of an attempt by a mentally disturbed passenger to blow up an aircraft in flight. This happens against a background of a soap-style mix of personal crises and administrative nightmares experienced by the airport staff in the course of a working day. The all-star project featured Burt Lancaster, Dean Martin, George Kennedy, Jacqueline Bisset, Helen Hayes, Maureen Stapleton, Van Heflin, and Dana Wynter. George Seaton was signed to direct and Ross Hunter was the producer.

Hunter, who had established himself with many hit films (including *Pillow Talk* and *Thoroughly Modern Millie*), did not initially envision Jean Seberg in *Airport*. He had wanted Angie Dickinson to play the role of Tanya Livingston, the character in charge of public relations at the airport. Universal, however, insisted Jean should be cast in the role, since she had a pay-or-play two-picture contract with the studio. In addition, her name would help the film's sale in the international market.

Jean knew of Universal's request and that Hunter did not want her in the film. This, together with the impressive roll of actors already signed for the film, added to her nervousness. Hunter said he and Jean eventually became great friends, "But only after I'd convinced her I was genuinely happy to have her in the cast." Hunter explained to her that she was not the only person in the film who had not been his first choice. Both Thelma Ritter and Jean Arthur had been selected to play Ada Quonsett before Helen Hayes was signed — and later won an Academy Award for her performance.

Jean's contract for *Airport* was the most lucrative of her career: $150,000, plus $1,000 a week in expenses for sixteen weeks, and a studio car at her disposal for the duration of the filming. After Lancaster and Martin, Jean received third billing, which is indicative of her standing in the film market at that time.

Whereas Martin and Lancaster received a percentage of the profits from the film, Jean did not. This was in part due to the combination of Hollywood sexism and her agent's negotiations over the studio's offers. As with all of her American films, she was given a straight salary, preventing her or her estate from making a claim to a share in any additional profits generated from future television, cable, or video/DVD sales.

Like many of her American roles, the part Jean had been given turned out to be a disappointment for her. When not standing next to Lancaster in the airport offices, she was chasing Helen Hayes, a smart and unassuming stowaway. Financial considerations apart, working with Hayes was one of the few rewards she derived from the film. "Helen Hayes reminded Jean of our grandmother," says Mary Ann Seberg, "and the role was something like our grandmother would have done." As her mother remembered, "Jean always idolized Helen Hayes as a teenager. She used to say if she could be half as good as she, it would be just wonderful."

Jean gave her high school drama teacher Carol Hollingsworth an autographed copy of Helen Hayes' autobiography in which Hayes inscribed to Hollingsworth: "Thank you for giving Jean such beautiful diction."

Location filming commenced at the Minneapolis-St. Paul International Airport in January 1969. Most of the cast and crew jetted to Minnesota, but Dean Martin, who played the principal pilot, took a train because he did not fly.

Problems with the production began almost immediately. John Findlater, a film actor who also spent two years on television's *Peyton Place*, played a Trans Global Airline ticket checker, and remembers the production. "We went to Minnesota for the snow," he says. "But there wasn't any snow. It had to be brought in."

Filming took place at night — "All night," Findlater says — until the morning sun began to rise. Interior shots of the airport's terminal were filmed, and several hours were spent on exterior scenes of the snow-covered runways in temperatures plunging to a wind chill of 43F degrees below zero. At times, the film froze in the cameras, thus slowing the schedule, and the cast and crew, despite wearing face masks, suffered in the cold. "I think it went rather smoothly, considering," Findlater concludes.

Money was not a problem for the $10 million production. "In a Ross Hunter production you are guaranteed there will be a certain polish to the film — which is a contradiction to many of my European films," Jean remarked. For greater authenticity, Hunter rented a $7.5 million Boeing 707 at $18,000 a day. The three calfskin, sable-lined coats designed by Edith Head which Jean wore ("trimmed with wolverine fur because snow won't stick to that," the designer elucidated) cost $2,000 each — two for Jean, in case of accidents, and one for her stand-in. Privately, however, Jean disliked the Head designed gray mini-skirted uniform she wore in the film, feeling it made her look like a clown.

Since Marshalltown is only a five-hour drive south of the Twin Cities, Jean made a quick trip home during a break in filming. "About 3:30 in the morning Mom heard the doorbell ring," recalls Mary Ann, "and she and my father went to the door. Jean and Celia had flown from Minneapolis to Waterloo and a cabdriver had driven them to Marshalltown. And Jean said to the cabdriver, 'Oh, come on in. Mom will make you breakfast.' So he came in and Mom made breakfast for them at 3:30 in the morning." She added, "I don't think my parents were upset. They were just happy to have her home for a visit."

After location scenes were completed in Minnesota, the *Airport* cast and crew moved to California, where a damaged Boeing was brought into Universal Studios for the filming of the jet's interior scenes. Before filming his scenes with her, John Findlater thought Jean Seberg was "a gorgeous sex symbol. When I was young enough to go crazy over sex symbols, I always though of her as being this sexy gal.

"She was almost like a Brigitte Bardot, although Jean wasn't running around naked all the time. That's how I perceived her. I thought, 'Wait until I work with her — she's going to be fabulous.'"

Filming a scene in Airport *with Burt Lancaster, John Findlater and Helen Hayes, 1969.*
AUTHOR'S COLLECTION

But when Findlater first met Jean Seberg he found his preconception was wide of the mark. "She was totally different. She had already been out, and she was having problems with Romain Gary. She was sort of frail and lonely at the time. She was very shy on this picture; she had a hard time on it.

"One scene we did together was with Helen Hayes and Burt Lancaster. Jean was giving Helen Hayes hell for stowing away on a plane." The scene, which lasts less than nine minutes in the finished film, took four days to shoot. "Jean was very nervous," Findlater recalls. "Helen Hayes was nervous, too. I don't know why. I was having a ball because I didn't have that much to do." In this scene Hayes was required to nibble on a sandwich. By the end of one day's filming she had consumed two heaped platefuls of chicken salad sandwiches. When it came time to break for dinner, however, the diminutive Hayes still had room for a serving of roast ham.

"The delays upset Lancaster — everybody wanted to get the picture done. It could be translated as a lack of professionalism, and people could get mad. Nobody got mad at Jean. No one was upset with her. Everyone was nice to her, and she was nice to everybody." The filming of her other scenes with Findlater, however, went smoothly.

When acting with Jean, Findlater was surprised to find she was not a stylized or a method actress. "She gets bigger and better pictures," Findlater thought to himself. "She keeps getting these great pictures, but not very good reviews. How does she do it?" Findlater also feels Jean was uncomfortable when "the [talent] agents came around. From their point of view, she was just being cooperative."

Jean also became a close friend and a great admirer of Maureen Stapleton during the filming. "Jean told me, 'Now there's a real actress,'" recalls Marshalltown friend Roger Maxwell. "Maureen could cry on-cue, and then when the scene was over, she'd immediately be laughing. Jean was very impressed."

Stapleton viewed Jean as "a misplaced saint." One evening she was at Jean's house when Hakim Jamal telephoned. Stapleton saw her "getting more and more agitated. Tears were in her eyes." Jean gave her the receiver so that she could listen to Jamal's appeal on behalf of his cause. Stapleton listened momentarily, then interrupted Jamal. "I told him 'You're a sonofabitch. Jean is working her ass off for you people, and you don't appreciate it,'" Stapleton said. "'Go out and get a real job, then I'll talk to you.' Jean wasn't too happy that I talked to him like that, but I couldn't help it. They all were using her."

"Oh my God, oh my God," Stapleton recalled Jean saying as she handed her back the receiver. "She was shivering into the phone, and you know what the guy said to her? 'Who was that woman who just cut me up? I like her.' But the guy was a shit. He abused Jean by taking advantage of her and her connections and then sticking it to her."

"She apparently didn't have a friend [in Los Angeles]," John Findlater believes. "I think she was alone a lot. I feel she had relationships with people here that were social. That didn't interest her because they were not deep — doing lunch or meeting with agents.

"Jean was always 'Can you help me?,' 'Can you be there for me?,' or 'Can I stand with you?' She needed a man, I guess. Someone strong to be with. I always saw it like that, and I guess I was the one on that picture. I wasn't exactly Clint Eastwood," Findlater adds, pointing out that his friendship with Jean was platonic.

While filming continued on *Airport*, Jean attended the Academy Awards ceremony at the Dorothy Chandler Pavilion on April 14, and made plans the same month for a fundraising party to benefit Hakim Jamal's Montessori school. James Bacon, a writer for the *Los Angeles Herald-Examiner*, recalled

Jean telephoning industry people she didn't know and inviting them to the event: "I am Jean Seberg, an actress. I don't know whether you have heard of me or not, but I would like to invite you to a fundraiser I am holding…"

"What we are striving to do," she told Bacon, "is to raise enough money to make it available to ghetto children who need it the most. As you know, the Montessori system was founded in Italian slums, but in this country, it is only for the children of the well-to-do." In his article Bacon observed ironically that Jean's initiative "sounds like a kind of Midwest neighborliness."

The fundraiser was held in her Coldwater Canyon home on April 16. Two rooms were filled with the celebrities who came to the house. Paul Newman and Joanne Woodward attended, as did Jane Fonda and Lee Marvin, with Vanessa Redgrave in the company of her lover Franco Nero. The event raised a few thousand dollars, not counting a $5,000 contribution from Jean's Marshalltown friend Bill Fisher.

Jean's Coldwater Canyon house also became a regular stomping ground for the Panthers, while Jean continued giving her time — and money — to everything from the group's Free Breakfast Program in Los Angeles to paying hospital bills for the delivery of babies. She was trying "to be a friend, and a good one."

"I'd watched her with this Black Panther thing," John Findlater says, "and I'd known she was having some publicity on her love life and her political life, so I thought of her as a 'Jane Fonda-type.' Besides being a pretty girl and an actor, she was involved in things political. Everybody [on the set] said she was going through something in her personal life. She was upset about what was going on in her life. Romain Gary's name kept coming up a lot during these problems. I don't know if he was a problem or if he was good for her. I just know his name would come up in regard to all of this."

Findlater and George Seaton had done a lot of comedy work in their careers. In an effort to help Jean relax and get her mind off whatever was troubling her, Seaton would conjure Findlater to perform a "little comedy shtick to get her to laugh and to lighten up the set." Jean laughed with each performance, but the effect soon wore off.

Ross Hunter recalled Jean going through "very traumatic times" during the filming. "There's no doubt [it] was an extremely difficult period for her. Many times the press wasn't kind to her. She was going through a great deal of agony and suffering, both personally and physically, although she never tried to let it show. She was always there, always trying."

Times were indeed traumatic for Jean. Apart from her problems with Romain and her involvement with the Panthers and the Montessori school, she knew there were blacks within those organizations who were either jealous of or disgruntled with the extreme elements with which Jean was involving herself. She also felt she was being spied upon, not only by black members of the organizations who questioned her sincerity, but also by the FBI.

Ross Hunter recalled Jean's fears when he received several 3:00 A.M. phone calls from her. "Many nights when she'd be so frightened she'd come sleep on the couch at my home," he said. "She always very sweet, very professional, very thoughtful. She was like a broken sparrow, but a terrific gal, right down the line."

This was also a busy time, especially May 1969. The first weekend of the month, she jetted back to Paris to visit Diego. ("I can't stay away from there for a very long time.") She undoubtedly also saw Romain during her brief stay.

According to Jean's FBI files, on May 7, 1969, while the Los Angeles police were arresting a mentally disturbed individual, Hakim Jamal and Jean were observed standing behind some bushes across the street from the place of arrest. Jamal was taking photographs of the officers with a camera equipped with a telephoto lens.

A few days later, Jean was back in Marshalltown. The Fisher family dedicated a theater to the community named after Bill Fisher's sister, Martha Ellen Tye. The state-of-the-art playhouse was to provide a worthy environment for plays and musicals, since Marshalltown had previously lacked adequate premises for such entertainment. To show her appreciation toward Bill Fisher, Jean took a three-day break from filming *Airport* and arrived in Marshalltown just one hour before the dedication ceremony.

With her hair pulled back and cascading to her shoulders, Jean's delicate beauty was evident, and the low-necked, robe-like gown she wore accentuated her features, especially the high cheekbones. "I owe everything to Bill Fisher and Carol Hollingsworth," she said from the podium to the black-tie audience. Jean then read portions of an essay by Mark Twain. "You know," she later said, "he wrote some very sharp protest things …

"[The readings] refute the Darwinian Theory that man has evolved to a higher order. Twain was very pessimistic about that. I sort of shook [the audience], I suppose. I thought it might be interesting to show them that protesting is not something new."

It is doubtful many of those in the audience understood Jean's reason for selecting the piece. "While we were, of course, glad Jean could be there, none of us could hear because she spoke too softly, and it was a difficult piece for the audience to follow at best," recalled Sandy Schlesinger, a Marshalltown acquaintance of the Seberg family.

"Marshalltown is beautiful this time of year," Jean told television and news reporters who were covering the event. She was also happy to be home to celebrate Mother's Day, and with Mary Ann and her family visiting from New Jersey, the family was together for the first time since David Seberg's death.

During the short visit, Jean drove around Marshalltown and was surprised her hometown had "gone hip." On the courthouse lawn, several hippies, varying in age from their teens up to thirty, gathered day and night. Some congregated there to converse; others met to purchase drugs. "But the drug use there on the lawn was conservative," one Marshalltown residents remembers. "It was a strange time. God-fearing people would slowly drive their cars by the lawn to gawk at the hippies, disgusted at the scene. Then at night these same people would go to a bar across the street and drink all

With Mary Ann, Ed, Grandma Frances Benson, Dorothy, and Mary Ann's daughter Sara holding Misty, 1969. COURTESY OF SEBERG FAMILY COLLECTION

night. They made no attempt to understand the hippies, and just shook their heads while getting smashed themselves. And there were 'prominent, upstanding citizens' who'd buy pot from the hippies, then go off to hobnob at the country club."

Returning to Los Angeles, Jean reunited with and received a gift from Jean-Claude Killy. Although the whirlwind romance with the skier did not progress as far as she might have wished, she did confide in Vony Becker. "She loved Killy very much," Becker says, "and he bought her a small car as a gift." Killy ordered the car from Detroit especially for Jean. "It's kind of crinkly green with all kinds of do-dads on it," Jean said. "And I don't have any insurance on it ..."

Jean also continued to help the Panthers and the Jamal family. That month she gave Hakim Jamal a personal check for $5,000, and on May 14, Jamal used it to open a checking-and-savings account at the City National

Jean Seberg — Breathless

Bank. By now, according to the FBI, Jean had contributed at least $10,500 to the Black Panther Party. The Bureau also reported that, two days later, on May 16, Jean arranged for the Panthers to view Costa-Gavras' film *Z*, which the Panthers were to receive sometime between July 3 and July 6. Jean proposed the group should raise bail money for imprisoned Panthers by playing the film, and she received permission from Costa-Gavras for the film to be shown in preview at universities. The print, however, was "lost" in customs and never recovered.

Jean's professional career was moving forward. The whispers concerning *Airport* were that it was going to be a blockbuster, and her next film, for director Nelo Risi, was to be made in Italy. While completing *Airport*, Jean was interviewed by Nathan Fain, a reporter for the *Houston Post*. Fain noted that Jean "shuffles images of herself like a blackjack dealer. She sits not far from the Universal Studios administration tower, which she jokes is what Stanley Kubrick's sphinx was in *2001: A Space Odyssey*. The much-interviewed Miss Seberg arrived late and apologetic, cool to see and warm of voice. She's beautiful. She ordered a salad, adding her life had been 'one long diet.'"

Jean told Fain she was looking forward to starring in Carlo Ponti's film *The Blue Planet*, in which she would play the widow of an astronaut who discovers areas of research to benefit mankind. "She tries to do something useful herself," Jean said, noting that no one had yet done a film about a woman who "rebels against the public widow image." Unfortunately for her, however, the plan fell through.

Jean's private life was as inconstant as her career. She had received many "offers" from men, including one from a Texas millionaire who invited her to his house because he liked the film *Lilith*. Jean declined. On the lighter side, however, Jean was seen speaking with Jack Webb at one of the few Hollywood parties she attended. Webb was the star of TV's *Dragnet*, and it was an open secret in the industry that he had remained a virgin most of his life. In a mischievous mood, Jean flirted with Webb and managed to entice him to nibble on her ear, if only momentarily.

In the close-knit Hollywood community Jean still felt lonely, realizing she had very few true friends in Los Angeles. When costume designer Edith Head threw a party for the cast of *Airport* Jean did not have an escort, so she telephoned John Findlater. "I really don't know anybody," she confessed to her co-star, "and I don't want to go alone. I want to go with a man. If you're not going with anyone, can I go with you?" Findlater told her he would be happy to take her to the party. After they hung up, he felt sorry for Jean. He always felt that, even if he had a date, he would have also taken Jean to the party because "she sounded so sad and frightened."

After Findlater picked Jean up at her Coldwater Canyon house, she asked him to go to the Beverly Hills Hotel to get Maureen Stapleton, who also needed a ride. The trio arrived at the party, where a mock-up of the 707 was prominently displayed. Jean danced with Ross Hunter and was greeted by actress Greer Garson and others while she sat a table with Jacqueline Bisset. Jean wore a Mexican dress and captivated everyone with her poise and beauty. "Jean was still very quiet, wasn't flashy, very reserved, and very sweet the whole time," Findlater remembers. "She looked dynamite. I've always remembered that."

19

"What little glamour I've seen in this glamorous business I've hated."
— Jean Seberg

In June 1969, G.C. Moore, the FBI official in charge of surveillance of extremist groups, recommended that "an active discreet investigation be instituted on American actress Jean Seberg who is providing funds and assistance to black extremists, including leaders in the Black Panther Party." A photograph and personal information about her was distributed to FBI field offices throughout the country, and the Immigration and Naturalization Service was instructed to search her luggage each time she left or entered the United States. Among others, the FBI list also included Shirley Sutherland, Jane Fonda, and Vanessa Redgrave. J. Edgar Hoover now regarded the Black Panthers as the single greatest threat to the internal security of the United States.

In *White Dog*, Romain Gary alludes to incidents in Jean's life during her civil rights activities: threatening phone calls; a pistol planted on a table in her house; and her cats mysteriously poisoned. Diego recalled the latter: "I was six when our cats were poisoned in Los Angeles. We adored those animals — that left its mark on me." Romain wondered if these things were the work of disgruntled Panther members. Jean felt it was the FBI.

When Jean left for Italy to film *Ondata di calore* (*Dead of Summer*), the FBI's Los Angeles office alerted the Washington headquarters that "subject departed Los Angeles one P.M. June Nine instant via TWA flight eight forty for Rome, Italy. Seberg exchanged Los Angeles to Paris ticket for one way ticket to Rome and is traveling under the name Mrs. J. Gary. Seberg reportedly will stay at the Excelsior Hotel in Rome.

"Bureau requested advise legat, Paris and Rome."

On June 16, 1969, the FBI placed on Jean Seberg an Immigration and Naturalization Service (INS) F-3 Stop, a notification procedure to track an individual's arrival into and departure out of the United States.

In the third week of June, the *Dead of Summer* crew left for location filming in Morocco. The film tells of a schizophrenic woman whose unhappy marriage reaches crisis point when she discovers her husband's penchant for young North African boys. Alone in their luxurious apartment in Agadir, she is on the verge of a breakdown and haunted by violent nightmares. At the end of a period of twenty-four hours, in which she struggles to make sense of her experience, she discovers that her husband is dead, and that she herself is the killer. "Morocco is a sad country," Jean wrote a friend. "The people live so terribly poorly and without much hope at all. It was very hot and dusty when we were there."

According to Jean's FBI files, a Panther member attempted to contact her in Azazik, Morocco. When the telephone operator told her that there was no such place, the Panther offered she may have the wrong spelling and would check it on a map. The Panther member did not try to make contact a second time.

As the film continued production into July, Jean found more cysts in her breasts and flew to Paris for a second operation. Fortunately, the cysts were benign, but her illness was a setback for director Nelo Risi, and because of rising costs he decided to take the production back to Rome. While recuperating, Jean wrote her parents on July 19 from the rue du Bac apartment: "I'm in very good shape, but the surgery had to be done as I had a local infection while in Morocco and it would have probably recurred during the months to come.

"Daddy, the sickness I have is a hormonal imbalance called recluse sickness, wherein my body tends to produce cysts, either mammary or ovarian. Most doctors are very much against a treatment with male hormones because of the unpleasant side effects. They removed many tiny cysts clustered together this time — the same as three years ago. Anyway, my general health is excellent, but I am a little tired — it's been two years of constant work as you know… In less than six weeks I've been from the U.S. to Rome to Majorca, back to Rome, to Paris, to Morocco to work, to Paris and now again to Rome. Too much chasing around!"

Jean rejoined the production and rented a villa on the outskirts of Rome for the remainder of filming. The villa was rumored to have been the love nest of Elizabeth Taylor and Richard Burton while filming *Cleopatra*. Diego visited for a couple of weeks, at which time Ed and Dorothy Seberg also flew in for a few days. Filming prevented Jean from seeing much of her parents, but they did make a visit to Venice and to the movie set. The Sebergs were surprised to find that Diego had mastered French, Spanish, and Italian, but spoke little English. It was not the kind of reunion any of them hoped for.

Foremost among their concerns was the state of their daughter's health. They witnessed first-hand how the physically and psychologically demanding role affected Jean, pushing her to a state of chronic fatigue. They also noticed she was taking sleeping pills at night.

Despite the ten-day delay Jean's illness had caused, *Dead of Summer* was completed in August. She was extremely satisfied with the results and it eventually became the film from the second half of her career she liked best. *Variety* applauded Jean's "tour-de-force performance ... On screen without respite from beginning to end, Miss Seberg thesps in virtuoso style... [a] grandslam performance."

"*Dead of Summer* is a one-woman show, a Seberg celebration," wrote Vincent Canby in the *New York Times*. "She is one of the movies' most interesting objects ... her beauty has 'set,' like plaster of Paris, attaining, curiously, a new perfection in definition as it has hardened. She moves with style, which is sometimes awkward, and behind that extraordinary mask, there is real intelligence."

Unfortunately, the film was not widely distributed. In the United States it played for only one week in New York.

After her parents left and Diego returned to Romain, melancholy set in, as Jean told columnist Roderick Mann: "Always in the back of my mind is the romantic belief in the perfect relationship, in the ideal family life. Right now I'm forcing myself to live in a kind of deep freeze. I run away if I see someone. Perhaps I've just become overly cautious from having hurt and been hurt, and finally realizing that love is not some sort of a game."

On August 22, the FBI circulated information on Jean Seberg to the Los Angeles Secret Service, the US Army division in Pasadena, and OSI, Morton Air Force Base. The sources providing information were kept confidential because, in the words of the FBI — more than thirty-five years after the fact — the identification "could adversely affect the internal security of the United States." The FBI requested "appropriate investigation be conducted to determine Jean Seberg's current whereabouts and her activities."

Jean spent the remainder of summer 1969 in "cool but sunny" Majorca with Diego and Romain. Romain wanted their marriage to continue, but, after all of the things she had experienced in the past few months, Jean needed rest more than anything. "Goodness, I'm glad that film's over," Jean wrote her parents during the vacation:

"I have never been so worn out — I'm just sorry you had to see me that way, as I know it upset you. I am beginning to feel human again, for the first time in a long while — sleeping regular hours with no pills, et al., and trying to lose some weight. So far, I've knocked off about four pounds.

"The days here just drift by. I don't do anything — makes me feel very guilty, as I'm just not used to it. Romain works awfully hard and seems happy as can be here. But if you're not a writer or painter, I should think one would get restless on this endless 'vacation.' At least, I'm beginning to squirm a little."

During the vacation, Jean and Romain discussed Diego's schooling, finding that the boy had fallen behind in his studies. Jean was convinced one of the reasons for this was her son's confusion of languages. Diego mostly spoke Spanish because he had spent a lot of time in Spain with his nanny Eugenia. Also, Jean noted her son was "never being left to play or concentrate on his own for even a few minutes." Diego was immediately given private lessons, and Romain warned Eugenia that if his son's studies did not make progress, Diego would be sent to a private school in Switzerland.

"I hope that'll make Eugenia realize how serious we consider all of this," Jean wrote her parents. "He's bright and there's no reason for it except bad working habits." The problem cleared and Diego remained in Paris the fol-

Appearing on The Dick Cavett Show *with guest Mort Sahl, 1969.*
COURTESY OF INDEPENDENT VISIONS

lowing year. But the vacation did not result in reconciliation for the Garys, and Jean filed for divorce in September. That same month Jean returned to the US to make a rare television appearance on *The Dick Cavett Show*. She appeared happy and friendly, without a hint of disappointment over the failure of her marriage, or the long-anticipated release of *Paint Your Wagon*, which was set for the following month.

When the time came for the *Paint Your Wagon* premiere on October 15 in New York, Jean was asked to attend. She politely declined, citing illness as the reason — "mostly exhaustion from doing four pictures in a row with only about two weeks rest."

This was true, but not the whole truth. In fact, there was also an element of disappointment. Jean had seen a cut of the film earlier and felt too many opportunities for humor had been wasted. "I haven't seen the final version," she wrote Dawn Quinn at the time. "Now, the public and critics shall have their say! I have mixed feelings." In addition, Maggie and Clint Eastwood attended the premiere. Jean did not want to be put into an uncomfortable situation, seeing her former lover with his wife.

The public, however, responded favorably to *Paint Your Wagon*. The film brought a new generation of Jean Seberg fans with the public and critics alike, with most noting Jean's beauty. Vincent Canby revealed: "… age is giving Miss Seberg a kind of gutsy quality that only makes her beauty more interesting. It's somewhat startling to hear the waif of *Breathless* break into song…"

"If *Wagon* isn't the best of all possible worlds, it comes as close as a Western musical can," the *Los Angeles Times* offered. "It's entertaining enough, hilarious enough and poignant enough to keep Lee Marvin, Clint Eastwood and Jean Seberg on the movie star map…Jean Seberg is beautiful and much more mature as an actress."

After its road show engagement and the preliminary reviews in which several critics yawned the film was too long, Paramount ordered half an hour of *Paint Your Wagon* cut from its 166 minutes length. For general release, the film was shown in the abbreviated version.

Helped by a $750,000 advance in New York and Los Angeles, *Paint Your Wagon* brought in $15,000,000 in rentals during its first North American run. Although it was ranked as 1969's fifth highest film rental, the film was considered a disappointment, since it failed to gross domestically what had been hoped. *Paint Your Wagon* was cheered abroad and easily made enough to put the film in the black, as Alan Jay Lerner confirmed in his autobiography. Contrary to the widespread myth, it was not a bomb, unlike several other musicals released in the same era, such as the Julie Andrews vehicle *Star!*, which cost $31 million and returned less than $8 million. *Hello, Dolly!* cost $40 million and raised only $25 million in film rentals.

20

"It's called show business, not show art."
— Jean Seberg

In the United States, tensions between the Black Panther Party and the law enforcement authorities increased. Jean followed the events from a distance, disgusted by many of the incidents, but continued to supply the Panthers with funds.

Money was something Jean did not have to worry about, at least not in late 1969. She was signed for $100,000 to appear in *Macho Callahan*, a somber and dramatic Western. It was the last time she would command a salary of this magnitude. Prior to signing the deal, she wrote her parents on November 10, 1969:

Well, it looks as if I'm going back to work—'back in the saddle again.' I've been offered a good part for good money in a western, to be shot entirely in Mexico, playing opposite David Janssen who, if I'm not mistaken, is one of Mom's favorites (*The Fugitive* on TV). I'm awaiting the final deal, but if it works, Celia and I will go to Mexico City in early December.

The hurting part is leaving Diego behind, but I think in February, he may be able to fly over to see you in Iowa with Eugenia (sorry), and that Celia and I can fly up from Mexico. He has about 2 weeks vacation in February which should coincide with the end of our film. For Christmas, his vacation is shorter and I think he'll go skiing. I really feel miserable about missing the holidays with Diego, but he doesn't seem to be upset and Romain feels I shouldn't let the opportunity go by.

The title of the film — if I do it — is *Macho*, which means 'virile' in Spanish. It will be rough — lots of horseback et cetera, but I chose this crazy profession so I guess I should do it as well as possible. Healthwise, I am rested and feel good. As Mom said in Rome, it's just the lack of a little romance that's missing!

Diego's party will finally be given this Thursday, on my birthday. About 16 children, with movies and, hopefully, a judo demonstration. I'll be busy with that tomorrow and Thursday. Then next week I'll fly to Rome to dub the Italian film [*Dead of Summer*] before leaving for Mexico. If it weren't for Diego I'd be awfully unhappy as Paris is gloomy and depressing. I just don't know how to make a home — it has to be here, I guess, because of Diego's schooling, but I'm so tired of Paris.

I hope they sent Granny a new check. How embarrassing! They changed the branch bank for my account and my business manager didn't tell me before I wrote the check. But it should be settled now.

I've been living a quiet life here — seen a few friends, though not too many. *Paint Your Wagon* is apparently doing good business in the States. No one has seen *Airport* yet.

I miss you. Will let you know if all this works out. Much, much love to the two of you and Granny, and if you see Carol Hollingsworth, give her my affectionate thoughts.

Much love,
Jeana

On December 2, Jean arrived in Mexico City with Celia in tow, and began work almost immediately. The filming entailed long hours, with Jean acting as interpreter between the Mexican crew and American cast, since she spoke Spanish fluently.

David Carradine, who had a small role in the film playing Jean's husband, recalls Jean as being "a great lady." In his memoirs, Carradine remembered a minor incident involving Jean, himself, and co-star Lee J. Cobb: "One day, just before a shot, the wardrobe people were fussing with my clothes interminably. I said, 'How do you make them stop?' Lee said, 'You say 'Basta' (enough)!' Jean said, 'No. You say, 'no es necessario' (It is not necessary).' Sweetness instead of a command. Like I said, a real lady. It broke my heart when I heard about her death."

Filming *Macho Callahan* primarily went smoothly, and Jean thought co-star David Janssen was "just so wonderful." In the film, Jean plays a vengeful widow who tracks down her husband's killer, Callahan (played by Janssen). After she confronts him, a struggle culminating in rape ensues, and now the widow inexplicably falls in love with Callahan. The fight sequence promised to be one of the "most savage man-woman fight scenes on film," according to director Bernard Kowalski.

"This isn't the ordinary man-woman fight you see in films," Jean explained. "This isn't a simple slap-around. It's a battle to the death. At least on my part, and David's character realizes after the first whack with the poker that he might have to kill me to stop me. It's pretty brutal, and I even shuddered when I first read the script. But it's true to life. A woman whose husband is murdered is apt to get pretty violent."

Jean's stand-in on the film was Joan Blunden, a young student on leave from the University of the Americas in Mexico City. Today, she is known in the U.S. as the former *Good Morning America* host Joan Lunden.

Diane Ladd, who played bit part as a saloon hostess, remembers Jean: "She was terribly sensitive, almost like a little girl. We shot in a village outside Mexico City one day, and they set up tables for the cast and crew to eat. These skinny dogs wandered over, and Jean started to feed them off her plate. Someone snapped that you don't do that — not when there were people going hungry. Jean looked awfully hurt and didn't eat for two days after that.

"I personally considered her a great lady and a wonderful human being. A lady of sensitive, thought-out, careful choice and depth, and select caring."

When shooting stopped for the Christmas holiday, Jean and Celia flew to Iowa for a three-day visit. The *Times-Republican* reported that Jean hoped to come home for a longer visit in the spring, and that *Macho Callahan* was expected to be completed in mid-February. She then planned to go on a skiing vacation with Diego, either in France or Switzerland.

The FBI reported her arrival in and departure from Iowa.

With co-star David Janssen in Macho Callahan. AUTHOR'S COLLECTION

Back in Mexico, Jean celebrated the New Year at a party where she met the famed Mexican writer Carlos Fuentes. The two had mutual friends scattered throughout the world, and spent most of the evening talking. "Jean Seberg was quite sophisticated when I knew her," Fuentes said years later. "There was nothing hick or infantile about her."

In the novel *Diana*, a thinly-disguised account of his acquaintance with Jean, Fuentes asked her where she would feel comfortable.

"In Paris, in Majorca," she replied.

"Los Angeles?" he asked.

"What ever happens there is the most important thing in the universe," she answered facetiously. "Only Hollywood is international, cosmopolitan. And boy, when you prove to them they aren't cosmopolitan, they hate your guts. They make you pay for it."

According to Fuentes, he and Jean had an affair lasting the first few weeks of 1970, while she was working on *Macho Callahan*. Fuentes writes how, during a banquet held in honor of the film crew, Jean sat next to a General

Cedillo. Later that evening the General told Fuentes, "Tell your girlfriend to be careful." Long after the party, Fuentes confronted the General about the comment. The General warned, "The FBI [is] everywhere ...Watch out."

In mid-January, filming resumed north of Mexico City in Durango. Mine workers were on strike at the time, and some of the poorer residents joined the strikers in protest. On January 20 the Mexican government parachuted troops in to calm the protesters. Jean's sympathies lay with the protesters when she witnessed the extreme contrast between the rich and poor, and she donated money to the strikers.

One of the protesters Jean helped was a man named Carlos Navarra, known as El Gato (the Cat). It was recorded in Jean's FBI file that she was rumored to have had an affair with him. A member of the *Macho Callahan* crew (who wishes to remain anonymous) does not remember El Gato, but recalls another man in Jean's life at this time. "Ms. Seberg was having an affair with a very respected and admired Caucasian man for whom she felt a great deal of love and wondered if she should marry. That man is dead now," the source confided.

While filming, Jean was contacted by Abe Greenberg of the *Hollywood Citizen-News* for an interview. Instead of talking about the *Macho Callahan* filming, she spoke of her career and acting. "You work very hard, then months will follow in which you do nothing and desperation sets in. Getting up early and doing difficult things is nothing. The worst part is not having difficult things to do and having no reason to get up early, which is generally the case."

When Greenberg asked her what advice she had for girls who wanted to follow in her footsteps with an acting career, Jean responded: "I would only ask someone...to question the depth of their need for it. I think it's too tough. There are too many things that have to be sacrificed along the way to make it all worth while.

"So much of acting is good luck that it's quite unfair and unjust."

Luck was certainly lacking for Jean Seberg in the case of *Macho Callahan*. When it was released, critics were scathing about both the film and the star. "Seberg looks poorly even before she's beaten up, acts worse and is even further hindered by a series of Barbie Doll wigs," the *Los Angeles Times* sneered. "At any rate, for whatever reason, *Macho Callahan* is a mess."

After the film completed production, Jean returned to Paris in early March and apparently rekindled her relationship with Romain. "At that time of the affair Jean went to see her husband in France, and while there, reunited with him," the *Macho Callahan* source continued, adding, "Jean confided that she and Romain had engaged in intercourse."

Soon after, Jean realized she was pregnant. This was a pregnancy whose consequences, without a doubt, contributed to her ultimate mental and physical breakdown.

CHAPTER SEVEN
1970-1971

"Everyone knows I'm here so it doesn't matter ...
I've got these 'little friends' who follow me ..."
— Jean Seberg, from a conversation recorded by the FBI

Pregnant with Nina, 1970. COURTESY OF INDEPENDENT VISIONS

21

"It is felt that the possible publication of 'Seberg's plight' could cause her embarrassment and serve to cheapen her image with the general public."
— FBI memorandum

The Garys' "ordonnance de non-conciliation" (statement of irreconcilable differences) came through on February 17, 1970 followed by an application for divorce the following month. According to legal requirements, each was required to provide proof their union was unsalvageable — usually by providing the worst offenses imaginable. Neither Jean nor Romain wished to publicly insult the other, and since they could not stop the proceedings, they remained civil in the matter. Romain said Jean had abandoned the matrimonial home and had refused to resume their life together. Jean blamed Romain for his authoritarian character, and the "humiliations, insults and violence" he had inflicted upon her before third parties. Custody of Diego was entrusted to Jean on the condition he continue attending the school where he was registered at the time. Romain was in charge of Diego each time Jean was away, as well as school holidays. Both were allowed to freely visit Diego at each other's homes, which the couple had agreed to do earlier.

Although legally separated in the spring of 1970, and despite the wall which separated the dwelling into two self-contained sections, Jean, Romain and Diego were very much together at the rue du Bac apartment. "It seemed the most sensible thing to do," Jean told Roderick Mann, "because this way we can both see our son at the same time, and he gets the security he wouldn't have if we lived apart. Of course, we're still great friends. Romain and I were never bored when we were married and we're not bored now."

Jean continued her involvement with various groups and causes, but primarily with the Panthers. Although involved in divorce proceedings, she was still Mrs. Romain Gary, and the child she carried was at least ostensibly and legally Romain's. Romain told reporters that the child was the "fruit of our reconciliation" after Jean returned to Paris from the *Macho Callahan* shoot.

On April 21, 1970, Elaine Brown of the Black Panthers placed a collect call from San Francisco to Paris, waking Jean at three in the morning. During the course of the call, Masai (Raymond) Hewitt also spoke with Jean. The FBI recorded the conversation and not only discovered Jean's pregnancy, but also deduced from it that Romain Gary was not the father of the unborn child:

Jean: I'm like in the fourth month so I have a nice long wait ahead. I guess it's that year, you see.

Hewitt: I guess it's all right.

Jean: I guess, yes. I think it's all right...I'm happy about this, really...I ran into a thing that scared me legally about my other son. I was afraid I was going to lose custody, you know, if my former husband got wind of it and got upset about it. And I talked to him about it and he was really very civilized and very nice about it.* So it's really good, you know. So everybody, sooner or later, I guess, is going to have a big tummy.

Hewitt: I'm not going to try to have anything to do with it.

Jean: Listen. I'm afraid of you. You're a liar.

Hewitt: I really didn't know.

Jean: No, but I'm really happy. That's kind of the best surprise you could have. That's terrific. She told you what I call you, didn't she?

Hewitt: Yes, but I can't remember.

Jean: Johnny Appleseed.

Hewitt: No, she didn't tell me that.

Jean: Yes, planting your little seeds around.

Misinterpreting this conversation, the FBI erroneously assumed Jean was pregnant by Hewitt. Had they investigated further, they would easily have discovered both that Hewitt had been in Los Angeles at the time of the baby's conception, and that Jean was not in California during the first months of 1970 when she became pregnant. In addition, the "planting your little seeds around" joke by Jean refers to the belief that Hewitt was sterile, disproved when he impregnated two women in a short period of time. She was apparently just teasing about the irony of Hewitt's pending fatherhood, but in its haste the Bureau had inferred something quite different and potentially sensational.

Perhaps because she was groggy, having been woken by the telephone call or, more than likely, believing that the conversation was being taped, Jean told Hewitt she was in "the fourth month" by April 21. But when Jean delivered her child at the end of August, which, according to the FBI memoranda, would have been her eighth month, the child would have undoubtedly weighed more than the three pounds it did when born. In several FBI transcripts Jean alludes to various dates as to the baby's due date and conception.

On April 27, Richard Wallace Held, case agent in charge of FBI-COINTELPRO activities against the Panthers, offered the following to headquarters:

"Bureau permission is requested to publicize the pregnancy of Jean Seberg, well-known white movie actress, by _____ [name is blackened out] by advising Hollywood 'Gossip-Columnists' in the Los Angeles area of the situation. It is felt the possible publication of 'Seberg's plight' could cause her embarrassment and serve to cheapen her image with the general public.

---

* Note: presumably the Eastwood affair.

"It is proposed that the following letter from a fictitious person be sent to local columnists:

> I was just thinking about you and remembered I still owe you a favor. So — I was in Paris last week and ran into Jean Seberg, who was heavy with baby. I thought she and Romaine [sic] had gotten together again, but she confided in me that the child belonged to _____ [deleted] of the Black Panthers, one _____ [deleted]. The dear girl is getting around! Anyway, I thought you might get a scoop on the others.
>
> Be good and I'll see you soon.
>
> Love,
> Sol

"Usual precautions would be taken by the Los Angeles Division to preclude identification of the source of the letter if approval is granted."

J. Edgar Hoover responded with a cable allowing the story's go-ahead on May 6:

"Jean Seberg has been a financial supporter of the BPP and should be neutralized. Her current pregnancy by _____, while still married affords an opportunity for such effort. The plan suggested by Los Angeles appears to have merit except for the timing since the sensitive source* might be compromised if implemented prematurely...to insure the success of your plan, Bureau feels it would be better to wait approximately two additional months until Seberg's pregnancy would be obvious to everyone."

However, this information was leaked to the *Los Angeles Times*, and Joyce Haber, whose gossip column was syndicated in a hundred newspapers, received the information. Known as the successor to gossip columnists Hedda Hopper and Louella Parsons, Haber was dubbed "Hollywood's No. 1 voyeur" by *Time* magazine, which added that Haber was "more intelligent, more accurate — and often more malicious — than her predecessors."

Haber once described Melina Mercouri as having "wall to wall hips, an ear to ear smile and more teeth than a pretzel has salt." She also wrote of Julie Andrews as having "a kind of flowering dullness about her." In a thinly disguised item using initials, Haber hinted that Andrews once said to co-star Rock Hudson, "But I'm the leading lady, dear."

Not knowing the truth of the new information on Jean Seberg, Haber opted to run a not-so-blind item, which provided the reader with clues to

---

* Note: The "sensitive source" is believed to be the FBI's wiretap at the Panther's headquarters.

the subject without revealing actual names. Using this procedure also protected Haber in the event the information was false. On May 19, 1970 the *Los Angeles Times* lead Haber's column with the headline: MISS A RATES AS EXPECTANT MOTHER:

"Let us call her Miss A, because she's the current 'A' topic of chatter among the 'ins' of international show-business circles. She is beautiful and she is blonde. Miss A came to Hollywood some years ago with the tantalizing flavor of a basket of hand-picked berries. The critics picked at her acting debut, and in time, a handsome European picked her for his wife. After they married, Miss A lived in semi-retirement from the U.S. movie scene. But recently she burst forth as the star of a multimillion dollar musical.

"Meanwhile, the outgoing Miss A was pursuing a number of free-spirited causes, among them the black revolution. She lived what she believed which raised a few Establishment eyebrows: Not because her escorts were often black, but because they were black nationalists.

"And now, according to all those really 'in' international sources, Topic A is the baby Miss A is expecting, and its father. Papa's said to be a rather prominent Black Panther."

Jean learned of the item and assumed that her conversation with Hewitt had been intercepted. She later said the shock of reading Haber's story was "severe."

On the same day Haber's item appeared, J. Edgar Hoover distributed memos of Jean's activities to Attorney General John Mitchell, Deputy Attorney General Richard Kleindienst, and John Ehrlichman, President Nixon's White House assistant for domestic affairs. Three weeks later, on June 8, *The Hollywood Reporter* carried part of the rumor, but named Jean: "Friends are wondering how long Jean Seberg will be able to keep her secret — or if she'll want to."

While the storm of gossip brewed in the States, Jean continued to live in Paris with Romain and Diego. She spent a lot of time with her son, and welcomed interviews. While the couple's divorce came through on July 1, she told the press they planned to remarry after the baby was born. One reporter who visited Jean in the rue du Bac apartment noted Diego "is living freely the life of a little American among two exuberant black cats and a big yellow dog, Sandy." The reporter noticed an empty bird cage in the apartment's entrance hall. It had once held a toucan named Billy the Kid, but which Jean had given to a Paris zoo because it made too much noise.

Unlike her secret pregnancy with Diego, Jean's second pregnancy was not concealed. She took long walks in the park with her son, shopped for baby clothes with friends, and attended social dinners with Romain.

Concerned for her own and her unborn child's safety in regard to the FBI and disgruntled Panther members, Jean hired a young Frenchman to act as her bodyguard that summer.

22

"Jean Seberg ... is a sex pervert."
— FBI memorandum

Although Jean had spent a few days in Marshalltown during the Christmas holidays, she wanted to visit her parents for a longer period of time. She also wanted Diego to experience an Iowa summer like the ones she had enjoyed as a child. On July 4, Jean and Diego arrived in Marshalltown and began their vacation at the Fourth of July celebration at the fairgrounds. Soon after, Mary Ann and her two daughters visited from New Jersey for a family reunion.

While Diego spent the time swimming, on pony rides, and playing with Mary Ann's daughters, Jean told her parents that she and Romain would not be divorcing, having now become reconciled. Diego was already eight years old, and Ed and Dorothy were delighted with the impending arrival of another grandchild.

During her stay, *Airport* was released. Although most reviewers were dismissive of the film, the movie-going public was not. With $45.3 million in gross receipts, it eventually became not only the top grossing film of 1970, but of Jean's entire career. She told Warren Robeson and the *Times-Republican* that Romain was in Paris working on an adventure script about the international drug trade for her, and that the film would be produced sometime after Christmas. Professionally and privately, all seemed well.

Lynda Haupert stopped by the Sebergs for a visit, and remembers Jean acting her usual self. "I had on a pair of clogs and a mini-skirt, and I was trim, my hair was up, and I looked the best I'd ever looked. Jean asked to try on my clogs, then said, 'Oh heavens, Lynda. They really are much too big for me,' with that sly smile of hers. It was kind of a put-down, but not really. More this attitude Jean took to let you know that she was amused by you, but that she'd been there already. It was a look she gave me all her life — kind of ironic and mocking, loving and superior all at once."

Jean and Diego returned to Paris on July 11. On July 15, *The Hollywood Reporter* printed another item: "Hear a Black Panther's the pappy of a certain film queen's expected baby, but her estranged hubby's taking her back anyway." Two weeks later, the Omaha department of the FBI sent headquarters copies of *Times-Republican* articles of Jean's recent visit to Marshalltown. "These articles were made available via mail to the Des Moines, Iowa Resident Agency of the FBI by *[blacked out]* Iowa."

Since Diego had been delivered by Cesarean section, Jean's doctors told her she would need the same operation once she was ready to deliver. Jean retreated to Majorca with Romain, Diego, and Celia, with the intention of resting. While on vacation, she attended the San Sebastian Film Festival, at which she was greeted with sustained applause. She presented awards to the winners, including the top prize to Nelo Risi for *Dead of Summer*, a result which naturally pleased her. Although her own performance was the linchpin of Risi's film, and despite the dissent of several critics, Jean saw the best actress prize go to Stéphane Audran for Claude Chabrol's *Le boucher* (*The Butcher*). If she felt any disappointment on that score she concealed it well.

With Dorothy and Diego in Marshalltown, 1970.
COURTESY OF MARSHALLTOWN TIMES-REPUBLICAN

Photographs of the event show her looking very pregnant but apparently in the best of health and spirits.

Meanwhile, back in the US, the FBI continued monitoring her. On July 24 a record was cataloged in Jean's FBI file: "*[blacked out]* stated that he had received a letter from Jean Seberg who was in Spain ... According to *[blacked out]* the BPP needed money; however, J. Edgar Hoover was causing trouble about prominent people who were helping the organization. According to *[blacked out]* Seberg stated that Hoover would probably give names the next time he makes a statement; however, it would make no difference to her."

Jean did not care if the FBI announced that she was a supporter of black causes, but the Bureau never made the alleged list public. On July 28, a SAC in Los Angeles removed the INS F-3 stop on Jean since she "is not known to be in possession of any BPP literature which would be of intelligence value to the Bureau."

Aside from the FBI, Jean's pregnancy was giving her problems in sleeping, and her concern over the snipes from the Hollywood gossip columns certainly didn't help matters. On the evening of August 7, an unconscious Jean was rushed by ambulance to the Juaneda Clinic in Palma, where doctors discovered she had taken a large quantity of pills. Her stomach was pumped, and both Jean and her unborn child were saved.

Romain told the press, "Jean awoke yesterday complaining of stomach cramps. She took some tablets to ease the pain, but her condition became worse. She nearly died in the ambulance on the way to the hospital. But she is feeling much better now." There was a rumor that Jean had taken an accidental overdose of sleeping pills. Another one whispered that it hadn't been accidental.

Several days later Jean spoke to the press from her hospital room. She didn't look suicidal. In fact, she glowed like most pregnant women. When a reporter from the *Daily Telegraph* asked her about her upcoming divorce from Romain, Jean replied, "It is wonderful. We are completely reconciled — ironically, just when our divorce papers are finally coming through...during the last eleven months things have changed and we are back together and very happy."

Concerned about the delicate pregnancy, Romain had Jean transferred to Geneva, where Hubert de Watteville, one of Europe's finest obstetricians, would be available in the event of a premature or complicated birth. After tests at the Geneva hospital, she went to the Blauherd Garmi Hotel in Zermatt, a fashionable ski resort near the hospital, again under strict orders to rest. Jean wrote her parents that the doctors "wanted to reassure me, and for me to escape the ghastly Spanish heat wave. The Professor Watteville confirmed that I am fine, just the risk of premature birth, for which he gave me progesterone shots, and I feel much, much better, except for missing Diego. It seemed silly to take him away from the sea he loves so much.

"Hope you had no stupid alarming press reports — they can be so irresponsible, never even checking facts. Write me in Paris and don't worry: except for my back aching, I feel great."

Newsweek in New York was interested in the latest adventures of the Garys. The magazine contacted their Paris correspondent, Edward Behr, who supplied information to the head office. Behr apparently noted that the story he submitted was not verified. For reasons not entirely clear, the final editing of the August 24 issue of *Newsweek* was not made by editor Kermit Lansner, who had injured himself in a motor bike accident. According to *Paris-Match*, there was a mix-up in procedure. Usually, Lansner marked unverified pieces with a green-ink pen, indicating the information is not finalized for print. After his accident, he contacted his secretary with instructions. The secretary could not locate a green-ink pen so she used a red-ink pen and marked two lines on the piece believing that would draw attention to it. But since the piece was not coded in green ink, the mark, regardless of color, was ignored.

Whether or not this explanation is true, it has not been determined who made the final choices for the edition that hit the newsstands on August 17. In the gossipy "Newsmakers" section of the publication, the dam broke:

"Can small-town girl from Iowa find happiness in Paris? It seems so, despite the ups and downs of her marriage. 'It's wonderful,' smiled movie actress Jean Seberg, 31, when reporters looked in on her in a hospital in Majorca where she was recuperating from complications in her pregnancy. 'We are completely reconciled — ironically just when our divorce papers are finally coming through.' She and French author Romain Gary, 56, are reportedly about to remarry even though the baby Jean expects in October is by another man — a black activist she met in California."

Jean was stunned when she received the magazine in Zermatt on August 19 and read the article. While the other publications implied the rumor, *Newsweek* had come out into the open, naming her and stating the rumor as fact. The same day, her furious husband informed her that they would bring a lawsuit against *Newsweek*. Jean then cabled her parents:

PLEASE DON'T BE UPSET BY NEWSWEEK ITEM ISSUE [August] 24 PAGE 31. WE ARE PREPARING HUGE SLANDER SUIT AND WILL WIN. MY NEW YORK LAWYER WILL CALL YOU TO REASSURE YOU IN TWO DAYS I AM WELL AND LOVE YOU ALL.

Jean's family was stunned when they read the *Newsweek* article. It only made matters worse when the *Des Moines Register* reprinted *Newsweek's* allegation, bringing the gossip in Marshalltown to a head. Concerned, Warren Robeson of the Marshalltown newspaper called the Sebergs for a statement. When the initial shock subsided, Ed Seberg told Robeson: "Jean tried to help a black activist group in California last summer. But when she found out they were trying to use her, she dropped them, and now they're trying to get back at her and hurt her."

"I was outraged," recalls Mary Ann Seberg. "I couldn't imagine that a nationally respected magazine could write something like that without having the correct information. It wasn't only *Newsweek*. There were other publications that came out about the same with the same information." Within a few days of *Newsweek's* story, over one hundred newspapers carried the same item. None of them verified the facts of the story.

On August 20, 1970, Jean could not sleep because of the recent events. Then the contractions began. A helicopter flew her to the Cantonal Hospital in Geneva, where doctors gave her sedatives to stop the contractions. Half a dozen reporters immediately swarmed to the hospital. Several more joined in the following days. On August 23, Jean gave birth by Cesarean section to a girl weighing just over three pounds. The child was put into an incubator and given less than a twenty percent chance of surviving.

After the delivery, Jean was wheeled into her hospital room to rest. Still groggy from the medication, she later said that several of her Panther friends were at her bedside, where they tried to take her credit cards and money. One of them handed Jean a gun to examine. "I took it and turned it over in my hands. Stupidly. Without thinking. My fingerprints were on it. He could kill anyone with that gun and furnish proof against me." Romain immediately cleared the room of all visitors, disconnected the telephone, and had guards stationed outside her door.

Whether or not Jean's recollection rang true or was simply a psychological reaction to the medication she was receiving, friends believe something traumatic happened in her room — something relating to Romain's taking charge, Jean's fear for the baby's life, or the consequences of the rumor.

On the morning of August 25, the baby girl lost her fight to live. Jean cabled her parents:

SAD NEWS BUT MY BABY GIRL BORN THREE MONTHS EARLY DIED THIS MORNING… LITTLE LUNGS NOT STRONG ENOUGH NEWSWEEK IS BEING SUED FOR MINIMUM 3 MILLION DOLLARS. I'LL WRITE. I LOVE ALL OF YOU.

Jean and Romain had named their child Nina Hart Gary: Nina, after Romain's mother; and Hart, after John Hart, Jean's ancestor who was one of the signatories of the United States' Declaration of Independence. To them, Nina was the victim of a sick, racist society. Immediately, Romain sent the following to *France-Soir*, entitled "The Big Knife":

"Since the age of 14, this daughter of the Middle West has supported the right to dignity of blacks of her country. Therefore, it was necessary at all costs to explain her horror of racism by sexual penchants. It was necessary at all costs to prove that a white woman who still believes in the American dream of justice and fraternity, the dream of Jefferson and Lincoln, was actually interested in blacks because they are, in the minds of crazed racists, the tempting symbols of the forbidden fruit."

Continuing, he laid the blame for Nina's death directly on *Newsweek*:

"Several hours after reading this infamy, Jean had to be transported by helicopter to the Cantonal Hospital in Geneva, where she has just given birth, 63 days prematurely, to a little girl who, at the moment I am writing this, is struggling against death with all her 1,700 grams of white flesh. This little spark of life is mine by all the laws of France. But *Newsweek* cares little for the laws of our country. This publication operates according to more convenient laws-those which, for 50 years, have assured the prosperity of the Mafia...

"It is three o'clock in the morning. We will have to wait, wait, wait, before knowing whether this attempt at slaughter in the Manson style ... will be rewarded with success. But already a Dantesque carnival of legal doctors, witnesses, and lawyers swirl about this little being, trembling in its incubator..."

At the end Romain added: "August 25, six o'clock in the morning. The doctor has just come in. The child is dead."

Romain's letter called forth numerous articles from both tabloid magazines and the "legitimate" press. "IT WAS MY DAUGHTER," SAYS ROMAIN GARY, splashed one headline. JEAN SEBERG WEEPS FOR HER BABY, KILLED BY HATRED was another. The majority of the French press came to Jean's defense.

Several American newspapers carried part of Romain's letter. As for *Newsweek*, editor Kermit Lansner said, "We deeply regret the loss that Mr. Gary and Miss Seberg have suffered and are profoundly unhappy that Mr. Gary would feel that we in any contributed to it."

The FBI obtained a copy of the French newspaper *L'Humanité*, which also printed Romain's letter. A translator provided the FBI with an English version of the piece. "The Big Knife" became "Murder, American Style" and added that Romain closed the letter "by saying that he is not trying to appeal to the readers' sympathy, but rather that he is 'bearing witness' to help people understand what is happening in America and why there is a revolt of young people 'in that country for which I will never give up hope.'"

Even more than the care of his former wife, however, Romain's most pressing concern appeared to be punitive justice. He sent Guy-Pierre Geneuil a telegram signed "Very urgent," to join them in Geneva. As soon as Geneuil arrived, Romain left Jean in the bodyguard's hands and returned to Paris — an act which many felt was unforgivable, given the circumstances of the past few days' events.

Geneuil took Jean to Lausanne, where they occupied two suites at the Beau Rivage Hotel. When the pair entered their suites, the first thing Jean asked of Geneuil was to search the rooms. "Jean thought there were microphones everywhere," he says. After taking down all of the framed pictures and thoroughly looking over every inch of the suites, Geneuil came up empty-handed. Despite Jean wearing a long wig and using the name "Madame Médard," as well as asking for discretion from the hotel staff, Geneuil says, "The FBI and CIA came anyway."

Jean spent her time recuperating with a visit by Diego and Eugenia, and by reading. It is likely she may have read the September 8 edition of the *Los Angeles Times* in which Joyce Haber reported: "Jean Seberg lost the baby which was born nine weeks prematurely. *Newsweek* …had reported that the baby's father was a black activist she met in California." She also wrote several letters. One was to a friend in Hollywood which read: "My little baby girl was born prematurely and died. That horrible gossip, just for a sensational new item, made it up. How can anyone be so malicious?" The item ended up in a gossip magazine.

Geneuil gave a vivid account of an extraordinary incident which took place in Lausanne. One day Diego asked his mother if he could go play in a small park adjacent to the hotel. Jean, who continued to wear her dark wig and glasses while at the hotel, told him he could, but only if he stayed close by and in her sight. The boy went to the side and sat down, playing with horse chestnuts that had fallen from the trees.

A hotel worker brought a telephone out onto the terrace, and informed Jean there was a party calling her long distance. Geneuil watched Diego as the worker plugged in the telephone and Jean took the call. A few seconds later, Jean slammed down the receiver.

"Guy-Pierre, someone just phoned to warn me that they're going to take Diego away from me!!" Jean screamed.

Geneuil was shocked. "Who?"

"The FBI!" Jean answered, almost hysterically. "Diego! Come here, quick!"

Geneuil turned to see the boy still playing with the horse chestnuts, not hearing his mother. At the same time, Geneuil noticed a Pontiac car driven by a white male coming toward Diego, stopping fifty meters from the boy. A woman, whom Geneuil remembered seeing earlier in the day, stepped out of the car and ran toward Diego. Instinctively, Geneuil sprinted toward the car. He saw the woman had grabbed Diego, and was trying to drag him into the car.

From the terrace, Jean was joined by Eugenia, who heard the boy's screams, and watched in horror the drama taking place in front of their eyes. They yelled to Diego while Eugenia helped Jean, still unhealed from the Cesarean section, get to the scene.

"Help me!" Diego screamed as he struggled to get away from the woman.

The woman ordered Diego to be quiet, but the boy refused. Then he bit the would-be abductor hard in her forearm. "You little son of a bitch!" she roared. Then Diego kicked her under her knee. The struggle caused the woman to fall on the ground, losing her hold on the boy. She then jumped into the car and the male driver sped off, just as Geneuil arrived on the scene.

Eugenia and Jean, whose wig and glasses had fallen off in the rush, came upon the scene seconds later. Diego threw himself into his mother's arms, shaking and crying. The attempted kidnappers were never seen again. It is unlikely that the pair had planned the kidnapping scheme on their own, since very few people knew that Jean was in Lausanne, let alone that Diego was there with her. In any event, Diego was immediately returned to the safety of his father and Paris with Eugenia.

Jean had Nina's body embalmed in Geneva and made arrangements for photographs to be taken of the child. Some showed the mother holding her daughter in her arms. Jean decided that her child would be buried in Marshalltown. Ed and Dorothy Seberg suggested burying Nina in Paris, since France was Jean's residence. They felt it would be best for Jean to put the entire episode behind and move on with her life. HOPING TO FOLLOW YOUR BEAUTIFUL SUGGESTION CONCERNING BURIAL. DECISION AWAITS MEDICAL AND LEGAL TESTS Jean cabled her parents, but she was adamant about burying her child in Marshalltown.

Despite the fact that Marshalltown had mixed feelings toward Jean Seberg, it was still home. "I feel that she had to prove to people that the child was white and that there was no substance to the rumors going around," says Mary Ann Seberg. "It was a very personal tragedy for her. I think that she felt that Marshalltown was a permanent place, and she wanted to make sure the child would be secure in the place she felt was home."

"It was something out of a movie almost," Lynda Haupert adds. "To think that sort of thing could actually happen to someone you know — it was amazing. Jean wanted the world, and especially Marshalltown to know that the baby was white, that those rumors were all lies."

In the second week of September, Jean and Guy-Pierre Geneuil boarded a jet in Geneva for the United States, starting on an extremely long and taxing journey. The pair's itinerary included stops at Zurich, Montreal, Chicago and Des Moines. Jean was extremely nervous and frightened. Only days before, three European airplanes bound for the U.S. had been hijacked by extremists of the Popular Front for the Liberation of Palestine. With one aircraft in Cairo and the other two in Jordan, the highjackers were threatening to blow them up, hostages included. At one point during their trip, Jean told Geneuil she wanted to go to Cairo and negotiate with the terrorists.

While awaiting their connecting flight in Zurich, Jean and Geneuil saw cowboy film star (and Iowa native) John Wayne. Geneuil recalled Jean became angry at the sight of Wayne. "That man, I hate him," she said in French. "He adhered to McCarthyism, witch hunts. He is as racist in person as he is in his films." Other film stars, including Joseph Cotten, were flying out of Zurich that day, apparently vacationing. Fans noticed the actors and asked them for autographs. Not one asked Jean for hers. She was virtually unrecognizable as she continued to wear her black wig and sunglasses.

On the jet, a stewardess served Jean a drink of scotch in a crystal glass. She swallowed two sleeping pills which put her to sleep until the plane touched down in Montreal. But while they were in Chicago waiting for the final leg of their journey, Geneuil says Jean got into a serious fight with a black policeman, calling him "a traitor." To Jean, her world, and the entire world, was falling apart. Geneuil interceded, and the confrontation was forgotten.

Ed and Dorothy Seberg met their daughter and Geneuil at the Des Moines airport, and drove them directly to Marshalltown. They put Jean in their room, and gave Guy-Pierre the spare bedroom. Ed Seberg resorted to a cot in the basement. The FBI was duly informed "by an unnamed source" that Jean had arrived in Marshalltown to make arrangements to bury her baby.

The next day, Ed Seberg drove Jean and Geneuil to the Mesquaki Indian settlement near Tama, a fifteen-minute drive east of Marshalltown. Again, Jean wore the long blonde wig. Jean spoke with a few of the Native Americans, asking what their needs were. She was clearly making plans to help them.

The main reason for Jean's return to Marshalltown, however, was to bury her daughter. Unbeknown to Jean, Nina's body was not on the plane when she returned to Iowa. For several hours, she and Geneuil frantically telephoned to locate the remains. Nina's body finally arrived in Marshalltown on Wednesday, September 16 — days after Jean's arrival. The oak casket was taken to Avey Funeral Home.

There, Jean asked Geneuil to lift the lid. Geneuil recalls she said to him in French, to "be careful. I think the CIA or FBI put a bomb in the coffin." Geneuil did as he was asked. "I was startled," he says. "There was a second lid made of lead. It was according to regulations for transport to America." He cut the seal and saw the baby. After everyone left the room, Geneuil lifted Nina out of the coffin, to make sure there was no bomb inside.

Jean then secured a photographer from the *Times-Republican* to take additional pictures. She was given the prints and negatives of the photos which, again, showed her holding the child.

Warren Robeson recalls seeing Jean at the time. "Jean began to feel harried. It was understandable, [but] I didn't think a great deal of it," Robeson says. "Later, when she was talking with her mother and the family lawyer, she said that the phone might be tapped. I was astonished. I think she thought the telephone had been tapped, but I didn't put it all together until after the FBI story came out. She thought she was being wire-tapped even here in Marshalltown."

An open casket wake was held on Thursday and again on Friday before the funeral service. Friends and neighbors were invited to call at the funeral home; some came to pay their respects to Jean. Others came to see what color the baby was. Several residents could not understand why she brought the child halfway around the world. "I wanted witnesses to the lie," Jean said in 1974 in explanation.

Jean invited Erma Morrow, a black woman whom she knew in Marshalltown, to come to the wake and funeral. Morrow had not heard the rumors of Nina's paternity. "It was a white baby with white and light blonde hair, and I didn't know the essence of it all. I just thought it was gracious that she invited me. I can just see that beautiful little, cotton white baby wrapped with pale pink roses in the coffin. I wish I would have taken a snapshot of it. I can remember it as if it were yesterday."

During Jean's stay, she went to Rabbi Sol Serber for comfort. "She was unhappy and disturbed. She felt that she had let her parents down. She knew all the gossip going around, and she was afraid it would hurt them," Serber says. "Jean was always this girl who went away from Marshalltown, but never really left."

The day before the funeral, Jean, Guy-Pierre, Serber and Marshalltown realtor Leo Knox drove to the Tama Mesquaki Indian settlement. Jean again spoke with the Native Americans and offered assistance, then broke down in tears, realizing nothing she could do could better the impoverished state of the Indians.

On returning to Marshalltown, Jean ordered the car to be stopped when she saw an injured dog lying on the side of the road. She got out of the car and cradled the dying animal in her arms. Far removed from the cool, sophisticated celebrity the public saw, Jean crumbled as she held the dog, overcome by a feeling of helplessness. The problems with the Indians, the minorities, the death of her daughter — perhaps it was a sense of the unfairness of things which overwhelmed her as she wept here on the open roadside.

The next day, on September 18, the funeral service for Nina Hart Gary was held at 3:30 P.M. at the Trinity Lutheran Church. About ten minutes after the service began, Indians from Tama arrived to pay their respects, as Jean had invited them to do the day before. Paton Price and Tom Malinchak, two of Jean's few Hollywood friends, flew in for the services. Phil Everly of The Everly Brothers singing duo attempted to make it there, but couldn't break a previous engagement.

Romain Gary, as well, was conspicuously absent. He had been taken ill just as he was boarding the plane in Paris, and the attendants would not allow him to fly. Romain was then taken to a Paris hospital. He cabled: PLEASE TELL ALL OUR FRIENDS HOW WRETCHED AND HEARTBROKEN I FEEL. PHYSICAL DISABILITY ALONE PREVENTS ME FROM BEING WITH JEAN AND ALL OF YOU AT OUR LITTLE GIRL'S BURIAL.

After the service, the mourners went outside. Erma Morrow recalls: "Mr. Avey [of the funeral home] and I came out of the funeral, and Jean came straight to me. Standing next to the casket, Jean said, 'I wonder why the Lord took my baby.' I told her, 'It was God's will.' A man pulled the car up, and there was a small commotion. I asked my brother who was with me, 'What's going on?' He said, 'There could be something in there — a bomb or something.'" The car was searched then deemed safe. "At that time prejudice was great, and they wanted to make sure the car was safe to travel in."

Nina Hart Gary was buried at Riverside Cemetery in the Seberg plot, only feet from David Seberg's resting place.

With Dorothy at the burial of Nina Hart Gary, 1970.
COURTESY OF MARSHALLTOWN TIMES-REPUBLICAN

"She had her detractors here, people who were jealous or whatever," said Marshalltown resident David Norris. "But she thought enough about her hometown to come home and dispel those rumors. She bit the bullet, didn't she? It took a lot of guts."

"Maybe it was the worst thing she did, bringing the child back," says Rabbi Serber. "Sometimes when you have to prove something, there are people who will use reverse psychology — 'You have to prove something? Why do you have to prove it?' It was too bad she had to prove it, but that really threw her — emotionally and in many other ways."

The *Times-Republican* carried a front page account of the service. Unlike the widespread news of the paternity rumor a few weeks earlier, only a handful of Iowa-area newspapers carried brief stories of the funeral. Nationally, Jean's loss went largely unreported.

The day after the burial Jean, Geneuil, Price, and Malinchak returned to the settlement near Tama so that she could thank the Indians for attending the services. Jean and Geneuil made several trips to this settlement over the next few weeks. Once, on the way back to Marshalltown, the pair saw a couple of young hitchhikers. Despite his objections, Jean offered the pair a ride. After leaving the two in a nearby town, Geneuil glanced in the rear where the couple had been seated. "There was a gun," he says. Using a piece of paper to keep his fingerprints off the gun, Geneuil picked it up, and once they arrived to Marshalltown, he threw it into a public trash can. As a precaution, he also emptied the ashtrays in case the hitchhikers had been smoking hashish during their ride. "Three hundred meters ahead of us," he says, "the police were waiting."

Later in the week, Jean drove to a 314-acre farm eighteen miles southwest of Marshalltown, near the community of Melbourne. "Jean had always loved farms in Iowa," says Mary Ann Seberg. "We used to go to my aunt and uncle's farm near Indianola when we were young — every summer for a couple of weeks. I think at the time when she was looking for investments, Iowa farmland looked like a very good investment."

In later years, Jean recalled a talk with Frances Benson shortly after she returned to Marshalltown for Nina's burial. "She told me so many things about her life," Jean wrote, including an episode in which Frances told her regarding the loss of her and her husband's farm. "Grandpa lost his farm in a swindle, and she thought he would go out of his mind…before moving to town with her husband, she herself prepared the final meal for twenty famished farmers who gathered the last Benson corn. [The Melbourne farm] was to be a kind of vindication." In October, Jean signed a ten-year contract to purchase the farm, with $20,000 in annual payments after putting down $40,000 of the $227,500 price.

Shortly after, Jean made another purchase in Marshalltown: a two-story, five-bedroom house on West Church Street, a few blocks from the house she grew up in. "Black students went to Jean and asked, 'Would you do something for us?,'" says Erma Morrow. "There were students living in the basements of white people, and they couldn't study." Jean met with Morrow and Leo Knox to discuss plans to purchase a house for the students. A house was found and Jean purchased it for $26,000 to house black athletes attending the Marshalltown Community College.

The house was a community effort with a handful of residents donating sheets, beds and furniture. McGregor's Furniture supplied used davenports. "It worked out at the right time," says Morrow.

"I went from rags to riches," Jean told Morrow, "and I didn't use my money. I hadn't thought about it." "Jean wanted to do something with the problems not only in America," says Morrow, "but in Marshalltown, and it took money to do all of this. We talked about Martin Luther King's program and how movie stars were pouring their money into his causes. Jean had a heart of beauty, and was fighting like hell against racism. And she was well liked in Marshalltown. She was their daughter."

Immediately, the house for the black students caused an uproar in the community. Harvey Baltisberger, who lived across the street from the house, informed Jean that loud music and parties disrupted the peace. Several residents complained to the police about car doors slamming.

Jean sent a letter to Baltisberger, explaining that the house "was purchased as a home for people brought in by the community to bring hopeful prestige on the athletic field to the community. They have immeasurable, and, I consider, inexcusable deficiencies in having a place to live. The purpose of the house is that they should have a home in our town in the true sense of the word..." The letter added: "I checked into the zoning laws of your neighborhood. A boarding house is a place where moneys are exchanged for living there, which is absolutely not the case in this instance. The United States has very specific laws as to open housing as well...I hope all goes well and I hope you will behave toward your neighbors as you want them to behave toward you."

"She felt to purchase this home would become a place for them to congregate, for black students," says Roger Maxwell. "And as a matter of fact, this continues with universities and colleges today. So she was right on time with her actions for black students."

"It was to be a community-type thing, and she wanted many different types of people to be involved in it — 'minorities,' if you will. It was a vision that she had, and she hoped that it would work out. There was some unsettlement in the community about it, and it just didn't work out," says Mary Ann Seberg. One person who was close to Jean says, "The biggest problem with the house was prejudice. I think people were just looking for an excuse for it not to work."

"The community didn't see it as a community effort because the students were black," says Rabbi Serber. "But Jean felt this was her investment into the community, to help make it a better place."

While home, Jean also wrote a letter to Charles Garry, formally resigning her future assistance to the Black Panther Party. She cited her reasons as mistrust of a majority of the party members, and her impending trial. She also included a plea for peace:

"I feel enough people have died — good people — and I will have no part of such games. There are many other reasons, but no need to go into more detail. I believed, I tried, I helped humanly when I could. I beg our mutual friends to take care of themselves, their brothers, sisters and children, as the divisions in this country become each day wider."

"I feel Jean got suckered in by people sometimes," says Lynda Haupert. "Maybe she got in so far with the Panthers that she really couldn't get out, not realizing or fully knowing what she was getting into. But all of the causes Jean supported, from the March of Dimes to the Black Panthers, were to help the downtrodden, to make a difference for the better."

Jean divulged more about her involvement with the Panthers to Rabbi Serber: "Jean said she learned a lot about discrimination and racism through the Black Panthers. It was quite an experience. There were certain episodes with the group she wished she hadn't gotten involved in, but she said she never regretted all that had happened."

"There were some good people in the group. Not all the members were militants," Jean told Serber. "I felt that my involvement would help society and the country confront the problems with discrimination."

23

"I feel Jean's problems at the end were a compilation of many things: her Puritan Midwest upbringing; being plucked by Preminger and knocked down by him; and then marrying Frenchmen...But the loss of her baby haunted her for the rest of her life."
— Lynda Haupert

Contrary to myth, there never was a press conference where Jean spoke about the recent events. Nor did Jean present her dead child to the press as has been reported through the years. Nina Hart Gary was not buried in a glass coffin, although at one point Jean said she wished she had been, so that the curious who did not attend the wake could see the child was Caucasian. The news media did not check the facts and simply added more drama to an already sensationalized story.

Following Nina's burial, Jean quietly recuperated at her parent's home. She had two more items of business before returning to Paris: accepting an invitation to attend Jesse Jackson's Operation Breadbasket service in Chicago; and a stop on the east coast to meet with a lawyer.

Jean called Roger Maxwell and invited him and his wife Bunny to attend Jackson's service. She also invited other members of the community, including a number of high school students. When the group arrived at the Marshalltown airport on October 24, only two airplanes were available. Jean had reserved three. Quite uncharacteristically, she told one of the pilots, "I was told there would be three planes for my group. When I ask for a service, I expect to get what I am paying for." But he was unapologetic and offered no explanation of the mix-up. One member of Jean's group suspected with hindsight that the pilot had been an informant for the FBI. Jean apologized to the students for the fact that they could not all go with her to Chicago.

At the Operation Breadbasket service, Jean sat on the stage to one side of the pulpit, while a youth choir sang with the audience of two thousand.

Afterwards, the group went to a restaurant for lunch with other members of Jackson's crusade. "Jean, Jean's bodyguard, my wife Bunny, and I were seated at this table with this woman we didn't know," continues Maxwell. "The lady stated that she brought greetings from someone in Los Angeles, and Jean knew the party. Jean then talked to my wife and me further. The lady then asked what brought us to Chicago. I commented that Jean had chartered two planes this morning for us and a party of us left Marshalltown to come to the service. She asked us what time we left and she seemed to be asking very particular questions — her line of questioning was more inquisitive.

"I asked her in return, 'You drove from L.A.?' and she said 'Yes.' I asked her 'When did you leave?' and she said 'Yesterday.'" At that moment, the Maxwells realized the woman was lying. She could not possibly have driven the distance from Los Angeles to Chicago in that time frame.

"Jean then asked my wife to accompany her to the restroom, and the lady said 'I'll join you,'" Maxwell continues. "Jean then returned and spoke to her bodyguard in French to remove the [woman's] purse — move it to another table. I think Jean thought there was a recording device in the woman's purse."

Geneuil placed the purse on another table. Then Jean returned to the restroom. "It was getting tense," Maxwell says, "so I went over a told one of Rev. Jackson's staff, a black woman, that she'd better check out the restroom.

"When they all came back, two of Jackson's security guards came over and asked the woman, 'Are you ready to leave?' 'But I haven't finished my lunch,' she answered. 'You are ready to leave,' they said and escorted her out of the building. Jean was somewhat shaken up, but I firmly believe that the woman was some kind of infiltrator."

The group from Marshalltown returned home, while Jean sent Guy-Pierre back to Paris. Jean then flew to New Jersey to visit Mary Ann and to consult with her lawyer in New York. "She was completely distraught, very frightened. She was withdrawn," says Mary Ann. "I remember we went to a shoe store and we were trying on shoes, and she said, 'You see that man over there? He's with the FBI and he's watching me.' She also told me that our telephone was bugged. The more I heard later, the more I believe she was right. I can't dispute that."

Jean spent her time with Mary Ann and her family, and wrote down some lines in memory of her Grandma Benson which were recently discovered. Dated October 15, 1970, they read:

> If she died tonight
> We would all cry seventy-two hours
> Some longer.

No one, I think, would notice
that she had been a thief...
stealing hearts with foolishness,
feeding peppermints and redhots...
tickling feet and rubbing backs.

Who could file a suit
that she had taken away so much?
She would turn,
cover her mouth, and say
"Why, Jeana, shame on you" —
AND CLIMB ON UP THE STAIRS

After Nina's death, Jean received several letters from her Marshalltown friend Dawn Quinn. While at Mary Ann's, Jean telephoned Quinn. "I was concerned with her state of mind," says Quinn, recalling the conversation. "She told me her doctors had put her on lithium, but I was really frightened for her. 'Don't worry about me,' Jean told me. 'I know I've been exploited by these people,' meaning the Black Panthers. But it was too late. The damage had already occurred."

Jean visited her lawyer in New York regarding a lawsuit against *Newsweek* and other publications for libel. She primarily wanted to bring suit against *Newsweek* in the US to exact higher damages. The lawyer informed her that the suit against *Newsweek* alone would be long, drawn out, and messy. He told her she could file a lawsuit, but that she would be "crucified" in the courts, that everything regarding her and her character would be made public, and that there were records of her activities. "I realized that it was perhaps not the time to be Joan of Arc," Jean later said, "and on top of everything, a lot of friends would have burned with me. No legal action in the US, I gave in.

"He said to me it would cost a million dollars and take ten years. He asked me if the bitterness was worth it. That's when I cracked up." Jean returned to Paris and kept to herself in the rue du Bac apartment. There she slowly unraveled.

Shortly afterwards, an exhausted Jean was admitted to a French nursing home for rest. "At one point, [the doctor] feared I would never snap out of this ghastly world I was hiding in," she confessed in a letter to Rabbi Serber. "My parents don't know about this. It was the result of many things — mainly the body insisting on its own time to recuperate rather than let me push it too fast and too far, plus the inevitable shock reaction, which hit even worse because it came so late."

Medication in heavy doses did little to ensure a swift recovery. Jean's bitterness over the injustice inflicted on her prevented that. "Faith helps," she told Rabbi Serber, "when you haven't lost it, which, alas, I pretty much have."

At this low point, Hakim Jamal reappeared in Jean's life. With him was his constant companion and acolyte, Gale Ann Benson, the twenty-five-year-old daughter of a former member of the British Parliament whom Jamal had renamed Hale Kimga—an anagram of their first names. The couple went to Jean's apartment not only to offer sympathy, but to ask for money. Romain, however, saw the pair and told them Jean had gone to Spain. But when Jamal and Benson went around the corner to eat at a café and decide their next move, they saw Jean's maid, Celia. Through her, the couple learned where Jean was.

Jamal visited Jean in the nursing home and told her how Romain and the doctors "were up to no good — look how the husband lied about where she was! — but he had come to help her and all would be well." Jamal ordered her bags packed and she was dismissed from the home. Jean returned to her apartment with Jamal and Benson.

According to Diana Athill, a confidant of Hakim Jamal, Jean was obsessed with the death of Nina. Jamal set out to "cure" her. "He took the pictures away from her and told her he was going to burn them," Athill recounts from what Jamal told her. "She wept, screamed, tried to scratch his face, but he persisted. She cried all day, but he went on and on until at last he tore the photographs up."

By Jamal's account, within a few days, Romain Gary summoned him to his place. In order to get Jamal away from Jean, Romain told him that he had heard the police were looking for him, and gave him a laissez-passer, which could speed his way out of the country. Immediately after this Jamal and Benson left France together. Jean returned to the nursing home. She never saw Jamal again.

After his return, Jamal appeared to have dealt with his own mental breakdown. During his illness, Jamal re-evaluated Jean's involvement in his causes and the black power movement. He recalled Jean asking him if he knew certain individuals in different organizations, and he interpreted her inquiries as attempts to spy on the Black Panthers. Once, a photographer friend of Jean's had turned up in Los Angeles and told her he had heard Che Guevara was in Brazil. Jean's friend had simply heard the news on the radio, but Jamal accused her of being a spy and believed she "commanded secret knowledge," which was, of course, nonsense.

Jamal wrote Jean a letter filled with venomous accusations, claiming she had used him in the black revolution and spied on black people. Jean replied in a note, written with "dignity and sense," expressing her shock and sadness at his unjustified attack. This was the last communication to pass between them.

24

*"When they said that that child was a black child, what difference does it make if
she had an affair? The disgrace was how we reacted to [the rumor] itself, rather
than, 'How dare they do that!'"*
— John Berry

In a radio interview Romain gave in 1975, he explained that "by the time
you're fifty, you've taken on the world. Several times over. You've lived. All
of a sudden you find yourself in the company of a young woman who's just
starting out, who wants to forge her own relationships with the world. That's
hard to bear. You see her making the same mistakes you made. She won't
listen to your advice. And the more advice you give, the more you begin to
resemble a sagacious papa. All of which means, after a certain period of time,
that a husband and wife have turned into a father and daughter. That's the
profound drama."

Roger Grenier feels the end of the Seberg/Gary union was the result of
her return to make films in the United States. "The marriage was good until
she returned to America," he says. "Her affair with Clint Eastwood. And the
Panthers — they taught her how to drink, and also obliged her [to provide]
money. Those contributed to the breakup of her marriage to Romain."

If they could not be lovers, Jean and Romain wanted at least to remain
friends. As Jean slowly recovered from her illness, she wrote to Dawn
Quinn in mid-December to tell her she was finally feeling "like someone
who is coming out of a long tunnel on the way to health." With Christmas
approaching, Jean wrote, "I am trying to be enthusiastic, but it is really not
easy, as so much has happened. However, we have a beautiful tree and the
excitement in Diego's eyes when he counts the presents makes it all worthwhile." In concluding, Jean said she felt society was still blind to its own
impending ruin: "It seems that people have to scream because no one listens
when they whisper."

In a memo dated December 29, 1970, the FBI had already placed Jean
Seberg on its Security Index — Priority 3. This labeled her as an individual
who "because of background is potentially dangerous; or has been identified as a member or participant in communist movement, or has been under
active investigation as member of other group or organization inimical to
the U.S." In other words, if a presidentially-declared national emergency
occurred (as happened in the hours following the September 11, 2001 ter-
rorist attacks on the United States), Jean would be one of those the FBI
would take into custody to "safeguard the republic."

In February 1971, having regained her figure, Jean began work on
Romain's second film, *Kill* in Spain. She hoped that this might prove the
box office and critical hit that *Birds in Peru* had failed to be. "I feel rather

like President Nixon," Jean said in a press release, "who seemed to be at the bottom of his career when he jumped straight to the top."

In this film, she plays the wife of an anti-narcotics agent (James Mason) who leaves their Swiss home for a mission in Pakistan. Unknown to the agent, his wife precedes him by one day and becomes involved with an American (Stephen Boyd) who has a personal vendetta against the traffickers. The twist-filled plot involves intrigue, chases and numerous killings. "There will be twenty-seven cadavers in my film," Romain told the press. "For me, drugs are the most terrifying means of abasement today. Drug traffickers are the worst sort of assassins. Since I can't kill them myself, I'll kill them in the movies."

Romain said that the film would be a reply to American accusations against France. "It is not true that the French police force is corrupt. On the contrary, it is the American police which is corrupt to a disturbing degree." Romain believed that if the United States and other governments failed to move against the international drug traffic, "it will be the youth of those countries who will take the law into their own hands to get rid of the traffickers."

The movie was also another chance for Romain to prove himself as a filmmaker. "I got so damned tired of seeing my novels brought to the screen as if they were pure crap," Romain said. "I have written seventeen novels, some good, some less good; but the three that have made it to the screen deserved better treatment." Evidently he was thinking here of *The Roots of Heaven*, *The Man Who Understood Women* and *Lady L.*, excluding the autobiographical *Promise at Dawn*.

Jean quietly added, "I like working for Romain. I think I'm a lucky wife to have a husband who writes such marvelous movie parts for women." Romain then announced his interest in making "a picture in America. Perhaps even in Iowa." In fact, this second foray into film directing was to be his last.

Friends of the couple felt Romain was cruelly making fun of Jean's past involvement with the civil rights movement when, in her first scene in the film, she wears a dark Afro wig and listens to a recording of jungle sounds. Exasperated with her role of hausfrau, she turns and blasts the wall with a shotgun. The film also included a love scene showing Jean's character fully nude. Jean's stipulation that she should not be required to do nude scenes in the film necessitated the use of a body double.

When released, the film did nothing to further either Jean's or Romain's film careers. "Visually harsh and needlessly brutal," *The Hollywood Reporter* sniffed, "...pretentiously written ... indulgently directed." In France, the film unfortunately opened the same week as *The French Connection*, which was hailed as one of the best films of the year, and to which critics compared *Kill* unfavorably.

Jean, however, felt Romain's intentions had been beyond reproach, and she wrote him a letter on January 22, 1971, shortly after the film was released, to console him over the critics' reaction. She had doubted whether she would ever find the strength to work again, and this had been literally a question of her survival, as he had well understood: "Romain my love, there's something you forgot concerning the film and the absurd reviews, but I haven't forgotten ... When you made that film ... it was partly with the aim of saving my life. In the literal sense ... And you knew that it was a question of survival

Dining with Romain, 1971. COURTESY OF SNORRAMYNDIR

for me to find that discipline and strength to work again. If you hadn't made that film at that moment it would not have been possible. It was a deed of love...because it was an enterprise undertaken for very noble motives ... I'll never forget that, never. And you must not..."

In late April 1971, Jean and Romain brought a suit against *Newsweek* in France. In addition to *Newsweek*, the suit also named *American Weekly* and the French periodical *Minute*. Romain and Jean wanted to get the trial over with as soon as possible so that they could put the past behind once and for all. Each of them asked for 500,000 francs (approximately $100,000) in damages from *Newsweek* for invading their privacy and casting a prejudicial light on Jean's career. A sum of $45,000 was asked for from each of the other two publications.

Newsweek immediately counter-sued, asking for one franc in damages for Romain's accusations printed in *France-Soir* shortly after Nina's death, in which he blamed the weekly for the child's demise. It was not to be the open-and-shut case that the Garys had predicted.

Several of Jean's friends felt the lawsuit against *Newsweek* was justified — it had, after all, printed an untruth. However, others felt the lawsuit was a waste of time. "I really made fun of them both," says *Diamonds are Brittle* director Nicolas Gessner. "Romain told me about the conspiracy of the FBI, the CIA and all that, slandering poor Jean, having this affair with a Black Panther. I said, 'Look, both of you are so keen on your anti-racial religion. Why should you be worried about her having an affair with a black man?' Romain was looking at me [with a] 'You're right' look, in a way.

"It was so inconsistent with what they professed, that they wouldn't be racist, but still being offended that she had an affair, that [the rumor] would destroy or slander her. Why should Jean or Romain, who were so open-minded, take this so much at heart? Jean was not a prudish saint. I told Romain, 'It's really out of character with both of you. Perhaps I'm too cynical about it.'"

But Jean did not go deeper into detail about her motives with Gessner. She simply wanted the truth to be made public. While Gessner and several other European friends remained on the Garys' side, others fell out of favor. Jean and Romain invited the editor of a publication for which Romain worked to dine with them in Paris. The editor, who was a mutual friend, declined because of their lawsuit. "The periodical of a hated rival," Jean later said, "had become a 'colleague' to defend."

The Garys remained committed, and when they appeared together at the Cannes Film Festival in May, it caused a "small flutter" with photographers and attendees, according to Earl Wilson. Shortly after, Jean, Romain, and Diego retired to Majorca for a vacation. Romain worked on a new novel while Jean and Diego went swimming and sailing.

Jean also read over scripts, and chose as her next role *Questa specie d'amore* (*This Kind of Love*), to be filmed in Italy by prize-winning author Alberto Bevilacqua. The central character of the story, Federico, is in a mid-life crisis, and contemplates the failure of his marriage to Giovanna (played by Jean), the spoiled daughter of a rich businessman. Federico contrasts his own compromises with the moral courage of his antifascist father, from whom he has become alienated. Giovanna suffers the grief of a miscarriage, but comes to a better understanding of her husband as he seeks to re-connect with his own roots.

Bevilacqua worked with actors well in advance before any filming began, and *This Kind of Love* was no exception. He had met Jean earlier while she was filming *Congo Vivo* and he was working on another film, and had wanted to work with her. Bevilacqua spent two months working with Jean, discussing the script to give her a complete understanding of the character. "She was just what I needed," Bevilacqua said. "An outside onlooker, but sensitive, not from a specific place, not thoroughly American but a woman with a European impress who's assimilated the old continent's decadence through carrying its spirit to the heart of the great American problems.

"She was an exceptional actress, a serious professional. She transformed into the Giovanna I had imagined: when the film was in progress she went ahead spontaneously."

In the film, art imitates life, or at least comes uncomfortably close to Jean's life. The prospect of childbirth brings Giovanna a new happiness, but this is cut brutally short when there are complications with her pregnancy. Federico and Giovanna speak fearfully of the struggle between life and death within her — a battle that is soon lost. One can only imagine Jean's difficulty in playing these scenes.

While in Italy for the film, Jean was visited by Nicolas Gessner. "I remember there was a director who wanted her for a part," Gessner says, "and she didn't want to do it. We were to have dinner with him, and she said, 'Look. Let's do this ... ,' and she set up a little game. I was to pretend I was her European cousin, knowing nothing about movies. And that's how we'd lead this other director on and see how he would explain things, and I was to be asking silly questions. And we did it. It was superb fun and the director never knew the truth."

Gessner had hoped for Jean to appear in his film, *Someone Behind the Door,* co-starring Charles Bronson and Anthony Perkins. "It was a good secondary part," Gessner says, "as the wife who runs off and betrays her husband [Perkins]. But Charles Bronson wanted [his wife] Jill Ireland in the film, so she got the role."

After completing *This Kind of Love,* Jean returned to Paris to prepare for the upcoming trial, which was to begin in October. Jean and Romain's main target was *Newsweek,* although Jean's primary motive was to make public the circumstances which led to the rumor appearing in print. She consented to an in-depth and revealing interview with reporter Sandro Ottolenghi for *L'Europeo* to discuss the lawsuit:

"It's clear from the way things were reported in [the *Los Angeles Times*] that the call between me and my friend had been overheard, recorded. But what I don't know, and can't understand, is whether the [person] responsible for the intercept had misunderstood, or else understood perfectly and preferred to switch things around afterwards.

"I can't explain to myself the motive for them wanting to attack me in that way. [It] was a serious responsible journal, objective, liberal, to publish a story of that kind, presenting it as fact without bothering to check it. Now I ask myself how far the American press, all the press, is free. Or whether it's controlled to the extent of 'having' to do harm to someone who is 'troublesome.' Then I've also asked myself how and why, by what route, the information from a telephone interception by the police or the FBI could have reached the newspapers.

"I don't want to believe in such a direct relationship between the government and the press, but it seems clear to me there has been an attempt to discourage someone from doing certain things, from getting involved with activities which it's thought must be nipped in the bud. Did I upset someone? Am I upsetting someone? No, I don't want to believe in people's wickedness, even when I have persuasive evidence of it.

"Primarily we're interested in bringing out the disreputable things behind this story. That's assuming we manage to get to the bottom of it, for we already realize that to challenge a publication so established and so 'official' as that is like taking on the US Treasury: it takes a lot of money and a lot of strength. They have done everything to deter us. They've cajoled and threatened. For example, they let Romain know that if he didn't see reason his books would no longer be published in the America.

"I don't want anyone to feel sorry for me. I've never asked for compassion. I only want to demonstrate, and understand, how they wanted to harm me."

The trial began in Paris is early October. On the fourth of the month, Romain addressed the court. "No one is more respectful than I of the rights and freedom of the press," he announced. "But there is a problem. Namely, knowing when this liberty becomes the fascism of the press. One is crushed when one has for an opponent a publication with a circulation of more than seven million. How does one fight that kind of pressure? The power of that kind of money? To give you a single example, I have been made to understand that as long as this trial continues, my books will not be published in the United States...I ask you, sirs, what article could possibly avenge the death of a tiny infant?"

Representing *Newsweek* was one of France's most prominent trial lawyers, Robert Badinter. He said the long trip from Majorca to Zermatt would better explain the loss of Nina than any *Newsweek* piece. "One would have to have the character, the anguish and the neuroses of Romain Gary and Jean Seberg to claim that two lines of print caused the death of this child, and then to qualify it as murder and defamation," he countered.

But Jean's doctor, Hubert de Watteville, stated "it was medically possible that a psychological shock [could] induce a premature delivery." Despite de Watteville's claim, on October 25, the court rejected Romain's accusation that *Newsweek* was the direct cause of Nina's death. It did, however, agree that both his and Jean Seberg's privacy had been violated. As for the countersuit, Romain was excused for his article in *France-Soir* on the grounds that he had a right to reply to the magazine's story. The French courts ordered *Newsweek* to pay approximately $11,000 in damages, plus fines. *Newsweek* was also required to publish the court's decision in its own publication and eight other newspapers.

The ruling was not what Jean or Romain expected. When *Newsweek* threatened to appeal, an out-of-court settlement was reached.

When Ed Seberg heard of the settlement, he said, "I feel like I should have this much or more damages for what the story did to my wife. She has been upset ever since."

The ruling was a partial moral victory, even if the damages were smaller than Jean had hoped for (since she had planned to donate the money to several causes), and if they had been unable to reveal before the court the individuals and motives behind the rumor. But nothing could undo the scandal and its consequences. Brooding on the loss of her child and a Hollywood career, she could not move on. Society, she felt, had turned on her.

In December 1971, Diego was sick with rheumatic fever and Jean was concerned about his health. Penicillin was prescribed to treat the illness. "The worrisome thing with this sickness is to make sure his heart isn't strained, and, of course, the problem of weight," Jean wrote her sister that month. "He had to take a heavy cortisone treatment and is all puffed up. But he's been very good natured about it all, and my fingers are crossed."

Jean admitted Diego was, as a fifth grade student, at an age where he fought with other children at school, and was learning foul language. "That will pass," she said. "Apart from that, the problem with an only child is to try to teach him not to be egocentric."

Jean also encouraged Diego to learn as much as he could. One day he told his mother he wanted to write a script. After she told Romain of their son's interest in film, he bought Diego a small Italian camera to inspire his budding curiosity. When Jean asked Diego to make a movie about Little Red Riding Hood, he replied, to her amusement, "No, no. I want to write a new screenplay!"

In December, Jean wrote Mary Ann Seberg a Christmas letter from Zermatt, where she was vacationing for five days:

> I had my usual ambitions this year of organizing well and getting a package off to you, but it is a frustrating business. I can't conceive what sizes the girls wear by now and almost anything else is heavy to ship. So I decided to send you a truly rare item: a letter from Aunt Jean! I am enclosing a check for you all to decide how you want to use, either on

individual packages or a group project, and I am enclosing all my love and wishes for the New Year to come.

1971 was a good year for me, after a very bad start. I was a pretty sick and troubled girl after my trip to the States, but work was salutary and friends have been a tremendous help. I did Romain's film "Kill" in the spring with James Mason and Stephen Boyd and then an Italian film in the fall. I ate so much spaghetti in Italy I looked like Aunt Eula, but I have since lost 10 pounds and am once again my glamorous, beautiful movie star self that you all know and love…

My big wish is to get back to Iowa and the farm and Uncle Bill and Alta with Diego… Maybe this summer. My love to all of you and I hope you are well and happy and that school is going well for the girls, with all their activities I can't tell you how much I enjoyed my stay with you last year — it was a real comfort and delight.

Merry Christmas and love —
Jean

Jean's holiday spirits were full as she humorously added at the bottom: "Save this letter as it is a museum piece!"

CHAPTER EIGHT
1972-1976

"America seems farther away to me than Singapore."
— Jean Seberg

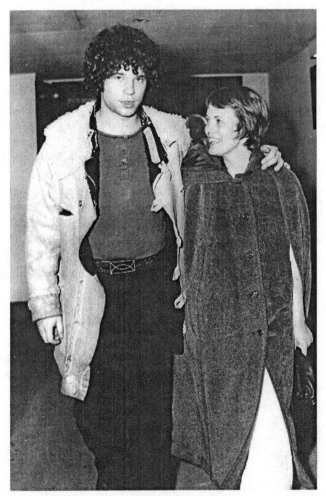

With Dennis Berry, 1972. COURTESY OF SNORRAMYNDIR

25

*"If you make a conscious decision to have a career and if it's creative
I don't see how you can give it up."*
— Jean Seberg

A reporter from *Elle* magazine interviewed Jean in her apartment in January 1972. Her appearance was vastly changed from the haute couture Jean Seberg of five years earlier. Now she dressed casually in denim jeans, tennis shoes, and Dorothy Bis cotton dresses. In the article, entitled "Jean Seberg: 'I chose the adventure of life,'" Jean was candid in the discussion of her life, career, and hopes for the future:

"I think about everything," she said. "That I will not be able to finish paying off the farm, that Diego won't be able to finish his studies…" She admitted she contemplated taking shorthand classes, telling herself she could always be a secretary. She also thought about being a florist, and at times, going to live on her Iowa farm "and really learning to work the land. It's a beautiful life." There was also the urge to extend her education, to learn Portuguese, to study piano, and there were screenplays she was working on too. Friends in the film world were encouraging her to try her hand at directing.

When asked point blank, "Are you preoccupied with growing old?" the thirty-three-year-old actress replied, "No. That worried me when I was ill a year ago, when I thought I was never going to get out of the situation. But now, I am discovering … in spite of society that wants everything to center on youth, all ages bring you satisfactions."

In the spring of 1972, Jean accepted an important role in *L'attentat* (*The French Conspiracy*), directed by Yves Boisset. The film was loosely based on the murder of Ben Barka, a fearless spokesman for Third World rights and exiled leader of the leftist opposition in Morocco, who disappeared after being picked up by two policemen in the prosperous St-Germain district of Paris. After the ensuing investigation, in which government officials and the SDECE (the French equivalent of the CIA) were implicated, public trust in the French government had been badly shaken. Jean's role was that of a hospital employee, with left-wing sympathies, who is also the girlfriend of Darien, the cat's-paw in the plot.

Jean was paid $40,000 for three weeks of work, taking the principal female role alongside Roy Scheider, Philippe Noiret, Michel Piccoli, Jean-Louis Trintignant, Gian-Maria Volonte and Michel Bouquet. To prepare for the role she lost weight, and sharply cut back her intake of both alcohol and tranquilizers.

For the beginning of the film, Boisset used footage of an actual demonstration against the Vietnam conflict which was held in Saint-Denis. The director shot the film himself, as Jean and Trintignant joined the column of protesters.

Boisset attempted to film on Paris streets on many occasions during the shoot, but was always turned down by the French police because of the politically sensitive nature of the film. This conflict came to a head when Boisset wanted to film outside the Brasserie Lipp on the Boulevard St-Germain, where the real kidnapping had taken place. Boisset alerted the international press to attend the filming, sensing another confrontation. Although not written into this scene, Jean appeared to lend her support to the director along with Trintignant, Piccoli, and Volonte. The police backed off, realizing the arrest of the four stars could result in embarrassing headlines, and the scene was filmed without official interference. When released later in the year, *The French Conspiracy*, her twenty-ninth film, became a box office hit in France and was Jean's last commercial success.

Jean began socializing more, and in the course of a few months was linked to aspiring filmmaker Ricardo Franco, André Previn's younger brother Stephen, and Fabio Testi, then one of Italy's rising young actors. One night when she was at Castel's, a trendy Paris discotheque, Jean caught the eye of Dennis Berry, another struggling filmmaker. "I was bowled over," Dennis recalled. He wanted to meet Jean personally, but felt the disco was not the best place for introductions. With the help of his friends and connections, he organized a party at a friend's home. Among those invited was Jean Seberg.

"She showed up with this macho Italian movie star Fabio Testi," Dennis said. "I was horrified. For the first time in my life I didn't have anything to say. I just gaped at her." Jean did the same. "Then," she later recalled, "I surprised myself by doing something I'd never done before in my life. I turned to him and said, 'Will you come over here and kiss me?' And he did."

The two talked for twenty minutes while Jean's date glared at the pair. Testi stormed out of the party in a rage, slipped on the stairs, and put his foot through a glass door. This night, one which Testi may have wished to forget, marked another turning point in Jean's life. Soon, she and Dennis Berry were seriously involved.

Twenty-seven years old with no money, Berry was American-born. His father was film director John Berry, who had been identified as a Communist during the McCarthy era. "Of course I know who named me. I certainly do," John Berry said. "Edward Dmytryk — Eddie Dmytryk. He was one of them. The others, I don't know for sure." Film director Dmytryk was also known as one of the Hollywood Ten.

To escape the wrath of Hollywood, and in order to support his family and continue making films, John Berry moved his family, including wife Gladys and six-year-old Dennis, to France in 1950 — "just as the list was to be made public."

"My reason for leaving the United States was because it was a period in American history when we were betraying one of the great ideas of our nation," John Berry explained from his residence in Paris, "and it was an atmosphere that I felt [had no concern] with my views about my country and my feelings for what was correct, ethically and morally.

"I left as a means of combating those ideas which I considered to be unacceptable, and continued my struggles against them from here. If I had stayed in the States, I certainly would have ended up going to prison."

John, however, held no ill-feelings toward the United States. "Not at all. That's my motherland. It's a country which I love — I've always said that. My motherland is America, and France is my wife or mistress. That's the way it is."

The transition to Paris for Berry was "difficult. I arrived here in 1950 and didn't officially start working until 1953. Dubbing, coaching English, I shot a television picture without my name on it and a full-length feature without my name [on the credits]."

John Berry's career included directing several plays and films in Europe and the United States. Among the films were *He Ran All the Way, Tamango* with Dorothy Dandridge, and *A Captive in the Land*, a joint U.S.-Russian production. Berry was also the model for Robert De Niro's character in the 1991 film *Guilty by Suspicion*. Shortly after completing *Boesman and Lena*, starring Danny Glover and Angela Bassett, Berry died in 1999 after suffering an attack of pleurisy.

Full of ambition, energy, and very talkative, the curly-haired Dennis Berry appeared in various small film roles. Among these was, by an ironical coincidence, *Promise at Dawn*, the 1970 film based on Romain Gary's account of his early life, starring Melina Mercouri. In the film, he played Romain Gary's friend.

Although acting helped pay his bills, Dennis wanted to make his own films. With his salary from playing a gangster in Borsalino, he made his first short film, *Jojo ne veut pas montrer ses pieds* (*Jojo Doesn't Want to Show His Feet*). The film brought Dennis critical acclaim and several honors, and he was named one of the most promising young filmmakers.

Jean found Dennis a breath of fresh air, a man with a devil-may-care attitude who, as she put it, "speaks fractured English with a Brooklyn accent." A heady romance ensued, and the couple saw each other every third day, all the while telling themselves they were not serious. "We decided: 'Let's settle things. If there's something between us, fine. Otherwise, we won't see each other again.' And we left for Saint-Malo in Brittany: three days walking on the beach, laughing, crying, until we realized, for reasons which still elude us, that we wanted at all costs to get married."

Three weeks after their first meeting, Jean and Dennis flew to Las Vegas to be married on March 12, 1972. With no American money on them,

Jean put the entire trip on credit cards, including the wedding rings. They were married at Chapel of the Bells around midnight by a former Iowan, a Reverend Peters, who recognized Jean's Marshalltown background. While they exchanged their vows, the minister's children were watching a movie on television in a back room. The movie was *Frankenstein*.

While Romain had a bouquet of flowers and a bottle of champagne waiting for the newlyweds, he also had Dennis investigated before the couple's return. "I asked around and everyone said he was penniless and a scrounger. I was convinced that he was another person using Jean. I could have killed him," Romain later ruminated. "Jean may pay the bills, but I reckon Dennis saves her a small fortune because he doesn't let her be taken for a ride. He has no expensive habits."

Unfortunately for the newlyweds, not everyone welcomed them with open arms. "Some of my oldest and dearest friends who had definitively classified me among the wives of diplomats have been astonished to see me in the company of this longhaired young man," Jean said. "And when I've introduced Dennis, saying that I loved him, they have thought I'd gone mad. They have assured me that it wouldn't last, and used all the cruel arguments which friends can find to show they have your interests at heart. Perhaps they weren't capable of understanding."

Jean's new father-in-law welcomed her into his family. He had known Jean for several years and had worked on François Moreuil's film *La récréation* as a technical consultant. "My relationship with Jean was a very loving, tender kind," John Berry said. While the two had endured similar experiences with the United States government, they never discussed what happened to either of them. "I rarely discussed politics with Jean," John Berry said. "Whenever you called into certain areas that were painful for her, the curtain would come down. Absolutely."

Soon after their return to Paris, Jean appeared in Fabio Testi's violent Neapolitan gangster film *Camorra!* As soon as her cameo role as the chief gangster's mistress was completed, Jean and her new husband left for a delayed honeymoon on the island of Capri.

When a reporter from *Elle* asked Dennis in the spring of 1972 if he and Jean were experiencing difficulties because of their vastly differing backgrounds, Dennis answered, "Why? That Jean is a big actress? So much the better. She helps me morally and financially. Love is an exchange. I only tolerate deep relationships, and for me, they are only possible through cinema."

Dennis admitted Romain Gary was "a guy I really like," but simply summarized Jean's marriages one by one. "The first was an accident of youth. The second, Romain, that was culture. Me — the bilingual ignoramus — that's the return to the source. I only have one simple image of Jean: That of happiness."

For a while, Jean was completely happy. Through Dennis, she discovered a new world — the artists. Not the established artists who lived in fancy villas; rather, the struggling artists who simply awaited discovery. Soon she found herself engulfed in a group of such people. "I only work with people who are very good," she maintained. "It's not charity. I feel I take as much as I'm receiving. The people I have around me also give me the courage to forget the disappointing things."

Jean was now more aware of people who used her name and status to further their own careers or goals. "I've known when I was hustled [in the past] and I've known why I let it happen." Witnessing the underground artists' ambitions and developing talents brought her a new confidence. She began to write again, working on scenes, short stories, and poetry. "If you keep busy, you don't go crazy," she said.

During the summer of 1972, Jean and her friend, the exiled Cuban film director Fausto Canel, wrote a screenplay entitled *Frontière Palace*. It was a lighthearted comedy about a film crew which arrives at a hotel in the French Alps, with a young hotel employee who falls in love with the star and follows her to Paris. Jean took scenes from her own life for the scenario, and the piece included barbs that were clearly aimed at Otto Preminger.

"Jean thought it was difficult to be an actress at that point in her life. She thought her film career was ending," Roger Grenier says. "She turned to writing poems and to other areas of writing. She showed me the script *Frontière Palace* and she asked me to write a French adaptation. I did it for her."

Jean received a grant from the French government to pay for one-third of the film's cost, but she was unable to raise the remaining funds. Paramount Pictures was interested in the script, and sent a telegram to Jean to begin negotiations for the rights. However, when Jean insisted Canel be allowed to direct the picture, Paramount refused the request and the project was shelved. "Nobody had seen Canel's pictures," Grenier says. "All his films were confiscated by Castro, so no one could see his works. But Jean was firm in her decision. She wouldn't change her mind. I suppose it was out of friendship."

Although Dennis Berry benefited from his wife's name (and her ex-husband's money), he continued trying to find film work, and also wrote a screenplay entitled *Le grand délire* (*The Great Frenzy*) for Jean to star in and himself to direct. His film would be, Dennis hoped, his "way of crowning her" as a star. Jean was reluctant to read the script because she "thought it would be bad and I love him too much." She eventually read her husband's work and was convinced the script would translate very well to the screen.

While Dennis looked for financial backers for the movie, Jean took a role in a Spanish suspense film, *The Corruption of Chris Miller*. Here, Jean plays Ruth, an English costume designer, who, aided by her neurotic stepdaughter Chris (played by singer Marisol), one night kills an itinerant hippie the women suspect of being a serial murderer. Jean didn't care for the script, but she needed the money.

Filming began that August in Spain, and Jean was additionally dismayed when director Juan Bardem wanted to age her in order to make the mother-daughter relationship more credible. Her fear that her makeup would be unflattering, however, proved unfounded. She still looked good on the screen.

In 1979, *The Corruption of Chris Miller* played in New York, where it was erroneously billed as Jean Seberg's last film. Reviewer Vincent Canby wrote: "... she gives an extremely sincere performance that is never particularly convincing. Once again, though, she gives dimension to a film of no great interest just because her presence is so unexpected. What, one keeps wondering, is this quintessentially American beauty...doing in the middle of so much quintessential European decadence?"

Roger Grenier remembers another film Jean planned to make for Juan Bardem, but the director-penned story "was a very bad script. No good. And we said that. Romain Gary originally offered, with me, to rewrite the script — to make it better — for free, only out of friendship to Jean. But the Spanish are very proud..." Grenier says. "The film was never made."

In October, using her salary from *The Corruption of Chris Miller*, Jean and Dennis bought an apartment in the rear of the rue du Bac complex, overlooking the courtyard. This allowed her to be still close to Diego, but just far enough away from Romain. She was still on friendly terms with her ex-husband, but her new marriage to Dennis lacked privacy, especially with Romain stopping by the apartment up to twice a day. "Although Romain is a charm and a delight, it is a strain on a young husband to have his wife's former husband dropping in every now and then for a can-opener," Jean explained. "And Romain did drop in occasionally — in a very civilized way, because he is a very civilized man."

Jean decorated the new apartment herself. In contrast to the marble or slate floors and ancient sculptures of her surroundings during the Gary years, the decor of her new residence was comfortably low key. The main living room had a color scheme of blue, pea green and emerald green, with a yellow ceiling and white woodwork. She had a set of white wicker furniture made especially for the room, and several plants added to the airy ambiance. As a final touch, Jean commissioned a special mirror, with a small silhouette of herself sitting on a rock alone, looking out onto a lake.

In December, Mr. and Mrs. Dennis Berry flew to Marshalltown for the Christmas holiday. There, Jean introduced her new husband to her parents and other relatives. Her family was not prepared for Dennis' flagrantly extrovert behavior.

"He was very outspoken," Velma Odegaard felt. "He took my brother's car

and wanted to drive it around town. He came back and was so unhappy —
sort of grumbling. He said, 'I have found out there are absolutely no poor
people in this town! No poor people!' Well, I didn't know what he expected.
We didn't know what to make of it. Nobody hardly said a thing. I wasn't
impressed with him. I thought he took advantage of Jean — just from my
feelings, from meeting him that short time."

At her parent's home with Dennis for the Christmas, 1972 holiday. AUTHOR'S COLLECTION

"He was anxious to have a good time and acted that he really liked Jean,"
says Mary Ann Seberg. "But he was, in a way, trying to run her life. And he
had so many aspirations that may or may not have included Jean." A close
friend of Jean's simply commented that Dennis Berry "was a spoiled brat,"
but Rabbi Serber remembers Dennis as "a nice young guy. They were happily married. She would sit on his lap and I could just see her eyes sparkle."

Jean's gift to her parents was a gift certificate for a trip to Europe. For
Dennis, she bought a Marshalltown High School letter jacket worn by athletes to publicize their accomplishments. Dennis wore the jacket, but he still
looked out of place in the tight-knit community.

After showing Dennis the Tama Mesquaki Indian settlement where Jean
donated $500 to help the Mesquaki Bucks basketball team purchase uni-
forms, Jean met with Sandy Schlesinger of the Marshalltown Community
Theater. Jean and Dennis discussed the possibility of presenting a play in the

Martha Ellen Tye Playhouse. "I'd love to do it as a 'thank you' to those in Marshalltown who helped me get my start and the many who have been so wonderful to me," Jean said. Dennis indicated he hoped to produce a play with Jean starring, and using some of the local theater people in the piece.

"In movie work there's a high, hard work for a short period, like a sprinter, then a chance to relax before the next scene," Jean theorized. "On the stage, you go all the way through a performance — like a long distance runner — each time." Unfortunately, Jean Seberg's return to the stage never materialized.

Before leaving for New Jersey for a short visit with Mary Ann and her family, Jean gave the customary interview to the *Times-Republican*. "We've gorged ourselves on mother's Swedish and German dishes and Maid Rites," she laughed. Diego stayed in Paris with Romain because of a problem with rheumatic fever, which Jean thought would be aggravated by the Iowa winter. "We were all together to open presents under the tree the night before we left," she told Warren Robeson.

"Please tell everyone I'm so sorry not to have had the chance to see more people. I want to wish all my friends a Happy New Year even though I didn't get to see them."

26

"At thirty-five [Seberg] is a very different person from the shy ingenue Otto Preminger discovered. Her obsession with acting has magnified, her self-confidence has stabilized...she has toughened up."
— Susan d'Arcy, *Films Illustrated*

Early in 1973, Jean awoke in the middle of the night and slipped in the dark hallway of her apartment, breaking her ankle. For the next three months, she wore a plaster cast while the injury healed. During her recovery she wrote her parents: "I'm getting along pretty well. Wednesday I went to the clinic and the x-rays look good, so they put a heel on my cast and I hobble around on my crutches. It was hard at first, but I'm almost a professional now. I just about wore Dennis out before that, as he carried me in his arms everywhere in the house and in and out of taxis. And there have been a stream of visitors to keep occupied. I'm writing a script — a Western with Dennis, so I while away a couple hours a day in front of this typewriter."

Unable to work while confined with the cast, she contemplated her finances. She wrote to several friends reminding them of money she had loaned them, hinting that she was having financial problems. Although Jean owned the summer house on Mykonos and the rue du Bac apartment, and was paying for the farm in Iowa, there was relatively little to show for the millions of dollars she had earned during her film career.

Throughout her life Jean sent $200 a month to Frances Benson, enclosed checks in letters to her family and arranged scholarships for relatives and friends. In New York for the premiere of one of her films during a hunger strike, she gave $20 bills to black children who lined her route to the theater.

"She did loan us money to make a down payment when we bought our first house," Mary Ann Seberg admits. "But it was done through lawyers and we paid the loan back through attorneys."

"Jean was never the type of person to insist on a lawyer," remarked Rabbi Serber. "That had to be Mary Ann's doing."

"Yes, my husband and I insisted on a lawyer," agreed Mary Ann.

That loan may have been the only one that was repaid. In the late 1960s, Jean's drama coach Paton Price borrowed $25,000 to purchase several acres of land in northern California. Although a wise investment, the money was never paid back to Jean, and the land has multiplied in value over the years.

Early in her career when a New York taxi cab driver had complained that he did not have a Christmas gift for his wife, Jean impulsively gave the driver the fur coat she was wearing. She helped her make-up lady with the purchase of a flower shop in Paris. Jean donated at least $10,500 to the Black Panther Party, in addition to several thousands to charities. And, rather than using tax shelters, she paid the full amount of income tax due each year to the United States government (up to 1970, as far as can be substantiated). Despite pleas from friends to invest her money more wisely rather than be subject to such high taxes, Jean felt it was her obligation to pay what she owed.

Jean also simply gave money away to friends. "I like to have friends laughing around me," Jean said in 1974. "I also like good food and good wine — so what if I'm the only one who can afford to pick up the check?"

"Jean was not a selfish person," says Mary Ann. "She wanted to make people feel comfortable and to help them. She made a lot of loans to many people, and I don't know if they ever remembered that Jean had given them anything."

It was Romain Gary who came through and helped Jean and Dennis with an allowance. "She was very, very impressed by Romain," Vony Becker says, "but in a way she despised him because he was very macho, and very worried about not having enough money."

"Romain helped Jean by giving her money two times a week," Roger Grenier adds. "He felt if he gave more she'd … [he throws his hands into the air]. They remained very, very close, and he became a father figure to her." Grenier recalls on one occasion while Romain was talking with him about Dennis Berry, he mistakenly referred to Dennis as "my son-in-law." Romain did once state publicly, "Having ceased to be my wife, Jean became my daughter."

In May 1973, Frédéric Mitterand, nephew of French socialist politician and future French President François Mitterand, held an appreciation for the actress, of whom he was an avid admirer. A banner reading WELCOME JEAN SEBERG hung outside his Olympic theater. While clips of Jean's films played onscreen, a band played American marches in an adjoining garden and guests munched on a buffet. Jean mingled with guests for about an hour, leaving only when her ankle began to trouble her. She appreciated Mitterand's efforts immensely.

On May 30, Jean attended her son's confirmation at Notre Dame. Because of Eugenia's influence, Diego wanted to be a Roman Catholic. "I guess the most important thing," Jean wrote her parents, "is that he has a religious formation, regardless of sect." Asked recently by an interviewer whether he identified more with his mother's Protestant or his father's Jewish background, Diego Gary opted decidedly for the latter. In his book *La nuit sera calme* (*The Night Will be Calm*, 1974), however, Romain Gary made his own position clear: "Where religion is concerned, I'm a non-believing Catholic. But it's perfectly true that I have always had a great soft spot for Jesus."

Although Jean did not formally practice her Lutheran religion in her later years (calling herself a "tortured Swedish Protestant, like Ingmar Bergman"), she kept a cross at her bedside and occasionally went to an empty church, where she would light a candle and sit for a while in thought.

"I believe in Christ, but not in most Christians I know, and I don't practice the religion in a formal way," she said. "I just think a lot of people don't live what they preach — and I don't either. I'm not pretending that I'm better than anybody else. But there was always a contradiction to me about the austerity of hell and damnation as I was raised to hear about it, and Christ's principles of love and forgiveness."

As a child, Jean attended summer Bible camps and had contemplated devoting herself to the Lutheran Church. She later concluded that "the constant preaching about man's guilt was a very bad thing" for her. One friend recalled that the man who taught Jean her catechism was a "screamer," and became so worked up at times that he "frothed at the mouth. Jean hasn't forgotten him, or the feeling of unworthiness he gave her. I think the experience may have had something to do with her reactions to Otto Preminger later."

"I was raised in a rather strict atmosphere. For a long time I lived waiting for the return of Christ on earth," Jean confessed. "Now I laugh at what people think." Romain, however, felt Jean's Protestant beliefs, with their "burden of guilt," weighed heavily in Jean's fate.

Ed and Dorothy Seberg decided to use their Christmas gift of a European vacation from Jean and Dennis that summer. Their travels included a trip to Sweden, where Ed's parents were born, followed by a visit to France. "Just let us know what you had in mind, and let me know your arrival date," Jean wrote her parents. "I'm having a check sent to you, as we promised you at Christmas, and with the poor value of the dollar, I'm sure you can make good use of it! Diego will be sad the football season is over, as that's something he would have really enjoyed doing with his grandpa, I think."

Jean also wrote of the prospects of acting:

"My leg is better — still tires me and hurts mornings, but the worst is over. I'm worried about finding a film to do, as I haven't worked all year.

"I have my fingers crossed as I'm up for a film in London with Michael Caine. The dates aren't sure and I'm not definite, but I hope it all works out Should know within the week. It's been so long since I've worked, I'm feeling pretty rusty."

Jean did not get this part, and furthermore missed out on a role she might have considered her second *Breathless*. François Truffaut was preparing a new film and had Jean in mind for a role as an actress. Although she had earlier been unable to play the leading female dual role in Truffaut's *Fahrenheit 451*, she still hoped to work with the acclaimed director who had championed her.

Truffaut tried in vain to contact Jean — telephoning her, leaving messages — but he never received a response from her. It is quite possible Jean never knew Truffaut wanted to speak to her about the project. Truffaut eventually gave up and cast Jean's *Airport* co-star, Jacqueline Bisset, in the role. The film was *La nuit américaine* (*Day for Night*), which won multiple awards, including the Oscar for Best Foreign Language Film and the BAFTA for Best Film.

Ed, Dorothy, and Kurt Seberg stopped by Paris in August 1973 for a few days. Before their return to the States, Ed and Dorothy announced to Jean and Dennis they had pledged $1,000 to Trinity Lutheran Church in Jean's name. Unknown to them, Jean could have used the money herself. In November she sold the farm in Iowa at a small profit. The sale was a disappointment, for with the farm, Jean's dream of retiring to a home in the country also disappeared. When she told Frances Benson, her grandmother tried to be reassuring. "Don't blame yourself, Jean," she said. "It just turned out that way. There aren't many people who really understand crops and cultivation."

In a 1974 interview with the London *Observer*, Jean outlined a scenario of how her life might have been had she not been discovered by Preminger. According to this, she planned to attend the University of Iowa, then tried to break into acting: "Because of all the sexual repression of my Midwestern upbringing I would have quickly got involved with some guy at the university and… I would have married him. It would have been a disaster, and we would have broken up.

"I would then have gone to New York to try and fulfill my ambition to be an actress, and probably married a second time, an actor or a director. And that would have been about it." Romain Gary added his opinion in that "To understand Jean, you have to understand the Midwest. She emerged from it intelligent, talented and beautiful but with the naivety of a child. She has the kind of goodwill that to me is infuriating — persistent, totally unrealistic idealism. It has made her totally defenseless. In the end it came between us."

The article also touched on Jean's association with the Black Panthers: "Jean now argues that she may have been 'used' but she knew it and was prepared to let it happen if the results were worthwhile. Gary puts it brutally: 'She was white and taken for a sucker.'" When the article appeared in Iowa, the *Des Moines Register* ran the story on page one with the headline "PARIS IS HOME TO JEAN SEBERG, HER 'AMERICAN DREAM' TURNED NIGHTMARE."

To the *New York Times* the following year, Jean admitted, "Around 1968 I got mixed up in a lot of things that had nothing to do with acting — a profession which was coming to mean no more to me than getting made up into one kind of Barbie doll or another. I officially broke with [the Black Panthers]. I've analyzed the fact that I'm not equipped to participate absolutely and totally."

In November 1973, Jean received another film offer. This project, called *Mousey*, had possibilities: it would be American-produced, with production taking place in England, and she would star opposite one of Hollywood's legendary leading men, Kirk Douglas.

"Mousey" is the nickname of a timid and introverted biology teacher whose wife (Jean) divorces him and remarries, taking their son with her. The son of whom he is so proud, however, is not his child: "Mousey" had married his wife after she became pregnant by another man. The loss of his wife and beloved stepson turns the humiliated man into a psychotic stalker bent on revenge.

"When I was offered *Mousey* I thought I should do it because it meant exposure in the States," Jean said. "Because of the scandal I don't imagine I'll work in America again. Also nothing much has ever been offered me from England, although directors write me sweet letters saying: 'We must work together.' It was quite a good woman's part." Jean also added that it was the first "really interesting" role she had been offered in a year.

The casting of Jean gave the director, Hollywood veteran Dan Petrie, Sr., the chance to work with a woman he had long admired. "I had met her at Cannes in 1961," Petrie recalled. "I was there with my film *A Raisin in the Sun*, and she was sort of the hostess to our little group, and Jean was sort of Sidney Poitier's 'date.' Roman Polanski was at our table, and he had not yet done *Knife in the Water*. Jean was just lovely, charming, and a beautiful woman. She really was.

"The casting director made a list of various people for the role in *Mousey*, and when I came across Jean's name, I suggested her. The fact that she was already in Europe and therefore we didn't have to pay huge transportation costs to bring her back and forth helped the budget. And the fact that there was name value also helped. Plus, I genuinely wanted to meet her again."

After shooting approximately half the movie on location in the eastern townships outside of Montreal, the cast and crew flew to London to film interiors and Jean's own scenes. Petrie met with her and reminisced about

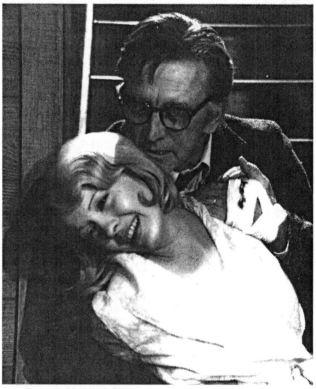

Mousey *with Kirk Douglas, 1973.* AUTHOR'S COLLECTION

their meeting in Cannes. "She had not remembered the details as vividly as I had," Petrie said; "Certainly not with my slant."

Petrie was pleased to have renewed his acquaintance with her, but found she was not the same woman as the one he had remembered from twelve years earlier. "Of course, we all change," he said, "but she was such a different person from this Golden Girl I had met at Cannes, who had such great social ease and a happy outgoing disposition, to this rather demure, careful individual. But she was still beautiful."

The month-long filming in London went smoothly, and Petrie recalled Jean got along "fine" with the cast and crew. He also felt Jean had done an acceptable job in her role. "It really wasn't a demanding role. She had to show 'fear,' and she could handle that quite easily," Petrie offered. "Jean seemed capable and able to do rather simple demands. But one had the idea it was a way she had of having an income, but her heart wasn't really in it. She came ready, with her lines memorized, and she didn't put any demands on me at all."

At one point during the production, while the crew prepared for a scene which required the use of a corridor, Petrie searched for a room to study the script without interruption. "It was in an office building, so I looked around and found this nicely appointed, quiet room — not an office, but more like a sitting room. So I went inside, sat down, and got my papers out." He was there for about fifteen minutes when the door opened and Jean entered the room.

"Oh, I'm sorry!" she said as she started to back out.

"No, no, no. Jean, come in," Petrie said. "Is this your room?"

"Well, yes," she replied. "They mentioned that I could use this. But you go ahead."

"No, no. Heavens. I've already tried to find a place to work," Petrie explained as he started assembling his papers, "and this was the only place. So please — it's yours."

"No," Jean refused. "You're absolutely welcome to stay here. Please, go ahead. Stay."

Petrie sat back down and returned to his work as Jean walked to the other side of the room and sat down. While she leafed through a magazine, Petrie glanced at her. "I just saw her there, nicely made-up and coifed for the role. And, I don't know why I said this, but I asked her, 'Jean,' and she looked up at me, 'why do you have such a poor opinion of yourself?' She looked at me for a second, then she just started to sob, a real outburst. It made me feel so terrible. I thought this 'together' person would have said, 'You think I have a poor opinion of myself? Well, I don't!'

"But she just fell apart. I dashed over, knelt down at her feet and embraced her. I said, 'Oh, please…I'm so sorry. I didn't mean…' Then she proceeded to tell me her story — the whole story of her life, from her childhood in Iowa, and the whole thing with Otto Preminger, who emerged in this conversation as a real villain. She alluded to the FBI, but didn't go into any great detail. She wanted to tell me in a way why she had been stripped of confidence in herself."

After talking for half an hour, the two were called to begin filming. Later, Jean invited Petrie to dinner with Dennis, who had accompanied her to London. Petrie remembered the evening was "very pleasant, and I must say, I liked Dennis. I had met his dad years before and was familiar with his work as a director." Petrie noted that while he "didn't notice any behavior on their part that set them apart as being 'wild,'" he did have concerns about Jean and Dennis's marriage "because of the age differential. There was something very boyish about Dennis, and something very ladylike about Jean. It seemed like a boy admiring an older woman."

Petrie also said Jean had not mentioned their conversation in the office. "She was back to being her guarded self, but still very pleasant and very sweet — there's nothing wrong with that — but I felt there was a facade."

Mousey was retitled *Cat and Mouse* for theatrical release outside the United States. In the States, the film marked Jean's television acting debut when it aired on ABC-TV as part of a weekly series of thrillers. "It wasn't very good," Petrie concluded. "We did our very best and made it as scary as it could possibly be, but I just don't think the script was too solid."

"I liked Jean a lot," Petrie stated. "She was careful. She was 'ladylike.' There was that aspect to her. When I heard some of the subsequent tales of her political involvement and so on, those things surprised me, because the person I met was almost 'demure.' My shock of reading of her downward journey — in a way it was shocking. But in another way, from what I experienced on that one occasion in the office, of a woman really in despair, I was not shocked with what happened."

On December 31, 1973, Jean celebrated the incoming New Year with Dennis. Happy and resolutely positive, "I'm going to live this year as if it were my last," she vowed.

27

"Am I right that Jean Seberg seems to have disappeared?"
— a fan to the *Los Angeles Herald-Examiner*, 1973

Early in 1974 Jean was approached by young experimental filmmaker Philippe Garrel, who wanted to use her in a film. Garrel had earned accolades for his works *Le lit de la vierge* (*the Virgin's Bed*), a 1969 modern Jesus parable starring Pierre Clémenti, and 1971's *La cicatrice intérieure*, featuring Clémenti and Velvet Underground singer (and Garrel's lover) Nico.

Garrel remarked in 2002 that he enjoyed viewing film footage before the editing process and had planned a similar project for Jean in 1974. Because of problems raising money for the project, Garrel decided to shoot on 35-millimeter black-and-white film, with no sound. As the film was originally conceived, Jean and other actors would in turn convey their individual solitude; but now Garrel decided that his film would focus predominantly on her. Not only did Jean donate her time and partially finance the film, but she also allowed Garrel and an assistant to shoot in her apartment for several days.

Berthe Grandval, a friend of Jean's, remembers Garrel visiting Jean often, discussing the film and spending several hours planning scenes. "He was very gloomy, very slender, very nervous, and very romantic," Grandval says.

Though produced with minimal resources, *Les hautes solitudes* (translated as either *The Outer Reaches of Solitude* or *The Extremes of Loneliness*) constitutes a great deal more than a glorified black-and-white home movie. It includes scenes of Nico from another film which Garrel never finished, as well as featuring Tina Aumont and Laurent Terzieff, all actors who had worked with Garrel before. Yet it is clear that their roles are secondary here. Garrel captured a fragile Seberg: blowing out a candle; having her hair combed; wiping tears away; delicately smelling a flower; gazing, deep in thought, out a window; expressions of agony, weariness, and resigned sadness.

Though the images of Jean Seberg reveal some of her private sorrow and loneliness as well as her beauty, some wondered why she appeared in a film which was so avant-garde. Her answer to that was that she considered herself "a journeyman actress. I'm not concerned with Art with a capital 'A,' and drama, and Academy Awards, and all that. But acting is my trade, my craft, and I have to go from city to city with my make-up case, the way some little old men go through the streets with sharpening knives."

"In the way that nobody in the art world knew quite where to go after Picasso broke through into cubism, young film makers haven't known where to go stylistically since Jean-Luc [Godard]," Jean said in 1974. "There are a lot of young directors, like Philippe Garrel, who are returning to images which speak without sound. It's almost going back to silent film making. And I think it's healthy. I don't think it's regression. It's part of rebirth and growing.

"Of course, it isn't everybody's cup of tea. It's certainly not something the masses are going to rush to watch. But it might be part of the beginning of a way of re-inventing cinema."

The finished film had little commercial value but played in art houses. "I don't think if I had used a French actress, the film would have been a success," Garrel commented in 2002, when the film was given a screening in Tokyo. "Jean [was] not French, but American. She [was] different from other actresses. Among the actresses who worked with me, Jean was the best."

In mid-March 1974 Jean vacationed with Dennis in Zermatt, Switzerland, spending her time relaxing and developing future film and writing projects. Jean sent Dawn Quinn a postcard while there:

Sweet friend — Since I never seem to write, "hello" and love to you all from this lovely Swiss village where I'm relaxing. No cars — just horses and sleighs. So pretty!

I have the white Bible you gave me so long ago by my bed in Paris. We are all well and happy — much love and hope all is fine.

— Jeana

While Dennis continued to secure financing for *Le grand délire*, an idea was presented to Jean that she readily accepted. Jean-François Ferriol, an aspiring actor, told Jean that he wanted to make a movie about Billy the Kid. Jean was intrigued with the idea and added the character of a fading sex goddess called "Star." "The figures are the cult figures of their respective ages," Jean said, "both now completely out of date. They represent the last two people left in the world. The film simply relates their last meeting." The title was *Ballad for the Kid.*

With Jean-François Ferriol in the film short, Ballad for the Kid, *1974.*
AUTHOR'S COLLECTION

Ferriol and Jean wrote the script "as a surrealistic film," Jean stressed, along with help from Dennis. Several of Star's lines were written by Jean herself, and they were autobiographical with touches of self-mockery: "Nobody believes in us. Nobody believes in us anymore," Star tells Kid. "We're has-beens." In another scene, the wind blows a crumpled newspaper to Kid's feet. He picks it up, sees a photograph of Star in the newspaper, and compliments her on its quality. She grabs it from his hands and tosses the newspaper away. "The press is a bore," Star says. "Mass media is a bore."

The $10,000 budget was split between Jean and Ferriol, with Jean acting, editing and directing at no cost, and there were no producer or writer fees. Filmed in seven days with a small crew, no insurance was taken out for the production. "It won't be that much different from a home movie," she said. "Everyone else is doing it — why not me, too? I want to find out if it's the kind of thing I want to do."

Once word got out of Jean's film, the press descended upon the film's location in a sandpit near Orly to record "Preminger's folly" turned director. The *New York Times* did a major profile of her, and photographs of Jean in a low-cut evening gown looking through the camera's viewfinder graced the pages of several French and British newspapers.

"People are making too much of this," she said of the press coverage. "It's just the realization of an idea I liked. It's not a big picture. I have no illusions about it. I'm not going to be onstage Oscar night. When it is shown to the audience, I would just like to say, 'Let me invite you into a little dream.'"

On the set, reporters noted how energetic Jean was, and how well she used her time preparing scenes while also encouraging Ferriol in his screen debut. "I haven't been burning to direct for years, or anything like that. It scared me a lot: I keep thinking of that precise French audience who know what they want," Jean told *Films Illustrated*. "I would like to do more. Many women directors will tell you that it is very difficult to get into the male stronghold. I had a name as an actress and I used it to get this working. I would say to anyone who wants to direct — go out, no matter how little money you have or how old the equipment is, go out and do it."

Jean wrote her family in July 1974 about the film:

> I've been all day every day shut up in an airless, dark room doing the cutting of my little film. It looks pretty good — at least I like it! The next big step is that I have to convince my 'Star' who wrote it with me and co-produced it that his French accent is just too strong. At first, I thought the idea of 'billy the kid' having a French accent was funny, but it really doesn't come off.

> The movie business is just disastrous right now. Half the films planned have been canceled, and everyone seems to have finance problems. The biggest success here right now is a 'skin flick,' and there seem to be more and more of them. You wouldn't believe the scripts I'm offered — and even in the half-way good ones there are objectionable scenes. I hope it's just a fad, but it makes it hard to find something worthwhile to do...don't want to get a spanking from my Pa.

Ballad for the Kid resulted in part from the absence of other film offers. "Various projects come up and then don't come out," Jean said. One was an

Italian film and another was an American movie with Tuesday Weld to be filmed in Connecticut. Both films fell through. "If I can get good work, it doesn't matter what kind of project it is," Jean offered. "People work because they have to work."

Still, Jean had reservations about ever working on another Hollywood film, even if an offer came through for her. "Usually when I go to the States — although *Paint Your Wagon* was an exception because it was a costume film — they tend to put some awful wigs on me — *Airport* is an example — and I become a wind-up plastic doll," Jean said in 1974. "Robert Rossen on *Lilith* is perhaps the only American director [with whom] I have really been able to communicate completely as an actress.

"The most stimulating thing about any of the American films I've done so far, I'm sorry to say, has been the money. On the whole I have fairly miserable memories of what I let be done to me when I go to Hollywood. I let them turn me into something I'm not. I seem to have no will, no way of coping — until recently. But now I've changed quite a bit."

It was at this time that Jean renewed her friendship with her *Bonjour Tristesse* co-star Mylène Demongeot. Jean and Jean-François Ferriol used the production house of Demongeot and her husband, Marc Simenon, to finish *Ballad for the Kid*. "She did a very good job with that film," Demongeot says today.

The completed project resembled a filmed one-act stage play, and with Jean's weight gain, her voluptuousness and portrayal of Star resembled a combination of a fading Marilyn Monroe/Tennessee Williams-type heroine. *Ballad for the Kid* was shown at several film festivals at the end of 1974. Unfortunately, despite its value as a curiosity, the film's commercial life was minimal. Perhaps what counted more was that Jean had crossed another threshold in her life.

"I realized the other day that I am 35 years old. I have therefore spent over half of my life walking around the back of and in front of cameras. It's strange for a woman to see her face and her very being change — recorded on film. And I begin to think that maybe there are one or two of all the things I've done — some of which are so bad — that one day my son is going to discover in the *Cinémathèque* or somewhere."

If Jean sounded emancipated by having made *Ballad for the Kid* and moving forward with other projects, she dismissed being labeled a "woman's libber." She did support women's right, but was perplexed at the notion of women wanting equality on all levels. "These days women seem to behave in a bizarre fashion," she remarked. "They are so concerned with not being regarded as sex objects that it makes them aggressive and distant, attempting to dominate men by a lofty rejection. It's a great pity because in this way they deny their own nature and impede its fulfillment. I hope this ridiculous fashion will pass, but I'm afraid men will have to show patience in the next fifteen years."

Dennis finally secured a government grant to cover part of the costs of *Le grand délire* and found financial backers, mainly through Mylène Demongeot and Marc Simenon, for the remaining costs. "Dennis had made three or four short movies which were very, very good," Demongeot says, "and we thought he was very talented. So we decided to produce his first [full-length] film.

"Then we saw Jean again. Of course, I saw the difference. She wasn't as sure of herself as before. And she'd drink too much. I know she'd drink big glasses of vodka."

While Dennis prepared to begin filming *Le grand délire* at the end of December, Jean was offered and accepted a role in the Italian drama *Bianchi cavalli d'agosto* (*White Horses of Summer*). Filmed partly in Rome, the work was beautifully shot and reunited Jean with her *Revolt in the Caribbean* co-star Frederick Stafford, but the limitations of the narrative meant it failed to achieve success, either critically or commercially.

The story turns around a married couple who spend most of their vacation arguing. The tension is apparent from the beginning and only intensifies with the appearance of a young journalist. The squabbling causes their son to run off along the nearby cliffs, where he accidentally falls to the rocks below, is badly hurt and rushed to a hospital. The parents wait outside his hospital room, unsure whether their son will live or die. Acting the vigil reminded Jean of the days after Nina's birth, waiting to find out whether her daughter would live. In addition, the pressures of acting and directing *Ballad for the Kid* earlier had taken its toll on her nerves.

Dennis arrived in Rome after he was informed Jean was experiencing difficulties. Signs of a breakdown were evident as she told her husband there were people chasing her. Dennis discussed the situation with Romain Gary over the telephone, and it was decided Jean should be returned to Paris. "Things just went wrong...," Roger Grenier recalls, from what Romain Gary divulged. "Gary told me 'It was impossible.'"

In Paris, Dennis admitted Jean into a clinic, where she was heavily medicated with barbiturates. Jean blamed this breakdown on *Ballad for the Kid*. "It was a mistake trying to direct and act at the same time. It made me completely schizophrenic. I just wanted to make a little Freudian film, but it turned out to be a round-the-clock struggle. I'd go home after the day's shooting and cry all night. People complicate the cinema so...Maybe I didn't work hard enough on it."

While Jean recuperated, Dennis continued fine tuning his screenplay. Mylène Demongeot sent a copy to her friend Sergio Leone for a critique. Leone was famed in America for the Spaghetti Westerns which launched the film career of Clint Eastwood.

Leone read *Le grand délire*, then telephoned Demongeot. "It's very good," he told her, "but there's work to be done with it to be good enough for a movie. Send me Dennis Berry." Demongeot and Simenon sent Dennis to Spain, hoping he would return with a finely tuned, polished screenplay. But Dennis disagreed with Leone's suggestions, and returned to Paris after six weeks.

He telephoned Demongeot shortly after: "Sergio Leone is a horrible man. I refuse to work with him."

But Leone had also telephoned Demongeot and Simenon, telling them: "Drop the movie. That Dennis Berry is a stupid guy. You shouldn't do the movie with him." Only because of their friendship with Jean — and because Jean wanted to do *Le grand délire* so badly — did Demongeot and Simenon decide to go ahead with it.

Jean and Dennis went to Switzerland in December with Demongeot and Simenon. For ten days, they stayed at a hotel ("Which resembled something like the one in *The Shining*," Demongeot laughs) where they tried to curtail Jean's drinking and help lose the weight gained from her hospital stay. "It was nice — we shopped and talked about the movie," Demongeot recalls, "but Jean didn't say much."

One incident in Switzerland caused the trio great concern. The room in which Jean was staying had a locked bar which was stocked with liquor. She did not have a key to open it, so she pried it open and drank the alcohol. Demongeot and Simenon then realized how far her drinking problem had stretched.

When the four returned to Paris, they worked on the final preparations for Dennis's film. At the end of the month, production began on *Le grand délire*, budgeted at approximately $2 million. Berry's finished screenplay tells the story of penniless drop-out Pierre (Pierre Blaise), who persuades his middle-class friends to turn their family mansion into a bordello after their father dies. The maid Marie (Isabelle Huppert) is to be the star attraction. Pierre falls for their American friend Emily (Jean), who is to join the enterprise, together with the mother (played by Dennis's mother, Gladys Berry), who will take over as maid. The plan succeeds, but it soon becomes clear that there is no place for the misfit Pierre, and he recognizes that it is time to move on.

With Dennis as director, there were tensions on the set — not only with Jean, but between him and almost everyone involved with the film. The first day of filming did not go well. "It appeared that Jean was drinking heavily," Marc Simenon remembered. "And with Dennis, she wasn't holding him back, but he couldn't get what he wanted. She was saying, 'Denny, don't tell me what to do.' Even though she was drinking and all that, she still was, more or less, boss.

"Denny had a strong temper, but she had a stronger temper. She had a strong character, a strong personality. When she said 'no,' it was no, and that was enough."

At the end of the first day's filming, Dennis announced he did not want the producers on the set for the remaining days of production.

"We did stay away," Demongeot says. "Marc always regretted it. He said, 'I should have stopped that movie immediately the first day.' Marc was a director, and Dennis a young director. He said, 'I cannot do that to a young man who's doing his first movie,' and he regretted that he didn't do it." Demongeot says that in addition to being banned from the set, being able even to view the rushes of film footage was difficult. "[Dennis] had a whole crew against him," Simenon felt. "And to have a crew against you, you're going to have problems."

Jean's taking direction was not the main problem on the film. She had, however, not lost all of the weight she had gained, and when Dennis asked her to do a nude scene, she balked. He, in turn, became furious and yelled at her. Still, she refused. The director/star relationship recalled experiences with Otto Preminger. "I found it quite hard work. Dennis was very rough on his mother and very demanding with us all," Jean remarked later. "Isabelle Huppert and I, who both worked with Preminger, nicknamed him 'Little Otto.'"

"Berry had an attitude that was unbelievable," one eyewitness on the set revealed. "Things didn't go well between him and Jean because he was quite rude to her. They had a lot of arguments. It was not a happy shoot."

On March 6, 1975, Jean wrote her parents:

> Here we are all fine. Denny is putting the finishing touches on his film and is gone early morn and home late at night, so I complain a little, but the truth is that I'm so happy he could finally get it done after such a struggle that I don't really mind. I'm writing a new screenplay with a friend, which helps to fill some of the long hours, and there are whispers of a film in Spain for the American market in June. Nothing sure, so touch wood, as business everywhere is lousy and I am just another of the millions of victims of that. We are living on a very tight budget, which in itself is a good lesson for me with all my past extravagances, and we don't really suffer that much: it just means paying more attention to things and not being such an easy 'hand out' to friends. Hard to say 'no' sometimes, but it must be that way.

When released, *Le grand délire* failed both critically and commercially. Some felt it was this film which brought an end to Jean's already fragile French career. *Variety* simply viewed the work as "an excessive first film" and called for "more cohesive" script writing, as the producers and Sergio Leone had advised.

"I was not pleased," Jean's French agent Olga Horstig-Primuz says of the film. "She always made a picture with her husbands and they were always bad pictures. Thanks to her, they could make a picture. But she was so influenced by them, and the films were terrible. It was funny because she had a lot of personality..."

Despite the problems, Mylène Demongeot feels *Le grand délire* is not without merit: "The casting was very good. Isabelle Huppert was excellent. The movie was not really bad. It could go on television very well today."

"It [was shown in] Paris for a week," Simenon stated. "It was, as we say, a flop. I haven't seen the film since it was released. It was as much Berry's fault — the script had gone backwards, and he was not able to direct Jean. [But] the film had some good things and charm, much because of Jean. She had a great presence on the screen. She was good."

In the remaining months of 1975 Jean and Dennis vacationed at her cottage in Mykonos. From time to time, she went through bouts of depression. A curious letter to the *Times-Republican* in 1975 showed her in an unfamiliar vein:

> I have written John Garwood thanking him for an article in his "Sighting Upstream" column of July 15, 1975. If you want to reprint this little item and use my letter, I would be very proud.
>
> Various forms of meditation are being exploited around the world and especially here in the United States. There is nothing new about the good physically and mentally attained through meditation, as any dedicated fisherman will tell you. To wander along a placid stream or one that bounds and bubbles over a rocky bed to drift at sunset on a pine-shored lake, there is peace and contentment you will find no other place. Harried business and professional men regularly seek the deep woods and faraway waters with fishing in mind, but actually they are searching for a place to rest and meditate away from the busy world and are better for it.
>
> Some of my best friends are fishermen, including Friends of Jesus, and my father (Ed Seberg). You are right, that is where perhaps one day men will come together (and women, too!) to find peace. I have a friend who is taking me fishing (soon).
>
> Jean Seberg
> 108 rue du Bac
> Paris, FRANCE

When the Berrys returned to Paris, Dennis founded an informal actors' workshop to help budding professionals explore other avenues in performance. In the months that followed, a dozen or so friends came to their apartment several times a week — some by motorcycle — to act out scenarios and discuss directors like Michelangelo Antonioni, while Jean served peanut butter sandwiches. She liked the play of ideas and took part in some of the workshop's improvisations.

But the idea of motorcycles in the quiet and exclusive rue du Bac complex did not sit well with most of its tenants. "Most of the people here hate us, either because we're radical leftists, or because of the motor scooters, or because we walk the dog without a leash," Jean said. "They're not the kind of people who are always running over here bringing me a chocolate cake — even though I have made great overtures. When one of them dies I write letters of condolence."

The lack of friendly neighbors — who had been amiable when she was Madame Romain Gary — obviously irritated and disheartened Jean. The reticence continued, for the following year she composed a poem:

> Nobody ever speaks
> Too many ghosts behind the doors
> The old lady across the way
> She died
> Nobody knew it
> I would like
> So much, so much
> To take a pumpkin pie to someone
> No one will want it
> We make too much noise

With no personal income, and with the failures of both Jean's and Dennis's films, decisions had to be made in regard to their financial future. Dennis wanted to move to the United States, where the opportunities for a young filmmaker were far greater than in France. Jean balked. "Most of our world is here in France," Jean reasoned. "Something in me is not equipped to be in America and play those games, selling yourself over martinis, being charming and gay and bright. It's not worth the fight. They always transform you into everything you aren't."

Another reason Jean did not want to leave France was Diego. In her divorce agreement with Romain, it had been decided that Diego would be raised and schooled in France. In addition, Eugenia, his nanny since birth, was dying of cancer, and Diego was not dealing well with his "second mother's" illness. Jean had a responsibility to thirteen-year-old Diego. She had felt guilty for leaving him in order to work on films in the past, and she admitted she could have been a better mother to him. But she would not desert him in order to move to the United States for a career that carried no guarantees.

Mylène Demongeot recalls a friend telling her about seeing Diego: "I don't remember who it was who told me, but I was told Jean was dressing Diego as if he were eleven [Diego was actually thirteen years old]. And they

With Dennis, circa 1975. COURTESY OF SEBERG FAMILY COLLECTION

said, 'Jean, you cannot do that. He's a young man and you disguise him as a little kid to make yourself younger. It's ridiculous! Be yourself! You have a kid, you have a kid! Let him act his own age.' 'No, no, no, no,' Jean said. 'He's only eleven.' So it was dropped.

"I saw him once around this time, but it was only a glance. Although [Jean and I] were very frank together, it was none of my business. But for the little boy, I thought, certainly he must be very unhappy. Perhaps not. I really don't know."

Diego Gary, however, denied having an unhappy childhood when, after many years of silence, he gave an interview to *Elle* in October 2004. He felt he was much loved as a child, and dismisses the story that he was abandoned, which was later circulated in the press. "[My parents] traveled a lot," he remembered. "They were involved in their respective careers, but I lived in exceptional circumstances with a governess who worshiped me. I was very spoiled, cherished, supported."

Diego retains a montage of vivid childhood memories of his parents. He remembered his mother singing Stevie Wonder's "You Are the Sunshine of My Life" to him many times. He recalled, too, how she taught him English by reading the *Herald-Tribune* out loud and played cards with him. His "official duties" included zipping the top of her dresses and buying her roses. She demonstrated tap dancing too, and sang "Happy Birthday" in a voice "as moving as Marilyn Monroe's." When he experienced his first hangover she was there to soothe him. Another image was walking Sandy the dog in the Bois de Boulogne. "My mother loved animals. We always had some at home."

Jean had given him the book *Catcher in the Rye* to read. When vacationing in Majorca she took him and many of his friends in her red Coccinelle (Ladybug) convertible to the football field. "She was beautiful, tanned, radiant," Diego wistfully recalled of this trip, "and I was so proud."

There could sometimes be disagreements. Jean would not stand for him being temperamental or showing disrespect, including the people who worked in their home. "Those were our only rows," Diego said. Once he had angered his father by forgetting Jean's birthday: "He practically threw me out." It was his mother who consoled him. They would sometimes exchange poems. "She was wonderfully loving, [but] I think her life began to fall apart when she lost my little sister. That was dreadful for her."

"Jean spent as much time with [Diego] as she could," says Mary Ann Seberg. "But he spoke Spanish very, very fluently, in addition to speaking French with his parents and English when he had to. I think their relationship was different from that of our parents because of the time limit and the logistics. The time they spent together seemed to be quality time."

The Sebergs were a very typical family of the 1940s and 1950s. Ed Seberg worked at the pharmacy, Dorothy was a housewife, and the family ate most of their meals together — as did most American families at that time. However, with economic changes beginning in the 1970s and middle-class American families needing a two-person income to sustain their standard of living, more and more families spent less time together than had the previous generation. In Jean's case, however, Diego accompanied her on-location with most of her films. Jean arguably spent more time with her son than the average American mother, considering that their time together multiplied when she wasn't working.

Romain's relationship with Diego was also close. One of the boy's teachers referred to his eminent father to shame him for misspelling words. Romain was incensed that his literary renown should be thus turned against his son. "He didn't want me crushed by his fame," Diego explains. As the boy grew older, Romain treated him as an adult, and told him about his work, friends, love life and experiences.

One day, when Diego was fourteen, he and his father were conversing. Romain had unexpectedly remarked: "One day your mother will kill herself."

28

"Every human being is a masterpiece, even with the defects."
— Jean Seberg

At the end of January 1976, Jean did an interview for Radio France with Jacques Chancel. In it she spoke about her life and career, but then a question inevitably touched on the published rumors about Nina's paternity. She did not evade the issue, but compared the "intrusive" American journalism unfavorably with that in France, adding that the item would not have mattered to her if it had been true. When Chancel asked her whether she could forgive those responsible for publishing the rumors, Jean paused. "I find that hard…"

Jean began devoting more of her time to writing. Clearly, Romain's influence had been pervasive during their years together, and this may in some ways have been inhibiting. But her own urge to write had always been present; Jean had already told Mylène Demongeot in 1957 that if she could not be an actress, she would become a writer.

"I have to do something. I couldn't just be a housewife," Jean told another interviewer. "So I have entered my literary phase. I can write as easily in French as in English. Perhaps I'll give up the movies altogether someday. I've never programmed my life. It's always been impulsive, instinctive. Things have happened to me — some good, some bad. Luck counts for so much, but I don't know if I believe in fate. What I find interesting now are the people who ask themselves questions. People who don't ask questions — the contented cows — don't interest me at all."

Unfortunately, few pages of Jean Seberg's writings survive. Several friends who had read pieces written by her, however, believe she had enough talent to become a successful author. "She was a helluva poet," John Berry said. "I think they were quite wonderful. She could write. She had everything going for her, but then she'd have that negative moral judgment of herself that I certainly never had [of her]."

In April 1976, Jean appeared in a German film adaptation of Ibsen's classic play *The Wild Duck*, entitled *Die Wildente*, which explores the consequences of the ruthless exposure of truth for a family with secrets. Jean had enjoyed the author's works since she was a child. When director Hans Geissendörfer approached Jean for the role of the photographer's wife, Gina, she accepted because she was won over by Geissendörfer's passion and commitment to the project.

"I hadn't even seen his earlier movies," Jean confessed in the film's pressbook. "I don't need to. I'm not much concerned about what a director had done previously. I decide to participate if I have a good feeling and a good impression of the director, and if the things he has told me about his movie have convinced me." She felt that "only three or four times" in the course of her twenty-year career had she worked with directors who loved their work and took it seriously. "Today I would rather not work at all than be involved with something I don't believe in."

"You're going to like me in this one," Jean wrote her parents. "I look just like G.G." [Granny Grunt, the the Seberg's nickname for Frances Benson].

In The Wild Duck, *1976.* COURTESY OF SNORRAMYNDIR

Concerned about her recent weight gain, Jean was relieved this would be hidden under the bulky costumes she had to wear for the role. While her part in the film was small, it was nonetheless a vital one, and Jean performed and looked well. Her hair was braided and worn on top of her head, bringing out her Scandinavian features, especially her prominent cheekbones — proving Otto Preminger had been wrong when, years earlier, he warned that if she gained weight she would lose this feature.

The role represented a new challenge to Jean as an actress, one that she welcomed. "It's no longer enough for me to be 'Jean Seberg' and look pretty and put on some silly cinematic airs," she said. Sand-filled weights added to Jean's shoes helped develop her interpretation of the character, one of a woman whose self-denial does not spare her from the tragic revelation of a past mistake.

The final scene of *The Wild Duck* is horrific. At the end, Gina's illegitimate daughter Hedwig climbs to the attic to sacrifice her duck at the instigation of her father's meddling friend Gregers. Instead, the girl sacrifices herself, and the parents come upon their daughter's dead body. Although not widely shown, the film was well-received by critics and most of Jean's notices were positive.

When Jean returned to Paris after completing the film, she received a letter from the United States Department of Justice. Dated June 6, 1976, the Department of Justice made arrangements through the Department of State for the letter to be personally delivered to Jean in Paris. The letter informed Jean that she had been an FBI COINTELPRO target.

The report issued by the Senate Select Committee on Intelligence detailed the methods the Hoover FBI had been using since 1947: paid informants, opening private mail, and lying. Anonymously referring to Jean, the Committee found: "When the FBI learned that one well-known Hollywood actress had become pregnant during an affair with a BPP member, it reported this information to a famous Hollywood gossip columnist in the form of an anonymous letter. The story was used by the Hollywood columnist."

The confirmation of the FBI's plot proved to Jean that she had indeed been watched and her privacy invaded, as she had long believed. These had not been the fantasies many people had supposed them to be. The damage, though, had been done, and rather than bringing any sense of relief the revelations simply fostered further anxiety.

By summer 1976, the Berrys' marriage had deteriorated to a series of misunderstandings and fights, with Dennis still unable to find work and Jean experiencing violent mood swings. Matters came to a head when Jean suffered a new breakdown. Dennis checked her into a private sanitarium, where special care was given behind locked doors. No visitors were allowed apart from him. Jean was once more prescribed lithium, which caused her to gain additional weight.

After a few days Dennis took Jean out of the sanitarium, and the two vacationed near Bonifacio, where he rented a house on a private beach. The time there proved cathartic for Jean and Dennis both, and the two decided to give their marriage another try.

Career-wise, Jean had been considered for another film, although it is unclear whether she knew about it. Donald Cammell was planning to direct the science-fiction thriller *Demon Seed* for MGM. According to Cammell's widow, China, he wanted either Jean or Julie Christie to play the lead role of a woman who is terrorized by a superintelligent computer which takes on human characteristics. For reasons unknown, the studio was opposed to the selection of Jean Seberg, and thus Christie was signed. Although the film was a modest hit, it had gotten a wide release in the United States, something which none of Jean's post-1970 films received.

Back in Paris, Jean requested a copy of her FBI file from the Department of Justice under the Freedom of Information Act. In November, she received a package which contained documents from her FBI file. She read each page and memorized passages, including the planned rumor and Hoover's proposal to neutralize her. After reading them and showing them to Dennis, she gave the documents to Romain to hold for safekeeping.

While Jean's correspondence with Marshalltown friends was infrequent in the final years of her life, she did write to Dawn Quinn at Christmastime:

> ... I was badly ill this year. I told my folks that I had viral hepatitis, so as not to worry them too much. The truth is I had a very bad nervous breakdown with persecution mania and the whole shebang. Don't ever let my folks know, dear Dawn, it will only frighten them, and they have had their worries...As for myself, it took months and I am in psychotherapy, but the worst is behind me, and Dennis and Diego supported me wonderfully. I take lithium, which as a nurse I'm sure you know. It's an effective anti-depressant...only problem is that it tends to make me put on weight.
>
> Diego is a delight, Dawn — tall and handsome and bright in school. He already has a little girlfriend. He and Dennis get along well and we all have some fun times together. As for Dennis, he is active with a TV project and with his second long film. It's been hard for him, and it's also been painful that he has brought in practically no money since we were married, but it really hasn't been his fault. I'm sure things will pick up in 1977. They just have to.
>
> When I hear you speak of your religious faith, I almost envy you. I lost mine somewhere along the line, and it saddens me as I know what consolation it can bring. But I still read from time to time the little white Bible you gave me so long ago and I think of you tenderly. I'll close now, but let's do keep in touch more often.
>
> I love you, my friend. Be strong.
> Jeana

This was the last time Quinn heard from Jean.

Jean Seberg — Breathless

CHAPTER NINE
1977-1979

"I used to believe in fairy tales, but part of me has become more realistic."
— Jean Seberg

With Romain and Diego. COURTESY OF HELEN MASON

29

"Jean needed help, but I don't think the people around her knew she needed help, or how to get her help."
— Mylène Demongeot

In mid-April 1977, Jean returned to Marshalltown during Diego's Easter break from school. It was her first visit to the United States in more than four years. The party comprising Jean, Dennis, Diego (then fourteen) and Diego's girlfriend was met by Ed and Dorothy at the Des Moines airport. In Marshalltown, Jean telephoned Carol Hollingsworth and spoke for awhile. "Jean said, 'Daddy's not letting me go anywhere' since she was home for a short time," Hollingsworth recalled. "We kept in touch several times a year — on my birthday, Christmas and in-between."

Frances Benson was almost ninety-six, and Jean treasured the moments spent with her during the visit. The year before, Frances had served as Grand Marshall of the Bicentennial Parade, riding down Main Street in an open convertible. "She had always been a serene woman, but toward the end she began to be fearful," Jean reminisced. "It was hard to understand her because she continued to joke about things. She hoped to remarry: she was looking for 'an old widower, very rich, if possible, of pleasant disposition.'"

Jean gave the *Times-Republican* a short interview: "We had hoped to come home for a visit last year, but I've been ill with infectious hepatitis for nearly a year," she explained. Jean told Warren Robeson of *The Wild Duck* and that there might be a chance to star in the upcoming Italian production *Let's Laugh* [the Italian film was actually never realized.] Jean also told Robeson, "I have a New York literary agent who is interested in my poetry and is encouraging me to do a few more poems to complete a book."

"I'm so sorry to have missed seeing so many friends, but time was just so precious," Jean said on her last day in Marshalltown. "Perhaps we can come back for a longer stay later this year."

After three days in Marshalltown, Jean and the others headed east to spend another three days sightseeing in New York and to visit Mary Ann Seberg and her family in New Jersey. Upon her return to Paris, Jean thanked Mary Ann:

> "This is just a brief note to tell you all what a jolly time we had during those (too) few days with you at Easter — from Great Adventure to church to the softball games (oh! — my aching muscles) and back again. The food on the table was delicious and the warmth in your hearts even more so. And

it's all inspired Diego to improve his English (hurrah!)

"I'll write at length soon — and Diego promised he would too, didn't he? But this was just to say from all four of us to you all, many thanks and — hey — when do we show you Paris?"

In Marshalltown with Frances Benson, April 1977.
COURTESY OF SEBERG FAMILY COLLECTION

Although Jean traveled to Marshalltown dozens of times in the 1950s and 1960s, this trip was only the fourth time she had returned to Iowa in the 1970s. It also marked the last time Jean visited the United States. Some Marshalltown residents believed Jean felt she was, after living in Paris and Hollywood, "too good" for Iowa. But that was not the case.

"I don't feel that it's atypical for anyone who gets to be her age and moves away not to visit home more often," says Mary Ann Seberg. "It's difficult to travel from one continent to another, and she wanted to spend more time with Diego. I think what concerned me more was that there were periods of time when we didn't hear from her, and that's because she was sick. But we didn't know about [Jean's illnesses] until much later."

With no film work lined up — and not especially wanting to work with her weight gain — Jean took on another cause in Paris. She unofficially devoted her time to helping the drug addicts on the Paris streets. "Drugs injected into the Paris scene much later than in the United States wreak havoc around us…" she wrote to Rabbi Serber. "Pathetic phone calls in the middle of the night, begging for money and love, mostly money, perhaps as a demonstration of love. At times, we refer to our house as 'the clinic.' At times, weary, we just withdraw and turn off the phone and don't answer the doorbell."

When Jean encountered addicts, she urged them to get help and put a few francs into their hands, hoping that it would go toward a hot meal rather than the next high. Jean opposed illegal drugs with a passion, and was trying to do her part in helping those less fortunate who were addicted.

Stories would circulate that Jean herself was addicted to one or another illegal, hard drug. According to her son and her friends, those stories were completely untrue. In several published interviews, both Jean and Romain were extremely vocal in their stand against illegal drugs and their effects. It was true that she took and came to depend on prescribed pills, but they were medication given to her under a doctor's professional care. They were to help her.

In August 1977 Jean learned that Frances Benson passed away. Her grandmother had suffered a stroke and was in ill-health for a short time. Despite her admiration and the strong attachment she shared with Frances, Jean did not return to Marshalltown for the funeral. "I didn't want to see her dead," she later explained.

In mid-October Jean wrote to Rabbi Serber, regretting that due to lack of finances, she had decided to sell the house in Marshalltown which she had purchased for black students. "I would definitely like to get it on the market as soon as possible. It has been many a day since I filmed with a really good salary, so the house has become a weight on my shoulders," she wrote. "I think of the house as a failure, which is sad."

Shortly after, she mailed Serber the papers necessary for the sale with a note of apology: "I do so wish I could say to you, Rabbi, take the house and use it as you feel best. But such is life — I'm not in that position at the present."

Income was not the only problem in Jean's life. Her marriage to Dennis was teetering badly, with many arguments culminating in physical fights. Jean told a few friends that Dennis hit her and had a violent temper.

One friend says Dennis Berry "hurt her whole life. He made her breakup with her friends and anything that dealt with her life with Romain. He was very jealous." Another claims Dennis would make Jean eat peanut butter and "other fatty foods to make her fat. She didn't need those mind games."

In addition, many of Jean's friends hold Dennis responsible (and dislike him) for allowing "freaks, drug addicts, hangers-on" into her home. Roger Grenier believes, "All those people took money from Jean. I think it was very unpleasant. She was a born victim."

"Whenever I would meet him on the street, I'd refuse to shake his hand," says one friend from the Romain Gary era who was *persona non grata* during the Berry years. "As soon as she hooked up with Dennis Berry, she went downhill quickly."

John Berry knew there were problems in the marriage. He felt the main problem was what had been put upon Jean before she met Dennis: "My point of view is, the bullshit values of America's success and the great need for celebrity, et cetera, had a great deal to do with the destruction of the pure aim that motivated her at the beginning. She was very bright; she wasn't just an actress or another great face. She was [a] very bright, sensitive woman.

"In France, of course, [it] was 'be beautiful and shut up.' There was always a problem with a woman being clever enough to hide her superior intelligence. Jean was always very straightforward. But when they said that [her daughter] was a black child, the disgrace was how we reacted to [the rumor], rather than saying, 'How dare they do that!' This was a terrible crisis in Jean's life because she had to deal with that judgment.

"I think she just lost faith in herself."

With fewer and fewer films being made in France, Dennis continued pressing Jean about moving to the United States where there were more opportunities. "Dennis had written a story that had gotten some attention in California," John Berry said, "and he was told to come and talk about it. I had a picture to make [there] and I said, 'Why don't we all go and [rent] a house?' Jean said if Dennis went to California, their relationship was over." Jean would not consent to the move. After his reasonings developed into extended arguments, Jean ordered Dennis out of the apartment. Shortly after Christmas, Dennis flew to Los Angeles to find work and spend time with his father. "Their relationship was over," John Berry claimed. "I approved of his leaving. The problem was he had a choice of devoting himself entirely to her life, and she did need that. I didn't think it was going to work out. Jean considered his leaving an act of treason — betrayal — when he left. It's very interesting, because they both really did suffer in that separation."

"I've changed enough to not expect everything to last," Jean offered in a 1974 interview, predicting the future of her marriage. "There are 120 reasons, besides an age difference, that a marriage can collapse. I'm aware there will come a time when Dennis will move on...Even if it ended with Dennis tomorrow, I would have received a tremendous amount from it."

Mylène Demongeot feels the separation was partially brought on by the *Le grand délire* disaster. "I think when you are a director, and a star, and you have a failure together, things become difficult because one tends to blame the other. Jean was not in good shape and he didn't know what to do with her. Dennis told us she was very fragile, was depressive, and not an easy woman to live with. But he didn't say much else about it."

"I stopped living with Jean because that's what she wanted," Dennis later claimed. "I didn't stop living with her just because she had mental problems. They were painful and destructive. But I would have lived it out to the end. Jean didn't want me to…She didn't want me to." Still, there are many who feel Dennis took the easy way out. "He didn't take care of Jean, and he used her," says one man who co-starred with Jean in one of her later films. "He loved her money more than he loved her. To leave her when he did was unforgivable." Jean informed her parents of the separation, and wrote to Rabbi Serber. "She said that she was very sad, but it wasn't killing her — it wasn't destroying her," Serber says. "She knew that it wouldn't work. She had to go on with her life, and he with his interests."

After Jean and Dennis separated, she remained close to his parents. John Berry thought she had grown into a "lady with all kinds of sensitivity and intelligence. The last period of her life she was under a terrible strain, but I saw a terrific growth in her. How impressed I was by the clarity she had about her own life. I always wanted her to write her story. She said it was too painful — the sense of loss.

"I don't think she ever [examined] the wonders of her life. She always dwelled on the negative terms. She had quite a life…What a life!"

Despite the encouragement, a friend recalls that John Berry made it a habit to use Jean's telephone "whenever he needed to call the United States, or place any other international call. And she had to pay the bill."

Harry Stein of *Esquire* also remembers Jean in this era of her life. "She was a remarkably fine human being, fragile as crystal but animated by spunk and vivid humor," Stein wrote in 1981. "…in her late thirties and by no means wealthy, she found herself examining other career options. She enjoyed writing [and] at one point she broached the idea of a monthly column from Paris for *Esquire*. But it was rejected, as were most of her other brave attempts to sell herself in this new guise.

"The easy sell, she knew, was an autobiography… But it was a notion she approached with great trepidation. 'My problem,' she told me one evening, 'is my parents. It would cause them such enormous embarrassment. I don't know. I think I'll wait…'"

In early January 1978, Jean once again allowed Philippe Garrel to use her apartment to film. This time Garrel filmed the experimental *Le bleu des origines* (*The Blue of the Beginning*). At the last moment Garrel asked Jean to replace a performer who was too stoned to work. Jean is virtually unrecognizable and received no screen credit.

Indeed, even after the departure of Dennis Berry, Jean's apartment continued to be a haven for what are deemed "the misfits of society"— alcoholics, drug addicts, homeless, mentally deranged people. "I guess I am a fellow traveler — at a distance — with what you might call 'leftist causes,'" Jean explained. "When people are in a jam, they sleep or hide here." Jean herself continued her reliance on the anesthetizing effects of alcohol to take her mind off things. "I am not an alcoholic," she said. "I just have a drinking problem."

A letter Jean wrote to *Libération* was published at the end of February 1978. Entitled "Love Letter to the Junkies," it was a vehement, rambling and incoherent piece which showed nothing of Jean's talent for writing. But it did reveal a state of mind which gave cause for concern:

To the drug dealers:
So much better the hit, so much better. Dirty seedy bastards…you're obscene.

…I feel like chatting. You'll smash my face in? (keep me from talking) Try it!

To the police:
I know that you have an unpleasant job. I know you're sick of it. Don't beat up my friends any more who are trying painfully to get out of their despair. Behave nicely, please! I beg of you. You know better than I where the coke is, who makes it, where it comes from and who profits by it. You know as well as I who protects whom and why and where the money goes. Be keepers of the peace. OF THE PEACE! That's noble. I implore you, I beg you.

To the French people:
Just one last thing, but an important one. Be kind to the Arabs and the blacks in France. Treat the Portuguese and the Spaniards kindly. They don't have an easy job. Talk to them kindly. Man to man. Like equals. There was a time when France had a reputation for that. A magnificent reputation…And now, with a thousand excuses, I am obliged to be demanding. I beg you. Do all that, and people will look on you with esteem. Don't do it and — and I say this quietly (important), politely, as a woman who doesn't know how to defend herself— that there are two Mohammeds (snigger) in my life. (Oh, I know. All the Arabs are called Mohammed.) One of them is "cafe au lait," American, famous, quick, but doesn't like to hurt people. The other is someplace else. Not far. Not close enough. But if I tell them softly that you are not being kind, they will come. They will get into planes. Be samurai, not beaters, of the sad Algerians or the victims of a cancerous society. In short, don't forget your catechism. (Even in public

school you learned it.) "Love your neighbor as yourself."
So behave yourselves, be calm. Love one another.

Each one of us sings the blues. Thank you.

P.S. I know that I'm going too far, but I'm unable to forget
this phrase of André Malraux: "Make men aware of the
greatness that they ignore in themselves."

In March Jean checked herself into another clinic for observation and
rest. The doctors strongly advised she should stop drinking and get her body
back into shape. Under medical supervision, she reported to a weight loss
clinic where she began a liquid protein diet. Looking ahead, she wrote to
Rabbi Serber, "The time is long, but I'll be proud of the new, svelte me."

Six weeks later Jean emerged model-thin. She had won this latest battle, curtailed her drinking dramatically, and, to celebrate her new look, once
again had her hair cut in the shorter *Breathless* style. She also filed for divorce
from Dennis shortly after her release. Unfortunately, the regime's results
were temporary. Some friends believe that this weight loss program — difficult enough for a healthy woman, but harmful for one in a frail condition —
is what pushed Jean over the brink. By mid-summer, the diet's true effect on
her health became evident.

The Sebergs were hoping for a reunion in summer 1978 as Diego and
Romain would be in the United States. Jean wrote her sister in July:

> ... As for me, I may be joining them there, but, confiden-
> tially, Mary, I had a very, very bad nervous breakdown and
> am convalescing and I wouldn't want the folks to see me in
> the trembling shape I'm in. It will just worry them to death.
> I am under doctors' treatment and heavy medication. So,
> with a saddened heart, I must absolutely count myself out
> of a family reunion. You'll just have to pretend to the folks
> that I am working on a film and couldn't get away. I know
> it's sad, but I beg you to understand, as I would want to see
> them well and strong and it's much better that all of you
> see only happy faces.
>
> So call or write Romain about the dates as you suggest and
> I'm sure something can be arranged for the kids, as Diego
> expressed the desire, too, to see you and his cousins.
>
> Don't worry about me as I will pull out of this, but please,
> please keep it a secret between you and me, will you? I love

you and miss you all…just need to "put the pieces together again." I think the severe diet I followed exhausted me and is partly responsible for my present burnt nerves.

My best to Ed and the girls, of course.

Much love,
Jeana

In August, Romain stayed at the Connecticut guest cottage of author William Styron (*The Confessions of Nat Turner*, *Sophie's Choice*) while Diego attended a tennis camp nearby. Styron decided to pay Romain a weekend visit and was surprised to find Jean had accompanied her ex-husband to the US. "[I was] shocked and saddened by her appearance: all her once fragile and luminous blond beauty had disappeared into a puffy mask. She moved like a sleepwalker, said little, and had the blank gaze of some-one tranquilized (or drugged, or both) nearly to the point of catalepsy," Styron was to record in his book *Darkness Visible*. He was touched, how-ever, by Romain's caring for Jean, "both tender and paternal." Romain told Styron Jean was being treated for the disorder that afflicted him, as he too was beginning to suffer from depression, although it was not incapacitat-ing. (Styron himself later battled depression after he gave up alcohol in 1985.)

After returning to Paris Jean spoke of returning to Marshalltown in 1979 for the tenth anniversary observance of the Martha Ellen Tye Playhouse, having been there for the dedication. She started to "put the pieces together again" by furthering her interest in writing short stories and drawing, fight-ing off the depression that at times engulfed her. She also began to venture outside her apartment and to stop for coffee at a café by herself, something she had not done in years.

"I was a teenager when I first met Jean in September 1978," recalls Jack X.*, "and I have always kept diffuse and mixed feelings of admiration, ten-derness, love maybe. But I think anyone approaching her was under her charm. I met her at Le Globe, and I didn't recognize her. She was having trouble translating French verses and asked me for help. She didn't reveal her identity. She just said she was 'an American tourist wishing to perfect herself in French literature.' Why not?

"She didn't wish to 'expose' herself in a public place, but at the same time, she didn't bear loneliness. We became friends and would meet infrequently at the same café. I was surprised by her talent of drawing. She was able to sketch the face of any customer coming into the café. I've always wondered

* Note: a pseudonym of an individual who wishes to remain anonymous.

what became of Jean's work — sketches, poems and song verses. She was a charming, average person."

Jean still kept herself informed of world events, reading with concern about US — USSR relations and the nuclear arms race. Now keeping her political opinions to herself, she sadly contemplated the progress of the human race.

Since it appeared that the black movement in the United States had played itself out, Jean turned her political energies to the Arab world and relations between Algerians and French citizens. Jean urged her parents to house several Iranian exchange students so that they could attend Iowa State University in Ames. The Sebergs begged off. They had sponsored a French student in the early 1970s, and although that had been a very successful arrangement, Ed and Dorothy felt they had already done their part.

Through the end of the year, Jean controlled her weight and her drinking, enjoying a glass of wine every now and then, but she continued to take prescribed pills to help her fall asleep at night. She made efforts to socialize, even though she preferred to avoid large crowds. In November, Vony Becker invited her to a party at her and her husband's home. "Jean was very beautiful — very thin and very short hair. She must have been on some kind of medication because she looked 'zonked.' She came to the party with a Spanish guy — Philippe Garrel — who was following her all the time. I don't know if he was a boyfriend or anything, but he'd follow her like a little dog."

When Jean learned Sammy Davis, Jr. would be playing in Paris in December, she attended the opening-night gala with a friend, Raymonde Waintraub. To Jean, Davis was a reminder of a better time in her past. After the concert, Jean and Waintraub went to a reception at Maxim's, where, when Davis saw Jean enter, he broke away and greeted her. For the remainder of the evening, Jean sat next to him and appreciated Davis's attentiveness, especially since there were others at the party with whom he could have chosen to spend his time.

Later that week, Jean and Waintraub went to see Liza Minnelli perform at the Olympia. When Minnelli finished her concert, the audience rose to its feet in a standing ovation. Jean joined the crowd, but then fainted. When leaving the hall, her legs buckled and she again collapsed. This was the beginning of her leg problems and would necessitate yet another trip to the hospital.

In the meantime, Jean continued to have money worries. Romain gave her an allowance for her expenses, but when unpaid merchants turned to him for sums owed to them, Romain took care of these bills too.

"With Jean, 'If I give you my word, you can count on it. If I offer a pledge, you can count on it.' The word 'promise' meant something to her," says Rabbi Serber. "If, for some reason, she had to break her word, it was like killing her. She would give you the shirt off her back if she thought you were down and out. Anyone could take advantage of her. And they did. And she paid for it in many, many ways."

In addition, Jean had few prospects for film work. The majority of scripts she was offered were either poorly written or pornographic — or both. Declining several offers to "act," Jean simply waited for the right script. When a production crew filmed location shots in France for the third sequel to *Airport*, entitled *The Concorde-Airport '79*, Jean could have easily appeared in a cameo of her *Airport* character, Tanya Livingston. She was available, but there was no role for her, and she was not asked to participate.

Hollywood had forgotten her.

Olga Horstig-Primuz says Jean did not have many film offers in the 1970s because of "the rumor that she wasn't particularly well," adding "when people get older, younger people arrive. The older you get, the more difficult it is to get parts. For women especially.

"She was a very good actress, but she didn't have a 'great' picture. *Breathless* was a big success, but after that she was in films that were not important," Horstig-Primuz believes, but adds that Jean never turned down a role that was to become a success with another actress. "A few times she declined scripts because they were not good. She had good judgment. Except with her husbands — then her judgment in scripts was not good."

Françoise Prévost blames the French producers and directors for failing to see beyond the fact Jean was an American, and that her accent was not pure Parisian. "Of course she was American, but she could have played a French girl coming from a French town," she offers. "In *Breathless* she was the typical American. In the other films she made in France, she could have played anything else. And I think it's too bad because I think the directors should have tried to avoid casting her as an American so she could have had more freedom to act."

But perhaps the most severe challenge Jean had to face at this point was the calendar. Her biggest critical hit film, *Breathless*, had occurred almost two decades earlier. The biggest role of her career, in *Lilith*, had materialized fifteen years previously. In almost all of her films, critics and the public alike had highlighted Jean's beauty.

"Jean always had a problem with age. She was always with someone much older or someone much younger. She kind of had a generation problem," Nicolas Gessner says. "She was so bright and perceptive, while at the same time very serious, very to-the-point. Still, with this little irony she had. That's why I was surprised she could never get over that problem with aging."

"Jean Seberg was known for her beauty. She couldn't stand getting old," Mylène Demongeot remembers. "She was very unhappy during that phase. And, as usual, the more you're unhappy, the more of a tendency you have to drink. The more you drink, the more your face ages. The more you hate yourself, the more you drink. It's a vicious circle. It happened to Simone Signoret…"

30

"The last years of Jean's life were pure hell."
— Carol Hollingsworth

On January 3, 1979, Jean checked herself into the Villa Montsouris for a rest. Here, she found the doctors unsympathetic and incapable of giving the help she needed. Abruptly, she had herself transferred to Bellevue, an expensive hospital on the outskirts of Paris. The paralysis in her left leg returned, and injections to help her to sleep proved ineffective. While there, she wrote a letter to Warren Robeson at the *Marshalltown Times-Republican*:

"Marshalltown's Jean Seberg writes from her Paris, France, home that she will probably return to the States only for occasional visits with her parents, for she is still chagrined to have learned of continuing prejudice against her and the black causes she has always defended.

"Miss Seberg says her pain is accentuated by the loss several years ago of her infant daughter, Nina Hart Gary.

"The actress and her son, Diego Gary…still plan on a visit to Iowa this coming summer. Beyond this statement, Jean says she does not wish to discuss returning."

"Jean never spoke badly about America. Never," Olga Horstig-Primuz says, "only about the FBI. She blamed them for everything." This accords with the consensus of all Jean's European friends.

While doctors at Bellevue could not pinpoint the exact nature of Jean's psychological problems, they found that physically she was in terrible shape. Her liver was damaged and her vision poor. Later that month Jean was transferred to a public hospital in Paris. Horrified by the conditions, she fled from the hospital to the safety of the rue du Bac apartment.

In February, she consented to an interview with the *International Herald Tribune*, and in this she stated for the first time publicly that the FBI had harassed her, and that she had the documents to prove it true. Jane Friedman's article read:

"Miss Seberg … says she is followed constantly in Paris. She said she received two threatening phone calls recently in which the caller identified himself as a representative of the CIA and warned that she is being watched. She said she was 'shot at' in December on a Paris street.

"She believes that the FBI or CIA is responsible for the alleged harassment. She talked about these incidents and the alleged 1970 FBI ploy partly, she said, because she fears for her life."

"It took me time in my own mind to decide how to get this out," Jean told Friedman. "I needed years to stamp it out and to bring it out again."

Jack X. recalls Jean's conversations with him at Le Globe, where they would sometimes meet two times a week. "She was upset that she didn't see more of her son, but she didn't go into detail. But she was very bright. She was always open-minded on many subjects, but the topic of social injustice came back very often, and she was pessimistic about the evolution of cinema."

A few days later, in early February, Jean flew to Algiers to meet with Abdul Aziz Bouteflicka, then Algerian Minister of Foreign Affairs. She claimed Bouteflicka telephoned her to come to Algiers and meet with him. Although Jean told several friends he sent her flowers and gifts, none recalls seeing the two together. Few believed Bouteflicka actually asked her to visit him.

According to Guy-Pierre Geneuil, Jean had told him she had been involved with Bouteflicka. "You know, little Frenchman," Jean confided, "I will soon be the first lady of Algeria." After the death of Algerian head of state Boumedienne on December 27, 1978, Bouteflicka believed he was going to succeed the leader. But with this development, Jean Seberg did not fit into his plans. Not only was she the former wife of Romain Gary, a prominent Jewish intellectual, but she was also an American woman, a Caucasian, with well-known liberal beliefs.

Bouteflicka learned through official channels that Jean was aboard a flight landing in Algiers. He did not wish to see her. Geneuil believes Bouteflicka was so angry about her appearance in his country that he "swore a vengeful hatred against her." Jean spent two days in Algeria before authorities ordered her back to France. Officially, the Algerian authorities found Jean's behavior "puzzling." Jean, however, said she had been expelled because of her former involvement with the Black Panthers. In the 1980s, Abdul Aziz Bouteflicka was found guilty of embezzling funds from the Algerian treasury, but by 1994 he was once again a leading force in the Algerian political scene.

After her return to Paris, Jean appeared to be having a further breakdown. Late one evening she stopped by Olga Horstig-Primuz's apartment unannounced. "She kept going to the windows. 'I'm followed! I'm followed!' She was not being followed at all," Horstig-Primuz recalls. "Maybe before, but not at that time. And she was always looking out the window. She telephoned Romain Gary, and he could tell she was affected because she kept saying the same things. It was sad, especially when one knew her from before. She was an intelligent, cultivated woman. She was wonderful. But at the end…"

Shortly after, Romain asked Dennis Berry's mother, Gladys, to sign Jean into Perray-Vaucluse, a sanitarium described as "a real snake pit." There, Jean lived among drug addicts, alcoholics, and the homeless. It seemed that the woman who a dozen years earlier had had the French public straining to catch a glimpse was of her was now living the very antithesis of that life of glamour.

"Either she was totally mad or she was acting," recalls Vony Becker, who visited Jean at Perray-Vaucluse. "I went to buy her a sweat suit so she'd look a little more energetic. She would just sit there in a robe…And she smoked heavily." Becker wept at her friend's condition, and that "our American star" had been reduced to this.

"She was there for some weeks," recalled Gladys Berry. "And [she was] very inert, flat on the bed with dead eyes and a dead voice. And then suddenly, I arrive one day and the nurse says, 'She's leaving on Saturday.' I went up to see her, and there she was. Very vigorous, not paralyzed at all, and full of life and vitality. I said to her, 'How did you … how did that happen?' She said, 'Just willpower.'"

After a month's stay, Jean was released from Perray-Vaucluse. Hospital officials wanted her to continue her recovery at a private hospital, but none would accept Jean because of her lack of finances. Even Romain Gary had stopped giving her money, having grown exhausted by this burden he had been carrying for the past several years. He commented to Lesley Blanch the anxiety was too much to bear. "There is no way out," he said to his former wife on the telephone. "It's her or me."

Jean called Vony Becker to take her home. Becker obliged, but was dismayed after spending some time with her. "I didn't realize how bad it was — what serious shape Jean was in," Becker says. "Jean asked me to do some shopping for her. I didn't have a whole lot of money, but I still wanted to help." Becker bought the food Jean asked for, but was shocked with the enormous amount Jean requested, "like she was going to feed a restaurant.

"Jean was going back home and wanted to be 'a star' again with the friends she had in this certain lifestyle," Becker continues. When she gave Jean the food, Becker received a hastily written poem by Jean. "It was very scary to see her like this with those people around her."

Jean's physical condition began deteriorating again, and she had gained weight. Her mental condition was unstable. "Her fantasies became real. She was in touch with reality — she'd know who everybody was, but she'd believe the fantasies," Gladys Berry said. "One day she came to my house and she said, 'I went yesterday to see Jean Claude in the hospital in St. Cloud, and while I was there I put on a white uniform and helped with an open heart operation.'

"It was as if she was omnipotent. She could do anything. Fix anything. She was on a high that night, but completely out of her mind."

John Berry agreed: "She was pretty disturbed toward the end. She really was. She was going to buy dress shops and selling the *Herald-Tribune*. At one point there was nothing we could do. There was simply no way I could reach her. Or any of us."

Philippe Garrel wrote that he heard Jean had received electroshock therapy treatments. It is not possible to ascertain when she might have received these controversial treatments, since the strict privacy laws in France naturally prevent access to personal records. If they did occur, they were probably administered during one of her hospital stays in 1979. Photographs taken during the first months of 1979 show her looking haggard and lifeless, with dark lines under her eyes. "[The treatments] had a tragic effect," Garrel concluded.

It was during this time that Jean's parents were informed (presumably by Romain Gary) of her mental and physical condition, although it is doubtful whether they were told the specifics regarding the treatment Jean was receiving. Ed and Dorothy were shocked by the news. They had no idea. When they spoke to Jean, they urged her to come to the United States for treatment. Jean begged off, assuring them that she would be fine. She still had ill-feelings toward the United States government and did not wish to receive help in the country that she felt was the root of her troubles. But she assured her parents she would visit them in the near future.

"I don't think she wanted her parents to see the state she was in and go back to Marshalltown," says Mylène Demongeot. "I wouldn't have gone if I were her...When you are 'Jean Seberg, actress,' coming out of Iowa and having a glorious life, you don't want to go back to everyone...How can you stand that sort of judging? It's better to stay anonymous in Paris than to go back there. You'd have to be very, very brave and have the courage [to publicly admit] your problem. That wasn't in Jean's character. She would have died of shame [if she went] back to Iowa and show them how she had everything, and then what she became."

Marc Simenon reveals that he had, in fact, several telephone conversations with Dorothy Seberg about Jean's drinking problems. "We spoke many, many times," he says. "I tried to help Jean. She was caught up by this disease, and alcoholism is a disease. It changes a person. They're not themselves anymore when they're caught up in this drug. I think she was an alcoholic. At the time, treatment centers were not available, etc., etc., etc." But Jean did not feel she was an alcoholic.

In early April of 1979, Jean began donating her time to SOS Amitié, an organization which provided a telephone hotline for people to call with their personal problems. Jean became one of the listeners. Perhaps it was listening to other people's troubles that helped Jean to start dealing with her own. Within a few weeks she was looking healthy again, rested, thinking positively, and looking ahead to the future.

"It was the spring of 1979, and I had not seen her in some time," Jack X. says. "I believed I wouldn't see her again. But one day she walked into

Le Globe, smiling, but very thin and her face was drawn. We spoke for awhile, and she told me she had to make a visit to the United States to her family."

During this time she ventured out to local restaurants and cafés, usually later in the day and staying late at night. For a few weeks, she lapsed into drinking heavily again, which caused her to rant about the injustices in the

Ahmed Hasni, 1979. COURTESY OF SEBERG FAMILY COLLECTION

world, primarily that of the treatment of Algerians in France.

One restaurant she frequented was La Médina, owned by a dark-skinned Algerian named Abdelkader (Kader) Hamadi. It was through Hamadi at his restaurant that Jean met his nephew Ahmed Hasni, in April 1979. Hasni later claimed he had met Jean on an airplane going from Geneva to Paris. When she tried to guess his nationality, he said it was love at first sight.

Perhaps to Hasni it was not simply love. He knew Jean Seberg from her films and status in France, and may have targeted her for financial gain. In the preceding months Hasni had reportedly employed his good looks to gain female conquests that he had later robbed. Although he said he was twenty-nine years old, and had, in fact, changed his identification card to reflect this, he was actually nineteen. Some who met him described him as a "romanticist," but many regarded him simply as an adventurer and habitual liar.

Hasni asserted he was a professional soccer player and an actor who had made eight films in Algeria. At other times he claimed to be the son of a rich Algerian merchant, whereas in fact his mother ran a steam bath in Oran. He also told Jean he had close ties with the political world in Algeria. Nothing could have been further from the truth, but Jean believed his stories. She called him "Sheriff."

In the spring, Jean wrote her parents telling them of her latest lover:

> ...Paris is full of tourists (flocks of Italians, especially, who are fleeing their country's violent political scene). Lots of Japanese, too. I received a beautiful coral, enamel and silver bracelet today from Abdul Arzing Bouteflika — we speak often on the phone...but somebody else is sneaking into my heart as a suitor — his cousin Ahmed Hasni Sharrif Bouteflicka, football player from Iran (his feet are as big as Ed's and insured for $70,000 — he trains with Beckbauer and Cruyf). We are writing a movie script together — He is also an actor and singer (eight films in Algeria and Africa)...
>
> Diego's exhausted with his term papers — just got over the chicken pox!!! As if he hadn't all the diseases a child can have.
>
> Love to you — still hoping to see you at Mary's — Kisses — Ol' Fat Jeana

To Jean, Hasni soon became a crutch; someone to talk with, someone who would listen to her problems, someone who would take care of her. He moved into her apartment and immediately took charge of what little money Jean did have. Shortly after, he began striking her, leaving bruises and marks. Photographs taken at this time show a tired, worn-looking Jean Seberg, in appearance well beyond her forty years of age.

Jean wrote her parents for the last time in May 1979:

> Dearest Family —
> Just a note to say that (Ahmed) Hasni Sheriff Bouteflika and I intend to reach Cherry Hill for the family reunion the Good Lord willing.
>
> Was out on film sets today — saw all my old friends and am getting money together for my script "Frontiere Palace," which I hope to direct — end of the year.
>
> Diego feels sad, but can't come yet as he has term papers.

Mother, what's your shoe size? A bit bigger than mine, I think — saw some wedgie-espadrilles I want to bring you. Still with money worries, thanks to Romain, but very happy.

I love you.
Jeana

(The film set Jean had visited was Studios de Billancourt, where director Costa-Gavras was editing the film *Clair de femme*. The reference to Romain and money worries stems either from their divorce agreement, in which Jean received no alimony or monetary settlement, or from the fact that Romain had recently stopped giving her money.)

On May 31, the Reverend Thomas E. Duggan of the American Church in Paris presided over a blessing between Jean and Hasni. Reverend Duggan confesses "it may seem hard to believe and reveals my own ignorance, but I had no idea who Jean Seberg was in terms of her career at the time I met her."

Hasni viewed this ceremony as a marriage, but in fact, it was not. Jean did not file the civil papers required in France before the celebration of marriage in the church. In addition, Jean was still legally married to Dennis Berry, so the "marriage" with Hasni had no formal significance. Reverend Duggan confirms, "According to the laws of France and the tradition of the church, Jean Seberg was not married to Ahmed Hasni." Jean did not inform her family or her friends of a marriage to Ahmed Hasni, which supports the view that she did not regard the blessing by Reverend Duggan as anything more than just that.

Jean soon learned that Hasni had no money, and that his family was by no means wealthy, as he had told her. Her resources continued to dwindle. While Romain accepted Hasni, if only because he was able to curtail Jean's drinking and pills, he tired of Hasni's habitual visits to ask for money. At last Romain put an end to these demands by throwing his ex-wife's boyfriend out.

Finding Romain refused to give her any more money, she turned to family and friends for help. "She told me she had a lot of money problems because she wasn't careful with her money. She'd give it to anyone who asked her," Mylène Demongeot says. "The man she took at the end didn't have any money, so she had to take care of them both with her money."

Mary Ann Seberg recalls receiving a late night telephone call from her sister around this time. "She had called and asked for some money, and there was a lot of noise in the background, including a man talking to her as she spoke to us," says Mary Ann. "Something just didn't sound right — her voice, the people in the background....I talked it over with my husband, and although Jean had loaned us money, and we had paid her back through attorneys, we didn't feel right about the whole situation. We felt something was going on…" She decided not to give her sister the money, solely because of the strangeness of the call. Had Mary Ann known the extent of Jean's problems, she would have helped. It was the last time the sisters spoke.

Vony Becker was another who received a call. Becker had already retired for the evening when her telephone rang, but she answered it.

"Can you give me some money?" Jean asked.

"Yes, probably," Becker replied, believing Jean was drunk. "[My husband] will be back and we'll see what we can do."

"You're just a spoiled rich lady," Jean replied abruptly.

"I was aggravated, but she would call all hours of the day or night," Becker remembers. Becker and her husband decided to give Jean half of the 5,000 francs she requested before delivering the remaining money. They wanted to see how the loan was going to be spent. "I went to the apartment on rue du Bac," Becker says. "Jean was like a 'star.' She had her maid, her 'hairdresser' and a lot of people around her. I brought half the money Jean asked for, and Jean played out the 'star' and gave around luxurious tips. I realized something was really wrong. She kept looking at me in a strange way. I was surprised.

"I don't think she was on illegal drugs. She had written to Simone Weill and said she was against drugs, and not to get involved with drugs."

Simone Weill was at the time the French Minister of Health. Another friend recalls Jean asking Romain Gary to deliver a letter to Weill concerning the illegal drug problem in France. But Romain threw it away, believing Jean's imagination was running wild.

Around the same time, Jean asked Roger Grenier to take her to a psychiatric hospital. "She explained to me she wanted to take the drug addicts there," Grenier says. "She was very mad, and I'm sure she was drinking too much, but drugs, I don't think so. There were many drug addicts around her. She explained to me she wanted to take the drug addicts to the hospital. 'Simone [Weill] telephoned me this morning and asked me to do that,' she said."

Grenier drove Jean to the hospital, and when she explained her reason for being there, the hospital officials did not believe her. "She was quite tired by then and wanted to go home," he says. When Grenier deposited Jean at rue du Bac, her maid took one look at her and said, "Something's wrong."

"Don't pray for me," Jean replied. "I'm quite well."

31

"I believe my career is going to start up again."
— Jean Seberg in 1979

It had been three years since her last legitimate film. As Marc Simenon says, "Word spreads quickly when someone has an addiction and problems," and Jean's problems were an open secret in the tight-knit French film industry. But just when Jean began to believe she might never act again she was offered a feature role from the producer of *Breathless* and *The Line of Demarcation*, Georges de Beauregard. *La légion saute sur Kolwezi* (*The Legion Parachutes into Kolwezi*) was to be an adventure film based on a true-life incident in which the French Foreign Legion was called on to rescue Europeans in the town of Kolwezi, Zaire, after it was overrun by rebels in 1978.

De Beauregard and Raoul Coutard (who had been the cameraman on *Breathless*) visited Jean in her apartment. They came not only to discuss the film, but also to see if Jean was healthy enough to act in the film. Coutard recalls that she "seemed tired, but otherwise healthy."

All seemed perfect. For one thing she would be working with people she knew, for another it had the earmarking of a quality production, and finally, given her financial plight, the role could not have come at a better time. However, her agent, Olga Horstig-Primuz, refused to be part of the agreement because she did not believe Jean would be capable of completing the film. Nothing daunted, Jean underwent a medical examination on behalf of the film's production company, Productions Bella, from which the doctor concluded she was indeed fit to work. Dispensing with representation by Horstig-Primuz, in July Jean signed the contract to play the wife of a Belgian mining engineer. Filming was set to commence in August, with nine days of filming at $2,000 a day.

In addition, there was the possibility of Jean reuniting with her *Bonjour Tristesse* co-star David Niven in the British production *A Nightingale Sang in Berkeley Square*, to be filmed later in the year. But first there was the Coutard/de Beauregard film to do, followed by the trip to Iowa as promised.

By mid-summer, Jean forswore all alcohol and prescribed medicines. She also continued writing. Contemplating her finances, Jean may have decided at this time to write her autobiography, despite the qualms she had earlier expressed both privately and in public. It is not known how far this progressed, but the majority of the notes for the project which have survived deal with her childhood, Nina's death and Otto Preminger. When Jean asked Romain to return her FBI file so that she might include portions of it in the work, he refused to give it back.

Meanwhile, Hasni had the desire to start a business in Barcelona and needed money. "She wanted to leave Paris," Aki Lehman says. "She had changed ever since she'd been living with this Hasni. He most certainly had a great influence over her."

Roger Grenier recalls Jean and Hasni visiting him at Gallimard. "She introduced him as an Algerian official — a general — and as the nephew of Bouteflika. I knew it wasn't true, but I didn't say anything. Romain was there and thought she was ill — all that belonged to a troubled mind."

Shortly after, Grenier quite unexpectedly met Jean in the street. "She was trying to avoid me," he says, but they exchanged a few words. "She told me something against Ahmed Hasni — something about his brain. After that, she said, 'Ahmed would be angry if I told you that because he is an officer.'"

It appears that Jean seriously contemplated moving out of Paris, and possibly France. She had in fact drafted a farewell letter to her adopted home, but had afterwards put it away. Reflecting a mood of bitter disillusionment, it read, in part:

> Dear friends and enemies: Greetings. Just a goodbye before I leave, letting you know some of my opinions. Why am I meddling? I'm a French citizen; I have the right to express my views...
>
> You have offered me hospitality, have given me work and "squeezed me dry" for twenty-three years. My son (a Frenchman) is completing his matriculation exams. I'm heaving a huge sigh of relief, and leaving you. Here's why, if it interests you at all.
>
> We French are grumblers, malicious and racist people. Oh, it's true, I've seen the odd smile and a little kindness even in the offices of the Prefecture. But not that often, not often enough. And I have had enough, too. Enough of the hands that thrust out greedily for a tip. Enough of the so-called French courtesy, which is made of ice...I have had more than I can take of the French cinema, which has no time for Jean-Luc Godard, to whom it owes so much, you might say everything. I have had enough of hearing my compatriots tell foreigners, with an air of self-satisfaction, that "if you don't like it here you can always go back to your own country." Actually not all of them are lucky enough to be able to return to their own land without fear. Sometimes the savage beast politics prevents that: or else starvation...
>
> Thanks for the nice memories, and no thanks for the rest. I have been cooked in this culture, which is turning rotten without the authentic flavor of Roquefort cheese. One day I'll come back to say hello in the hope that someone will answer. Happy holidays! Don't forget to fasten your safety belts, and don't, I beg you, abandon your animals. Thanks, Jean Seberg

In July, Jean sold the rue du Bac apartment to Dr. Marion Bouilhet for 400,000 French francs. Bouilhet, who made a down payment on the apartment, remembers Jean telling her that she needed money, and that she wanted to get away from Romain Gary. "She felt watched," Bouilhet says. Whenever Jean left the complex, she passed by Romain's apartment in order to enter the street. It was said Romain lifted the curtains to see who entered and exited the building.

"She couldn't stand it," Bouilhet says. "She wanted to move. The reason she stayed was because of her son." Jean left several pieces of furniture at the rue du Bac apartment, and her remaining possessions were put in storage. Reportedly, the money from the sale went into a briefcase.

She and Hasni then left on vacation to Majorca where the couple argued so violently Jean fled to Puerto Andraitx for several days. Then, preferring not to return to Paris, she decided to visit Eugenia Munoz' daughter, Mabel, in Barcelona. Jean learned Hasni had been there three days earlier but had already returned to Paris.

Jean stayed in Barcelona for a few days. She was photographed at this time while sunbathing. A close-up of her face reveals no dark circles around her eyes. The haunted expression has disappeared, and her familiar classic looks appear restored.

Despite the difficulties in their relationship, and especially severe strains in recent months, Romain Gary still showed concern for Jean. He made sure she was safe, even if he relied primarily on the reports of third parties by this stage. When he had not heard anything about Jean for several days, he became anxious. He located Jean at Mabel's home to tell her that Georges de Beauregard needed to discuss the upcoming film, since production was shortly to commence. Mabel confided in Romain regarding Hasni's visit, saying that he "terrified" her. Concerned, Romain told Mabel to inform the Spanish police.

A friend from this time later told *France-Soir* that Jean arrived at her place one night alone, "as if she were running from some danger she didn't dare confide in me. She seemed terrorized. Safe at my place, she quickly reverted to the normal, warm, well-balanced woman I had always known. The menace that she seemed to feel hovering over her lessened. But all during her stay, the sadness and anguish never left her. When she departed to make her film, I had the impression I would never see her again."

Jean returned to Paris and was met at the airport by Georges de Beauregard. Jean confessed to him the situation with Hasni, including the fact that he had stolen 60,000 francs from her, and told him that she had decided to move to the United States after the film was completed. De Beauregard spirited her to a hotel and informed the police of her whereabouts, asking that her location should not be divulged, above all not to Ahmed Hasni, who was by now searching for Jean.

On August 3, de Beauregard collected Jean at the hotel. The producer noted she was impeccably groomed and elegantly dressed, and that she looked like the movie star she once had been. De Beauregard then drove Jean to the airport to put her on the eight-hour flight for Guyana, where production on the film was to begin.

However, they arrived at the airport only to be greeted by Ahmed Hasni.

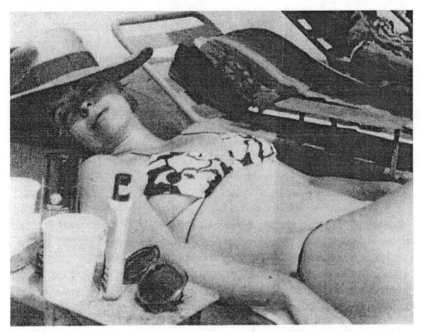

One of the last photographs taken of Jean Seberg, 1979. COURTESY OF HELEN MASON

He knew Jean was scheduled to leave that day, and insisted on accompanying her to Guyana. Neither wanted him to travel with them to the film location, but neither could think of a convincing excuse. Then de Beauregard remembered that Hasni, an Algerian, needed a visa in order to go to Guyana. Since he didn't have one, he could not join the film crew and Jean.

After finishing her scheduled one-day shoot on-location, Jean returned to Paris the following Tuesday and stayed in another hotel, reserved and paid for by de Beauregard. She was not scheduled to return to the film until September 6, when the production team returned to Paris. In the meantime, Jean opted to spend her time alone, writing, and working on her memoirs. But Hasni had in his possession portions of what she had already written earlier. When Jean went to retrieve her work from him, Hasni would not let her leave. "She was trapped, and he wouldn't let her go," a friend said.

On August 9, Jean and Hasni checked into the hotel du Pont-Royal, close to where Romain lived. Two days later, the pair moved to the more modest hotel Alexander. This was followed by Jean renting a small first-floor apartment at 125 rue de Longchamp. The dwellings, at a cost of approximately 4200 francs a month, were largely short-term leases.

The events of the last couple weeks of Jean's life are unclear. Little firm evidence exists, and it is impossible to corroborate Hasni's accounts to the press claiming that Jean made three separate attempts at suicide. In one of these, he alleged, she tried to jump out of the apartment window.

Hasni said that in the early afternoon hours of August 18, she tried to throw herself in front of an oncoming subway train at the Montparnasse station. "Jean told me about it," he said. "She pretended she had fainted but I know she tried to kill herself." Friends of Jean, however, believe that she might have gotten dizzy and had fallen, or could accidentally have been pushed.

As a train was entering Montparnasse station, the driver suddenly saw a woman falling from the platform onto the track. The driver instantly braked while cutting off the power. Jean was lying below the first car. She was pulled out and sat on a bench, where it was discovered she had not been seriously injured. She was, however, understandably in a state of shock, as witnesses testified.

Jean was taken to the Cochin hospital, where she was admitted. X-rays showed no damage, although she had suffered some contusions. She was given sedatives and kept overnight for observation.

Jean spent her final days at 125 rue de Longchamp, with the ever-present Hasni. In the latter days of August, she met two old friends quite by accident: Mylène Demongeot and Nicolas Gessner. She saw Demongeot at a restaurant one evening and had, as Demongeot recalls, a good talk. "For her, I was a stable person. In a way, I am a well-balanced person. And in that way, she liked to be with me," Demongeot says. "But at times she wouldn't speak with me because I wouldn't accept all the big reasons she'd tell me, to explain why she'd [live as she was]."

That evening, Demongeot thought Jean was in very bad shape. "She was shivering — trembling — and very, very depressed," Demongeot remembers.

"Jean, you cannot stay like this. You have to go to the clinic," her friend told her. "You have to do something with yourself. You cannot [continue] shivering like that."

Demongeot says that her own sister-in-law had committed suicide two years earlier, and that evening, Jean kept switching the conversation back to this woman. "That's horrible what happened to her. That's terrible. I think about it all the time. Why didn't you do something for her?" Jean asked.

"Jean, do something about you. Don't stay like that. It's bad. You've got to do something to make yourself well again and beautiful. You're a nice girl. Take care of yourself," Demongeot pleaded.

She told Jean of a doctor friend who had a clinic, and she tried to persuade her to admit herself there for help.

"I have money problems ..."

"That's OK. The man is nice — no problem. He can cure you." Demongeot asked Jean if someone could take her to the clinic.

"No...," Jean replied. "But I promise I will do it. I'll go."

The pair talked for half an hour and had one drink before leaving. Even though Demongeot was preparing work on a film, Jean never mentioned the de Beauregard film. She did, however, sing a few lines of the lullaby "Rock-a-bye Baby" to Mylène. Jean remembered it was one of Mylène's favorites since she had introduced her to it while working on *Ballad for the Kid*.

This was the last time Mylène Demongeot saw her. "If I had an extra week in Paris, I would have taken her to the clinic myself. I felt really guilty about it..."

Around the same time, Nicolas Gessner also spoke with Jean and Ahmed Hasni, whom he saw in a restaurant. "I met her briefly with Ahmed Hasni," Gessner remembers, "and what struck me when I first met him, was, 'Gee, she's gone back to her first husband.' My very first reaction. He looked like François Moreuil, in a way."

But what struck Gessner about Jean was that she "was frighteningly fat, but she still looked nice. And she knew that I knew [about the weight gain]. How could this have happened? Was it unavoidable, or did she let herself go? There was this unspoken 'Look at the way I look,' and my unspoken, 'You look all right.' She was wearing a blue-gray dress with a checkered pattern to hide her figure." *

Gessner spoke with Jean for a few minutes, and mentioned he was leaving for Los Angeles shortly on business. "She said, 'I'm going to give you the number. Call my parents in Marshalltown and tell them that I'm well. Tell them I'm doing well.'

"I thought that was so strange. Why didn't she pick up the phone and call? What's going on here? I said, 'OK. Give me the number and I'll call them up.' But she didn't give me the number. Did she already know something? Did she already intend something?"

At some point at the end of August, a frightened Jean telephoned Romain Gary, who was then living with the singer Jacqueline Danno at 108 rue du Bac. Romain answered the phone, and upon hearing the hysterical voice of his former wife, refused to speak with Jean. Danno took the receiver and attempted in vain to calm Jean. "Jacqueline, you have to help me!" Jean begged. "I am caught in the biggest Algerian drug network — help me!

* Note: In Europe, and especially France, the terms concerning weight gain differ from usage in the United States. From the photographs of Jean in a bathing suit taken one month earlier, she appears approximately twenty pounds heavier than her usual weight, which made her look heavier on her short frame, but far from what Americans term "overweight."

They're covered with snow! Romain has to warn Jacques Chirac [then mayor of Paris]! At any moment they can kill me!"

Danno attempted in vain to calm her, but Jean slammed down the receiver. Worried, Danno relayed to Romain what Jean told her. But Romain dismissed Jean's story, explaining that it was merely a fabrication of her imagination.

On August 27, Jean went to Dr. Michel Rothman, complaining of insomnia and concerned she would be unable to complete filming her scenes the following month. The doctor prescribed Temesta, a tranquilizer, and two sleeping pills, Nembutal and Nuctalon, which he advised her to alternate.

Two days later on the evening of August 29, Marion Bouilhet telephoned Jean from the rue du Bac apartment at eight P.M. She called to ask Jean about a cooker which was not working properly. Bouilhet called once again that evening, at around eleven o'clock. Jean told her she and Hasni had just returned from seeing a film. The one they had selected was, not surprisingly, *Clair de femme*, adapted from the novel by Romain Gary, and directed by Jean's friend Costa-Gavras.

The film was about a man whose wife is dying from a terminal disease and sends him away so that he will not witness her death. As he wanders the city, helpless and emotionally floundering, he has a chance encounter with a woman who has suffered a comparable loss. The two form a bond, forged from their common despair.

Jean had desperately wanted to play the role of this woman Lydia, playing opposite Yves Montand, but it was given to Romy Schneider. The film was a modest success for those involved, and although its reviews were poor this was a rare occasion when Romain did not feel betrayed by a screen version of his work. Jean not only felt excluded, but also angry, accusing Romain of exploiting her life once again, as he had in previous novels.

"That movie really upset her," Bouilhet recalls of this last conversation. "She found it humiliating, somehow, that another woman played...part of her being. Jean wasn't drunk or anything, not at all. She spoke clearly and calmly." The conversation ended at around eleven-thirty. Apparently, Bouilhet telephoned a third time around midnight with a short question.

Sometime after, Jean and Hasni went to bed. She did not take any sleeping pills, despite having had her most recent prescription filled. Early in the morning of August 30, Hasni alerted the police that Jean and her car had disappeared.

Shortly after eight o'clock that same morning, Bouilhet telephoned Jean's apartment once again, despite having just spoken with her a few hours earlier. Hasni answered the call. He told her that he and Jean had an argument and that Jean had left while he was asleep. "She's gone," he told her. "She's disappeared without her skirt."

Hasni's response surprised Bouilhet. "How can anyone disappear at night without the partner noticing?" she asked herself.

CHAPTER TEN
1979-1981

"I went through the woods for a walk in the rain...
And as I walked, my soul was freed from pain."
— from a poem written by Jean Seberg at the age of eighteen

32

"Jean Seberg was destroyed by the FBI"
— Romain Gary

Ten days later, on September 8, 1979, just as the sun set, Jean's body was found in her Renault car on the rue du Général-Appert, an avenue barely two blocks long, and less than three blocks from her apartment. The official version was that the car was discovered by two policemen when one of them looked inside and saw a bulky object wrapped in a blue blanket, wedged between the front and back seats. When he opened the door, inside lay the remains of Jean Seberg, wrapped in the blanket and decomposed almost beyond the point of recognition. An empty bottle of mineral water and an empty tube of barbiturates lay next to her.

There had been a delay in a press announcement that Jean was even missing. By the time a release reached the States, her body had already been found. The next day the Paris newspapers attempted to reconstruct the story of her disappearance:

> She got up sometime before six A.M. the morning of August 30. Wrapping herself only in a blanket, she took her car keys, a two-month supply of barbiturates recently renewed by her pharmacist, and a bottle of mineral water. She left the apartment, got into her Renault automobile and drove it just around the corner to the rue du Général-Appert. She parked the car, climbed into the back seat and curled up on the floor. Then she took the pills with the mineral water, swallowed them, then pulled the blanket over her head and waited to die.

A note was found at the scene. Written in French on blue stationery and folded into four, it was addressed to Diego: "Forgive me. I can no longer live with my nerves. Understand me. I know that you can and you know that I love you. Be strong. Your loving mother, Jean." The note eerily recalled the last one Romain Gary received from his mother, in which she closed: "Be strong, be resolute. Mama."

In the United States, the news media immediately reported that Jean Seberg had committed suicide. A well-known right-wing radio commentator announced Jean's death on his radio show, going into detail on how she had overdosed on barbiturates, on her failed marriages and on her "undistinguished film career." The announcer then went into a commercial, praising his sponsor for making an American product.

The majority of the news media showed restraint and a degree of sympathy in broadcasting Jean's death. Nobody, however, troubled to inform Jean's family of her death — or even that she had been missing. In New Jersey, Mary Ann and her husband were spending the day working in the yard when a neighbor stopped by and asked if they had listened to the radio that afternoon. Mary Ann said they hadn't, since they were either gone or working outside all day. "I think you better go in and listen. There's been a story about your sister being missing..." the neighbor said. The couple went inside their house, turned on their television set and tuned their radio to a Philadelphia station. When no report concerning Jean was broadcast on the radio, Mary Ann's husband telephoned the station. Even after he identified himself as Jean's brother-in-law, "They were very reluctant to say anything," he recalls. After several seconds, however, he was told Jean had been missing and was found dead in her car.

The last time Ed and Dorothy Seberg spoke to Jean was at the end of July, as they had spent the month of August vacationing. Back home in Marshalltown in September, the Sebergs were relaxing at home listening to an Iowa football game. Immediately after he received the information, Mary Ann's husband called to tell them of their daughter's death. A few minutes later, a news bulletin during a break in the game publicly announced Jean Seberg was dead.

At this time, Diego Gary was vacationing in San Francisco and was scheduled to return to Paris the following day when he learned of his mother's death. He later watched the news on the television set in his hotel room and saw images of the scene, with her covered body lying on the pavement. On the flight home, Diego recalls he obtained the daily edition of *France-Soir*. There, in the confines of a jet, he read the headline "The Suicide of a Lost Star" and the reporting of his mother's last weeks alive. Diego says that experience was devastating and it put him off from future air travels.

Dennis Berry had returned to Paris from California just before the discovery was made. A concerned John Berry had informed Dennis that Jean was missing and he paid for his son's return ticket. But the reasons why neither Romain nor any official from the American embassy in Paris had notified Jean's family of her death are unclear. Two days had passed since the discovery of Jean's body before the U.S. Embassy in France belatedly informed the Sebergs of Jean's death. The official who spoke with them on the telephone was vague regarding the cause of and events leading upto her death. (The U.S. Embassy refuses to reply to several requests made by the author to explain the circumstances.)

The news of Jean's death spread like a fire fanned by high winds. Many of Jean's relatives, neighbors, and friends in the United States and in Europe learned of her death by the news media before family members could tell them personally. Carol Hollingsworth and Lynda Haupert found out while listening to the radio. "I think it was appalling that at least the next of kin wasn't notified before anything was released," Haupert says. "It was horrible."

The shock of Jean's death, and especially the possibility of this being a suicide, troubled the minds of several people who knew her personally. "Had Jean reached a point in her life, [as] the giving person that I knew," questioned Rabbi Sol Serber, "that finally, after she felt 'I've gone as far as I can. I can't make a better society, and if I can't go further and I want to, but the frustration's too great' — perhaps she said, 'The End'?"

Film critics were also shocked by Jean's death. "One of the things that struck me when I first read about her death was the realization of how much I liked seeing her in various, mostly forgettable films," wrote Vincent Canby, "even though I don't think I ever gave her much credit as an actress. She seemed to be no driven, self-dramatizing, show-biz superstar, crying all over the public's shoulder as she invited fans to celebrate her misery, nor was she your average American girl."

While many close to Jean remained silent, Ahmed Hasni continually appeared in news articles around the world. He told the Associated Press that Jean had "wanted to kill herself for some time," and that "she didn't want to see anybody. She had even talked of stopping work." This contradicts comments in the last letters Jean sent to her parents, and is hardly consistent with the fact that she was still working on the de Beauregard film.

Hasni added that after watching *Clair de femme* Jean was despondent. "In a way, it was the story of Jean's and Romain's life," he said. "The memories added to her depression." In fact, Jean was reportedly more incensed than depressed after viewing the film. She may or may not have found another portrait of herself here, but in any case the words and situations drawn from Romain's intensely personal novel probably struck too many chords and touched on some raw nerves. She may well have felt that this was a role which should have been hers. Perhaps, all in all, watching this film brought home to her how much her life had changed, and not for the better.

On September 10, Romain Gary held a press conference in the offices of his French publisher, Gallimard. Diego sat silently by his side. Obviously mourning, with eyes red and his voice breaking, Romain announced, "It isn't *Clair de femme*, a film that has nothing to do with the life of Jean Seberg, which is the indirect cause of the death of my son's mother. It is the FBI. Jean Seberg was destroyed by the FBI."

Romain had debated whether or not to divulge the FBI documents publicly. Jean herself, according to Romain, was, like him, "torn" between the desire to make the information public and concern not to appear anti-American. "The American dream, and where she came from," he said, "was very strong."

In the lobby of Gallimard, Romain produced documents from Jean's FBI file and revealed the 1970 smear campaign to the reporters. "When an important American magazine published this rumor launched by the

FBI, Jean became like a crazed woman. She never got over the calumny, and that's why she lost her child at birth...She wanted the child to be buried in a glass [sic] coffin in order to prove that it was white. From then on, she went from one psychiatric clinic to another, from one suicide attempt to another. She tried to kill herself seven times, usually on the anniversary of her little girl's birth.

"From 1961 to 1969 I lived day and night with a perfectly normal woman — neurotic, perhaps — a movie star has fragile nerves — but healthy. After this incident, she became psychotic...she was obsessed by this dead child." Romain later added that during his years with Jean before the FBI and Black Panther era, "she never had a single breakdown" and she did not drink heavily.

But Romain exaggerated the alleged suicide attempts in relation to the anniversary of Nina's death. Confidants believed this claim was made solely for dramatic effect. Whatever the truth, because of Romain's statements, Jean Seberg was now effectively presented before the news media as a new St. Joan in her own right, sacrificed for political motives. "I owed it to Jean," Romain later explained. "She asked me that if anything happened to her — she thought she might be killed — I was to produce these documents. Besides, my son asked for it, too. Now I'm bloody happy I did it. I am at peace with myself because I did manage to set the record straight and her image will forever remain very pure."

No American journalist attended Romain's press conference. When it concluded, a skeptical French writer asked Romain if he was sure the FBI documents were not fakes. "I lost my temper," Romain recalled shortly after. "They thought it was a creation of a writer's sick mind." The day after, a French newspaper dismissed Romain's claims by writing: "Gary no longer knows what to do to stay in the spotlight."

Jean's parents and family spoke with Dennis Berry, Diego and Romain Gary on the telephone several times regarding the funeral arrangements. Not once did Romain mention to them the press conference he had held. The Sebergs' request for their daughter to be returned to Iowa and buried in Marshalltown — which Jean desired and once predicted years earlier — was met with resistance. The family conceded primarily because it was Diego's wish for his mother's remains to stay in France. In turn, they arranged for a memorial service to be held in Marshalltown simultaneously with the funeral proper in Paris.

Dennis Berry arranged the funeral, and his father contributed toward the cost. "I remember the dignitaries were to be aligned," John Berry recalled, "and I remember Dennis saying that if it wasn't done in a certain way, there would be no funeral because [Hasni] wanted to be in the car directly behind Jean [which is usually reserved for the spouse of the deceased]. But Dennis was still her husband."

The arrangements made by Dennis Berry were accepted, and Romain and Diego Gary were invited to take part in the procession. Romain also helped to pay for the funeral and also with the invitation list. François Moreuil was not approached, nor would he have gone, he says, if invited by Romain Gary.

In the years since their divorce, François Moreuil saw Jean only once, and that was quite by accident in the 1960s. "I saw her in a club, said 'hello,' and that was it. She was with Romain Gary," he recalls. "All I know is that she was not in very good shape at the end of her life," François says. "And I was sad about that. She was not the girl I knew."

François did not plan to attend the funeral for several reasons. His life with Jean had ended almost twenty years earlier, and they had had no contact in the intervening years, save for that one meeting. In addition, François had remarried, and did not feel his presence would be appropriate.

"When Jean died, my mother said, 'You have to go to the burial.' But I said, 'No,'" François says. "She said, 'Yes. You have been married in the church. You have to go.' And again, I said, 'No.' We went back and forth, and finally I decided to go. And I went with my mother."

The burial took place on September 14. At the memorial service in Marshalltown, Pastor Warren Johnson told family and friends that "we need to remember the happy days of Jean — a beautiful, radiant person...Her life was not for naught. She brought joy to many and sought to bear the burden of social injustice." The minister also said, "Just as Joan [of Arc] sought to lift the siege of Orleans, Jean sought to lift the siege of poverty and want."

The poem "Beside Still Waters" was read, referring to Jean's childhood joy of playing by the Iowa River, behind the Veterans' Home. The music selected included two items Jean herself had chosen for her daughter's funeral: "I Believe" and "The Impossible Dream."

At the same time, in Paris, a private funeral service was being held in the chapel of rue du Bac. The burial then took place at Montparnasse Cemetery, with around two hundred people in attendance, including Georges de Beauregard, Jean Eustache, Simone de Beauvoir, and Jean-Paul Sartre. "It was very strange," Roger Grenier remembers of the burial. "It was like out of a gangster movie — three black Cadillacs — one with Romain and Diego and one with the Dennis Berry family. I was there at the cemetery, and a French actress came up to me, crying, 'Jean and I — we had the same psychiatrist!'"

Bouquets of flowers from all over the world arrived and were placed along the east walls surrounding the cemetery. The sheer number of flowers was so great that they extended for the length of a block. A casket spray of lilies, daisies and yellow roses entirely covered the mahogany coffin, and cascaded down all four sides to the ground. In front of the casket, the composed Diego stood beside his father, who was visibly shaking, his face drawn. Dennis Berry was positioned in the front row, as was Ahmed Hasni. Some of Jean's friends complained out loud about Hasni's presence there.

Several people from the French cinema attended, including Jean-Paul Belmondo, who stood close to Romain. Belmondo looked around the group to see who else was there. At the back of the crowd, fifty yards away, he saw François Moreuil and his mother. Belmondo then openly left Romain's side and joined François.

The burial at Montparnasse Cemetery in Paris, 1979.
COURTESY OF INDEPENDENT VISIONS

Curious sight-seers and onlookers soon joined the ceremony, almost doubling the size of the crowd, while newspaper photographers elbowed to get better shots of the mourners. At times, the clicks from the cameras drowned out the murmured prayers. One person attending the service described it as a "surreal, Fellini movie."

Back in Marshalltown, as the family left the church to return to their Kalsem Boulevard home, a typewritten statement by Ed Seberg was distributed to reporters waiting outside Trinity Lutheran Church:

"Jean attempted all of her life to be of help and comfort to any who were in need. The dogs and cats she would bring home when she was a child, saying, 'They followed me.' The Indians, the Blacks, the friends, the relatives and others, any who thought she would help them. And she did.

"She lived her convictions until the people in our world showed they did not understand her convictions. Then she gave up."

At the end of the service in Paris, Diego, and each of Jean's husbands laid a single pink rose on the casket. Dennis Berry placed two additional roses "for her mother and father who were too upset to come." His statement was true to a degree. The fact is, however, the family was not invited to attend the services in Paris.

Romain had been vocal in his interviews regarding Jean's upbringing and he blamed much of Jean's problems on the religious beliefs she was taught as a child. This reproach apparently extended to Ed and Dorothy Seberg and their decision that she should be raised as a Lutheran.

"Romain strongly discouraged the family from going to the funeral," Mary Ann's husband says. "It was ten years since David's death, and [Ed and Dorothy] hadn't gotten over his death. To lose him, then Jean…They were devastated by Jean's death." The family was heartbroken, but the wish they not attend the funeral was shattering. Rather than cause a scene by appearing — or worse, be denied access in front of invited guests — at the funeral, the Sebergs conceded only after much discussion and debate. Thus, the service in Marshalltown.

Diego, however, never forgave his relations in the United States for not attending the funeral. While they wrote him often, Diego's communication with the family was sporadic at best, with years passing between letters. "My father had influenced me against them," Diego told an interviewer a quarter of a century later. "I broke off with them because they didn't come to the funeral."

Diego apparently did not know it was his father who asked them not to be present at the funeral. Nor did Diego ever ask his mother's family why they had not attended.

33

"I'm bitter … I'm bitter."
— Ed Seberg, after learning of the FBI's investigation

The next day, newspapers around the world carried the funeral and the FBI's admission as front page news. *The Marshalltown Times-Republican* headlined on page one: FBI PLANTED SEBERG BABY STORY.

The shock of the FBI's admission was felt across the world. The major television networks first covered the news of Jean's death, followed six days later by Romain's allegations of an FBI smear campaign. When the FBI admission became public, CBS News alone broadcast nearly three-and-a-half minutes on the story. Other news media around the world followed suit with lengthy articles and front page headlines, including the *New York Times* and several French and British newspapers.

"After the FBI admitted to planting that rumor, I thought it was horrible," says Lynda Haupert. "It makes you almost ashamed to be an American when you find out [that] happened to Jean, who was a real caring person. Her activist activities were always because she was trying to do the right thing. And when you're trying to be a good person and do the right thing and get knocked down for it, it's unforgivable."

Later in the day of September 15, Bill Fisher stopped by the Seberg house to express his sympathy. Completely out of character, Ed Seberg said to Fisher, "If you hadn't submitted Jean for that contest, none of this would have happened." Shortly after, Ed apologized for his outburst.

Strangely, one source who worked closely with Bill Fisher at Fisher Controls in Marshalltown says that during the investigation of Jean there was a warning that "All government orders placed at Fisher Controls would be canceled [by the government] unless the Fisher family discontinued all connection to Jean, on both a social and a private level. The plant couldn't have survived without the governments' orders for parts, so the family did what they had to."

Countless news organizations telephoned the Seberg household over the next few days, asking for statements. Three days after the funeral, Ed said to a reporter, "I'm bitter...I'm bitter." His voice broke four times during the five-minute conversation, audibly choking back tears. A few years later, Ed said, "If this was true, why didn't [the FBI] shoot her and get rid of her instead of having all of this travail that's gone on since?"

"Our family always believed in the government and believed in the flag, and we just could not imagine that the government would intrude into people's lives. In the first place we didn't understand why they'd be doing this, and we couldn't understand that they could do this to destroy someone," says Mary Ann Seberg. "It affected all of us a great deal..."

When Jean's files were made public, then-FBI director William H. Webster publicly vowed: "The days when the FBI used derogatory material to combat advocates of unpopular causes have long since passed. We are out of that business forever." A month later Webster said, "I accept the responsibility that the bureau thought it was a good idea. Whether it was ever implemented or not, there was a program. I don't want to weasel out of responsibility in that way. We take our responsibility, but we try to make our point that that was a program of long ago and we're not doing it any more."

New York Daily News columnist Liz Smith called the Seberg-FBI story "the most horrible" of the year. Countless editorials damning J. Edgar Hoover were printed for several months to come. Richard Cohn of the Washington Post wrote: "[The rumors] were planted by the bureau because then-director, J. Edgar Hoover, the only contemporary racist to have the honor of a Washington building named for him, hated black militants..." Donald Kaul wrote in the Des Moines Register: "There were rumors about Hoover, that he was homosexual. You never read about those rumors as fact or fiction in Newsweek."

One Marshalltown resident said, "When we were growing up we were taught to respect the FBI as the highest form of law enforcement. We've been disillusioned. It was always happening to someone else. Now it's happened here."

"Until now, we didn't know the FBI was involved," said Warren Robeson in 1979. "We just thought it was that damned gossip columnist. It's a shame it came after her death, but she's vindicated at least. Now the FBI director says it won't happen again. But it's too late for Jean, isn't it?"

As for Joyce Haber, who ran the rumor as a blind item in the *Los Angeles Times*, she insisted that her source was "a journalist." "I am beginning to wonder who my best friends are," Haber said after the FBI revelation. "Obviously, if I knew then what I know now, I wouldn't have printed the item. It's absolutely shocking and appalling. I can now have no trust in anybody."

Jim Bellows, who was Haber's immediate boss at the *Los Angeles Times* when the story was printed on Jean, says the FBI was behind the rumor. Bellows, however, suggested Haber to rewrite the column without naming names. He says the story made him "nervous," and was concerned about possible libel action if the *Times* used Jean's name.

For years he regretted failing to verify the story with Jean or someone close to her.

The Strange Death of Jean Seberg: Suicide or Murder?

"What I would have liked to know is the circumstances of Jean's death," says Mylène Demongeot today. "I tried to learn more about it because we are friends with the police, but learned only what I read in the newspapers."

Many inconsistencies have been exposed concerning the days Jean Seberg was missing as well as the circumstances of her death. The official report states that Ahmed Hasni informed the police of Jean's disappearance after dawn on August 30. John Berry, however, claimed he was the one who went to the police after he was informed Jean did not arrive to an appointment.

"I and my wife at that time, we went to the police. We were the ones who reported it. And I spoke to Dennis in California and asked him, 'Where could she be?' He told me of a few places she might have gone to. We checked them and couldn't find her. And the police were about as interested in me as..." Berry shook his head as he recalled the incident. The police dismissed him.

"It took a few days before [the police] became interested. I said that they should go out and look for her."

Apparently, on the morning of Jean's disappearance, Ahmed Hasni had reported to and was interviewed by Chief Inspector Jean-Pierre Lucchiani. Romain Gary was informed, and a missing person notice was issued by the criminal investigation department.

Although the official report from the Paris police stated Jean Seberg's body was found by two policemen who just happened, quite accidentally, to find her car while driving along the rue du Général-Appert, two other accounts surfaced as to how her remains were discovered.

The first occurs on the evening of September 8 in which Roger Desfarges was walking his dog along the rue du Général-Appert. The dog pulled him

The rue du Général-Appert where the car was discovered. AUTHOR'S COLLECTION

in the direction of the white Renault and Desfarges opened the unlocked back door next to the street. He saw a bulky object, firmly wrapped in a blanket on the floor behind the front seat. Desfarges investigated and discovered the remains of a woman. He immediately ran a few steps to relate the shocking discovery to concierge Mata Phéli and her husband, and then to the authorities.

The second story begins around ten o'clock in the morning of September 8, 1979, when a traveling businessman, identified only as Boniface, walked to his vehicle in front of #17 rue du Général-Appert. He saw his car was blocked in by a car, the bumpers of both vehicles touching. On the other side of his car, he noticed another car, a white Renault, had done the same, thus preventing him from moving his vehicle. He glanced at the car, and then noticed a strange odor seemed to be coming from the Renault.

Boniface walked inside building #17 and asked the concierge if the owner of the vehicles lived there. Then he mentioned the odor coming from the Renault. The pair walked out to investigate the matter. The concierge noticed a bulky object on the rear floor, wrapped in a blanket. The pair slowly lifted a corner of the blanket and saw underneath it, the body of a woman.

While the concierge ran back to his apartment to alert the police, a journalist happened to walk onto the scene. He learned that inside the car were the remains of Jean Seberg. Just as they had done many times during her life, the news media overstepped the bounds of taste and ethics when the journalist produced a camera and photographed her in death.

In this story, police officers were slow in responding to the caretaker's call. Inexplicably, it took more than ten hours before authorities arrived. The nearest police station was only one and a half blocks from the scene.

In fact, the police did not publicly reveal Jean Seberg's disappearance until September 7, the day before her body was found. The reason for the delays in making a public announcement of her disappearance and of the police reporting to the scene of the discovery, are a matter of speculation. Jean's involvement with the plight of Algerians, coupled with her psychological problems, was such as, in the words of Guy-Pierre Geneuil, "touched, for the first time, [on] the entourage of Romain Gary and de Gaulle," and would cause great embarrassment to that group.

Another disturbing question is why the police failed to find her earlier. She was, after all, one of the best-known actresses in France. In addition to the nearby police station, the embassies of Yugoslavia, Morocco, Guinea, Niger, and Pakistan, as well as her apartment, were all within three blocks from where the car was discovered. One block away from the site is Paris college number nine, Dauphine.

The police in the 16th district said it was not surprising to them that the car had not been noticed earlier. "The rue du Général-Appert is a seldom used road," an officer told *France-Soir*. "The cars belonging to the [Seine] river side residents remain parked all day long in front of the buildings. An abandoned car is only ticketed when it is improperly parked or when, after several weeks, it looks as if it were abandoned."

Initially, investigators believed the car had been moved to the street where it had been found, since it would be unlikely the body could have gone unnoticed on such a public thoroughfare. However, according to the British *Daily Telegraph*, the caretaker from a nearby building said he noticed Jean's car had been parked at the same spot for several days.

The French police speculated that someone might have moved the car after Jean's disappearance was announced. Eventually they dismissed this hypothesis, and noted that dust and leaves had settled on the car, proving that it had not been moved in some time. However, close examination of photographs and film footage shot shortly after the discovery show no dust or leaves on the car. In fact, the white exterior of the Renault appears to be quite clean — almost sterile. Possibly, for sanitary reasons, the car was disinfected before authorities removed it from the scene. But could vital evidence such as fingerprints on the vehicle have been destroyed by following this procedure before it had been fully examined?

The French police were also unhappy about the way Jean's body was positioned in the car — wedged on the cramped floor between the front and back seats. It did not look "natural."

But the dosage level of barbiturates which was found in her system appears to have been the major factor in her death. Since 1970 Jean had been given various prescriptions and doses of valium, barbiturates, and lithium to combat her depression. When she was taking lithium, it had to be monitored carefully, with frequent blood level tests and varying dosages. However, it seems she was not monitored as closely as she should have been.

One source believes Jean suffered from bi-polar disorder, and that French physicians did not know how to treat the disorder properly. Additionally, with her several visits to various care facilities, dozens of doctors attempting to "cure" her, coupled with various medication, Jean may have been inadvertently poisoned by overmedication. Instead of helping her, the drugs played havoc with Jean's behavior.

Berthe Grandval remembers Jean taking medication three months before her death. At that time, the corners of Jean's mouth turned black "like ink. It was a bad sign to her," Grandval recalls. "It was almost like arsenic." Hasni personally blamed the doctors who he felt prescribed Jean "dangerous barbiturates when in a state of severe depression."

The question of why Hasni himself didn't find Jean persisted. He had successfully searched for her all over Paris earlier when she left him. He had a control over her, a jealous possessiveness. Most disturbing is the conversation Dr. Marion Bouilhet had with Hasni the morning of Jean's disappearance. Hasni told Bouilhet, "She's gone. She left without her skirt." How did Hasni know Jean "left without her skirt" if he had not seen her leave the apartment — if she had indeed left the apartment on her own? And if he did see Jean flee, why didn't Hasni prevent her from leaving, as he had done on previous occasions? He was obsessed with her, and he had told Jean's former mother-in-law, Gladys Berry, that he would never allow Jean to leave him. Hasni warned others he "would burn Jean if she ever took another man."

But precisely what happened in the span of six hours, from the moment she ended her conversation with Bouilhet shortly after midnight on August 30 until six A.M. the same day when Jean allegedly fled, is something which has never been satisfactorily explained.

Ahmed Hasni spoke freely and openly with the French press after the discovery of Jean's body. The version of their last weeks together which he gave to the media concentrated on Jean's three alleged suicide attempts.

He also recounted their last hours together. He said Jean did not take any sleeping pills the evening they retired before her disappearance. He did claim that, after he turned off the light and Jean had begun to drift off to sleep, a black cat leaped into the apartment through an open window. "It jumped on the table," Hasni said. "I could see its phosphorescent eyes in the dark. I turned the light back on and said to Jean, 'Did you see that black cat?' Jean didn't just get up. She lunged out of bed and ran to caress it. All of a sudden, the animal disappeared." Hasni then offered that in Algeria, "There are birds as black as crows. Whenever they perch on the roof of a house and caw seven times in a row, it is said that someone in that house has only seven days to live."

He also remarked Jean did not want to see anyone, even though she gave an interview to José Gerson a few days before her disappearance. Gerson was compiling a book on "The Education of Parents" and asked Jean for her comments. She spoke about the FBI, racism, her marriages ("I've experienced disappointment three times. That doesn't prevent me from hoping, from confronting life") and plans for the future including the de Beauregard film, writing and society. "I'd like to say to women: 'Live, emancipate yourselves, love your children," Jean offered. "Don't believe that being a feminist means being aggressive, hysterical or masculine."

Hasni asserted to officials in a September 2 interrogation that he had no idea where Jean could be found. But in the days following Jean's disappearance, Fernand Fenix, who resided at 46, rue de la Faisanderie, noticed a group of four men talking around a parked white Renault car down the street from his home. One of the men, whose description matched that of Hasni, appeared very nervous and attempted to open one of the car's doors, only to be stopped by another man in the group.

Few things are absolutely clear about the death of Jean Seberg, but one thing is certain: She had expressed the wish to begin a new life, and suggested it would not include Ahmed Hasni.

As for the initial suicide ruling, it seems odd that Jean would have made plans for the next several months and then kill herself. Velma Odegaard remembered that Jean was going to visit her and other relatives in Iowa that fall, and had purchased a pair of shoes for her mother. Jean also told Alain X. that she was going back to the United States for a visit, probably after she finished the de Beauregard film. She had even mentioned to the producer that she was planning to move back the United States. A cousin from Marshalltown wrote Jean he would be stopping by for a visit while touring Europe in the fall. Most importantly, she was to return to the film she had already started in August — a film which she felt would revive her career — and possibly make the film with David Niven as well. It seems improbable that someone contemplating suicide would make plans to travel, work, shop, and receive house guests.

Then, too, there is the alleged suicide note. Jean was an ardent correspondent, and this letter could have been written at any time, possibly during

Jean's hospitalization at Perray-Vaucluse in February 1979. The note could be read as an apology to Diego, for when she was hospitalized, she had telephoned Diego several times. Later Jean learned her calls had frightened her son. Perhaps the note was written at that time, or earlier, but never sent. Investigators could not determine when it was composed.

Among Jean's papers were numerous notes and letters, including the work on her autobiography, screenplays and poems, and a letter in which she announced that she planned to move away from France. An unidentified friend who saw the actual note to Diego remarked: "She was lucid when she [wrote it]. I knew her handwriting. The note she left to her son was perfectly controlled."

Most of Jean's Paris and Marshalltown friends also question whether she did in fact commit suicide. "Even with the note they found that Jean allegedly wrote. It was strange that it didn't refer to herself and Diego as 'mother' and 'son,' but rather 'Jean' and 'Diego.' That just didn't ring. It didn't sound like something Jean would do," Warren Robeson says. "If Jean did commit suicide, I feel it could have been prevented. And I lay that at Hasni's feet."

As for the possibility of suicide, John Berry felt he didn't "know what the answer would be to many people, like Marilyn Monroe's death. So many different things you hear, I mean, how can you believe this woman would kill herself? How can you believe Jean would go out and poison herself? Well, when you know her, it's possible that she might give up. But you can't really believe that. I really don't know."

In the months following her death, however, the Paris police and the French public began to doubt the suicide theory. Once the autopsy report was released, it revealed that Jean had a shockingly high percentage of alcohol in her bloodstream — nearly eight percent per liter of blood. Even in the most hardened drinkers, between five and six percent would normally induce coma. The question is therefore how, in that state of intoxication, could Jean Seberg have driven her car? No liquor bottles were found in or around the Renault, disposing of the possibility that she drank the alcohol after she had parked the car. It was unlikely that she consumed the alcohol elsewhere. Hasni told the police he did not know where or how Jean had obtained the alcohol.

Additionally, relatives said Jean could not see, let alone drive, without her eyeglasses. The eyeglasses were discovered in her apartment at rue de Longchamp, along with a briefcase filled with money and her driver's license, which she had reported lost months earlier. The French police reported that there were no signs of a struggle in Jean's apartment when they searched it, although this was not done until several hours after the report of her disappearance.

An interesting side note is the testimony of John Finaly, who had noticed Jean's car parked on the rue du Général-Appert and peered through the window several days before the discovery of her remains. He had seen something wrapped in a blanket. He had informed the caretaker of number 24, who happened to be an employee of the police department, but no further action was taken. Finaly remembered the car from an earlier incident three weeks prior. It had been double parked in front of a pharmacy at 130 avenue Victor-Hugo. The Renault attracted Finaly's attention because the driver pulled away at the same moment Finaly drove up to it. He noticed two men inside. In the following days, Finaly noticed the same car parked on several roads in the neighborhoods near rue de Longchamp, including the rue du Général-Appert. Had the men Finaly saw patronized the pharmacy on Victor-Hugo, and if so, what did they purchase?

When the French press suggested Jean's death might not have been a suicide, Romain Gary told a reporter, "My son is very disturbed because of the latest news. I promised him I would not talk about it. I will never write about her or speak about it again. Nothing can undo anything that has been done. It's quite shameful to bring the matter up again. I know her death has a certain American social importance, but I just want her to sleep in peace."

Despite Romain's public comment, Jean's death case was re-opened by the Public Prosecutor's Office of the Paris Tribunal on June 25, 1980. Two charges were filed by Romain. The first was to look into the cause of Jean's death against "persons unknown" for "non-assistance of a person in danger." The charge indicated French police may have suspected that someone stood by and allowed Jean to take her own life, rather than trying to get medical help to save her—or conceivably even that someone forced her to take her own life, or watched as Jean Seberg was murdered.

Guy-Pierre Geneuil firmly believes Jean was murdered. "Jean said she was caught up in the 'gears' of drug trafficking between France and Algeria," Geneuil told *France-Soir*. "She knew too much. She was afraid."

The second charge was directly aimed at Ahmed Hasni for theft and fraud. Many of Jean's possessions, including her writings, personal mementos and jewelry, and various pieces of framed paintings and artwork worth several thousand dollars, were taken by Hasni. Neither Jean's friends nor her family know what became of the briefcase filled with money from the sale of her rue du Bac apartment.

Ahmed Hasni was traced by the French police in September 1980 and interrogated. He said his occupation was a male model, and admitted he had stolen 50,000 francs from Jean. He acknowledged he sold the pieces of artwork to dealers and kept the money. Hasni was freed on 10,000 francs bail on October 10, 1980, then was arrested and was sentenced in court on March 4, 1981 where he was sentenced by default to two years imprisonment. Hasni appealed the verdict twice, having his sentence reduced to eight months.

None of Jean's personal belongings were recovered from Hasni, including an obsidian head given to her by André Malraux that she treasured. Some of her writings have been sold in Paris antique stores, having undoubtedly originated from Hasni. Jean's jewelry, as well as her collection of artwork, were most certainly peddled, and are probably now in various wealthy homes with no trace of where they originated. The only items Diego has of Jean's, aside from his father's personal effects, are those she had with her when she died. None of Jean's friends knows of Hasni's current whereabouts, although it is believed he lives in Algeria.

"We don't know what the truth is about Jean's death," John Berry concluded. "And we never will."

34

"I have said all I have to say."
— Romain Gary

Leïla Chellabi became Romain Gary's partner in 1979 and lived with him in the rue du Bac apartment. She was born in Casablanca of a French mother and Turkish father, and had met Romain at a dinner given by mutual friends. Two days after their meeting, Romain telephoned Chellabi, and the two began seeing each other.

Chellabi recounted how after Jean's death she heard her voice call her in the apartment, and that Romain had admitted hearing it also. In the fifteen months after Jean's death, Romain had quietly slipped out of society. To justify his seclusion, he told people he was working on a new novel, but this was not the case. Romain had lined the walls of his office with photographs of faces. One board was covered entirely with photos and magazine covers of Jean and Romain.

Françoise Prévost, who had starred with Jean in her early French films, had successfully turned to writing novels. As is the norm in the publishing world, a photograph of her appeared on her book's jacket. "I got a letter from Romain Gary saying he loved this picture of me," she says, "and wanted this picture to go on the wall of his office. It was filled with pictures of well-known people — only their faces. This is strange, I thought. He said he loved the look and this was an interesting face." A majority of the pictures on display were of Jean, taken throughout the years.

Although Romain sold Cimarron in 1974 with the stipulation that he could visit one month out of the year, he went back there for only one brief stay. Increasingly he spent his time closeted at the rue du Bac, where Jean's bedroom was still preserved as it had been when she moved out over a decade earlier — as if she might one day return.

Romain talked about Jean compulsively to anyone (except the news media) who came to visit. A relative remembers, "He was very anxious and when I asked him why, he said he would never forget how his ex-wife's reputation had been dirtied. He missed his ex-wife more than he divulged."

Not only did Romain mourn Jean's death, but he also reproached himself for not helping her more in the final months of her life. Both of these feelings added to his depression. "Something was missing there," Françoise Prévost says. "He surely could have done something to protect her."

"There was 'something' Jean and Romain had going between them, despite her marriage to Dennis," says Rabbi Serber. "She was in love with Romain,

Jean Seberg and Romain Gary, circa 1962. COURTESY OF SNORRAMYNDIR

and there was a tie, even in the way he wrote to me in his concern of her. There was a chemistry. Whatever it was, no one knows. They had something between them that kept them together even when they were apart."

"Despite the routes their lives took, Romain was," according to Lynda Haupert, "the great love of Jean's life." After his mother's death, perhaps none of all the women in Romain's life affected him as deeply as Jean did, whether as his wife or as the "daughter" he felt she had become for him.

To Jean's *The French Conspiracy* director Yves Boisset, Romain had said many times prior to her death, "For me, Jean is so important I would do anything to save her. I can bear it that she left me and went with another man, but I don't think I could survive if she died." Earlier in 1980, author William Styron lunched with Romain at the Brasserie Lipp. Here, Romain had revealed to Styron that "despite their difficulties, his loss of Jean had so deepened his depression that from time to time he had been rendered nearly helpless."

Friends believed Romain's sense of the meaninglessness of things must have overwhelmed him. "He was in a deep depression, and was being nursed for the depression," Roger Grenier reveals. In addition, Grenier says that Romain "also had trembling hands. I thought he had Parkinson's disease."

Romain had just returned from a holiday with Diego in Greece when he went out to dine alone in Saint-Germain-des-Prés. One person who saw Romain there was Nicolas Gessner. "I was going out when I met him," Gessner remembers. "There's a front part and a back part, with a corridor in-between. And he was sitting at this table in the corridor, next to the stairs that led to the toilets.

"I said, 'Hello, Romain,' and he said, 'Look how they treat me. They give me the table next to the loo.' He was Romain Gary. They knew him. He could have said, 'Give me another table.' But he was sitting there, and being downbeat about being so badly treated. This was kind of a joke, because he could have had the best table.

"I said, 'How are you?' and he said, 'I'm fine... I'm tired...'"

On December 2, Roger Grenier remembers Romain had telephoned to Geneva for someone to pick him up at the airport, as he planned to travel there. This was his close friend Suzanne Salmanowitz, who had agreed that he might stay with her. Romain also telephoned a nurse, went to a meeting concerning his income tax, and returned to the rue du Bac. There, he wrote a letter, photocopied it, and mailed a copy to his publisher. Returning to his apartment, he walked into his bedroom. He placed a copy of the letter he had just mailed at the foot of his bed as he lay down. He then put the muzzle of a revolver in his mouth and pulled the trigger.

"No connection with Jean Seberg," Romain's letter read. "Lovers of broken hearts are kindly asked to look elsewhere. Obviously, you can put this down to nervous depression. But then, it must be added that the same depression has been going on since I reached manhood and has not prevented me from successfully carrying out my literary endeavors.

"Why then? Perhaps one should look for the answer in the title of my autobiography, *The Night Will Be Calm*, and in the last words of my last novel.... 'I have said all that I have to say.'"

Romain had wanted a grand funeral with his former comrades-in-arms at St-Louis-des-Invalides. Diego planned the ceremony, but there was no conventional funeral service, since Romain was effectively an atheist. Singer Anna Prucnal sang a Polish lullaby, which Romain's mother had hummed to him as a child, and a model of an elephant was placed on the coffin because he loved them so much.

To Diego, who spoke to a journalist from *Paris Match*, in retrospect there seemed nothing astonishing about his father's end. He explained that Romain had prepared him for the painful experiences life might bring. "He always repeated what his mother had written to him in her last letter: 'Be strong, my son.' So I'm not really surprised by his final act. I accept and I respect it."

Romain had given instructions over the previous months concerning the future of his literary works, the house, Diego, and even his death. This did not alarm Diego, since Romain frequently spoke to him in this manner. "If he hadn't thought I wasn't strong enough to stand such a test, he wouldn't have done it. I think it was the philosopher Alain who wrote: 'When a man has nothing more to build, he is unhappy.' And my father considered he had nothing further to build, nor to say, nor to do… He considered I'd grown into a man, so he left." Diego compared Romain to the legend of the elephants in *The Roots of Heaven*: when one of them feels he has become old, he leaves the herd and goes off alone to find a place to die. "My father departed like the elephants do."

Diego Gary also firmly rejected the notion that grief over Jean's death had been the cause of his father's suicide. "I insist, absolutely no connection between his suicide and my mother's. The death of my mother was for the two of us a closed matter…He supported her to the end and helped her in every way possible…He never abandoned her. I went to see her whenever I wanted, that's to say almost daily. My father was very much affected by her death, but at no moment did it, even in part, have a bearing on his."

Concerned for their grandson, Ed and Dorothy Seberg extended an invitation to Diego offering him to stay with them for awhile. On January 23, 1981, Diego wrote them:

> Right now I'm feeling kind of low and tired. I may — one of these days — leave Paris where I have too [many] memories to carry.
>
> Maybe I'll come to the States, and then visit you.
> I figure we have different thoughts about living, the world.
> We may be very different each one from each other. You can see: I can't even speak English right!

Just anyhow, I'm sure you are having some hard lives too, as I wanted to send a little gift of love. Hope Iowa is nice, hope that you are not feeling too sad.

Please, don't worry about me: I'm tired, yet strong.

I'll write again to you, with a clearer mind.

Love
Diego

In June 1981 it was revealed that it had after all been Romain Gary who wrote the 1975 Goncourt prize-winning novel and the three others which appeared under the name of Émile Ajar. Paul Pavlowitch, a second cousin whom Romain described as his nephew, came forward and admitted that his "uncle" had persuaded him to be his accomplice in an elaborate piece of deception. "At the end of 1972, Romain Gary told me that he planned to write something else under another name," Pavlowitch disclosed. "Nobody else was in on the secret." In publishing his account of the hoax, *L'Homme que l'on croyait* (*The Man You Believed*), on July 1, Pavlowitch was stealing the thunder of Romain's own literary testament, *Vie et mort d'Émile Ajar* (*The Life and Death of Émile Ajar*), with which he had planned the posthumous revelation of his extraordinary feat of authorship.

The claim by Pavlowitch was not completely true. Romain had told a handful of people that he and Ajar were one and the same. Diego, Jean, Dennis Berry, and Roger Grenier and the Agids all knew the secret, as did Romain's secretary Martine Carré and his lawyer Gisèle Halimi. In fact, when "Ajar's" first novel, *Gros-Câlin*, was published, it was Jean who had telephoned Romain while he was vacationing in Majorca to tell him the preliminary reviews were excellent. All who knew of the Ajar enterprise understood, however, that absolute discretion was vital to its success.

The book in the center of the Goncourt controversy was *La Vie devant soi* (*Life Before One*; English title: *Madame Rosa*). Hailed by some as a masterpiece when first published, it was bitterly attacked by the French press when it was awarded the highly coveted prize because of its "sordid" plot about a Jewish boy living with an ex-prostitute.

The use of a pseudonym had been nothing new for Romain. In 1958 he had published the satirical novel about the United Nations, *L'homme à la colombe,* under the name Fosco Sinibaldi, because as a French diplomat he could not use his real name. In 1974 his adventure story, *Les Têtes de Stéphanie* (*A Direct Flight to Allah*), had appeared under the name *Shatan Bogat*. Both François Bondy and Roger Grenier know of at least two thrillers of which Romain penned under a pseudonym, and Bondy suspects there were others. In *Promise at Dawn* he had, after all, described how even as a child he had tried out the fabulous pennames he would one day adopt.

There was a handful of people who suspected Romain was Ajar. In fact before *Gros-Câlin* was in early draft form, Romain wrote the title on the cover and had it sitting among other papers. A visiting friend noticed the title, and when the book was published under Emile Ajar, the friend went round telling everyone that Romain was Ajar. But it was in vain, as respected critics and publishers agreed that Romain was "incapable of writing such a brilliant work" and that he was "a writer who has come to the end of the line."

The uproar in France which followed the unmasking of Romain as the true author centered on the principle that a writer may win this prize once only. He had already accepted the Goncourt for *The Roots of Heaven* more than twenty years earlier. Roger Grenier explains why Romain chose to write under a pseudonym: "He was not a writer in that he was not a stylist. He was an important writer in France, but it got to the point where booksellers and critics would say, 'Yes, it's another Gary book. We know, we know,' meaning the same formula.

"He was afraid to be classified as 'old.' He wanted to be 'new.' Gary was afraid that part of the French and Europe thought he wasn't an asset."

But Émile Ajar was new, and a huge success — "more than Gary," Grenier says. And it soon became necessary to produce him. The people wanted to know the writer. "Gary took his nephew, Pavlowitch, to be Ajar, and he paid him money to do that."

For Pavlowitch, as his book makes clear, what had begun as an adventure turned into something more akin to nightmare when the deception got completely out of hand. He and Jean were friends, and she had warned him not to let himself be exploited. She had referred to her own treatment in *White Dog*, describing Romain as an "ogre" capable of consuming everyone: "It was warm and without bitterness," Pavlowitch said. "Jean was gentle. She bore no grudge against Romain. She still loved him. She thought that was just a matter of legitimate defense."

If some critics were furious at having been duped, there were also those who felt Romain had achieved a dazzling coup, and at the same time taken the literary establishment down a peg. Shrugging off the controversy Françoise Prévost says, "He deserved to win a second Prix Goncourt. Why not? Who cares if Romain wrote under a pen name?"

Leading a quiet life, far from the public eye, Diego Gary released a rare press announcement to comment on the sudden controversy. In it, Diego wrote: "The sensational aspect about Ajar's real identity should not mask the essential fact — Romain Gary's greater dimension as a person and author."

Epilogue

*"Jean Seberg was a very bright, delicate girl. Not fragile at all.   For me,
'fragile' is what breaks in two. Jean's delicacy had a tough sinew...
Like a flower coming through a rock."*
— Roscoe Lee Browne

*"There are no equivalents to Jean Seberg. She was magic. A superb person.
She was unique, and that's not exaggerated."*
— Nicolas Gessner

"Jean Seberg? Never heard of the guy."
— Marshalltown resident

Today, Diego Gary spends a majority of his time in Spain. Protecting his own privacy, he is active in administering his father's literary estate at a time when it has been the focus of intense new interest. Diego has spoken publicly about his parents only twice since their deaths. He is impatient of stories suggesting he was unloved by them, and although he experienced difficulties in dealing with their deaths, he honors their respective legacies to the literary and film worlds. "I feel an immense respect, a very great admiration for my parents," he said. "They were good people. I'm proud to have known them."

Diego recalls the countless people his mother helped, whether friends, neighbors, filmmakers or others. Director Claude Berri divulged to Diego that when he was starting out Jean helped finance his classic *Le Vieil homme et l'enfant,* a fact that was not widely known. "Her kindness, her almost excessive generosity," Diego says, "gets forgotten."

He still owns the rue du Bac apartment of his childhood, but leases it. Although not choosing to live there, he retains it because of the many good memories it holds — especially of Christmas, when his mother had Christmas trees brought in and spent days decorating the apartment.

Following his divorce from Jean Seberg, François Moreuil eventually developed a production company and either wrote, directed, or produced more than three hundred hours of television programming. His six-hour documentary series on Charles de Gaulle was shown in nineteen countries, and in 1990 the series won the prestigious Prix Vauban. Although his present wife is not an actress, she was raised in an environment similar to his own. They have been married for more than twenty-five years and live comfortably in Paris.

Dennis Berry continues to work in the entertainment industry, mainly directing television programs, including some in the United States. He, too, lives in Paris, with his wife Anna Karina, former New Wave star and ex-wife of Jean-Luc Godard.

Mary Ann Seberg and her husband, Ed, have been married since 1958. The union produced two daughters and several grandchildren. Both retired, Mary Ann and Ed travel extensively. Jean's brother, Kurt, lives quietly in the Midwest.

Ed Seberg seldom spoke publicly about Jean after her death. His bitterness toward the FBI never diminished. When Ed did talk about Jean, he usually concentrated on the fun times, such as when he and Dorothy visited Jean during *Paint Your Wagon*. Jean had put them up to stay at a first-class hotel, and Ed tried to appear sophisticated as he walked into the lobby carrying his luggage. Suddenly, the suitcase popped open and his clothes went, in Ed's words, "flying all over the lobby."

In September 1984, the unofficial mayor of 13th Street died of cancer. People have said that Ed never was his usual self after Jean's death.

In the years which followed Jean's death Dorothy Seberg's behavior changed. In 1989 she was diagnosed with Alzheimer's disease and was moved to an upper-class, private nursing home in Marshalltown, where she received excellent medical care. In 1996, she suffered a debilitating stroke and died in March 1997. For years she waited and hoped for a visit from her only grandson — who never came.

When Dorothy was admitted to the nursing home, Mary Ann packed her mother's personal belongings, which included memorabilia from Jean's career. When Jean died, the family did not receive any of her personal possessions from Paris. All they had left were her letters, scrapbooks of news clippings, and photographs. Believing that the State Historical Society of Iowa would appreciate the items for their collection of famous Iowans, Mary Ann telephoned them to offer her sister's memorabilia. The person at the society asked, "Who's Jean Seberg?" Mary Ann eventually donated a majority of the items to the Marshall County Historical Society.

Much of Marshalltown remains unchanged since Jean's last visit in the 1970s. The 25,000 population has not fluctuated significantly, although it is more integrated today with the immigration of Mexicans. A good deal of city planning went into the community as the downtown still has the look of an era gone-by. A majority of downtown buildings remain as they have for decades, including the *Times-Republican* office building. Although demolition was contemplated, the courthouse was finally restored in the 1980s to its former majestic appearance. The southern part of the city has expanded through the years. A shopping mall, several single-story buildings, and the discount stores Wal-Mart and K-Mart were built in this area, as have numerous fast food establishments that now line the main highway.

The Seberg Pharmacy closed in 1989, several years after Ed Seberg sold the business. Although the building has seen many different businesses come and go since then, the "Seberg Pharmacy" sign hung outside as a reminder of the Seberg name until the mid 1990s, when it was finally removed.

Jean Seberg is remembered in her hometown only through the efforts of a few individuals. A display of framed movie posters hangs on the east wall in the new Marshalltown High School auditorium, thanks to a donation by speech/drama instructor Tom Laville. Through the years, the Jean Seberg Award had lost its significance, and if a student announced (s)he was going into a related field of the entertainment industry, they would simply become the recipient. Laville reorganized the award and renamed it The Jean Seberg/Mary Beth Hurt Award. Hurt, a three-time Tony award nominee, was also raised in Marshalltown and had been baby-sat when she was Mary Beth Supinger by Mary Ann Seberg. It was rumored Jean Seberg had also sat for her.

For all its years of Seberg fervor during her life, Marshalltown seems to have neglected its famous daughter. There has been one Jean Seberg Festival, which was held in 1992, organized primarily by non-residents of the town. There is no plaque commemorating the premiere of *Saint Joan* at the Orpheum Theater, nor is there any sign to record that she helped dedicate the Martha Ellen Tye Playhouse. There is a small, but permanent Jean Seberg display at the Marshall County Historical Society, and a wall of framed movie posters in the lobby of the high shool auditorium alongside those of Mary Beth Hurt and others.

The feelings of Marshalltownians toward Jean have changed throughout the years. Some believe the town has disowned Jean Seberg, embarrassed by her activism and her life. Mary Beth Hurt said, "The feeling there is what happened to Jean served her right and that the FBI did the right thing." Merle Miller, author of the Harry Truman account *Plain Speaking*, who was another former Marshalltown resident, said, "There is very little pity for Seberg among those people."

But other Marshalltownians have a different view. Shirley Borton told the *Los Angeles Times:* "I was raised on the wrong part of town, and I wasn't the kind of girl people like the Sebergs would admire. But Jean was just darling to me. She should have stayed right here."

"The majority of the people who were around during Seberg's time are either dead or have moved away," one resident says. "The people here just have no idea who Jean Seberg was, or what kind of a career she had." In fact, when the dates for the Marshalltown showing of *Paint Your Wagon* were announced in early 1970, Ed Seberg stopped by the theater to make reservations. "Seaberg — Seaburg — Seeburg? How do you spell that?" asked the girl at the ticket office. The Marshalltown girl had no inkling that Ed was the father of the actress in the film.

Jean was an all-American girl, who believed in democracy and in the American dream. But her faith in both disintegrated, and her faith in humanity lessened. Someone once asked her, "If you had to do it all over again and not have been an actress, what would you have done?" Jean quietly replied: "A veterinarian. Animals can't tell you what's wrong. You have to be sensitive to them. But people will always tell you their problems. Sometimes I get tired of people telling me what's wrong all the time."

A close friend of Jean's concluded: "I wish we had more like her. It doesn't matter what anyone says — most people who make derogatory comments really didn't know her. I guess it's easy to judge, isn't it?"

Occasional Jean Seberg film festivals have taken place in Chicago and New York, and undoubtedly there have been film festivals in other cities in the past, such as the November 1983 series at London's National Film Theatre. Several critics have re-evaluated her acting career and now acknowledge her talent. *Lilith* was preserved and given a 2006 showing at New York's Museum of Modern Art. The *Monthly Film Bulletin* stated *Lilith* is "one of the finest films about madness ever made." *Entertainment Weekly* reviewed the home video release of *Saint Joan*, grading it with an A- and calling it "a charming intimate spectacle...[Seberg is] a stunning Joan." *Bonjour Tristesse* is now hailed a masterpiece. A fortieth anniversary theatrical release of *Breathless* confirmed its standing as an important and groundbreaking film. In fact, the London anniversary showing of *Breathless* sold out on many occasions. Hollywood has not forgotten Jean entirely. Through the American Film Institute, she was nominated by the film industry as one of the Greatest Film Star Legends of all time in 1999.

In France, Jean is still regarded as the quintessential American girl in Paris, the free spirit — in fact, there is a French hard rock music band called "Jean Seberg." Articles on style in French women's magazines continue regularly to feature the ageless "Jean Seberg look." Yet, side-by-side with Belmondo, no one more powerfully conveys the feeling of a given moment and place than Seberg, in her *New York Herald Tribune* T-shirt. The respect the French held for Jean was so great that on the day of her funeral, programming on French television was pre-empted to pay homage to her by showing *Bonjour Tristesse.*

As for the film Jean was working on at the time of her death, the role was recast and Jean's scenes were cut. Georges de Beauregard and Raoul Coutard felt Jean had been exploited by many who knew her — and several who did not, as well. They both agreed Jean's footage in *Le légion saute sur Kolwezi* remain private, despite the fact they were pleased with how she photographed as well as her performance. True to their word, the footage of Jean remains unseen.

At Montparnasse Cemetery, a flat, black granite slab with a cross covers her grave. A sign reads: JEAN SEBERG 1938-1979, and the simple, contemporary marker looks oddly out of place among the ornate and elaborate tombstones and statues which surround it. Although not particularly imposing and almost hidden, it commands attention when found. Scarcely a day passes when someone doesn't stop and linger at the site. Some are sightseers visiting the cemetery, who come upon it accidentally or are alerted by the guidebooks, but others are fans who have made a special effort to find her final resting place among those of so many others.

Rarely does a week pass without some new gift of sorts appearing on the marker. It may be fresh roses, silk flowers, or ceramic figures. Sometimes it can be a candle or an origami figure of a bird. Trinkets and coins from all over the world, including South America, Asia, and the United States, appear. Frequently handwritten messages are left there, pledging remembrance in any of a multitude of languages.

Every so often, the mementos are gathered by the groundskeepers and tossed out. They are considered an eyesore among the venerable old stones.

But, then, another week passes bringing another stranger with some offering — and perhaps, too, another promise never to forget.

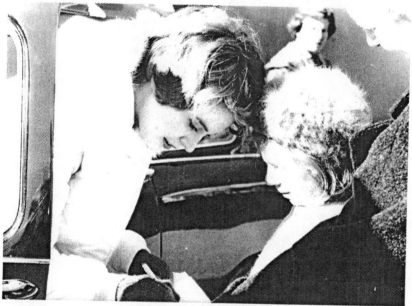

Signing an autograph for a young fan, February 1959. COURTESY OF SNORRAMYNDIR

Jean Seberg — Breathless

Acknowledgments

While one name is printed on this book as the author, it was the combined effort of many people to make this book a realization. This was no small task. Several years of research included reading thousands of news articles, spending several months traveling in Europe and the United States, locating and viewing Jean's films, reading her personal letters, and seeking out those people closest to Jean Seberg.

I recognize the generosity and help of many people including: Nicole Bacharan, Jean and Vony Becker, Jim Bellows, John Berry, Manoah Bowman, Lucille Carra, John Crome, Michael Coates-Smith, Mylène Demongeot, Sherrie Denning, Donatello and Fosco Dubini, Rev. Thomas Duggan, Elaina Eller, Robin Evans, John Findlater, Nicolas Gessner, Dana Good, Roger Grenier, Maurice and Chantal Guichard, Lee Hadley, David and Lynda Haupert, Carol Hollingsworth, Olga Horstig-Primuz, Independent Visions, Frederic Jones, Jude of the *St. Jean* Website, Irvin Kershner, Leo Knox, Bernard Kowalski, Joan Kufrin, Diane Ladd, Rosemarie Larson, Irv Letofsky, Marge Ludwig, Marshalltown *Times-Republican* and David Dawson, Kathy Martin, Helen Mason, Roger Maxwell, Gerald McGee, Larry McGee, Marian McGee, Perry McGee, Wilt Melnick, Erma Morrow, Dawn Quinn, François Moreuil, Richard Ness, Betty Nocella, Velma Odegaard, Ben Ohmart, Ann Okerstrom, Annette Oswald-O'Donnell, Jerry Pam, Douglas Peterson, Dan Petrie, Sr., Jenny Pickman, Françoise Prévost, Jeff Quam, A. Rebillard, Warren Robeson, Jean Russell Larson, Bob Sandin, George Schaefer, Sandy Schlesinger, Rabbi Sol Serber, Marc Simenon, Dale and Pauline Smith, Snorramyndir, Bill and Kathy Stahmann, Maureen Stapleton, Jeff Stein, Ray Walston, Bob Willoughby, Kathie Willson, Gail Yeisley Rhodes.

To the staffs at many libraries including the Bibliothèque de l'arsenal, Bibliothèque Nationale de France, Bibliothèque Centre Pompideu, Conservatoire National des Arts et Métiers, the Parks Library Iowa State University, the Margaret Herrick Library Beverly Hills, the Elma Public Library, and the British Film Institute.

To those individuals who granted me interviews with the provision I keep their names confidential, I have respected your wishes.

I must add a special thank you to Mary Ann Seberg for her help and kindness, and without whom many who personally knew Jean would not have met with me. And lastly, to my parents, family and friends for their unending support and patience over the years with this project. I am grateful to all of you and others. Thank you for helping make this book possible.

Garry McGee

Jean Seberg — Breathless

Selected Bibliography

Several newspaper articles were from the collections of Frances Benson, Pauline Smith and Michael Coates-Smith. In some instances, complete source data was not recorded.

[MTR-Marshalltown (Iowa) *Times Republican*; DMR-Des Moines (Iowa) *Register*]

"Actress in coma riddle," *Daily Mail*, August 10, 1970 page 1

"Actress Jean Seberg, Iowa Native, Found Dead," DMR, September 9, 1979 page 1+

Alpert, Don. "Jean Seberg: Out of Fiery Furnace," *Los Angeles Times Calendar*, February 14, 1965

Alpert, Hollis. "The Joys of Uncertainty," *Saturday Review*, December 29, 1962

_____. "Preminger Stunt won role for Jean," *Philadelphia Inquirer*, December 16, 1962

"Another Dirty Trick by The FBI," *Newsweek*, September 24, 1979 page 45

"Attornies for Jean Seberg Blast Moreuil," MTR, September 24, 1960

Auboyneau, Olivia. "Mais comment est morte Jean Seberg?" *Quotidien*, December 12, 1979

Bacon, James. "French Love Iowa's Star," *Los Angeles Herald-Examiner*, April 27, 1969

Bart, Peter. "Jean, Once a 'Has Been,' Back in Hollywood," *New York Times*, 1965

_____ . "Paris to Hollywood with No Stop at Marshalltown," *New York Times*, March 20, 1965

_____ . "Well, what's an interview for?" *New York Times*, March 27, 1966

Barthel, Joan. "Jean Seberg Loses Her Innocence," *Cosmopolitan*, May 1969, pages 110-13

Besozzi, Ludovico. "A 12 anni ero una Pantera Nera," *Oggi*, May 6, 1972, pages 78-80, 83

Bondy, Francois. "On the Death of a Friend," *Publisher's Weekly*, AR Bouken Co., Philadelphia, PA, December 19, 1980

"Busy Week for Jean Seberg as She Prepares to Marry," MTR, September 4, 1958

Cameron, Kate. "Movie Chat: London to Zululand," *Sunday News*, September 22, 1963

Canby, Vincent. "The Sad Life of Jean Seberg," *New York Times*, September 23, 1979 pages 19, 29

_____ . "A Summer in Spain," *New York Times*, November 30, 1979

_____ . "Screen: Nelo Risi's 'Dead of Summer'," *New York Times*, March 10, 1971

Cartwright, Otis. "What Jean Seberg Learned About S-E-X," unknown

Chaigneau, Jean-Francois. "Le fils de Romain Gary explique: 'Il a fait de moi un homme, il pouvait partir," *Paris Match*, December 19, 1980 pages 108-11

Champlin, Charles. "A Return in Triumph for Miss Seberg," unknown, 1965

_____ . "Julie Sommars Escaped Limelight with Her Youth Intact," *Los Angeles Times*, October 24, 1989

_____ . "Thoughts about the Seberg Tragedy," *Los Angeles Times*, September 12, 1979

Clarke, Sue. "My life has been a roller-coaster," *Photoplay* (UK), March 1974 pages 29, 59

Coleman, William A. "The Fall and Rise of Jean Seberg," *American Weekly*, April 16, 1961

Conrad, Shawn. "Fond Memories All That's Left at Seberg Pharmacy," MTR, September 30, 1989

Couderc, Claude. "Jean Seberg: 'Aprés l'amour, je découvre l'amitié'," *Paris Jour*, January 25, 1972

Dahl, Arlene. "Jean Seberg Adopted by Franch as Own Star," unknown

D'Arcy, Susan. "Adieu Tristesse," *Films Illustrated*, August 1974 pages 490-3

Deming, Angus, and Scott Sullivan. "Romain Gary's Surprise Ending," *Newsweek*, December 15, 1980 page 59

Die Wildente: Ein film von Hans W. Geissendorfer nach dem gleichnamigen Theaterstuck von Henrik Ibsen. 1976.

Dorsey, Hebe and Phil Hilts. "Jean Seberg--Romain Gary's Tale of FBI Documents and an American Idealist," *Washington Post*, September 17, 1979 pages B1, B11

Douin, Jean-Luc. "Jean Seberg 'Au fond de moi je ne suis qu' une fille de la campagne'," *Telerama*, July 21, 1982 Pages 18-20

_____. "Les Hautes Solitudes," *Telerama*, December 12, 1974

Driancourt, Christophe. "Seberg: La Piste Des Trafiquants De Drogue," *France-Soir*, August 22, 1995 pages 2-3

E.J., "The great Killy flees to America for love," *Stop*, January 1969

"Entrega de los premios del XVIII festival de cine de San Sebastian," *Hola*, July 25, 1970 pages 32-3+

Evans, Peter. "Preminger's Pre-Production Rehearsals Are Worth It," *Kinematograph Weekly* 1957

"FBI admits planting rumor about Seberg's pregnancy," DMR [AP report], September 15, 1979

"FBI Planted Seberg Baby Story," MTR, September 14, 1979 [local and AP reports]

"FBI Thanked in Seberg case," DMR AP report, September 16, 1979

"The FBI vs. Jean Seberg," *Time*, September 24, 1979, p.25

Fain, Nathan, "Home From Europe, Jean Seberg Found Marshalltown 'Hip,'" *Houston Post*, May 14, 1969

Ferris, Irene. "Jean Seberg, Idolized, Is Saddest American," Women's News Service, November 1961

Fieschi, Jean-André. "The Unique Film," *Cahiers du cinéma* no. 7, January 1967

Fireman, Ken. "Whispers: What happened when the FBI 'neutralized' Jean Seberg," *Free Press*, 1979, pages 1B & 4B

Fitoussi, Michele. "Je suis fier de mes parents," *Elle*, October 18, 2004, pages 80-2, 84, 86

"Fragments d'un journal par Philippe Garrel," *Cahiers du cinéma*, September 1991, #447, page 39

"French Seek Algerian Friend of Jean Seberg," MTR [AP report], June 25, 1980

"French Probe Jean Seberg Death Case," MTR [AP report], May 1980

Friedman, Jane M. "Actress Says FBI Plotted to Smear Her," *International Herald Tribune*, February 7, 1979

Gale, Patrick. "Jean Seberg the Tragic Gamine," *Marie Claire* (Australia), May 2000 pages 261-6

Gardner, Paul. "Rossen's Trip into 'Lilith's' Clouded World," *Montgomery County Sentinel*, May 9, 1963

Garrett, Gerard, and Maureen Cleave. "Mr. Shaw Finds Freedom," *Evening Standard*, September 27, 1963

Gary, Romain. "The Big Knife," *France-Soir*, August 1970

"Gary's Note: No Seberg Death Link," MTR [AP report], December 1980

Gerard, Lou. "Washed Up at 20, Jean Seberg is a Star Again — At 21," *National Enquirer*, August 7, 1960, vol. 34, no. 7

Giuffredi, Enrico. "E'stata Uccisa," *Gente*, September 28, 1979

Gow, Gordon. "Re-birth," *Films and Filming*, June 1974

Graham, Sheilah. "Jean Seberg has Mixed Feelings on Film Career," North American News Alliance, circa January 1958 unknown

_____ . "Jean Seberg's New Outlook," *Hollywood Citizen-News*, June 10, 1965

_____ . "Jean's Fed Up with Paris and Preminger," DMR [AP report], November 12, 1961

_____ . "Like A Ship Adrift," North American News Alliance, June 5, 1969

_____ . "Movie Gadabout's Diary," North American News Alliance, unknown

Grant, Lee. "Did Gossip Kill Her?" *Los Angeles Times' Calendar*, September 23, 1979

Greated, Arthur. "'Joan of Arc' Gets Burnt," *Daily Mail*, February 1957

Greenberg, Abe. "Jean Seberg Owes Career to Brando," *Hollywood Citizen-News*, January 6, 1970

_____ . "A New Career for Jean Seberg?" *Hollywood Citizen-News*, July 24, 1968

Greene, Lee. "Ah, Such Sweet Sorrow," unknown

Grenter, Cynthia. "In Gallic 'Style'," unknown

Gussow, Mel. "The Seberg Tragedy," *New York Times Sunday Magazine*, November 30, 1980 pages 51-53+

Haber, Joyce. "Jean Seberg at 29: the Quality of a Roaring Mouse," *Los Angeles Times* reprint, December 8, 1968

_____ . "Jean Seberg Explains Breakup of Marriage," DMR [From Los Angeles *Times*], August 28, 1969.

_____ . "Miss A Rates As Expectant Mother," *Los Angeles Times*, May 19, 1970

Halphen, Philippe. "L'actrice Jean Seberg menacée pour avoir recueilli des Noirs," *France-Soir*, December 12, 1968

Hamel, Therese. "Jean Seberg et Romain Gary," *Marie France*, January 1968 pages 58-61

Hamill, Pete. "For caring about other people, Jean Seberg paid with her life," *New York Daily News*, reprinted in DMR on October 23, 1979

_____ . Unknown *Saturday Evening Post*, June 15, 1963

Harris, Radie. "Broadway Ballyhoo," *Hollywood Reporter*, October 20, 1967

Heffernan, Harold. "Her 87-Year-Old Grandmother Is Inspiration for Jean Seberrg," North American Newspaper Alliance, July 1968

_____. "Iowa's Jean Seberg Gives 'Adopted' Hippies a Bath," DMR [North American News Alliance report], November 7, 1968

Hérisse, Marc. "Jean Seberg: 'J'en ai assez des superproductions, je voudrais tourner avec Ingmar Bergman," *France-Soir*, May 24, 1970

Heymann, C. David. *RFK*, Dutton, New York. 1998

Houston, Penelope. "After the Lost Generation," *The Financial Times*, September 27, 1963

Howell, Georgina. "Jean Seberg," *Vogue*, October 1990 pages 364-72, 439

Hutchinson, Tom. "Preminger gets tough with ST. JOAN," *Picturegoer/Film Weekly*, February 23, 1957

"In the French Style...At Midnight," *Daily Cinema, September* 25, 1963

Incerti, Corrado. "E'Facile Diventare Regista." *L'Europeo*, April 20, 1972

"Innocence Abroad," *Newsweek*, June 6, 1963 page 95

"Inséparables depuis leur divorce," *Paris Jour*, August 28, 1970

"Inside the FBI," Connaught Films/BBC 1994

"Iowans Gasp at Francois' Short Trip," DMR, September 1958

"Is it true what they say about Otto?" *McCall's*, March 1965, pages 107, 176-9

Jacobs, Lois. "Stage, Screen Stars Add Glitter to Playhouse Opening," MTR, June 5, 1969

Jalon, Allan M. "A Faulty Tip, a Ruined Life and Hindsight; A journalistic lapse allowed the FBI to smear actress Jean Seberg." *Los Angeles Times*, April 14, 2002

"Jean honored; she may visit soon," MTR, April 4, 1958

"Jean Loses Her Baby," MTR, August 25, 1970

"Jean Married at 4 P.M.," MTR, September 5, 1958

"Jean Marries Romain Gary in Corsica," MTR, October 1963

"Jean, Parents on Separate CBS TV Shows," MTR, 1957

"Jean Plans Slander Suit," MTR, August 20, 1970

"Jean Returns to Paris After Visit Here," MTR, May 1961

"Jean Says Magazine Amplified Contents," unknown

"Jean Seberg a épousé son 'retour aux sources'," *Elle*, May 15, 1972

"Jean Seberg Aids Indian Cagers," MTR, January 29, 1972

"Jean Seberg & Ex Sue 3 Mags," *New York Daily News* [UPI report], April 26, 1971

"Jean Seberg avait déjà tenté de se suicider en se jetant sous le métro," *le Figaro*, September 10, 1979

"Jean Seberg Back in U.S., Finds Masher, Detectives," DMR circa 1963

"Jean Seberg: 'Deux hommes grenouilles me protégeaient des bandes de requins'," *France Soir*, June 6, 1972

"Jean Seberg: Elle gagne un procès né d'un atroce malentendu C'est une victoire amère," *Paris-Match*, November 6, 1971

"Jean Seberg, French Mate Reveal Rift," *Hollywood Citizen-News*, September 17, 1968

"Jean Seberg, Gary Win Libel Damages," MTR, October 26, 1971

"Jean Seberg Globe Nominee," MTR, February 1965

"Jean Seberg, 'Heroine' of Stranded Ferryboat," Long Beach *Press-Telegram* [UPI report], January 26, 1963

"Jean Seberg Hospitalized, But 'Getting Along Fine,'" MTR, August 11, 1970

"Jean Seberg Is Granted an Iowa Divorce," DMR, September 22, 1960, page 9

"Jean Seberg Is Wed to Author Gary, 49," DMR [AP report], October 1963

"Jean Seberg: 'J'ai choisi l'aventure de la vie'," *Elle*, January 24, 1972

"Jean Seberg Loses Baby; Sues Newsweek Magazine," DMR, September 8, 1970

"Jean Seberg mariage heureux, divorce heureux," *Marie Claire*, May 1975

"Jean Seberg: mieux vaut un vieux décor qu'une aventure douteuse," *Le Figaro*, October 30, 1972

"Jean Seberg Plans Divorce from Gary," MTR, September 17, 1968

"Jean Seberg Plans Occasional Visits," MTR, January 30, 1979

"Jean Seberg pleure son bébé tué par la haine," *Paris Jour*, August 28, 1970

"Jean Seberg préfère tourner en Europe," *Tribune de Genève*, January 6, 1965

"Jean Seberg Rescued From Grounded Ship," MTR, January 27, 1963

"Jean Seberg Tells Parents of Split," MTR, September 6, 1978

"Jean Seberg to Remarry Ex-Husband," *Daily Telegraph*, August 11, 1970 page 13

"Jean Seberg tourne pour son mari," *France-Soir*, December 14, 1974

"Jean Seberg's Despondent Ex-Spouse Dead," DMR [AP report], December 1980

"Jean Seberg's Film Winner of International Film Festival," MTR, July 15, 1970

"Jean Tells Wallace She Won't Quit," MTR, January 6, 1958

"Jean Weds in Vegas; Plans City Visit Soon," MTR, March 14, 1972

"Jean Will Make Movie in Africa," MTR, September 5, 1961

"Jean's Film: 'Even Paris Is Startled,'" DMR, April 26, 1960, page 11

"Jean's Parents Await Burial Word," MTR, September 10, 1979

"Kite Flying, Bird Watching Helps Jean Recover," MTR, April 1959

Kleiner, Rick. "Romain Gary Wants His Movie Censored," MTR [NEA report], unknown

Kobler, John. "Jean Seberg: the Dream and the Nightmare," *Cosmopolitan*, March 1985, pages 246-9, 265

Kondo, Miyuki. "Silent fragments of Seberg's true-life pain and loneliness," *Cinema-Guide*, June 28, 2002.

Kyria, Pierre. "Jean Seberg … A bâtons rompus," *Combat*, July 16/17, 1966

L. J.-P., "La fin tragique de Jean Seberg — décomposition," *l'Humanite*, September 10, 1979

"L'actrice Jean Seberg poursuit deux hebdomadaires en diffamation," *Le Soir*, May 22, 1971

"L'actrice Jean Seberg retrouvée morte dans sa voiture e Paris," *L'évènment*, September 10, 1979

La Badie, Donald W. "Everybody's Galatea," *Show*, August 1963, pages 77, 98

Lamberto, Nick. "Jean Seberg Buys Home for Athletes," *Des Moines Register & Tribune*, January 6, 1971

"Les accusations de Romain Gary," *L'Aurore*, September 11, 1979

Lewin, David. "Seberg at 25 'I'll Never Be Bullied Again'," *Daily Mail*, September 18, 1963

Lewis, Kevin. "Jean Seberg of Iowa and Paris," *Films in Review*, April 1980, pages 226-9

Mann, Roderick. "She's the Darling of Paris," *London Free-Press* unknown

_____ . "Jean Never Bores Me Says Mr. Gary," *Sunday Express*, October 23, 1967

_____ . "Jean Seberg: la femme qui a toujours l'air D'être 'la maîtresse'," *Cine Revue*, August 8, 1974 pages 32-5

_____ . "Why I'm glad my St. Joan was a flop — by Miss Seberg," *Sunday Express London*, September 2, 1962

Marchant, Jean-Pierre. "Ski Bum Killy Blows Jean Seberg and Husband," *Confidential*, vol 7, #3, March 1969 pages 15-16, 82.

"Marshalltown denies it had no pity for Seberg," DMR [from AP], 1980

McCormick, John. "What Have They Done to Ed and Dorothy Seberg's Daughter?" *Los Angeles Times' Calendar*, September 23, 1979.

Mills, Bart. "Jean Seberg Today," *New York Times*, June 16, 1974

"Moreuil Won't Accept Jean's U.S. Divorce," MTR [AP report], September 23, 1960

"My husband and I are to part, says Jean Seberg," *Evening News*, September 17, 1968, page 1

"New Charges Filed...," MTR [AP report], 1980

"Newsmakers," *Newsweek*, November 4, 1963

"Newsmakers," *Newsweek*, August 24, 1970, page 36

"Newsmakers," *Newsweek*, July 1, 1974

"'Newsweek' condamné pour diffamation envers Jean Seberg et Romain Gary," *Le Monde*, October 27, 1971

"Nympho in a Home Movie," *Time, December* 1968

Osborne, Robert. "Rambling Reporter," *Hollywood Reporter*, April 22, 1992

Ostrow, Ronald J. "Extensive Probe of Jean Seberg Revealed," *Los Angeles Times*, January 6, 1980 page 12

Ottolenghi, Sandro. "Perche ho fatto causa a *Newsweek*," *L'Europeo*, October 28, 1971 pages 74-7, 79

Oulahan, Richard. "A Touching, Tortured Lilith," *Life*, October 2, 1964

Paley, Stanley. "An intimate interview with Jean Seberg," *Cahiers du cinéma* no. 7, January 1967

Paley, Stanley. "The Shooting of *Lilith*," *Cahiers du cinéma* no. 7, January 1967

Pantel, Monique. "Jean Seberg: êtra femme et metteur en scene ne pose aucun problème'," *France-Soir*, June 21, 1974

Parsons, Louella. "Jean Seberg Denies She'll Wed Otto," DMR [AP report], February 1959

_____ . "Jean Seberg: the Great Transformation," AP report, 1965

"Person to Person," CBS-TV 1960

Porter, Bob. "Seberg Has 'Good Year'," *Dallas Times Herald*, May 27, 1969

"Pour leur recontre Paris, Jean Seberg et son fils ont parlé espagnol," *France Soir*, October 23, 1966

"Premiere Set For Seberg Drug Film," MTR, January 19, 1972

Prévost, Françoise. "Les problèmes de Jean Seberg: Je préfère vivre 20 ans avec lui que 40 ans avec un autre..." *Marie Claire*, February 1, 1965 pages 70-7

"Rambling Reporter," *Hollywood Reporter*, June 8, 1970

Ibid. July 15, 1970

"Radioscope de Jacques Chancel avec Jean Seberg" *Radio France*, January 29, 1976

Rawls, Jr., Wendell. "FBI Admits Planting a Rumor to Discredit Jean Seberg in 1970," *New York Times*, September 15, 1979 pages 1, 6

Reed, Rex. "Some Iowa Folks May Think She's Lost," *Times-Democrat* [from New York *Times*], August 18, 1968

Robeson, Warren. "Actress Jean Seberg Ends Brief, Sad Visit to City," MTR, May 1, 1968

_____ . " 'Cat Is Out,' Says Jean in Admitting Marital Rift," MTR, July 1960

_____ . "Jean Ends Happy Visit," MTR, July 11, 1970

_____ . "Jean Spends Time Shopping, Resting While Visiting Family," MTR, February 6, 1962

_____ . "Jean Vacations After Busy Year," MTR, May 1966

_____ . "Jean Seberg Ends Holiday Visit At Home," MTR, January 1, 1973

_____ . "Jean Seberg Makes Brief Visit," MTR, April 15, 1977

_____ . "Jean Seberg Received Wide Acclaim," MTR, August 7, 1986

_____ . "Jean Seberg May Return Here To Perform In Stage Play," MTR, January 3, 1973

_____ . "Jean Seberg Visits; 'No Marital Change'," MTR, December 2, 1968

_____ . "Jean's Baby Daughter Buried; Crowd Hears Brotherhood Plea," MTR, September 19, 1970

_____ . "Lilith Not A Pretty Picture," MTR, November 1964

_____ . "New York Critics Disagree on *Bonjour Tristesse*," MTR, January 1958

_____ . "T-R City Editor Tells Nation about Marshalltown's Jean Seberg," MTR, September 17, 1979

Roche, France. "Jean Seberg: 'Le cinéma de papa c'est confortable, mais je reviens en Europe chercher un vrai role pour mes 32 ans," *Paris Presse*, April 14, 1970

Roddy, Joseph. "The Restyling of Jean Seberg," *Look*, July 3, 1962

Ronan, Margaret. "The Lively Arts: Jean Seberg Asks Her Own Questions," Senior *Scholastic*, November 15, 1968.

Rummel, Larry. "Jean Seberg's Acting Is Tops," unknown 1964

Ryan, Jack. "Jean Seberg-Woman Between Two Worlds," *Family Weekly*, September 22, 1963

Sarris, Andrew. "Films," *Village Voice*, January 17, 1963

Schauer, Philip K. "And Bonjour Jean Seberg," *Los Angeles Times*, February 7, 1958

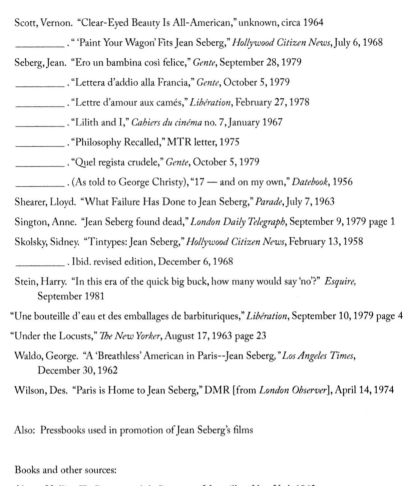

Scott, Vernon. "Clear-Eyed Beauty Is All-American," unknown, circa 1964

_____ . " 'Paint Your Wagon' Fits Jean Seberg," *Hollywood Citizen News*, July 6, 1968

Seberg, Jean. "Ero un bambina così felice," *Gente*, September 28, 1979

_____ . "Lettera d'addio alla Francia," *Gente*, October 5, 1979

_____ . "Lettre d'amour aux camés," *Libération*, February 27, 1978

_____ . "Lilith and I," *Cahiers du cinéma* no. 7, January 1967

_____ . "Philosophy Recalled," MTR letter, 1975

_____ . "Quel regista crudele," *Gente*, October 5, 1979

_____ . (As told to George Christy), "17 — and on my own," *Datebook*, 1956

Shearer, Lloyd. "What Failure Has Done to Jean Seberg," *Parade*, July 7, 1963

Sington, Anne. "Jean Seberg found dead," *London Daily Telegraph*, September 9, 1979 page 1

Skolsky, Sidney. "Tintypes: Jean Seberg," *Hollywood Citizen News*, February 13, 1958

_____ . Ibid. revised edition, December 6, 1968

Stein, Harry. "In this era of the quick big buck, how many would say 'no'?" *Esquire*, September 1981

"Une bouteille d'eau et des emballages de barbituriques," *Libération*, September 10, 1979 page 4

"Under the Locusts," *The New Yorker*, August 17, 1963 page 23

Waldo, George. "A 'Breathless' American in Paris--Jean Seberg," *Los Angeles Times*, December 30, 1962

Wilson, Des. "Paris is Home to Jean Seberg," DMR [from *London Observer*], April 14, 1974

Also: Pressbooks used in promotion of Jean Seberg's films

Books and other sources:

Alpert, Hollis. *The Dreams and the Dreamers*. Macmillan, New York 1962

Anissimov, Myriam. *Romain Gary: le caméléon*, Denoel, Paris 2004

Athill, Diana. *Make Believe: A True Story*. Steerforth Press, South Royalton, Virginia 1993

Benson, Frances. *Eight Weeks of Ecstacy* [private memoirs, Seberg family collection]

Bona, Dominique. *Romain Gary*. Mercure de France, Paris 1987

Brown, Elaine. *A Taste of Power*. Pantheon, New York 1992

Carradine, Keith. *Endless Highway*. Journey Editions, Boston 1995

Casty, Alan. *The Films of Robert Rossen*. Museum of Modern Art, New York 1969

Current Biography, 1966 pages 360-3

Dubini, Donatello and Fosco Dubini. *Jean Seberg: American Actress*, Tre Valli Filmproduktion Zurich/Dubini Filmproduktion Koln 1995

Evans, Robert. *The Kid Stays in the Picture*. Hyperion, New York 1994

Fuentes, Carlos. *Diana, the Goddess who Hunts Alone.* Farrar, Straus and Giroux, Inc., New York 1995

Frischauer, Willi. *Behind the Scenes of Otto Preminger.* Michael Joseph, London 1973

Gary, Romain. *King Solomon.* Harper & Row, New York 1983

_____ . *Promise at Dawn.* New Directions, New York 1961

_____ . *The Talent Scout.* Harper & Row, New York 1961

_____ . *White Dog.* The New American Library Co., Inc. in assoc. with the World Publishing Company, New York 1970

Gary, Romain with Francois Body. *La nuit sera calme.* Editions Gallimard, Paris 1974

Geneuil, Guy-Pierre and Jean-Michel Dumas. *Jean Seberg: ma star assassinée.* Edition 1, Paris 1995

Gentry, Curt. *J. Edgar Hoover: the Man and the Secrets.* Plume 1992

Graham, Sheila. *Confessions of a Hollywood Columnist.* William Morrow & Co, New York 1968

Hilliard, David, and Lewis Cole. *This Side of Glory.* Little, Brown and Co., Boston, Massachusettes 1993

LeRoy, Mervyn, as told to Dick Kleines. *Take One.* Hawthorn Books, Inc., New York 1974

Lerner, Alan Jay. *The Street Where I Live.* WW Norton & Co., New York   1978

Logan, Joshua. *Movie Stars, Real People and Me.* Delacorte Press, New York 1978

Manso, Peter. *Brando the Biography.* Hyperion, New York 1994

Parrish, Robert. *Hollywood Doesn't Live Here Anymore.* Little, Brown and Co., Boston 1988

Preminger, Otto. *Preminger: An Autobiography.* Doubleday & Company, Garden City, New York 1977

Previn, Andre. *No Minor Chords: My Days in Hollywood.* Doubleday, New York 1991

Reemes, Dana M. *Directed by Jack Arnold.* McFarland, Jefferson NC 1988

Richards, David. *Played Out.* Random House, New York 1981

Schickel, Richard. *Clint Eastwood,* Alfred A Knopf, Inc., USA. 1996

Shnayerson, Michael. *Irwin Shaw A Biography.* GP Putnamm's Sons, New York 1989

Styron, William. *Darkness Visible: A Memoir of Madness.* Vintage Books, 1990

Wallace, Mike. *The Mike Wallace Profiles* CBS-TV 1981

Zec, Donald. *Marvin — the Story of Lee Marvin.* St. Martin's Press, New York 1980

Index

Academy Awards (Oscars) 59, 112, 129, 153, 180, 183, 238

Airport 9, 180-183, 185, 187, 193, 202, 246, 269

Arnold, Jack 69

Backfire (Échappement libre) 123-124

Ballad for the Kid 244-247, 283

Beatty, Warren 111-113, 115-119

Becker, Vony 84, 121, 123-124, 140, 145, 155, 168, 170, 186, 236, 268, 272, 277

Behr, Edward 204

Belafonte, Harry 42

Bellows, Jim 294

Belmondo, Jean-Paul 71-75, 82-83, 114, 123-124, 291, 310

Benson, Frances (grandmother) 15-17, 22, 39-40, 66, 86-89, 126, 137, 156, 186, 213, 236, 238, 255, 260-262

Bergen, Candice 170

Berry, Dennis 227, 229-238, 241-244, 247-252, 256-257, 260, 262-264, 266, 271, 276, 287, 289-291, 294, 302, 305, 307

Berry, Gladys 229, 248, 271-272, 297

Berry, John 219, 229-231, 254, 263-264, 272, 287, 289, 294, 299, 301

Bevilacqua, Alberto 222-223

Birds in Peru (Les oiseaux vont mourir au Pérou) 146, 148-150, 152-154, 170, 219

Black Panther Party 174-177, 184, 186-188, 192, 198-200, 206, 214-215, 218-219, 236, 239, 271, 289

Blanch, Lesley 80-81, 94, 100-104, 108, 119, 219

Boisset, Yves 228-229, 303

Bonjour Tristesse 9, 45-46, 50-53, 56-59, 63, 71, 310

Bouilhet, Marion 280, 284, 297

Boyd, Stephen 220, 226

Brando, Marlon 23, 29, 52, 54, 99, 158-160, 174

Brasseur, Pierre 148

Breathless (À bout de souffle) 9, 71-75, 83-84, 86, 92, 96, 102, 110, 124, 128, 154, 192, 238, 266, 269, 278, 310

Brown, Elaine 177, 198

Browne, Roscoe Lee 61-62, 307

Cahiers du cinéma 59, 70-71, 112, 126

Camorra! 231

Canel, Fausto 232

Cannes Film Festival 46-47, 97-98, 105, 222, 239-240

Carradine, David 194

Cassel, Jean-Pierre 93-94

Chabrol, Claude 70, 110, 138, 144, 203

Clair de femme 276, 284, 288

Cohn, Harry 72

COINTELPRO 175, 199, 256

Columbia Pictures 62, 65, 67-72, 75, 84, 97, 99, 104-105, 108, 111, 116, 118, 125, 151, 154

Congo Vivo 99-100, 105, 111, 273

Connery, Sean 136

The Corruption of Chris Miller (La corrupción de Chris Miller) 232-233

Costa-Gavras 187, 276, 284

Coutard, Raoul 74-75, 83, 278, 310

Crome, John 150-151

Darrieux, Danielle 148

Davis, Sammy Jr., 169, 174-175, 266

Day, Doris 70, 130

Dead of Summer (Ondata di calore) 9, 188-190, 203

De Beauregard, Georges 72, 278, 280-281, 290, 310

De Broca, Philippe 84, 93-94

De Gaulle, Charles 7, 80, 101, 114, 122, 160, 296, 307

De Watteville, Hubert 204, 224

Demongeot, Mylène 51, 53, 55, 120, 246-250, 252, 254, 260, 263, 269-270, 273, 276, 282-283, 294

Desmond, Paul 49, 51, 56

Diamonds are Brittle (Un milliard dans un billard) 133-134

Douglas, Kirk 239-240

Druker, Harry 87, 91, 145

Duggan, Rev. Thomas 276

Eastwood, Clint 151, 161-162, 164-169, 192, 219, 247
Evans, Bob 49, 171

Federal Bureau of Investigation (FBI) 9-10, 14, 131, 175, 179, 184, 187-188, 190, 195-196, 198-199, 201-202, 204, 207, 210, 219, 222, 256, 270, 288, 292-294, 309
Ferriol, Jean-François 243-246
Ferzetti, Gabriele 99
Findlater, John 181-184, 187-188
A Fine Madness 135-137
Fisher, J. William (Bill) 32, 65, 184-185, 293
The Five-Day Lover (L'amant de cinq jours) 9, 84, 93-96, 105, 127
Fonda, Jane 62, 76, 117, 150, 152, 184, 188
Fonda, Peter 112, 116-117, 119
The French Conspiracy (L'attentat) 228-229
Frontière Palace 232, 275
Fuentes, Carlos 195-196
Furse, Roger 43

The Girls 150-151
Garrel, Philippe 242-243, 264, 268, 273
Garrison, Sean 109, 128
Gary, Alexandre Diego 106-107, 111, 120, 122, 124-127, 132-133, 135, 140-142, 145, 147, 150, 153, 156, 166-167, 170, 178, 185, 188-191, 193, 195, 198, 201-204, 207-209, 219, 222, 225, 228, 233, 235, 237, 251-253, 257, 259-261, 266-267, 275, 286-292, 301, 303-307
Gary, Nina Hart 197, 206, 209-213, 215, 218, 224-225, 247, 254, 278, 289
Gary, Romain 79-82, 85, 88, 90-91, 93-98, 100-106, 108, 114, 117-122, 124-125, 127-131, 133, 135-150, 152-157, 159-161, 166-167, 170, 178-179, 182, 184, 188, 190-191, 193, 196, 198, 201-202, 204-207, 211, 218-225, 230-231, 233, 235-237, 239, 247, 253, 259, 267-268, 271-272, 276-278, 280, 283-284, 286-290, 292, 294, 300-306
Geissendörfer, Hans 254-255
Geneuil, Guy-Pierre 207-210, 212-213, 216, 271, 296, 300
Gessner, Nicolas 121, 133-135, 222-223, 269, 282-283, 303, 307
Gielgud, John 40, 42-43
Givenchy 47, 52, 88, 120

Godard, Jean-Luc 70-75, 83, 90, 110, 243, 279
Golden Globe Awards 9, 129
Le grand délire 232, 247-250, 263
Le grand escroc 110
Grandval, Berthe 242, 297
Grenier, Roger 153, 219, 232-233, 236, 247, 262, 277-279, 290, 303, 305-306

Haber, Joyce 151, 153, 167, 200-201, 207, 294
Hamill, Pete 10, 158
Hart, John 15, 137, 206
Hasni, Ahmed 274-276, 278-284, 288-291, 294, 297-301
Haupert, Lynda 19-20, 25, 27, 29, 49, 51, 55, 63, 65, 66-67, 81, 102, 112, 153, 156, 165, 202, 209, 214-215, 287-288, 292, 302
Les hautes solitudes 242-243
Hayes, Helen 43, 180-182
Held, Richard Wallace 199
Hewitt, Raymond "Masai" 198-199, 201
Hitchcock, Alfred 127, 131-132
Hollingsworth, Carol 31-33, 35-36, 38, 40, 46, 58, 71, 76, 107, 122, 139, 144, 149, 181, 185, 260, 270
Hoover, J. Edgar 7, 10, 131, 179, 188, 200-201, 203, 256-257, 293
Horstig-Primuz, Olga 250, 269-271, 278
Hunter, Kim 112
Hunter, Ross 181-181, 184-185, 188
Huppert, Isabelle 248-250

In the French Style 104-108, 115, 119
Ives, Burl 78, 89

Jackson, Jesse 215-216
Jamal, Dorothy 174-175
Jamal, Hakim 174-177, 179, 183, 185-186, 218
Janssen, David 193-195
Johnson, Rev. Warren 8, 14, 290
Jones, Frederic 113-114, 116-120, 137

Kennedy, Jacqueline 61, 114-115
Kennedy, John F. 61, 114
Kennedy, Robert 160-161
Kerr, Deborah 46, 51-53, 55
Kill 219-220, 226
Killy, Jean-Claude 169-170, 178, 186
Kowalski, Bernard 194

La Roche, Guy 64
Lancaster, Burt 180, 182-183
Lansner, Kermit 204, 207
The Legion Parachutes into Kolwezi (La légion saute sur Kolwezi) 278, 310
Leone, Sergio 165, 247-249
Lerner, Alan Jay 151-152, 162, 164, 166, 192
LeRoy, Mervyn 109, 127-128, 130-131, 139
Let No Man Write My Epitaph 75, 78-79, 130
The Line of Demarcation (La ligne de démarcation) 138, 278
Lilith 9, 106, 111-117, 119, 125-126, 129, 187, 246, 310
Loewe, Frederick 151
Logan, Joshua 76, 151-152, 162-165, 169
Los Angeles Times 131, 153, 167, 192, 196, 200-201, 207, 233, 294, 309

Macho Callahan 192, 194-196, 198
Maddox, John 31, 34
Malinchak, Tom 211-212
Malraux, André 97-98, 114, 127, 144, 266, 300
Marisol 233
Marquand, Christian 62
Marvin, Lee 151-152, 162, 164-166, 169, 184, 192
Mason, James 220, 226
Maxwell, Roger 183, 214-216
Moment to Moment 109, 127, 129-130, 132-133, 137, 139
Moreuil, François 41, 55-73, 75, 78-79, 81-82, 88-89, 91-92, 124, 231, 290-291
Morrow, Erma 211, 213
The Mouse That Roared 41, 68-69
Mousey (Cat and Mouse) 239-240, 242

National Association for the Advancement of Colored People (NAACP) 24, 95
Navarra, Carlos 196
New York Film Festival 125
Newsweek 59, 90, 204-208, 217, 221-225, 293
Nico 242-243
Niven, David 46, 51-53, 55, 278

Odegaard, Velma (aunt) 10, 16-17, 20, 154, 168-170, 233, 298
O'Neal, Patrick 136
Operation Breadbasket 215

Paint Your Wagon 9, 49, 151, 153-154, 156-157, 161-162, 164-167, 169-170, 191-192, 246
Pam, Jerry 169
Paramount Pictures 49, 151-152, 156, 163-164, 171, 192, 232
Parker, Suzy 62-63
Parrish, Robert 104-108
Pavlowitch, Paul 170, 305-306
Pendulum 154-156
Peppard, George 154, 156
Petrie, Daniel Sr. (Dan) 239-242
Playtime (La récréation) 84, 88-91, 95-96
Poitier, Sidney 97-98, 239
Preminger, Otto 39-45, 47-53, 55-63, 67, 69, 92, 97-98, 111, 118, 130, 232, 249
Prévost, Françoise 88, 90, 269, 301-302, 306
Price, Paton 70, 211-212, 236

Quinn, Dawn 22, 27, 29-30, 38-39, 56-59, 66, 90, 95, 99, 105-106, 115, 130, 135, 174, 192, 217, 219, 243, 257

Revolt in the Caribbean (Estouffade à la Caraïbe) 140-141
Rich, Claude 133-134
Richer, Paul 27, 89
Risi, Nelo 187, 189, 203
The Road to Corinth (La route de Corinthe) 144
Robeson, Warren 28, 45, 59, 87, 102, 130, 205, 210, 235, 260, 270, 294, 299
Rossen, Robert 111-113, 116, 118, 125, 138, 246

Sagan, Françoise 45, 50-51, 59, 62, 84
Sabrina Fair 28-29
Saint Joan 8, 31, 33-34, 36, 39-40, 42, 44-52, 59, 70, 97, 118, 130, 154, 310
St. Laurent, Yves 111, 120, 128
Salamanca, J.R. 111-112
Salinger, Pierre 160
San Sebastian Film Festival 202-203
Schaefer, George 154-156
Seale, Bobby 175-176
Seaton, George 180, 184
Seberg, David (brother) 16, 58, 66, 86, 97, 103, 154-155, 212, 292

Seberg, Dorothy (mother) 9, 14-16, 18, 20-22, 33, 36, 45, 58, 65, 85, 90, 96, 103, 107, 128, 136, 154-155, 168, 177, 181, 186, 189, 203, 210, 212, 238, 268, 273, 287, 292, 308

Seberg, Ed (father) 9, 10, 16, 18-21, 33-36, 39, 45, 58, 60, 85-86, 96, 103, 107, 136, 139, 155, 166, 177, 186, 189, 205, 210, 225, 253, 268, 273, 287, 291-293, 308-309

Seberg, Kurt (brother) 9, 15-16, 54, 58, 86, 97, 103, 154-155, 212, 292

Seberg, Mary Ann (sister) 9, 14-20, 22-23, 25, 33, 35, 43-44, 46, 48, 58, 663-64, 66, 81, 95, 103, 115, 125, 130, 132-133, 140, 149, 156-157, 180-181, 186, 202, 205, 209, 213-214, 216-217, 234-236, 253, 260-261, 276-277, 287, 293, 308, 309

Sellers, Peter 68-69

Serber, Rabbi Sol 211-212, 214-215, 217-218, 234, 236, 262, 264, 266, 268, 288, 302

Shaw, Irwin 104-105, 107-108, 115

Shepperton Studios 42, 57, 68

Simenon, Marc 246-250, 273, 277

Smith, Pauline 28, 37-38, 96

Sommars, Julie 33-34

Southern Christian Leadership Conference 158, 176

Stafford, Frederick 247

Stapleton, Maureen 180, 183, 187

Stein, Harry 264

Strasberg, Lee 61

Studios de Billancourt 107, 145, 276

Styron, William 267, 303

Sullivan, Ed 36

Testi, Fabio 229, 231

This Kind of Love (Questa specie d'amore) 222-223

Time Out for Love (Les grandes personnes) 84, 90, 95

Trintignant, Jean-Louis 228-229

Truffaut, François 59, 70-71, 84, 90, 124, 238

Ungaro 150

United Artists 32, 151

Universal (studio) 127-128, 130-131, 139, 146, 151, 180-181, 187

Valère, Jean 84, 90

Wallace, Mike 47, 63

Walston, Ray 152, 162-164, 166, 169

Warner, Jack 131, 136

Webster, William H. 293

White Horses of Summer (Bianchi cavalli d'Agosto) 247

Widmark, Richard 35, 40

The Wild Duck (Die Wildente) 254-255, 260

Willoughby, Bob 39, 45

Woodward, Joanne 112, 135-136, 152, 184

CPSIA information can be obtained at www.ICGtesting.com
Printed in the USA
LVOW10s1212030314

375796LV00003B/58/A